Counseling E...
A Multifaceted Approach

edited by
DAYA SINGH SANDHU

AMERICAN
COUNSELING
ASSOCIATION

5999 Stevenson Avenue
Alexandria, VA 22304
www.counseling.org

Counseling Employees: A Multifaceted Approach
Copyright © 2002 by the American Counseling Association. All rights reserved. Printed in the United States of America. Except as permitted under the United States Copyright Act of 1976, no part of this publication may be reproduced or distributed in any form or by any means, or stored in a database or retrieval system, without the prior written permission of the publisher.

10   9   8   7   6   5   4   3   2   1

American Counseling Association
5999 Stevenson Avenue
Alexandria, VA 22304

Director of Publications
Carolyn C. Baker

Production Manager
Bonny E. Gaston

Copy Editor
Elaine Dunn

Cover Design
Martha Woolsey

Library of Congress Cataloging-in-Publication Data

Counseling employees : a multifaceted approach / editor, Daya Singh Sandhu.
     p.   cm.
   Includes bibliographical references.
   ISBN 1-55620-197-4 (alk. paper)
     1. Employees—Counseling of   I. Sandhu, Daya Singh, 1943–

HF5549.5.C68 2002
658.3'85—dc21   2002016403

This book is dedicated to
all those who work to live
and also to
all those who live to work!

Contents

Section 4: Special Problems

Section 5: Special Programs

Foreword

Counseling Employees: A Multifaceted Approach makes an important contribution to the counseling literature. Daya Singh Sandhu has assembled a group of authors from diverse perspectives and backgrounds to address multiple issues affecting worker satisfaction and productivity. The book provides an excellent overview of issues that challenge contemporary workers. The chapter authors address a diverse range of concerns adults encounter in various work settings, and the issues addressed in the book are both timely and important. For example, a theme contained in several chapters is the emerging meaning of work in the postmodern workplace. It is clear that the postindustrial wave bringing technological advances and new workplace scenarios (such as contingent workforces engaged in "on demand" work projects) has resulted in many workers reevaluating the meaning they find in their work. Substantial numbers of downsized workers result in questions pertaining to the role of work in people's lives. Many contemporary workers express reluctance to sacrifice everything for their work when the employers they work for are so willing to sacrifice them. Thus, many people now search for ways to achieve more balanced participation in their life roles. Whereas many workers in the last century "lived to work," today workers express a growing desire to "work to live."

This issue, in particular, becomes even more salient after the terrorist attacks of September 11 in the United States. Since that date, many career counselors report encounters with clients seeking answers to deep questions about their work activity. Many people now have a heightened sense of the fragility of life, and there is an emerging sense that engaging in work activity that is personally meaningful is an important career goal to achieve. Therefore, many workers now acutely realize that questions related to the meaning of work are really questions about the meaning they experience in their lives. Finding purpose in work activity is a goal that an increasing number of workers seek to achieve. Thus, many people now conceptualize work differently. They now conclude that work activity reflects outcomes from decision-making processes dedicated to resolving the question, "How will I spend the most precious commodity I have (i.e., my time alive on this earth)?" Few things are more personal to us than our career choices. Chapters such as the one addressing spirituality in the workplace (chapters 2 and 3) become an important resource for stimulating our thinking about how these deeper questions might be explored.

Concerns and issues encountered generally in life, but that also have important implications for worker productivity, are also addressed in *Counseling Employees*. For instance, complex issues such as violent behavior, substance abuse, and depression are important topics covered in this book. Obviously, these are problems in living that create problems in working. Moreover, they are issues that require informed and sophisticated interventions. Chapters addressing these topics seek to provide readers with strategies for helping workers cope with contemporary issues in living so they can be happier and more productive in their work.

Another strength of *Counseling Employees* is that, rather than taking a more academic approach to addressing issues confronting workers, the authors provide substantial practical advice for helping workers cope with workplace issues. Moreover, the authors address worker concerns from a holistic perspective. For example, postmodern strategies for helping workers cope with work-related concerns are offered in chapters such as those addressing dual-career couples and assessment processes. Thus, authors offer creative and current strategies for helping workers. It is also refreshing to note that the practical advice provided by the authors is based on the relevant research literature.

Readers will also be impressed with the fact that the chapter topics highlight the demographic diversity that characterizes today's workplace. Authors offer insights into important factors counselors must be aware of as they assist people of color, workers who are disabled, workers who are lesbian, gay, or bisexual, and reentry workers engage in productive and satisfying work lives while coping with the prejudice and discrimination they encounter.

I am confident that readers will find this book to be an extremely useful resource for understanding concerns of adults in the contemporary workplace and in identifying strategies for enhancing worker productivity and satisfaction.

—Spencer G. Niles
Professor of Education and
Professor-in-Charge
Counselor Education Program
Pennsylvania State University

Preface

Although the old axiom says "Work to live, don't live to work," the fact is that work matters significantly to people. It has numerous financial, social, and psychological benefits (Witmer & Sweeney, 1992). Many people's self-worth is inextricably tied to their work, and it is through work that their lives have meaning (Dollarhide, 1997). When work does not go well, however, or when an employee's life is unsettled and personal problems spill over into the workplace, it becomes the job of the manager or supervisor to "fix the problem." This can mean counseling the employee directly or referring the employee for help.

When the work environment is healthy, everyone benefits. Unfortunately, the work environment is not always healthy, and this can have a negative effect on the self-esteem of employees and their psychological well-being. Competition, in-fighting, blocked careers, fear of becoming unemployed, and unfulfilling work are just a few examples of what can cause the workplace environment to become unhealthy (Krohe, 1994). The effects of an unhealthy work environment can be costly to both the employee and the employer. High burnout can lead to lower levels of productivity. A hostile work environment causes low morale and can lead to higher staff turnover. Increased levels of stress can cause serious health problems, which result in high absentee rates. Job dissatisfaction can lead to any number of problems, including depression.

According to Johnson and Indvik (1997), much of the depression Americans experience comes from work, and it is because of an unhealthy work environment. An employee's personal and family problems can also have a negative effect on the workplace. At times it is virtually impossible to separate the personal and professional from the institution. Many employees struggle with alcohol and drug problems but may be reluctant to discuss the problem with their employer for fear of losing their jobs or being stigmatized. Parents may find it hard to reach an appropriate balance between work and family. This is especially true with new parents and parents who are returning to the workplace. And with 50% of all marriages in the United States currently ending in divorce, there are more single parents in the workplace than ever before. Child illnesses and elder care are two additional family issues employees deal with that can lead to absenteeism and stress in the workplace. Kofodimos (1995) wrote that programs designed to alleviate work–personal conflict of employees often fail because they only concern themselves with the symptoms and not the causes of these conflicts.

Another factor confronting workplaces of today is the changing workforce itself. The women's movement and antidiscrimination legislation enacted during the 1960s contributed to record numbers of women and minorities entering the workforce. Women constitute nearly half of the workforce today (Wallis, 1992). The U.S. Bureau of the Census (2000) estimates that by 2025, the White population in the United States will drop to 62% of the population (from 75% in 1990), whereas Blacks, Asian/Pacific Islanders, American Indians, and Hispanics will constitute the remaining 38%. By 2050, the population of Whites will drop further to 52%, whereas Blacks, Asian/Pacific Islanders, American Indians, and Hispanics will increase to 48%. This demographic shift will result in corresponding shifts in workplace demographics. Additionally, there are currently 17.2 million Americans of working-age with nonsevere disabilities (U.S. Bureau of the Census, 2000) whose employment could significantly impact the work environment. And, as a result of budget shortages and workers seeking greater job flexibility, the workplace has become increasingly reliant on temporary workers, which is an additional dynamic that has altered the workplace.

Along with these changes in the workplace have come policies that protect the rights of employees. Laws in place no longer allow for managers to willfully discriminate against racial minorities, women, gay men and lesbians, people with disabilities, or the elderly. Legislation such as the Americans With Disabilities Act, the Family Leave Act, and affirmative action require managers to be knowledgeable about laws affecting their individual employees. And sexual harassment policies require managers to monitor the workforce environment to ensure that a hostile environment does not exist toward women, gay people, racial minorities, and other groups.

All of these factors—blurring of the personal and professional at work, the changing workforce, and the legal issues affecting the workplace—suggest that the workplace is a complicated setting and that the job of a manager or supervisor has changed and become more complex. Many employers have acknowledged this changing workplace, and the rise of Employee Assistance Programs (EAPs) has been one response to these changes. Most EAPs began in the 1980s as a way to help employees who had drug or alcohol problems (Wilson, 1997). Since then, however, EAPs have grown to the point where over 8,000 of them exist in North America alone. In addition to drug, alcohol, and personal counseling, many EAPS now include health and wellness workshops as preventative measures to relieve stress (Crawley, 1995). College campuses have also been known to turn to counselors for help in resolving the personal differences that can create dysfunctional departments (Wilson, 1997). In regards to higher education, institutions wishing to improve the learning possibilities for students must become vitally interested in both the personal and professional development of the faculty (Sanford, 1980).

Unfortunately, not all workplaces have EAPs at their disposal to refer employees for help. Nor do most supervisors have the counseling skills required to counsel the employees who turn to them for help. Even if mangers or supervisors do have some level of counselor training or expertise, it would be difficult for any one person to be knowledgeable about all of the topics and issues confronting the workforce in the new millennium. For these reasons, it is imperative that a book on counseling employees be written that can provide guidance for the managers and supervisors who are attempting to counsel their employees in these changing times.

With the contributions from the elite professionals from the field, I aspire to present this book to those who are interested to meet the counseling needs of their employees. To acquaint readers with the characteristics of this book and introduce salient themes of all chapters, I present an overview of contents below.

Overview of Contents

This book is divided into five major sections that focus on the various perspectives, needs, and concerns of employees in the workplace. Each chapter is placed under each of the five sections

Section I: *Work and the Workplace: Their Impact on the Lives of the Workers* consists of four chapters that focus mainly on personal and spiritual values of the employees and their interactions with their workplace. Chapter 1 highlights the importance of guiding employees to find meaning in their work. Salience of work in life span development and various assessment methods to determine perceptions of mattering in the workplace are discussed. Chapter 2 addresses significance of spirituality in the workplace. It also examines the relationship between work and spirituality and concludes with a model of workplace spirituality and career counseling. Chapter 3 focuses on spirituality as an integral part of employees' total personality. It also demonstrates how spirituality can be beneficial for the employees and the organization in developing teamwork, customer focus, and empowerment of the employees. Chapter 4 discusses strategies to explore clients' values, responsibilities, and choices to reduce stress in the workplace. An analysis of the organizational issues that have stressful effects on the employees is also presented.

Section II: *Special Tools* includes three chapters that focus on various strategies to address problems of the employees and the organizations. Chapter 5 summarizes strategies of motivational interviewing and discusses its practical applications. This chapter also illustrates how motivational interviewing techniques can be used as a powerful counseling style to bring about necessary behavioral changes in the workplace. Chapter 6 discusses the "Adlerian construct of the lifestyle" as an effective tool to analyze and understand the behavior of employees in the workplace. Also, several instruments and intervention strategies are presented to understand and resolve conflicts between organizations and their employees. Chapter 7 discusses the effects of the human problems on the employees and their place of work. This chapter also suggests an eight-step process to identify work-related problems and to help design a plan of action to resolve those problems.

Section III: *Special Populations* is the largest section of the book and focuses on issues relating to eight specific employee populations. Chapter 8 explores the career development and other work-related issues of ethnic minorities. Specifically, this chapter discusses personal problems, social conflicts, and other concerns, such as perceived discrimination, by ethnic minority workers that affect their performance. Chapter 9 identifies employees with disabilities and discusses what factors affect their employment. The chapter also suggests resources for the EAP counselors to create and maintain a friendly work environment for employees with a disability. Chapter 10 introduces several issues that affect gay, lesbian, and bisexual employees in the workplace. Intervention strategies to address issues relating to homophobia for the improvement of workplace morale, interpersonal effectiveness, and productivity are discussed.

In chapter 11, the concerns of delayed or reentry workers are discussed. This chapter addresses issues of homemakers who had to change their identity to that of a worker. It also discusses expectations, motivations, sex role socialization, and perceived structure of opportunity for delayed and reentry workers. Chapter 12 focuses on the special career development needs and issues of displaced homemakers. Also, practical applications for career counselors are suggested to facilitate their transition into the workplace. Chapter 13 presents the EAP counselors with pragmatic intervention strategies to assist dual-career couples with their unique career needs and relationship dilemmas. This chapter applies a narrative or storied approach for counselors to illustrate three practical steps of deconstruction, coconstruction, and reconstruction.

Chapter 14 identifies acculturative stress among expatriates and sojourners who are faced with cultural conflicts and adaptation challenges. It also describes an adaptation and treatment protocol to minimize acculturative stress among international business travelers. Chapter 15, the final chapter in this section, highlights the role of temporary workers in the labor market. This chapter also explores transition concerns of these employees. A description of a typical temporary worker is presented, and suggestions are made about counseling prospective candidates for temporary employment.

Section IV: *Special Problems* discusses special problems of employees in four chapters. Chapter 16 explores how the contemporary practice of performance ranking is negatively affecting career development of the employees. The overemphasis on performance ranking causes competition but does not foster much-needed collaboration in the workplace. Chapter 17 addresses problem of depression in the workplace. The authors discuss the nature of depression and explain how the symptoms of depression are manifested in the workplace. They also examine causes of depression and discuss various treatment and prevention methods that employers can use to deal with it. Chapter 18 discusses the impact of alcohol and other drugs in the workplace. Various prevention and intervention strategies are presented. A new approach developed by the authors—DASH, an acronym for Denial, Awareness, Surrender, and Help—is introduced and illustrated with case examples to help substance-abusing white-collar employees. Chapter 19, the last chapter in this section, focuses on managing the effects of violence on the employees. The history of violence in the workplace, its effects on employees, and debriefing following critical incidents are discussed. Necessary training and qualifications of EAP personnel are also suggested.

Section V: *Special Programs* focuses on special programs to assist employees. This section includes two chapters. Chapter 20 describes the historical foundations of EAPs. It also discusses important issues as they relate to higher education and suggests some necessary steps for successful implementation of such programs on college and university campuses. Finally, Chapter 21 discusses the ways EAPs can be evaluated to improve their effectiveness. Higher priority is given to those evaluation methods that are systematic and continuing, not those evaluation methods that are random and sporadic.

—*Daya Singh Sandhu*
Louisville, Kentucky

References

Crawley, A. L. (1995). Faculty development programs at research universities: Implications for senior faculty renewal. *To Improve the Academy, 14,* 231–243.

Dollarhide, C. T. (1997). Counseling for meaning in work and life: An integrated approach. *Journal of Humanistic Education and Development, 35,* 178–187.

Johnson, P. R., & Indvik, J. (1997). The boomer blues: Depression in the workplace. *Public Personnel Management, 26,* 359–365.

Kofodimos, J. R. (1995). *Beyond work–family programs: Confronting and resolving the underlying causes of work–personal life conflict* (ERIC Document Reproduction Service No. 383 973). Greensboro, NC: Center for Creative Leadership.

Krohe, J. (1994). An epidemic of depression. *Across the Board, 31*(8), 23–40.

Sanford, N. (1980). *Learning after college.* Orinda, CA: Montaigne.

U.S. Bureau of the Census. (2000). *National population projections.* Retrieved from http://www.census.gov/population/www/projections/natsum.T5html

Wallis, C. (1992, Fall). The nuclear family goes boom [Special issue]. *Time,* 42–44.

Wilson, R. (1997, August 1). Colleges get psychological help for dysfunctional departments. *Chronicle of Higher Education, 43*(47), A10–A11.

Witmer, J., & Sweeney, T. J. (1992). A holistic model for wellness and prevention over the life span. *Journal of Counseling and Development, 71,* 140–148.

Acknowledgments

First and foremost, I would like to thank God Almighty for His help without whose Will not even a blade of grass moves in this universe. There are too many persons to be mentioned here who directly or indirectly made the publication of this book a reality. Mere mention of these persons' names is no way sufficient to compensate them for their help. I will always remain indebted to them.

First, I would like to thank all the contributors for their hard work, dedication, and their chapter contributions. I am also grateful to them for having enough trust in me to serve as their editor. I sincerely appreciate these contributors' profound insights into employee and career counseling and related issues. Above all, I am thankful for their cooperation and patience.

I thank Carolyn Baker, Director of Publications at the American Counseling Association, for her encouragement and guidance at every step in the preparation of this book. I also appreciate and thank Dr. Cheryl B. Aspy and Dr. Christopher Sink for their most valuable comments and scholarly suggestions. I am also thankful to Elaine Dunn for her editorial comments and suggestions. I would also like to thank Dr. Spencer Niles for taking time from his very busy schedule to write the Foreword to this book.

I also appreciate and thank Rose Wade and Karen Barnes for their secretarial help. Last but not the least, I would like to express my gratitude to Rob Longwell-Grice, my graduate assistant, for the library research assistance, proofreading, valuable comments, and suggestions.

Finally, I thank my lovely wife Ushi for her moral support and encouragement. For those I inadvertently missed or who helped me indirectly, please accept my thanks and apology.

—*Daya Singh Sandhu*
Louisville, Kentucky

About the Editor

Daya Singh Sandhu, EdD, NCC, NCCC, NCSC, CPC, is chairperson and professor in the Department of Educational and Counseling Psychology at the University of Louisville. He received his BA, BT, and MA (English) degrees from Punjab University, India. After moving to the United States in 1969, he received his MEd from Delta State University, Specialist in English degree from the University of Mississippi, and Doctor of Counselor Education from Mississippi State University. He has more than 30 years experience in education, both at the secondary and the university levels. He taught English, mathematics, physics, and chemistry in India. In the United States he taught English for 11 years in public schools and also served as a high school guidance counselor and agency testing coordinator for 7 years with the Choctaw Agency, Bureau of Indian Affairs Schools, in Philadelphia, Mississippi. Since 1989, he has taught graduate courses in counselor education and counseling psychology at Nicholls State University and the University of Louisville.

Dr. Sandhu has a special interest in school counseling, multicultural counseling, neurolinguistic programming, and the role of spirituality in counseling and psychotherapy. Previously, he has published four books, *Numerical Problems in Physics, A Practical Guide for Classroom Observations: A Multidimensional Approach, Counseling for Prejudice Prevention and Reduction* (as a senior author), and *Empowering Women for Equity: A Counseling Approach* (as a second author). Dr. Sandhu also edited or coedited four more books, *Asian and Pacific Islander Americans: Issues and Concerns for Counseling and Psychotherapy, Faces of Violence: Psychological Correlates, Concepts, and Intervention Strategies, Violence in American Schools: A Practical Guide for Counselors,* and *Elementary School Counseling in the New Millennium.*

Dr. Sandhu has also published more than 50 articles in state, national, and international journals. His first book was in Punjabi poetry, *Satranghi Pingh.* Dr. Sandhu is also an experienced presenter and professional workshop trainer. He has made more than one hundred presentations at the international, national, state, and local levels. His presentations have focused on a wide variety of subjects that can be broadly classified under school counseling and multicultural counseling.

Dr. Sandhu has also received numerous honors and awards for his professional accomplishments. Such accolades include the following: 2000 College of Education Alumnus of the Year Award at Mississippi State, 2000 Multicultural Teaching Award at University of Louisville, 2000 AMCD Research Award, 2001 President's Distinguished Faculty Award for Outstanding Research and Creative Activities, 2001 Kentucky Counselor Educator of the Year Award, and Fulbright Research Award for India 2001–2002.

About the Contributors

Kimberly K. Asner-Self, EdD, is an assistant professor in the Department of Educational Psychology and Special Education within the School of Education and Human Services at Southern Illinois University, Carbondale, Illinois. Dr. Asner-Self coordinates the Council for the Accreditation of Counseling and Related Educational Programs (CACREP)-accredited Community Counseling Master's program, a program that produces community counseling generalists including future Employee Assistance Programs counselors. She has also coordinated several job development and placement training programs for rehabilitation professionals interested in enhancing their employment placement skills with people with disabilities.

Patricia A. Cluss, PhD, is a licensed psychologist, the associate director of the Western Psychiatric Institute and Clinic's Behavioral Medicine Program, and assistant professor of psychiatry at the University of Pittsburgh School of Medicine. Her clinical and research interests are in the area of women's health and mental health issues and in behavior change strategies for individuals and health care providers. She is a certified motivational interviewing trainer and has initiated the University of Pittsburgh School of Medicine Motivational Interviewing Interest Group, a collaboration of health professionals who are using motivational interviewing in their work with individuals in various settings in the medical center.

Kathleen M. Connolly, PhD, holds undergraduate and graduate degrees in psychology, human services, counseling, and counselor education from Loyola University of Chicago, DePaul University, and the University of North Carolina at Greensboro. Her training has also included extensive work in the areas of organizational change and behavior. Dr. Connolly is the founder and president of Acumeans, Inc., located in Charlotte, North Carolina, where she provides counseling, psychotherapy, and corporate consulting. Acumeans, Inc. contracts with other management consultants seeking expertise in assessment and interpersonal dynamics. Dr. Connolly is also a part-time faculty member in the Department of Counseling, Special Education, and Child Development at the University of North Carolina at Charlotte.

Paige N. Cummins, PhD, NCC, is an assistant professor of Human Resources at East Central University in Ada, Oklahoma. Currently, she teaches in the Graduate Counseling Program. Her teaching interests are in group counseling and supervision. She is certified in basic critical incident stress debriefing. Dr. Cummins's practice and research interests are in eating disorders, group counseling, attachment, and grief. She has published articles about preparation for group counseling and attachment and adjustment to college.

John M. Dillard, PhD, is a professor in the Department of Educational and Counseling Psychology at the University of Louisville, Louisville, Kentucky. He has written several books and journal articles on the topic of career development and career planning across ethnic and cultural groups. Dr. Dillard is the author of one of the original books on multicultural counseling and is currently revising his book, *Lifelong Career Planning*.

Mary H. Guindon, PhD, is assistant professor and chair in the Department of Counseling and Human Services at Johns Hopkins University and also coordinates programs in organizational counseling, an innovative specialty area combining counseling skills with organizational development and behavior principles. She has published articles and made numerous presentations at national and international professional conferences. She has more than 15 years private practice and consultation experience providing workshops and consultation services in educational, corporate, governmental, hospital, and community settings. She is a licensed psychologist, a licensed clinical professional counselor, and a National Certified Career Counselor. She is past president of the New Jersey Mental Health Counselors Association, past president of the

New Jersey Association of Counselor Education and Supervision, and a Fellow in the Pennsylvania Psychological Association.

Michael E. Hall, PhD (Counseling Psychology, Pennsylvania State University) and Certified Career Management Fellow (International Board for Career Management Certification's highest designation), is in independent practice in Charlotte, North Carolina, where he provides organizational career development services. He is also director of Executive Career Management (The Transition Team–Charlotte) and adjunct faculty member of the graduate counseling program in the University of North Carolina at Charlotte. A member of the International Association of Career Management Professionals and the American Counseling Association, Dr. Hall has been most active within the National Association of Career Development, serving on the editorial board of the *Career Development Quarterly* and as a frequent conference presenter. Previously, he spent 12 years in higher education (associate director for Counseling, Career Services, and affiliate assistant professor of Counseling Psychology at Penn State) and as a contingency provider for a national career consulting organization (Career Development Services at Rochester, New York). Dr. Hall's professional life began with an 8-year stint as a school psychologist in Columbus, Ohio.

Patrick H. Hardesty, PhD, is an associate professor at the University of Louisville and a licensed counseling psychologist. He received his doctorate from Northwestern University, where his research focused on the role of part-time work in adolescent development and career development. Dr. Hardesty developed specialties in adolescent development, career counseling, and assessment. He currently leads two research teams, one investigating the criteria people use, under differing conditions, to select jobs and the other studying the role of social support in reducing high school dropouts. In the past, he has worked on federally funded grants to reduce drug abuse among elementary and middle school students. Dr. Hardesty maintains a private practice treating a variety of client concerns. He is also an industrial consultant on issues of employee selection and development.

Debra A. Harley, PhD, is an associate professor in the Department of Special Education and Rehabilitation Counseling and coordinator of the graduate program in Rehabilitation Counseling at University of Kentucky, Lexington, Kentucky. Dr. Harley has authored more that 40 refereed journal articles and book chapters and has made 26 national and international professional conference presentations.

Nancy E. Huenefeld, PhD, is a licensed psychologist in Washington state and has been in the mental health field for 14 years. Her main expertise areas are in trauma (rape, sexual assault, suicidality, and posttraumatic stress disorder), grief and loss issues (divorce, loss of job, death, and life transitions), multicultural issues, and career issues. She works as a counselor at Seattle Central Community College. She is area chair and teaches in human services for the University of Phoenix, Washington Campus. She is in private practice. Dr. Huenefeld enjoys community work and is on the board of the Seattle Crisis Clinic and Southeast Youth and Family Services. She earned a BA from University of Arizona, an MS from University of Kentucky, and a PhD in Counseling Psychology from the Pennsylvania State University.

Kathleen M. Kirby, EdD, is an associate professor and clinical training director of the Department of Educational and Counseling Psychology at the University of Louisville. She is also the clinical supervisor of the Learning Improvement Center housed within the School of Education at the University of Louisville. She is a licensed psychologist who formerly worked for 20 years as a social worker in the child welfare system. Her interests include psychological assessment and counseling of children adopted after infancy, ethnicity and adoption, women's issues, self-concept formation of individuals from marginalized groups, gays, lesbian, bisexual, and transgendered individuals, and Native Americans. She specializes in treating children and families.

Pamela J. Leconte, EdD, is an assistant professor in the Department of Teacher Preparation and Special Education within the Graduate School of Education and Human Development at George Washington University, Washington, DC. Dr. Leconte coordinates the Collaborative Vocational Evaluation Training program, a master's level training for vocational evaluators working to serve people with disabilities to match them with training, careers, and employment. She is a past president of the Vocational Evaluation and Work Adjustment Association.

Joseph A. Lippincott, PhD, is an associate professor and director of intern training at Kutztown University Counseling Services in Pennsylvania. He is a certified clinical specialist in adult psychiatric/mental health nursing, with an MS (Psychiatric Nursing) from Rutgers University and a PhD (Counseling Psychology) from Lehigh University. Dr. Lippincott has extensive experience working with international populations in a variety of clinical settings. He has presented papers on cross-cultural treatment issues at international conferences in the United States, Canada,

Argentina, China, Turkey, and Scotland, and has published articles in journals of the American Medical Association and American Psychological Association.

Ruth B. Lippincott, JD, is a corporate in-house commercial attorney at the headquarters of Air Products and Chemicals, Inc., a company with operations in over 30 countries and 17,000 employees around the globe. Ms. Lippincott has traveled to over 30 countries and has worked with her corporate clients and with customers in North and South America, Asia, Australia, Europe, and North Africa. She has presented training on international business topics within her company in the United States, Europe, and Asia and has presented papers on cross-cultural issues at international conferences in Turkey and Scotland.

Robert M. Longwell-Grice, MEd, is a doctoral candidate in the Department of Educational and Counseling Psychology, University of Louisville, Kentucky. His program area is college student personnel, and he has worked extensively in the field of student affairs. His research interests include issues of multiculturalism, research and assessment in student affairs, and the experiences of first-generation college students

Eugenie Joan Looby, PhD (University of Georgia), is an associate professor of counselor education and assistant dean in the College of Education at Mississippi State University. Her primary research program focuses on diversity and gender issues, sexual trauma, family, violence, and eating disorders and body image perceptions among African American females. She has conducted numerous workshops and state, regional, and national presentations on these topics. Dr. Looby is also a member of numerous honor societies and professional organizations, including Chi Sigma Iota and the American Counseling Association. She serves on the editorial boards of *Counseling and Values* and *the Journal of Counseling & Development*.

Octavia Madison-Colmore, EdD, NCC, LPC, LMFT, NCSC, is an assistant professor at Virginia Polytechnic Institute and State University, Counselor Education Program, Northern Virginia Graduate Center in Falls Church, Virginia. She received a BA in psychology from Hampton University, an MEd in agency counseling from Lynchburg College, and an EdD from Virginia Polytechnic Institute and State University. She has 15 years of experience as a clinical practitioner specializing in the treatment of substance abusers. Dr. Madison-Colmore has presented at numerous conferences on topics relating to substance abuse and multi-culturalism and, more recently, was invited to teach a course on substance abuse at Tainan Woman's College of Art and Technology in Tainan, Taiwan.

John McCarthy, PhD, is an assistant professor in the Department of Counseling at Indiana University of Pennsylvania. He completed his predoctoral internship at the University of Florida Counseling Center and has also served on the faculty at Slippery Rock University, Chatham College, and St. Bonaventure University. He has received training in motivational interviewing and been an active participant in the University of Pittsburgh Medical Center Motivational Interviewing Interest Group. His other interests include multicultural counseling, cognitive therapy, and creative approaches in counseling.

Betty Milburn, PhD, is associate director of counseling at the Student Counseling Service, Texas A&M University, College Station. She received her bachelor's degree in psychology from the University of Texas at Austin and her master's degree in psychology and her doctorate in educational psychology from Texas A&M University. Dr. Milburn has over 20 years of experience in counseling, supervision, and administration.

James L. Moore III, PhD, is an assistant professor in the Department of Counselor Education at the Ohio State University in Columbus. He received his BA in English Education from Delaware State University and earned both his MEd and PhD in Counselor Education at Virginia Polytechnic Institute and State University. He has a biography listed in *Outstanding Young Men in America* (1998 edition) and is a member of numerous professional and honor societies, including Alpha Kappa Mu, Phi Kappa Phi, Phi Delta Kappa, Kappa Delta Pi, and Chi Sigma Iota. The Delaware Association of Teachers of English recognized him for his exceptional contribution to English Education with its Outstanding Achievement in English/Language Arts Award (1995). In addition, he has served in a leadership capacity in various professional organizations. Dr. Moore has presented at numerous state, regional, national, and international conferences. Many of his presentations and papers have been directly or indirectly related to Black males.

Steven J. Morris, PhD, is an assistant professor in the Department of Educational and Counseling Psychology at the University of Louisville and a licensed psychologist in Kentucky. He received his PhD in counseling psychology from the University of Illinois at Urbana-Champaign. His research interests include depressive cognition, depressive personality styles, and representations of the self.

William Morton, EdD, graduated from Nova University and has worked with children and families in a variety of settings since 1966. He is the executive director of Warren Family Homes, Inc., in Whitby, Ontario, Canada, and has a private counseling practice.

Don Pazaratz, EdD, has been in clinical practice in Oshawa, Ontario, Canada, since 1977. He has served as a consultant to numerous small businesses. He is also president of Hayden Youth Services in Oshawa.

Paul R. Peluso, PhD, NCC, LPC, LMFT, is director of Outcome Research and a marriage and family therapist for the Odyssey Family Counseling Center in Georgia. He has also been an organizational consultant for private corporations and government agencies. He has coauthored articles and facilitated trainings on the use of family therapy techniques and Adlerian principles in organizational settings. In addition, Dr. Peluso is on the adjunct faculty of Mercer University in Atlanta.

Debra S. Preston, PhD, LPC, NCC, NCCC, is an associate professor and school counseling program coordinator in the Department of Psychology and Counseling at the University of North Carolina at Pembroke. Dr. Preston received her doctorate in counseling from Virginia Tech. Her areas of specialty include school counseling and career counseling. She has served as president both of the North Carolina Association for Assessment in Counseling and of the North Carolina Association for Counselor Education and Supervision.

Scheryl Price, MEd, is the director of Career and Student Development at Southeastern University. She is a graduate of George Mason University, where she earned an MEd in agency counseling. She serves as the national corporate recruiter for a large high-tech company; coordinator of diversity programs and outreach programs, including welfare-to-work, stay in school, college access, and at-risk-youth programs; corporate trainer on wellness, self-development, and professional development; and adjunct faculty member. She is an active member in the following organizations: National Association of College Employers, Virginia Counseling Association, Virginia Clinical Counselors Association, Virginia Career Development Association, National Career Development Association, and Washington Technical Forum. She has many years of experience in the counseling profession with specialties in the treatment of substance abusers and career development.

Sherry Knight Rossiter, PhD, LPC, NCC, sees approximately 600 employees annually in her work as a corporate career counselor and works with many other clients remotely through her Web site at www. CareerAgility.com. Her counseling style is direct but respectful, immensely practical, and spiritually based. She is the coauthor of *Change Careers—Change Your Life* published in 2001 by VocationLab LLC. Prior to making a midlife career transition, she was a commercial airplane and helicopter pilot and flight instructor, and now she provides counseling support to pilots and passengers who have survived aviation-related trauma. She has been a Licensed Professional Counselor in private practice for 12 years and is a frequent workshop presenter.

Kevin B. Stoltz, MS, NCC, LAPC, is an academic coordinator and career consultant at Georgia State University. He has over 20 years experience in business, industry, and management. He has provided consultation to various state and federal agencies. Currently, he teaches organizational principles at an international leadership institute and is on the adjunct faculty of Mercer University in Atlanta.

Work and the Workplace:

Their Impact on

the Lives

of the Workers

1

....

Work: Meaning, Mattering, and Job Satisfaction

Kathleen M. Connolly

ounselors are often faced with the task of helping their clients integrate work and life to guide them toward a deeper sense of meaning in both areas (Dollarhide, 1997). Such integration is not only for the good of the individual but also for the good of the workplace and society at large. When individuals are unable to experience a meaningful connection between work and life, they become despondent (Fox, 1994). The despondency in society today is traced to the alienation of the worker from the deeper meaning of life expressed through work (Fox, 1994). Without meaning, "people learn they are not needed in the universe. Feeling unneeded, in turn, engenders self-hatred and the deadening of the self found in alcohol and drug abuse, crime that leads to prison, and other forms of self-punishment" (Fox, 1994, p. 60). Thus, the importance of guiding individuals to find meaning in their work, and ultimately in their lives, has become an important mental health issue (Moomal, 1999) and one that professional counselors are well suited to pursue in their work with clients.

While counselors are well prepared to help clients cope with the psychological pressures associated with the world of work, they must also grow increasingly aware of the workplace variables that shape their clients' experiences as members of a constantly changing workforce. Job satisfaction is a critical workplace and psychological variable that is thought to mark the degree to which individuals experience meaning, wellness, and life satisfaction (Connolly, 2000; Judge & Watanabe, 1993; Spector, 1997). The nature of today's workforce, however, is unpredictable and not conducive to providing the comprehensive benefits and satisfaction that theorists have suggested are necessary for individuals to obtain meaning and satisfaction through their work (Dollarhide, 1997; Fox, 1994; Frankl, 1984; Shain, 1996). Downsizing, reengineering, rapid technological change, and flatter organizational structures are a few of the challenges posed to workers that potentially serve to leave them lacking a sense of satisfaction and meaning in the workplace (Harvey & Brown, 1996).

This chapter begins with an overview of the salience of work in life span development. Satisfaction with work, that is, job satisfaction, is explored with an emphasis on the relationship between it and meaningful work. The concept of mattering is introduced and defined as a way in which individuals create meaning, in this case, in regard to the workplace. Assessment methods for determining perceptions of mattering are discussed, and implications for counseling are suggested.

Work

In the broadest sense, work incorporates everything that is done to sustain and contribute to life for oneself and others and incorporates a broad spectrum of activities (Adler, 1927/1954). Work is considered to be any activity one engages in that generates material or immaterial products or outcomes, including raising children, composing music, or engaging in leisure pursuits (Adler, 1927/1954; Shain, 1996). In this chapter, however, work is defined traditionally as those activities performed that render monetary compensation as a function of being employed, either by oneself or by an organization.

Adler (1927/1954) claimed that work was one of three essential tasks individuals confront over the life span; the other two major life tasks are friendship and love. The extent to which individuals successfully accomplish these tasks is central to determining success in life (Adler, 1927/1954; Dreikurs, 1953). Work is considered the most crucial life task because it determines individuals' ability to provide for and contribute to self, others, and society (Adler, 1927/1954; Herr & Cramer, 1996; Myers, Sweeney, & Witmer, 2000). Successful accomplishment of the work task is essential for individuals to obtain a sense of worthiness, competency, belonging, and meaning in life (Adler, 1927/1954; Herr & Cramer, 1996).

Dreikurs (1953) purported that individuals' ineffectiveness in fulfilling the work task signaled serious illness. The loss or absence of work creates feelings of "despair, disillusionment, and anger" (Amundson, 1993, p. 147) and poses threats to individuals' ability to find meaning in life (Amundson, 1993; Amundson & Borgen, 1987; Herr & Cramer, 1996). The effects of unemployment further support the importance of work, as researchers have found increases in murder, suicide, mental illness, coronary heart disease, substance abuse, divorce, and domestic violence associated with the loss of work (Amundson & Borgen, 1987; Herr & Cramer, 1996; Pelletier, 1994). However, these debilitating effects do not appear to be solely by-products of the loss of work but have also been associated with dissatisfaction with work. In fact, Palmore (1969) suggested that job dissatisfaction results in a shortened life span.

Dissatisfaction with work is associated with poor physical and psychological health, including coronary disease, stress, anxiety, and depression (Amundson & Borgen, 1987; Begley & Czajka, 1993; Bluen, Barling, & Burns, 1990; Fox, Dwyer, & Ganster, 1993; Jex & Gudanowski, 1992; Lee, Ashford, & Bobko, 1990; O'Driscoll & Beehr, 1994; Palmore, 1969; Pelletier, 1994; Spector, Dwyer, & Jex, 1988). Conversely, individuals who report experiencing job satisfaction report fewer physical and psychosomatic symptoms (Begley & Czajka, 1993; Fox et al., 1993; Lee et al., 1990; O'Driscoll & Beehr, 1994).

Job Satisfaction

Job satisfaction, defined as the extent to which individuals are satisfied with their job or how they feel about different aspects of their job, is the most frequently studied concept in organizational behavior research (Cranny, Smith, & Stone, 1992; Spector, 1997). The assessment, study, and optimization of job satisfaction is a social responsibility given the relationship between job satisfaction and employee health and life satisfaction (Spector, 1997). The importance of work to individuals and society overall suggests the need to ensure that, as workers, individuals reap the economic, psychological, and social benefits of work and are protected from the consequences of dissatisfaction with work, including increased physical and psychological illness (Dreikurs, 1953; Herr & Cramer, 1996). However, as workers are increasingly removed from the ability to make meaning through their work, they lack the opportunity to experience job satisfaction (Fox, 1994; Frankl, 1984).

Job satisfaction has been related to myriad physical and psychological health variables as well as workplace variables (Cranny et al., 1992; Spector, 1997). The research and conceptual literature on job satisfaction is voluminous, with nearly 300 articles published yearly (Spector, 1997). Results of such research continue to support well-established relationships between job satisfaction and employee health. Such relationships have been posed in many different models of job satisfaction. A complete review of the literature and models of job satisfaction is beyond the scope of this chapter; however, one model in particular supports the importance of both work-related and psychological variables in regard to the experience of job satisfaction. The *job characteristics model* (Hackman & Oldham, 1980) is presented here to reinforce counselors' understanding of the psychological and workplace variables thought to mediate and predict job satisfaction.

Job Characteristics Model

The job characteristics model suggests that certain characteristics of jobs induce critical psychological states that in turn lead to increased motivation, decreased turnover, and increased job satisfaction (Hackman & Oldham, 1980; Spector, 1997). This model purports that any job can be described in terms of five core dimensions, defined as follows: (a) skill variety, the degree to which the job requires diverse activities, thus requiring the worker to use different skills and abilities; (b) task identity, whether the job requires completion of a whole or identifiable piece of work; (c) task significance, the degree to which the job has a substantial impact on the lives or work of others; (d) autonomy, whether the job allows the individual to express a degree of freedom, independence, and decision making in regard to scheduling the work and determining how to proceed with the tasks; and (e) feedback, the degree to which an individual receives information or evaluation regarding the effectiveness of his or her performance.

According to the job characteristics model, the presence of skill variety, task identity, and task significance leads workers to feel that their work is meaningful. Autonomy creates a sense of responsibility within the worker, and feedback creates knowledge about the results of one's work. These psychological states—meaningfulness of work, responsibility, and knowledge—are thought to engender satisfaction within the worker (Hackman & Oldham, 1980) and are moderated by growth need strength. Growth need strength is an individual's desire for fulfillment of higher order needs such as meaningfulness, autonomy, or personal growth.

Hackman and Oldham (1980) purported that for employees to gain a sense of meaningfulness and thus satisfaction with their work, skill variety must be present. Indeed, Stimson and Johnson (1977) found that the relationship between task repetitiveness and satisfaction was consistently negative. This suggests that employees who continually perform the same task are likely to feel unchallenged and unsatisfied (DeSantis & Durst, 1996), perhaps because the repetitiveness of the task lacks meaning (Hackman & Oldham, 1980). Connolly (2000) found a positive relationship between job satisfaction and skill variety and found it to be the strongest predictor of job satisfaction compared with age, gender, education, feedback, and job tenure. Skill variety has also been found to be related to employees' perception of mattering to their workplace (Connolly, 2000).

In addition to skill variety, the job characteristics model purports that the presence of task or job significance, that is, whether the job has an impact on others or society, is an important component of finding meaning and thus obtaining satisfaction with work (Hackman & Oldham, 1980). Voydanoff (1980) concluded that self-expression was an important variable in the analysis of job satisfaction, and that workers who perform tasks that are high on attributes such as skill variety, job significance, autonomy, and feedback from their job experience greater levels of job satisfaction than workers for whom such attributes are not present.

The job characteristics model supports the notion that components of the job itself are not sufficient to produce or preclude job satisfaction, but personal needs, psychological states, and perceptions are also related to and mediate the experience of job satisfaction. The idea that individuals' personal needs or characteristics are directly or indirectly related to whether they experience satisfaction with their work has been examined by counselors, primarily in relation to career development (Super, 1990), wellness (Connolly, 2000; Myers et al., 2000; Witmer & Sweeney, 1992), and the concept of mattering (Connolly, 2000).

Mattering

The importance of being needed, feeling significant, and making meaning in life has been referred to as *mattering* (Rosenberg & McCullough, 1981). Individuals need to feel they matter to others in order to make meaning in their lives. They need to feel that others pay attention to and take interest in them, consider them important and care about what they think and do, and are dependent on them for their potential participation and involvement (Rosenberg & McCullough, 1981; Schlossberg, Lassalle, & Golec, 1988). People who perceive they matter are more likely to report feeling significant and a sense of belonging to society (Amundson, 1993; DeForge & Barclay, 1997; Gossett, Cuyjet, & Cockriel, 1996; Rosenberg & McCullough, 1981; Schlossberg et al., 1988). Moreover, people who perceive that their work matters are more likely to experience wellness and job satisfaction (Connolly, 2000).

The construct of mattering consists of four components: attention, importance, dependency, and ego extension. Attention is described as the most elementary form of mattering. This is the feeling that one commands the interest or notice of another person. Importance is the feeling that we are important to the other person or are the object of his or her concern. Dependence is the notion that we are bonded to society not only by virtue of our dependence on others but also by their dependence on us:

> Mattering also is important for society, for it is a significant source of social cohesion. It is frequently held that one of the main forces binding people to society is their dependence on others. Humans cannot survive, or even be truly human, without other people. But perhaps equally important is others' dependence on us. (Rosenberg & McCullough, 1981, p. 180)

Another component of mattering is ego extension. This is the belief that others are interested in our successes and disappointments, actively follow our progress, and are concerned with our fate (Amundson, 1993; DeForge & Barclay, 1997; Rosenberg & McCullough, 1981; Schlossberg et al., 1988).

There are two types of mattering: interpersonal, that is, mattering to specific individuals; and general, that is, mattering to the larger community or society (DeForge & Barclay, 1997; Marcus, 1991; Rosenberg &

McCullough, 1981). In determining the meaning of interpersonal mattering, it is not necessary to corroborate individuals' beliefs about their significance to others with the reports of significant others themselves. It is
the individuals' perception, right or wrong, of how much they matter to
others that defines this concept (DeForge & Barclay, 1997; Rosenberg &
McCullough, 1981; Schlossberg et al., 1988). In general mattering, the
perception of how much people feel they matter to others is also considered. This concept implies the importance of developing a sense of social
cohesion and belongingness to a larger social entity. For example, general
mattering is likely to exist when people believe that they matter to society,
their communities, or their workplaces (DeForge & Barclay, 1997; Rosenberg & McCullough, 1981; Schlossberg, 1997).

The opposite of mattering is marginality, which is defined as the perception that one does not fit in, is not significant, and is not needed
(Rosenberg & McCullough, 1981; Schlossberg et al., 1988). Marginalization can occur during transitions such as changing or losing a job, returning to school, or entering retirement (Rosenberg & McCullough, 1981;
Schlossberg, 1997; Schlossberg et al., 1988). In these instances, marginality is often considered a temporary condition that is likely to subside
following the transition.

The loss of a job and searching for employment can be a nonmattering,
marginalizing experience, marked by feelings of despair (Amundson,
1993). Probably the most contemporary reflection of nonmattering experiences in the workplace includes those of downsized or laid-off employees. These individuals who find themselves suddenly unemployed are at
risk for compromised physical and mental health (Amundson & Borgen,
1987; Herr & Cramer, 1996; Pelletier, 1984). Counselors who work with
these employees as their clients are likely to find moderate to severe
depression, anxiety, relationship discord, and other emotional problems
(Amundson & Borgen, 1987).

Mattering and Mental Health

Researchers who have investigated mattering support the importance of
both interpersonal and general mattering (Amundson, 1993; Connolly,
2000; DeForge & Barclay, 1997; Rosenberg & McCullough, 1981;
Schlossberg et al., 1988). Empirical research results support a positive
relationship between mattering and global self-esteem or self-concept.
Notable, however, is that although there is a relationship between matter-

ing and self-concept, the formation of self-concept is independent of individuals' perception of mattering (Rosenberg & McCullough, 1981).

Other psychological or mental health variables found to be inversely related to mattering include depression, anxiety, a variety of somatic symptoms, and the propensity to be involved in delinquent behavior (Rosenberg & McCullough, 1981). Connolly (2000) found a positive relationship between mattering and a holistic wellness concept that embodied the dynamic process of experiencing physical, psychological, occupational, and spiritual health.

Mattering is a critical factor in coping with the emotional challenges associated with work, including job satisfaction (Amundson, 1993; Connolly, 2000). Individual psychology and Adlerian theory describe solutions to address the challenges likely to emerge in the workplace that grow out of such fundamental principles as social interest (Dreikurs-Ferguson & Laube, 1999). For example, individuals' basic need to want to belong and contribute, that is, social interest, has an impact in the workplace. When individuals' needs for affiliation and belonging are met, they are more likely to experience not only satisfaction with work but also overall improved physical and psychological well-being.

Mattering also involves feeling appreciated by others (Schlossberg et al., 1988). Employees who report feeling appreciated by their supervisors are more likely to experience job satisfaction (Herzberg, 1987; Herzberg, Mausner, Peterson, & Capwell, 1957). In fact, "appreciation by supervisor" was found to be to be an aspect of job satisfaction that was ranked substantially higher than "delegation of authority" or "technical competence and aptitude." The importance of appreciating employees can be central to encouraging and motivating employees, thus improving the overall productivity and success of an organization. Counselors involved in organizational change and development should understand that an organizational culture in which employees experience appreciation and a connection to the workplace is conducive to meeting a broad range of employee needs, including job satisfaction (Adler, 1927/1954; Dreikurs-Ferguson & Laube, 1999; Gerhart, 1987; Schlossberg, 1997). By working with employees and employers to discover ways to increase mattering in the workplace, counselors are well positioned to contribute to increasing overall job satisfaction among employees. Moreover, career, employment, and employee assistance counselors are in a unique position from which the tenets of mattering can be used to increase positive counseling outcomes both in and outside of the organization.

Implications for Counseling

Counselors providing individuals with career, employment, or employee assistance counseling are encouraged to create an environment that supports the tenets of mattering, thus helping clients to feel important, appreciated, needed, and accomplished within the counseling relationship itself (Amundson, 1993). "Through involvement in mattering experiences, people meet their basic needs for relationships and meaning in life" (Amundson, 1993, p. 147). Moreover, investigating mattering and non-mattering experiences as part of the counseling process can help both counselor and client develop an understanding of the client's meaning-making experiences and overall worldview.

Although the importance of mattering is not necessarily new to counselors, naming mattering as a meaning-making process is somewhat novel. Because mattering is a perception, it becomes part of an individual's construction of his or her reality. In counseling, clients' perceptions are continually sought out, validated, and challenged. Perceptions of mattering are a way in which individuals create meaning through their experiences. The General Mattering Scale (Marcus, 1991), discussed below, is a viable means for assessing clients' perceptions of mattering, both in the workplace and in other areas of lifestyle functioning.

General Mattering Scale

Counselors can use the General Mattering Scale (GMS; Marcus, 1991) to assess the degree to which clients perceive they matter, to whom, and in what contexts, thereby guiding clients toward meaning making. The GMS (Marcus, 1991) is composed of five items: (a) How important do you feel you are to other people? (b) How much do you feel other people pay attention to you? (c) How much do you feel others would miss you if you went away? (d) How interested are other people generally in what you have to say? and (e) How much do you feel others depend on you? Respondents are instructed to answer according to a 4-point Likert format ranging from 4 = *very much*, 3 = *somewhat*, 2 = *a little*, to 1 = *not at all*. Scores range from 5 to 20. The higher the score, the higher the respondent's perception of mattering.

Connolly (2000) and Deforge and Barclay (1997) performed studies of internal consistency on the GMS and computed Cronbach alphas of .86 and .85, respectively. These psychometric analyses support use of the

GMS in both research and clinical assessment arenas. Factor analysis also revealed support for the validity of the GMS (Connolly, 2000).

By definition, the GMS measures general mattering but can be adapted to reflect whatever context is of interest to the counselor or client. When using the scale as a paper-and-pencil instrument, the counselor should provide instructions to direct the respondent to answer the items in reference to a particular context, such as work. For example, if a counselor was interested in determining a client's perception of mattering in the workplace, instructions might read like this: "The following questions are designed to measure the degree to which you feel like you matter to others in the workplace. Please answer these items in relation to how you perceive yourself in your work setting."

The GMS can be included with a battery of paper-and-pencil instruments in an effort to assess a client's overall functioning and can also be used as an informal assessment instrument. In the latter situation, the counselor could simply ask the questions in an open-ended style to elicit client exploration.

To begin helping individuals integrate work and life, counselors can use mattering as a way of exploring the core dimensions of work and the critical psychological states described in the job characteristics model. If clients can become more aware of their needs in regard to meaning and mattering in the workplace, they may be better able to distinguish between a job and job dimensions that may or may not serve to meet those needs. Guiding clients to examine how skill variety, task identity, task significance, autonomy, and feedback can shape the degree to which they experience a sense of meaningfulness informs the process of integrating work and life. When the counseling process invites this discussion, clients are more likely to be able to discriminate between what they experience in the workplace and what they need to create meaningfulness in both work and life. Both the client and the counselor can become better aware of the psychological variables operating in the client's world of work and their impact on his or her satisfaction with work and life.

Conclusion

In and outside of the workplace, assessing clients' perceptions of mattering can be considered an intervention in itself, as it can engender a discussion of how clients' make meaning and where they perceive a lack meaning in their lives. Such a discussion may also unveil cognitive distortions or destructive thoughts that may be diagnostic of depression or other emotional problems. Helping clients to cope with their role as worker and the increasingly complex nature of work in our culture is no small task. Attempts to synthesize work and life are not futile, as the worker role, while all encompassing to some and elusive to others, is regarded as a critical part of development over the life span. Those who find meaning in their work are more likely to accomplish the task of work successfully and thus experience job and life satisfaction in addition to holistic wellness (Connolly, 2000; Wrzesniewski, McCauley, Rozin, & Schwartz, 1997).

References

Adler, A. (1954). *Understanding human nature* (W. B. Wolf, Trans.). New York: Fawcett Premier. (Original work published 1927)

Amundson, N. E. (1993). Mattering: A foundation for employment counseling and training. *Journal of Employment Counseling, 30,* 146–152.

Amundson, N. E., & Borgen, W. A. (1987). Coping with unemployment: What helps and hinders. *Journal of Unemployment Counseling, 24,* 97–106.

Begley, T. M., & Czajka, J. M. (1993). Panel analysis of the moderating effects of commitment on job satisfaction, intent to quit, and health following organizational change. *Journal of Applied Psychology, 78,* 552–556.

Bluen, S. D., Barling, J., & Burns, W. (1990). Predicting sales performance, job satisfaction, and depression by using the achievement strivings and impatience–irritability dimensions of Type A behavior. *Journal of Applied Psychology, 75,* 212–216.

Connolly, K. M. (2000). The relationship among wellness, mattering, and job satisfaction. *Dissertation Abstracts International, 61*(5-A), 1750.

Cranny, C. J., Smith, P. C., & Stone, E. F. (Eds.). (1992). *Job satisfaction: How people feel about their jobs and how it affects their performance.* Lexington, MA: Lexington Books.

DeForge, B. R., & Barclay, D. M. (1997). The internal reliability of a General Mattering Scale in homeless men. *Psychological Reports, 80,* 429–430.

DeSantis, V. S., & Durst, S. L. (1996). Comparing job satisfaction among public and private sector employees. *American Review of Public Administration, 26,* 327–339.

Dollarhide, C. T. (1997). Counseling for meaning in work and life: An integrated approach. *Journal of Humanistic Education and Development, 35,* 178–187.

Dreikurs, R. (1953). *Fundamentals of Adlerian psychology.* Chicago: Alfred Adler Institute.

Dreikurs-Ferguson, E., & Laube, H. (1999). Individual psychology and organizational effectiveness. *Journal of Individual Psychology, 55,* 109–114.

Fox, M. (1994). *The reinvention of work: A new vision of livelihood for our time.* San Francisco: Harper.

Fox, M. L., Dwyer, D. J., & Ganster, D. C. (1993). Effects of stressful job demands and control on physiological and attitudinal outcomes in a hospital setting. *Academy of Management Journal, 36,* 289–318.

Frankl, V. E. (1984). *Man's search for meaning.* New York: Washington Square Press.

Gerhart, B. (1987). How important are dispositional factors as determinants of job satisfaction? Implications for job design and other personnel programs. *Journal of Applied Psychology, 72,* 366–373.

Gossett, B. J., Cuyjet, M. J., & Cockriel, I. (1996). African American's and non-African American's sense of mattering and marginality at public predominantly White institutions. *Equity and Excellence 29*(3), 37–42.

Hackman, J. R., & Oldham, G. R. (1980). *Work redesign.* Reading, MA: Addison-Wesley.

Harvey, D., & Brown, D. R. (1996). *An experiential approach to organization development.* Upper Saddle River, NJ: Prentice Hall.

Herr, E. L., & Cramer, S. H. (1996). *Career guidance and counseling through the lifespan* (5th ed.). New York: HarperCollins.

Herzberg, F. (1987). Workers' needs. *Industry Week, 234*(6), 29–31.

Herzberg, F., Mausner, B., Peterson, R. O., & Capwell, D. F. (1957). *Job attitudes: Review of the research and opinions.* Pittsburgh, PA: Psychological Service of Pittsburgh.

Jex, S. M., & Gudanowski, D. M. (1992). Efficacy beliefs and work stress: An exploratory study. *Journal of Organizational Behavior, 13,* 509–517.

Judge, T. A., & Watanabe, S. (1993). Another look at the job satisfaction–life satisfaction relationship. *Journal of Applied Psychology, 78,* 939–948.

Lee, C., Ashford, S. J., & Bobko, P. (1990). Interactive effects of "Type" A behavior and perceived control on worker performance, job satisfaction, and somatic complaints. *Academy of Management Journal, 33,* 870–881.

Marcus, F. M. (1991). *Mattering: Its measurement and theoretical significance.* Unpublished manuscript.

Moomal, Z. (1999). The relationship between meaning in life and mental well-being. *South African Journal of Psychology, 29,* 36–41.

Myers, J. E., Sweeney, T. J., & Witmer, J. M. (2000). Counseling for wellness: A holistic model for treatment planning. *Journal of Counseling & Development, 78,* 251–266.

O'Driscoll, M. P., & Beehr, T. A. (1994). Supervisor behaviors, role stressors and uncertainty as predictors of personal outcomes for subordinates. *Journal of Organizational Behavior, 15,* 141–155.

Palmore, E. B. (1969). Physical, mental, and social factors predicting longevity. *Gerontologist, 9,* 103–108.

Pelletier, K. R. (1994). *Sound mind, sound body: A new model for lifelong health.* New York: Simon & Schuster.

Rosenberg, M., & McCullough, B. C. (1981). Mattering: Inferred significance and mental health among adolescents. *Research in Community Mental Health, 2,* 163–182.

Schlossberg, N. K. (1997). A model of worklife transitions. In R. Feller & G. Walz (Eds.), *Career transitions in turbulent times* (pp. 93–103). Greensboro, NC: ERIC-CASS.

Schlossberg, N. K., Lassalle, A., & Golec, R. (1988). *The mattering scale for adults in higher education* (6th ed.). College Park: University of Maryland Press.

Shain, M. (1996). Work, employment, and mental health. In R. Renwick, I. Brown, & M. Nagler (Eds.), *Quality of life in health promotion and rehabilitation: Conceptual approaches, issues, and applications* (pp. 327–341). Thousand Oaks, CA: Sage.

Spector, P. E. (1997). *Job satisfaction: Application, assessment, causes and consequences.* Thousand Oaks, CA: Sage.

Spector, P. E., Dwyer, D. J., & Jex, S. M. (1988). Relation of job stressors to affective, health, and performance outcomes: A comparison of multiple data sources. *Journal of Applied Psychology, 73,* 11–19.

Stimson, J., & Johnson, T. (1977). Tasks, individual differences, and job satisfaction. *Industrial Relations, 3,* 315–322.

Super, D. E. (1990). Career and life development. In D. Brown, L. Brooks, & Associates (Eds.), *Career choice and development: Applying contemporary theories to practices* (2nd ed., pp. 197–261). San Francisco: Jossey-Bass.

Voyandoff, P. (1980). Perceived job characteristics and job satisfaction among men and women. *Psychology of Women Quarterly, 5,* 177–185.

Witmer, J. M., & Sweeney, T. J. (1992). A holistic model for wellness and prevention over the lifespan. *Journal of Counseling & Development, 71,* 140–148.

Wrzesniewski, A., McCauley, C., Rozin, P., & Schwartz, B. (1997). Jobs, careers and callings: People's relations to their work. *Journal of Research in Personality, 31,* 21–33.

Spirituality in the Workplace: An Overview

Eugenie Joan Looby and Daya Singh Sandhu

he topic of spirituality in the workplace has infiltrated corporate America and has become the focus of published books, self-help literature, journal articles, workshops, seminars, academic conferences, symposiums, training sessions, university courses, topics on course syllabi, articles in magazines such as *Time, Newsweek*, and *Business Week* among others, television news shows, and Web sites (Adams & Benzer, 2000; Eaton, 1998; Robbins, Biberman, & King, 1999; Skelton, 1999). It has been suggested that this flourishing interest in spirituality is a consequence of the 1990s, with its increasing levels of isolation, spiritual emptiness, and existential frustration. Individuals are experiencing a spiritual renaissance and are seeking wholeness in body, mind, and spirit. They have become satiated with material goods and desire to feed their souls, especially in the workplace.

The workplace occupies a significant portion of people's lives and provides personal, social, and community fulfillment. Many individuals are therefore looking to the workplace to sustain them, to help them find a renewed sense of community and belonging, and to integrate their souls into their work. According to Sperry (1998):

> Many individuals are creative and meaning seeking, and spirit is the creative, meaning-seeking part of being human. Soul is the connective link between conscious and unconscious, between self and others, and between the material and the spiritual. Thus, the measure of soul in one's life is the measure of belonging and connectedness. Work can be thought of as an expression of the spirit at work in the world through individuals. As such, work is the expression of one's soul or inner being. (p. 2)

This chapter addresses spirituality in the workplace. It begins by examining the relationship between work and spirituality. This is followed by a discussion of what workplace spirituality means. Next, reasons for the rising interest in spirituality are articulated. Then, important principles of spirituality are outlined. Spiritual violence in the workplace is explained, along with suggestions for integrating spiritual practices in the workplace. The chapter concludes with a model of workplace spirituality and career counseling implications.

Work, Wellness, and Spirituality

Wellness/health has been analyzed as having several dimensions. The literature documents that optimum levels of wellness/good health depend on a balance between the following six dimensions: physical, social, emotional, intellectual, psychological, and spiritual (Depken, 1994; Hettler, 1984; Whitmer & Sweeney, 1992). While most models of health now include a spiritual dimension, it was not until recently that its impact on health has been realized. Osman and Russell (1979) believed that the spirit is a legitimate aspect of individual and corporate life and a legitimate dimension of well-being that cannot be ignored. For example, strong levels of spirituality have been found to enhance a person's ability to cope with traumatic or negative life circumstances such as illnesses, losses, or death (Kennedy, Davis, & Taylor, 1998).

Spirituality is woven into everyday experience and cannot be separated from the individual. Some individuals attempt to compartmentalize their identities by divorcing the career persona from other areas of their life, believing that one does not impact the other (Dorn, 1992). Others select careers for financial gain, for upward mobility, and to impress and please others rather than for achieving personal, occupational, or environmental congruence. Although these careers may offer material and social benefits, they may deprive individuals of the spiritual connections necessary for occupational fulfillment. For example, consider the following statements that are made quite frequently: (a) Another day, another dollar; (b) It is just a job; (c) I am doing this until something better comes along; (d) I hate to go to work; (e) I am overworked and underpaid; (f) I am doing it for the money; (g) I am working to get a bigger home, a new car, and the children's tuition paid; and (h) It pays the bills. These statements reflect the emptiness that some individuals may feel about their work. Integrating personal spirituality into everyday work activities can be the spark that ignites meaningfulness and purpose within individuals. Therefore, what is workplace spirituality, and what are some issues that it raises?

A Definition of Workplace Spirituality

Words such as faith, the divinity, meaning, peace of mind, harmony, principles, mystery, service to others, self-satisfaction, piety, well-being, optimism, relationships, play, experience, connections, freedom, ritual practice, forgiveness, hope, knowledge, learning, present-centered, and purpose (Banks, 1980; Chapman, 1987; Depken, 1994; Egbert, 1980; Fahlberg & Fahlberg, 1991; Greenberg, 1985; Hettler, 1984; Ingersoll, 1998; Moberg & Brusek, 1978; Satir, 1988; Seaward, 1995; Whitmer & Sweeney, 1992) are often used to define spirituality.

There has been much discourse regarding the differences between religion and spirituality. According to Kelly (1995):

> A typical distinction between religion and spirituality is found in a demarcation between spirituality as a personal affirmation of a transcendent connectedness in the universe and religion as the creedal institutional and ritual expression of spirituality that is associated with world religions and denominations. (p. 4)

Thomas (2000), on the other hand, saw little distinction between religion and spirituality. He stated:

> Spirituality is something universally human, that all people are spiritual, that spirituality and religion are practically synonymous, that spirituality, therefore, is as much concerned with the outer life (of the body, community, institutions, liturgy, tradition, doctrine, ethics, and society) as with the inner, and that spirituality is as much concerned with the public life of citizenship and work as with private life. (p. 267)

Spirituality in the workplace may have less to do with seeking a higher power and more to do with seeking fulfillment through work. This does not imply that religious feeling is lacking. Instead, individuals may have little faith in corporations as purveyors of religious fulfillment and are seeking ways to bring passion and meaning back into their work (Vogl, 1997). Spirituality has to do with principles such as honesty, integrity, accountability, ethics, trust, communication, values, mission, and cooperation (Laabs, 1995).

The spirituality-at-work paradigm has evolved into a challenging debate about its meaning. To some in corporate America, the concept is cryptic, confusing, ambiguous, hard to define, hard to measure, hard to quantify, and intangible. Given the emphasis on linear thinking, the scientific approach, and huge profit margins, spirituality at work was thought to have little impact on achieving company goals. Until recently, corporate America has not embraced spirituality for several reasons. Spirituality could be equated with religion, could border on harassment, could disrupt the work environment, could infringe on religious freedom, could border on discrimination, could result in proselytizing to others, may not relate to the company's mission, should be private, could co-opt the function of churches, could result in preferential treatment of employees, and could easily distort its practices (Laabs, 1995; McLaughlin, 1998; Vogl, 1997).

Laabs (1995) contended that while Title VII of the Civil Rights Act of 1994 prohibits religious discrimination against employees, the statute does not allow for companies to permit religious practices that disrupt the company's daily operations. Managers, however, struggle with respecting religious beliefs and allowing individual decisions at work based on religious practices and principles. Additionally, some companies are not altruistic enough to sacrifice personal beliefs for high profit margins. Furthermore, while management may think that creating a more spiritual workplace has value, they are not sure how it fits, where it fits, or how to integrate it into their corporate mission.

Despite these concerns, spirituality is beginning to infiltrate the workplace. Some employees are choosing to bring their values and personal identities to work in an attempt to bring congruence, meaning, and wholeness to their lives. According to Labbs (1995):

> As companies have downsized, restructured and reorganized themselves into oblivion, they've been left with skeleton crews who, quite literally, feel lifeless, tired, and sucked dry. Managers struggle to manage work

forces with little energy, creativity or commitment. In short, people
have been disembodied from their spirits and left feeling less than
whole, less than human. And there seems to be no end in sight. (p. 61)

Some companies and organizations are therefore being challenged with
how to retain valued employees, how to increase productivity, and how to
promote job satisfaction. Indeed, the workplace seems to be one of the
places that is emerging as the delivery system for modeling values people
want to integrate into their lives. Instead of asking how much money they
will make, employees want to known if the company's values are congruent with their own.

Institutions and corporations such as The World Bank, Tom's of
Maine, World Vision, Xerox, Taco Bell, Pizza Hut, Wal-Mart, Deloitte &
Touche, Chick-Fil-A, Aetna, Exxon, and Timberland, to name a few, continue to extol the virtues of spiritual values in the workplace (Conlin,
1999; Laabs, 1995; McLaughlin, 1998; Neal, 1998). Conlin (1999)
reaffirmed the increased interest in spiritual concerns:

> That's not to mention the 10,000 Bible and prayer groups in work-
> places that meet regularly, according to the Fellowship for Companies
> for Christ International. Just five years ago there was only one confer-
> ence on spirituality in the workplace; now there are about 30. . . . The
> number of related books hitting the store shelves each year has quadru-
> pled since 1990 to 79 last year. (p. 152)

It is evident that there is a spiritual yearning to find meaning and purpose in the workplace, as well as to create healthier corporate cultures that
allow individuals to reach their full human potential. Conlin (1999) felt
that the spirituality movement in the workplace may be symptomatic of
societal trends:

> With more people becoming open about their spirituality—95% of
> Americans say they believe in God or a universal spirit, and 48% say
> they talked about their religious faith at work that day, according to the
> Gallup Organization—it would make sense that, along with their brief-
> cases and laptops, people would start bringing their faith to work.
> (p. 152)

As a consequence, there may be as many definitions and ways of
expressing spirituality in the workplace as there are employees and corporations (Laabs, 1995). Suffice it to say that spirituality is an individual
experience, the manifestation of which takes many forms. Such expression
may involve interactions with others that include love, honor, respect, sacrifice, compassion, and caring; social, community, and environmental

responsibility; creating an organization that embodies integrity and strong moral and ethical values; engaging in meaningful, life-enhancing activities; being interconnected with others and the universe; personal fulfillment and helping others; developing a relationship with a higher power; sharing outward expressions of faith with others; and engaging in organized religious activity. The common denominators are making connections and finding meaning and purpose in life.

The Search for Meaning in the Workplace

The search for meaning in the workplace is not a new phenomenon. Most people desire to engage in work that provides connections with others and personal fulfillment. Meaningful work has been equated with high levels of performance and productivity. Spirituality is slowly finding itself spreading to corporate America because of concerns about the dehumanizing effects of the work environment and a quest for personal integration and fulfillment of human potential. Mitroff and Denton (1999) conducted a seminal study of spirituality in the workplace. They conducted extensive interviews with senior executives and human resources executives in major corporations all over the United States and discovered the following:

> People are hungry for ways in which to practice spirituality in the workplace without offending their co-workers or causing acrimony. They believe strongly that unless organizations learn how to harness the "whole person" and the immense spiritual energy that is the core of everyone, they will not be able to produce world-class products and services. (p. 83)

Participants were asked to delineate what provided the most meaning and purpose in their jobs. The most important things were realizing their potential, affiliation with a good and ethical organization, interesting work, money, good colleagues, serving humankind, service to posterity, and community service. Mitroff and Denton (1999) concluded that "beyond a certain threshold, pay ceases to be the most important, and higher needs prevail. The desire for 'self actualization,' as Abraham Maslow calls it, becomes paramount" (p. 85).

Mitroff and Denton's (1999) study also gleaned important information about other workplace issues related to spirituality:

- Participants express their intelligence and creativity instead of their emotions at work.

- Most participants wished to express and develop their whole selves at work.
- Most participants listed values such as integrity, honesty, good relationships, trust, honoring a commitment, and support for family and others as values that govern their lives, and rarely were those values compromised at work.
- Participants viewed their companies as caring, ethical, and profitable and saw no dichotomy between being ethical and being profitable.
- About 30% of the participants viewed religion and spirituality positively; 2% had positive views of religion and negative views of spirituality; 60% had positive views of spirituality and negative views of religion; and 5% had negative views of religion and spirituality.
- Many of the participants believed in a higher power, wished that they could express their spirituality at work, but were ambivalent about how it should be fostered.

Mitroff and Denton (1999) also sought participants' definitions of spirituality. Defining features included nondenominational, informal, inclusive, universal and timeless, ultimate provider of meaning and purpose, feeling of awe, sacredness, interconnectedness, inner peace and calm, unlimited faith and willpower, the end in itself, and the existence of a supreme guidance force.

Mitroff and Denton (1999) also found that participants were "unaware of models that could be used to foster spirituality appropriately in the workplace. Instead, they were seeking models or guides that would allow them to implement spirituality programs"(p. 86). The study also provided five models of religious or spiritual organizations:

- The religious-based organization may feel positively about religion and spirituality or positively about religion and negative toward spirituality (e.g., Mormons).
- The evolutionary organization begins strongly aligned with a specific religion and then becomes more universal (e.g., YMCA).
- The recovering organization adopts the twelve-step method to encourage spirituality (e.g., Alcoholics, Gamblers, Narcotics, and Overeaters Anonymous).
- The socially responsible organization is guided by strong spiritual values that become part of the corporate mission. The goal is social responsibility (e.g., Ben & Jerry's).

- The values-based organization is guided by a philosophy not aligned with any religious or spiritual doctrine (e.g., Kingston Technologies).

Mitroff and Denton (1999) discerned that each model represented individual ways of finding meaning and purpose in life, that one was not superior to the other, that each has its strengths and limitations, and that no one model was applicable to all organizations. They discovered that because each model was the consequence of a critical event, it was built on a foundation of hope. Each model was guided by its own vocabulary and fundamental principles, particularly how to run an ethical business. Finally, individuals who perceived their organizations as spiritual viewed their organizations as better than their less spiritual counterparts. Mitroff and Denton concluded that ways of integrating spirituality into management should be developed because organizations may not survive without finding ways to address employees' spiritual needs.

Reasons for the Growing Interest in Spirituality

A review of the literature indicates many reasons for the rising interest in spirituality in the workplace (Conger, 1994; Handy, 1994; Neal, 1998; Pulley, 1997; Robbins et al., 1999; Rutte, 1996; Vaill, 1989). The following are the most frequently cited.

Fear in the workplace: Factors such as corporate downsizing, technological advancements, rapid changes in the workplace, management's ability to obtain a cheaper labor force in other countries, the weakening powers of trade unions, and the demand for skilled laborers send the message that job security is no longer guaranteed. This results in workplace uncertainty, anxiety, and fear.

Corporate downsizing and restructuring: This may streamline operations and increase profits but has resulted in layoffs, loss of livelihood, and greater demands on remaining employees. These factors contribute to employee stress, anxiety, lack of creativity, and job uncertainty. For some employees, the layoffs may have created better opportunities. Other employees experience loss of company loyalty, little creativity and motivation, and a weakening of the human spirit.

Lack of a spiritual connection with the workplace: In some organizations, there is little company loyalty, no job security, lack of appreciation or respect for core human values, lack of community, and lack of trust and faith in management. In such a climate, it is difficult to find meaning and purpose in work.

The aging of the baby boomer generation: The baby boomer generation, which represents the largest segment of the workforce, is in mid-life. Some individuals are discovering that materialism is no longer fulfilling and are more concerned with the legacy that they will leave behind. This generation is reexamining and assessing the meaningfulness of their lives, and spiritual connectedness is an emerging theme.

Science versus spirituality: There is a realization that there are mysteries about life that are not measurable. Science does not provide the answers to everything; there are some things that cannot be explained by human manipulation. Realizing that there is a power greater than man helps individuals to understand the unexplained.

Popular culture: Book sales, articles, magazines, Web sites, conferences, university courses, workshops, symposiums, motivational speakers, public interest in spiritual concerns, articles, compact discs, television shows, and organizations devoted to spiritual issues have made spiritual concerns a new profession.

Time management: Workplace demands have left less time for individuals to participate in formal religious activities on a consistent basis. Therefore, these needs may remain unfulfilled.

Women in the workplace: There are more women in the workplace. Because women may be perceived as more sensitive and nurturing, they may focus more readily on spiritual values than do men.

The technological age: With the many advances in technology, there may be necessity for a reduced workforce. Furthermore, for those who work with machines instead of people, there may be fewer opportunities for human contact in the workplace. In such an environment, finding ways to nurture the spirit and connect with others may become very important.

Lack of purpose: Many companies are so consumed with focusing on product and profit that promoting human dignity and respect becomes unimportant. Employees may feel little shared purpose or company loyalty. The work environment may become unsettling because of the loss of human kindness, the loss of human spirit, the loss of energy, and the loss of motivation. Hence, employees may be forced to seek validation elsewhere.

Gap between management and employees: Workplace fragmentation and lack of community have led to toxic workplace environments.

Employees are seeking work environments that are more congruent with their inner values, where they are valued and respected, where there is company unity and loyalty, and where work brings not only financial but also spiritual fulfillment.

Productive employees: Some companies have realized that one way to get more productive employees is to incorporate spiritual values into the workplace. This may enhance organizational performance. Several companies are presently incorporating spiritual values in their mission statements.

Self-actualization: Individuals have the innate need to strive toward self-actualization. If individual goals for success have been met, then the natural tendency is to pursue other existential issues that focus on values, meaning, purpose, and spirituality.

Corporate greed and employee boredom: Workers are being turned off by corporate greed and are reacting against a workplace philosophy that emphasizes profits over people. Employees are also searching for something that will inspire and motivate them, especially if work has become repetitive, mundane, and tedious.

Creating a more spiritual environment is the responsibility not only of management but also of employees. Table 2.1 outlines principles that can be adopted to promote job satisfaction, reduce employee turnover, and create a new mission and sense of purpose in the workplace (see Taylor, 2000).

Spiritual Violence in the Workplace

Spirituality at work starts with each employee. When the essence of the employee's spiritual soul is violated, the result is spiritual distress. The consequences may be manifested in harmful and dysfunctional behaviors inflicted on self and others. Incidents of workplace violence remain the focus of national news. For example, the first sentence of a news story written by *Seattle Post–Intelligencer* reporter Tom Paulson (1999) reads, "The day before a gunman opened fire in an office in Seattle's Wallingford neighborhood, killing two employees and wounding two others, a copier repairman killed seven co-workers in Honolulu" (p. 1). Unfortunately, workplace violence seems to have become the norm not the exception.

Workplace violence in the United States is reaching epidemic proportions. Because one's self is so intimately interwoven in work, the workplace becomes the ideal place in which to vent rage, frustration, anger,

TABLE 2.1   TWELVE PRINCIPLES OF SPIRITUALITY IN THE WORKPLACE

Creativity	Creativity means allowing individuals to break out of molds, finding new ways of doing, thinking, and believing, and breathing life into the workplace. When employees enjoy their work, they are more productive and happier. Stifling creativity means stifling human potential.
Communication	Effective communication is the glue that holds individuals together and fosters teamwork and understanding. The ability to express ideas, thoughts, and feelings honestly and to be heard fosters a healthy respect and valuing of each individual.
Respect	Respect for self and others, including peers and management, fosters teamwork and mutual sharing of goals. Lack of respect leads to antagonism, negativity, and discord.
Partnership	Partnership involves taking responsibility for tasks, fulfilling obligations, accepting different viewpoints, agreeing to disagree, and working together for the mutual benefit of company goals. Lack of partnership leads to discord, poor collaboration, and incongruent goals.
Vision	Vision means seeing all that is possible and probable, a strong desire to grow and expand, persistence, and setting goals. Lack of vision breeds stagnation.
Flexibility	Flexibility means to change as circumstances permit, to be resilient, to recognize strengths and weaknesses, to do things differently, and to accept the ideas of others. Lack of flexibility results in rigidity and accepting the status quo.
Energy	Energy is excitement in work. It stems from being creative, being able to express ideas freely, and being appreciated by peers and management. Negative energy translates into loss of productivity and toxic work situations.

(continued)

TABLE 2.1   *(continued)*

Fun	People who enjoy life have a reason for being, an attitude of excitement, and reverence for each day. This is translated into everything that they do, including their work. They see value in everything and allow their lives to unfold. They are not afraid to live. Spirituality is the attitude that one has about living.
Finding self	When individuals are in harmony with themselves and the universe, their lives are richer.
Values training	Values training means ensuring that there is a match between individual's values and company values, and ascertaining that individuals will not be placed in work situations that compromise their values.
Relational management	This means matching company and individual goals, creating trust, eliminating hidden agendas, and modeling integrity, respect, and positive relationships in the workplace.
Stress management	This includes finding a balance between work and personal life, developing effective time management skills, and taking care of mental and physical health.

threats, and otherwise lash out at others. The United States Department of Justice surveyed 45,000 households between 1992 and 1996 and discovered that almost 2 million Americans experienced violent acts or threats of violence in the workplace (Watkins, 1998). Furthermore, workplace slayings constituted one out of every six job-related deaths (Watkins, 1998). Common reasons usually cited for workplace violence include termination, layoffs, disputes, and disciplinary action; however, the underlying cause of physical violence is spiritual violence.

Wallace (1999) purported that in addition to physical acts, violence frequently involves abusive acts of an emotional or psychological nature that can limit or deny certain rights, freedoms, or liberties to others. Abuse of power is perpetuated when violence creates change that denies the spirituality of the connection with others. Spiritual violence is an act or acts that undermine or violate the spiritual dimension of human nature. Workplace violence therefore becomes a consequence of spiritual violence.

Acts of spiritual violence are manifested in the workplace in many different ways, some of which include but are not limited to the following:

- Sexual harassment
- Being forced to do a task for which the employee is not trained
- Assignment of tasks that violate employees' personal, moral, ethical, and religious principles
- Unsatisfying and oppressive job conditions
- Lack of company loyalty and trust in management
- Employed in a company that engages in unethical business practices
- Being forced to work on the Sabbath or other religious holidays
- Being passed over for raises, promotion, or other benefits
- Having other employees or management take credit for work that the employee accomplished
- Stifling of creative ideas and not being allowed a voice
- Termination without just cause, layoffs, downsizing, and loss of livelihood
- Wage disparities
- Feeling threatened, devalued, disrespected, and mistreated by supervisors or other employees
- Little opportunity for growth
- Lack of interconnectedness and being forced to engage in meaningless work
- Being placed in demeaning positions
- Prejudice and discrimination
- Self-worth and contributions to the organization never validated
- Loss of hope and spirit

A Spirituality of Work That Works

There are several things that companies can do to enhance and nurture spiritual responsibility in the workplace and decrease acts of spiritual violence. These practices should be automatic and focus on promoting human respect and dignity. According to Kennedy (1999), management should take some responsibility for preventing incidents of spiritual violence in the workplace:

> As a consequence, managers—even those with deeply held faith commitments—do not have a duty, as managers, to pursue or ensure

the spiritual development of their subordinates. They do, however, have a duty to make sure that the structures and activities of the workplace are not hostile to this spiritual development, and where it does not conflict with the legitimate goals of the association might possibly support such development. (p. 5)

Kennedy (1999) delineated specific practices that can promote and enhance the spiritual climate of the workplace. These practices should serve as guiding principles for workplace environments that value individual worth. These include but are not limited to the following:

- Engage in practices and produce work products that promote human well-being and ensure that the employees understand what goods are served by their work.
- Do not force employees to make difficult choices between work and family responsibilities, sick children, medical emergencies, and other critical concerns.
- Do not penalize employees for making choices consistent with their cultural values, beliefs, traditions, and customs instead of the job.
- Do not exploit employees for the benefit of company profits.
- Do not foster environments in which employees may be forced to violate their moral, ethical, religious, and personal values for the benefit of the company. Such practices could include lying, cheating customers, producing inferior products, selling inferior goods, and refusing to serve customers of a particular religion, sexual orientation, gender, nationality, race, or social class.
- Foster a sense of community among employees and management.
- Do not create environments that foster unnecessary and unhealthy competition, that value some employees over others, and that support organizational distrust.
- Be attentive to the vocational gifts of each employee and provide support, resources, and opportunities for those gifts to bloom.
- Be attentive to the religious concerns of employees, including allowing them to celebrate religious holidays and honoring their request not to work on sacred days.

Rutte (1996) believed that there are several benefits that can accrue from creating a more spiritual workplace. Such benefits include but are not limited to the following:

- More creativity and full expression of human potential

- Authentic communication and deeper levels of trust
- Increased ethical and moral behaviors
- Company and customer loyalty
- Community, interconnectedness, and valuing of self, others, and work
- Pleasant and energetic work environment
- Appreciation and respect for self, others, and diverse talents
- Passion about job
- Good mental health and peace of mind
- Work that has meaning and satisfaction
- Increased productivity

A Model of Spirituality

A model is a step-by-step procedure that can be followed to yield desired results. Both career counselors and career consultants can use the components of this model, both individually and in combination with each other, to develop and enhance the spiritual dimensions of workers and leaders alike. Because of the inordinate number of definitions provided to explain spirituality, this model is built on the consensus definition agreed on at the Summit on Spirituality convened in 1995 by the Association for Spiritual, Ethical, and Religious Values in Counseling, a division of the American Counseling Association:

> The animating force in life, represented by such images as breath, wind, vigor, and courage. Spirituality is the infusion and drawing out of spirit in one's life. It is experienced as an active and passive process. Spirituality is also described as a capacity and tendency that is innate and unique to all persons. This spiritual tendency moves the individual towards knowledge, love, meaning, hope, transcendence, connectedness, and compassion. Spirituality includes one's capacity for creativity, growth, and the development of a values system. Spirituality encompasses the religious, spiritual, and transpersonal. ("Summit Results," 1995, p. 30)

We use several keywords from this definition to demonstrate various ways in which career counselors can highlight the significance of spirituality in the workplace and enhance employee spiritual development. These keywords include love, meaning, connectedness, and creativity/development. This model is neither exhaustive nor comprehensive but serves as a reference point for beginning conversations that focus on workplace spiritual issues.

Love

Love in the workplace means compassion. Most organizations are structured in a hierarchical manner. Words such as *dominance* and *power* generally describe relationships between employees and their supervisors. In a spiritually oriented workplace that focuses on love and compassion, power over employees changes to power with the employees. For example, career counselors should assist management with creating environments that value equality of all employees. Career counselors should help management to develop strategies that value diversity, recognize individual talents, and appreciate the contributions of each employee to the company's mission and goals. Career counselors should devise strategies that focus on effective communication among employees and also between management and employees. Career counselors should also assist with planning activities that tap into the creative talents of employees in the workplace and that include different voices. Ultimately, if employees feel that their voices matter, then work and their contribution to an end-product become more meaningful.

Meaning

Some employees are yearning to find meaning in their work that transcends material gains and personal rewards. It is the meaning in work that dignifies life. Organizational discontent is usually caused by meaningless and purposeless work. To create a workplace where everyone shares a sense of purpose, it is important that trust, honesty, and values as spiritual concepts are explored (Leigh, 1997) and practiced. When there is external and internal congruence, then work becomes a preoccupation in which individuals immerse themselves (Bloch, 1997). Career counselors should assist employees with selecting work environments and occupations that are congruent with their spiritual and moral values. Career counselors should assist employees with choosing occupations and work environments that may provide personal fulfillment. Career counselors should encourage employees to develop positive relationships in the workplace and should also encourage employees to contribute to building community in the workplace.

Connectedness

Traditional support networks and relationships are weakening, and many spiritual sources of solace such as extended families, church, and civic groups are becoming less influential. Many individuals are looking to their workplace to fulfill their spiritual thirst for connections to others

(Brandt, 1996; Mirvis, 1997). Nagai-Jacobson and Burkhardt (1989) conceptualized spirituality as a harmonious interconnectedness with self and others. In many work environments, however, this interconnectedness between management and employees never develops (Hampden-Turner, 1970). Career counselors should find ways to create interconnectedness among employees, their coworkers, and supervisors because synergy, created through interconnectedness, "catalyzes, unifies, and unleashes the greatest powers within people" (Covey, 1989, p. 262). Career counselors should encourage employers and employees to develop shared goals that are congruent with the company's philosophy. Career counselors should encourage employers and employees to focus on respect, communication, teamwork, and rewards in the workplace. Such practices may help to foster company loyalty and positive work environments.

To produce world-class services and products, organizations should learn how to harness the whole person and the immense spiritual energy that each person possesses (Mitroff & Denton, 1999). Career counselors should therefore help employers and employees develop strategies that help to address employees' workplace physical, emotional, and spiritual issues. Career counselors should help employees to conceptualize work as a part of their lives, not apart from it. Career counselors should also assist management with techniques for building community in the workplace and ensuring that employee spiritual development is not compromised. Addressing the whole individual helps to create coherence, meaning, and purposefulness in work.

Capacity for Creativity, Growth, and Development

Corporations are challenged with creating work environments that can promote employee creativity and satisfaction. Work is the expression of an individual's soul. Career counselors, career educators, and career development specialists should focus on the spiritual dimension when preparing people for work. Career counselors should assist management in creating work environments that promote creative thinking and expression. Career counselors should also help employees to find ways of expressing their spirituality creatively and without offending others.

Conclusion

Today's workplace is in transition. Downsizing, technological advancements, globalization, changing demographics, cutbacks, competitiveness and corporate greed, little job security, and lack of company loyalty are some of the many factors that have contributed to unfriendly work environments. Some employers are acknowledging that to promote job satisfaction, to retain valued employees, and to attract the best and brightest, creating a workplace congruent with employee values and beliefs may be the best way to enhance productivity.

Employees are also striving for wholeness, meaning, and interconnectedness in their work and may not be willing to compartmentalize their identities and values and deposit them outside the office doors. Instead, there is a widespread spiritual yearning for fulfillment and purpose in the workplace. Spiritual connectedness can inspire, motivate, encourage, and give new mission to work. Integrating spiritual practices into the workplace can promote trust, the development of shared goals, creativity, understanding, and community.

Career development, approached from a spiritual perspective, acknowledges the whole person and recognizes that the workplace provides the ideal venue for individuals to connect with each other on deeper levels and express their spirituality. Career counselors, career educators, and career development specialists should focus on the spiritual dimension when preparing individuals for work. They should help in the creation of work environments that promote creative thinking, respect individual spiritual development, and nurture humanity. After all, rediscovering and nurturing the human spirit should be an important component of workplace satisfaction.

References

Adams, T. B., & Benzer, J. R. (2000). Conceptualization and measurement of the spiritual and psychological dimensions of wellness in a college population. *Journal of American College Health, 48*, 165–173.

Banks, R. (1980). Health and spirituality dimensions: Relationships and implications for professional preparation programs. *Journal of School Health, 50*, 195–202.

Bloch, D. P. (1997). Introduction. In D. P. Bloch & L. J. Richmond (Eds.), *Connections between spirit and work in career development: New approaches and practical perspectives* (pp. vii–xii). Palo Alto, CA: Davies-Black.

Brandt, E. (1996, April). Corporate pioneers explore spirituality. *HR Magazine, 41*, 82–87.

Chapman, L. S. (1987). Developing a useful perspective on spiritual health: Love, joy, peace and fulfillment. *American Journal of Health Promotion, 2*(2), 12–17.

Conger, J. (1994). *Spirituality at work: Discovering the spirituality in leadership.* San Francisco: Jossey-Bass.

Conlin, M. (1999, November 1). Religion in the workplace: The growing presence of spirituality in corporate America. *Business Week.* Retrieved from http://www.businessweek.com/careers/content/jan1990/b3653001.htm

Covey, S. R. (1989). *The seven habits of highly effective people: Restoring the character ethic.* New York: Simon & Schuster.

Depken, D. (1994). Wellness through the lens of gender: A paradigm shift. *Wellness Perspectives, 10,* 54–69.

Dorn, F. J. (1992). Occupational wellness: The integration of career identity and personal identity. *Journal of Counseling & Development, 71,* 176–178.

Eaton, H. (1998). Spirit, community, and leadership at work. *High Technology Careers Magazine.* Retrieved July 17, 2001, from http://www.hightechcareers.com/doc.298/lifestyle298.html

Egbert, E. (1980). Concept of wellness. *Journal of Psychosocial Nursing Mental Health Services, 18,* 9–12.

Fahlberg, L. L., & Fahlberg, L. A. (1991). Exploring spirituality and consciousness with an expanded science: Beyond the ego with empiricism, phenomenology, and contemplation. *American Journal of Health Promotion, 5,* 273–281.

Greenberg, J. S. (1985). Health and wellness: A conceptual differentiation. *Journal of School Health, 55,* 403–406.

Hampden-Turner, C. (1970). *Radical man: The process of psychosocial development.* Cambridge, MA: Schenkman.

Handy, C. (1994). *The age of paradox.* Boston: Harvard Business School Press.

Hettler, W. (1984). Wellness: Encouraging a lifetime pursuit of excellence. *Health Values, 8*(4), 13–17.

Ingersoll, R. E. (1998). Redefining dimensions of spiritual wellness: A cross-traditional approach. *Counseling and Values, 42,* 156–166.

Kelly, E. W., Jr. (1995). *Spirituality and religion in counseling and psychotherapy: Diversity in theory and practice.* Alexandria, VA: American Counseling Association.

Kennedy, R. (1999). Can we conceive a management spirituality without faith? *Department of Management, University of St. Thomas.* Retrieved July, 17, 2001, from http://www.stthomas.edu/cathstudies/cst/mgmt/goa/kennedy.html

Kennedy, J. E., Davis, R. C., & Taylor, B. (1998). Changes in spirituality and well being among victims of sexual assault. *Journal for the Scientific Study of Religion, 37,* 322–328.

Laabs, J. J. (1995). Balancing spirituality and work. *Personnel Journal, 74*(9), 60–68.

Leigh, P. (1997, March). The new spirit at work. *Training and Development,* 26–33.

McLaughlin, C. (1998). *Spirituality at work.* Retrieved July 17, 2001, from http://www.projectearth.com/pages/workplace.html

Mirvis, P. H. (1997). "Soul work" in organizations. *Organization Science, 8,* 193–206.

Mitroff, I., & Denton, E. (1999). A study of spirituality in the workplace. *Sloan Management Review, 40*(4), 83–93.

Moberg, D. O., & Brusek, P. M. (1978). Spirituality well being: A neglected area in quality of life research. *Social Indicators Research, 5,* 303–323.

Nagai-Jacobson, M., & Burkhardt, M. (1989). Spirituality: Cornerstone of holistic practice. *Holistic Nursing Practice, 3*(3), 18–26.

Neal, C. (1998). The conscious business culture. *Creative Nursing, 4*(3), 5–7.

Osman, J., & Russell, R. (1979). The spiritual aspects of health. *Journal of School Health,* 49, 359.

Paulson, T. (1999). Shipyard shooting: Workplace violence becoming epidemic. *Seattle Post–Intelligencer.* Retrieved July 17, 2001, from wysiwyg://21/http://wwwseatlep-i.com/local/work04.shtml

Pulley, M. L. (1997). *Losing your job—reclaiming your soul.* San Francisco: Jossey-Bass.

Robbins, L., Biberman, J., & King, S. (1999). *Origins, framing and teaching of management and spirituality.* Retrieved July17, 2001, from http://mars.acnet. wnec.edu/Eam/Ann...delphia1999/Papers/RobbinsLee.html

Rutte, M. (1996). *Spirituality in the workplace.* Retrieved July 17, 2001, from http://www.cop.com/info/rutte01.html

Satir, V. (1988). *The new people making.* Mountain View, CA: Science & Behavior Press.

Seaward, B. L. (1995). Reflections on human spirituality for the worksite. *American Journal of Health Promotion, 9,* 165–168.

Skelton, H. (1999). *What is spirituality in the workplace?* Retrieved July 17, 2001, from http://www.spiritualityatwork.org/articles-etc.htm

Sperry, L. (1998). Executive leadership, character and spirituality at work. *Organizational and occupational psychiatry.* Retrieved July 17, 2001, from http//www.aoop.org/Spr98work.htm

Summt results in formation of spirituality competencies. (1995, December). *Counseling Today,* p. 30.

Taylor, B. (2000). *Seven principles of spirituality in the workplace.* Retrieved July 17, 2001, from http://www.itstime.com/rainbow.htm

Thomas, O. C. (2000). Some problems in contemporary Christian spirituality. *Anglican Theological Review, 82,* 267–282.

Vaill, P. (1989). *Managing as a performing art: New ideas for a world of chaotic change.* San Francisco: Jossey-Bass.

Vogl, A. J. (1997). Soul-searching: Looking for meaning in the workplace. *Across the Board, 34*(9), 16–24.

Wallace, H. (1999). *Family violence: Legal, medical and social perspectives.* Needham Heights, MA: Allyn & Bacon.

Watkins, T. (1998, July). Workplace violence troubles 1.7 million Americans a year. *Cable News Network.* Retrieved July 17, 2001, from http://www.cnn.com/US/9807/27/workplace.violence/

Whitmer, J. M., & Sweeney, T. J. (1992). A holistic model for wellness prevention over the life span. *Journal of Counseling & Development, 71,* 140–148.

3

Developing the Whole Employee: Some Practical Applications Regarding Spirituality in the Workplace

Betty Milburn

This chapter explores reasons for growing interest in spirituality in the workplace. It also provides definitions of key concepts, characteristics associated with spirituality, and ways that spirituality can be nurtured. In spite of interest in spirituality, there appears to be uncertainty about how to address this aspect of employees. For this reason, counseling applications for dealing with the spiritual dimension of both organizational leaders and employees are also provided in this chapter.

Factors Related to Spirituality in the Workplace

The workplace and the structure of one's work life are undergoing profound changes. Downsizing, right sizing, telecommuting, project contracting, outsourcing—these are just a few terms demonstrating that change, uncertainty, and stress are staples of today's work environment. How does one cope with such complexity and chaos? There are numerous ways, but the crux of any coping method is that it provides reassurance. Reassurance that everything will work out okay; reassurance that the event or situation will be survived; reassurance of the ability to deal with whatever is necessary; reassurance that something positive will result from the struggle or pain. To engender confidence, reassurance must be based on a higher authority. Hence the burgeoning interest in spirituality, because spirituality is the connection to one's soul, which in turn is the connection to the universe.

Additional reasons for the emerging interest in spirituality in the workplace exist. Herriot (1992) stated that individuals bring many roles to work; they come with expectations of the organization, and they have differing values and needs. Mitroff and Denton (1999) found that people do not want to compartmentalize their lives. Conger (1994) noted that the workplace is one of our most important sources of community because places that used to provide support no longer fulfill that function as well. For example, many people do not know their neighbors, families are scattered across the nation and globe, and hectic lifestyles limit time available for participation in civic organizations.

Another factor related to spirituality in the workplace is the emphasis on quality of work life in many organizations. My workplace has a Quality of Work Life Vision Statement (TAMU President's Executive Committee, 1992) that affirms people as the institution's most valuable resource. The statement affirms the importance of encouraging employees to achieve personal and professional goals, the right of all individuals to be treated with respect and dignity, and the needs that people have at work, such as adequate resources, training, and *understanding with regard to family-related responsibilities*. This type of emphasis on employees as the primary asset of the organization results in the necessity to view employees in their entirety. The spiritual dimension is now being acknowledged as one facet of every human being, thus further normalizing spirituality as appropriate for consideration in the workplace.

Even so, both organizational leaders and employees seem unclear about how to address spirituality in the workplace. Everyone knows that separation of church and state has been a guiding principle of the United States, and that has generalized to the work environment. People seem afraid to talk about their spirituality or religious beliefs because they do not want to be perceived as insensitive to differing views or as sharing something they should keep private.

Spirit, Soul, Spirituality, and Religion

There are differing opinions about the similarities and differences between religion and spirituality. Some view them as one and the same, whereas others view them as distinct entities (Hinterkopf, 1997; O'Hanlon, 1998). Further complicating the concept are the notions of soul and spirit. Moore (1997) viewed soul and spirit as distinct, whereas Briskin (1996) seemed to view them as synonymous, defining soul as the "multiplicity of selves within each of us" (p. 5). Briskin further wrote about four core themes related to soul: connection to unconscious, vitality, the place where opposites join, and "a spark of the divine, a bridge to the qualities of a supreme being or a cosmic aspect to consciousness" (p. 11).

Webster's New World Dictionary (1994) defined *spirit* as "the life principle, especially in man, originally regarded as inherent in the breath or as infused by a deity" and as "the thinking, motivating, feeling part of man, often as distinguished from the body" (p. 1293). The definition of *soul* is "an entity which is regarded as being the immortal or spiritual part of the person and, though having no physical or material reality, is credited with the functions of thinking and willing, and hence determining all behavior" (p. 1281). I view spirit and soul as the wick and wax of a candle. They are two separate features of the object, yet must come together to light the flame of a person's entirety.

Spirituality is about certain core values or characteristics, regardless of one's religious beliefs or lack thereof. Conger (1994) identified themes of spirituality: selfless love, compassion, respect and concern for well-being and life, and reverence for the universe. Other writers add understanding that all things, people, and events are connected (Garfield & Toms, 1997; Guillory, 2000) and an abundance mentality (Guillory, 2000).

Religion refers to a "specific system of belief and worship" (*Webster's New World Dictionary*, 1994, p. 1134). Religion is one of many paths to foster spirituality. Spirituality is the path to connecting with the authentic self, or soul, which in turn is the connection to the Universe, Supreme Being, or whatever name one chooses to use for the Great Mystery.

Benefits of Nurturing Employee Spirituality

Why nurture the spiritual dimension of employees? Trott (1996) found that employees with higher levels of spiritual well-being demonstrated high levels of self-efficacy, organizational commitment, and adaptability. The converse was true for employees with low levels of spiritual well-being. Furthermore, creativity, especially with regard to the flash of insight and the incubation period, can be considered a spiritual process. Also, passion is associated with one's spirit, and soul "speaks to timeless longings for meaning and purpose" (Briskin, 1996, p. 28). Certainly creativity and passion are desirable qualities for the organization, and fulfilling purpose or finding meaning in one's work is a way for employees to meet the need to belong. Another chapter in this book deals with meaning in work, but it is important to note here that purpose is a spiritual concept.

Native American beliefs seem to provide a useful distillation of this discussion on spirituality.

> In the beginning were the Instructions. We were to have compassion for one another, to live and work together, to depend on each other for support. We were told we were all related and interconnected with each other....The Instructions during that time, at the beginning, were to live and respect one another even with all the differences, different cultures, different languages. (Wall, 1993, p. 2)

On purpose, "the Creator has His things for us to do while we're here visiting, and it's set up before we are even born" (Wall, 1993, p. 152).

Characteristics of Spirit-Based Leadership

Employee values, needs, and life circumstances assert themselves daily in the workplace. Following are some examples of employee requests that occurred in a period of a few weeks in a relatively small organization.

"I just learned that a client of mine was hit by a car while he was running and is in intensive care. Is it okay for me to miss the meeting this morning? I want to go to the chapel and say a prayer for this person."

"I have the chance to participate in a Bible study tour abroad for a week. I know this is our busiest season, but this is an opportunity of a lifetime. May I have the time off?"

"My mother is having health problems, and I must make some decisions about the type of care she needs. I can only do this by observing her for an extended period of time. I know my absence will increase the workload of the rest of the team, but I am the only one who can make this decision and deal with her business holdings."

"I know how busy the summers are for us, but I really want to start taking summers off to spend with my child. Is this an option you are willing to consider?"

"My work is extremely demanding, and I already have trouble accomplishing everything I want to in a timely fashion. But I really want to add one more responsibility. I think this particular activity would be beneficial to me personally, and I also feel I can make a positive contribution to our division through my participation. Will you support my involvement on this team?"

Organizational leadership can respond to such employee needs in many ways; some nurture employee spirit whereas others demoralize. One common response is to consider the bottom line or the impact on production or service. But leadership based on higher (spiritual) values will base decisions on spiritual principles. Scott (1994) stated that using rational thinking as the primary or only basis for decision making ultimately stifles spirit. Guillory (2000) argued that organizations that are supportive of employees exhibit high performance. He further stated that high performance is spiritually driven. The spiritual principles he identified are listed below.

1. We are all *inherently* equal as human beings.
2. Dignity, respect, and trust *voluntarily* govern our behavior.
3. We are each responsible and accountable for *every* condition on this planet.
4. This planet is *fully abundant* to support the needs of everyone.
5. We are *one* with all that exists. (Guillory, 2000, p. 132)

These principles lead to the behaviors of teamwork, quality assurance, continuous improvement, environmentalism, customer focus, diversity, and empowerment. To Guillory (2000), integrating humanistic principles, practices, and behaviors with sound business functioning is the essence of spirituality in the workplace. Cox (1996) stated the formula for nurturing spirituality in the workplace a bit differently, but the underlying theme is the same: "Making yours a resonant, growing, soulful organization boils down to this: Allow spontaneity; encourage intellectual passion; honor and reward truth, even when painful; break down barriers; recruit talented people; and value their independent thought and abilities" (p. 131).

Rolbin (1996) added the importance of clear direction from the leadership and flexible rules. She also said that people "need to be managed by someone who is not afraid of them or their knowledge—someone who can let, indeed encourage them, to soar" (p. 31). Rolbin identified

10 ways leaders can encourage people's spirits to be engaged at work. These are summarized in the paragraphs below with occasional commentary or elaboration.

First, Rolbin identified strong, committed, visionary leadership as absolutely essential. Moreover, the leaders of the organization need to work together; lack of communication and coordination negatively impact morale. Leadership working together seems like basic common sense, but my perception is that it is more often absent than present. In my own work environment, where the leadership team members are all highly trained in communication skills and the importance of communication, I have been amazed at the number of issues, both large and small, that have resulted from lack of coordination and communication. I can only imagine the communication problems that exist in organizations in which communication is not at the core of their daily work with clients.

Second, Rolbin exhorts leaders to treat employees with respect and as equals. Again, this is common sense and a philosophy most have been exposed to almost since birth, and certainly throughout the years in the educational system. Yet, there exists an extreme gap in the stated value and the behavior that is observed. Often, it is the support staff who are treated as less than equal. Examples run the gamut from less funding for training and professional development to not consulting them about changes that directly impact their work.

Third, communication is crucial. Employees need accurate information provided in a timely fashion. It is also imperative to have access to the people above them in the organization.

Fourth, find ways to show employees that they, and the work they do, are valued. An essential part of valuing employees is giving them recognition for their good work. Another component is supporting them when they want to try new ideas. On the opposite end of the continuum, it is important to expect mistakes and to help employees learn from them rather than placing blame. Looking for win-win solutions is key in demonstrating support for employees.

Fifth, Rolbin noted the importance of putting people in positions for the right reasons. It is quite demoralizing to see people promoted or hired for positions without the requisite qualifications or experience. Likewise, it is equally disheartening to possess skills or knowledge but not be asked or allowed to use them to solve problems in the organization.

Sixth, listen without judging, and ask questions that help the employee think through whatever problem the employee is experiencing. The employee should solve the problem; the role of the manager is to provide guidance by listening and questioning.

Seventh, managers must do their job, which is to deal with organizational politics and difficult situations that interfere with employee functioning.

Eighth, leaders need to have a vision and to be fully engaged themselves, thus modeling enthusiasm and helping employees to feel that they have joined in a mission larger than their job title that will truly make a difference. Leaders should expect and encourage outstanding work.

Ninth, managers must provide employees the tools and resources needed to accomplish the job. This includes adequate budget, equipment, information, training, timelines, and decision-making authority.

Finally, Rolbin stated that managers need to be secure with themselves, thus eliminating the possibility of feeling threatened by the expertise and accomplishments of their employees.[1] Security also allows them to speak the truth, regardless of what others might think or want to hear as well as permits them to "stay the course" in difficult times. Security further provides a framework from which to objectively sift through feedback, both positive and negative, to discern what, if any, adjustments are needed. McDermott (1994) also listed a strong sense of personal identity as a spiritual resource for leaders, which allows them to depersonalize negative feedback.

Guillory (2000) posited depth self-knowledge as the essential first step for leadership. He suggested that such knowledge can only be attained through inner work, which results in contact with one's soul. Palmer (1994) likewise stressed the importance of inner work in his examination of the dark side of leaders. He identified five shadow areas of leaders: insecurity; belief that the universe is hostile, which makes life a battle; belief that only the leader is ultimately responsible for everything that happens; fear, especially of chaos; and denial of death. Palmer stated that leaders must deal with these issues through inner work to keep from projecting them onto the organization.

Three other characteristics of spirit-based leadership must be highlighted. One is a service orientation that includes service to all stakeholders, including clients, employees, the community, and the world. An

---

1 From *Surviving Organizational Insanity: Keeping Spirit Alive at Work*, by S. Rolbin, 1996, pp. 51–68. Ottawa, Ontario, Canada: Lightkeeper. Copyright 1996 by Sharon Rolbin, PhD. Adapted with permission.

overwhelming majority of books and articles I read on spirituality in the workplace emphasized the importance of a service mentality, which flows from one's spirituality. Discussions about vision, mission, purpose, and meaning are all rooted in the concept of service that transcends mundane work activities to allow people to make a positive difference in the world. This is spirit aflame and a little understood fact: Soul is easiest found in the routine, daily, common tasks in life if only we approach them as sacred and focus on the service we provide through our labors.

The second characteristic that must be highlighted is integrity. Orsborn and Toms (1997) suggested that integrity is the result of acting in congruence with one's deepest beliefs. Nair and Toms (1997) addressed having a single standard of conduct for all aspects of life. Kanungo and Menlonça (1994) addressed ethics, stating that ethics is integral to spirituality. Again, integrity is a prerequisite for leaders who wish to nurture spirit in employees; their conduct must honor deeply held spiritual values such as honesty, sincerity, justice, and service. The behavior of leaders, not their words, demonstrates to employees acceptable actions and the values the organization holds most dear.

Last, humility is a requisite characteristic of spirit-based leadership. Humility, combined with a strong sense of both security and identity, allows the manager to receive input and criticism and learn from each person and situation. It minimizes the need to assert one's authority or to "be right." It fosters flexibility and openness to different ideas and makes the leader more approachable.

Counseling Applications for Organizational Leaders

It is imperative that leaders in organizations be firmly grounded in their own spirituality, which means they understand their purpose, know their deepest values, and are employed in positions congruent with them. Counselors working with leaders should help them explore these areas. Discussion should focus on the time being spent daily on their spiritual development and the methods they are using. The goal is to help leaders uncover their authentic selves, which can be a difficult task because of the myriad expectations placed on them from various sources. Most people have attained leadership positions by conforming to and fulfilling expectations, often with little thought to their true selves. Thus, another topic of exploration is expectations. Discussion of values and gaps between values and behavior, particularly in the workplace, is another important focus for counseling. The goal is to help leaders consciously choose actions and responses aligned with their spiritual principles, even when it is not convenient or expedient. Career counseling may be necessary if their position does not mesh with their purpose and values, because finding other employment is preferable to letting their spirits diminish.

Leaders who consider higher values in the conduct of their roles view themselves as providing service to their employees. This service goes beyond the typical procurement of resources and dealing with organizational politics to sincere concern about the well-being of employees and their personal and professional development. Thus, helping leaders explore ways to utilize skills and interests of staff, even when they are outside the realm of essential job duties, could be another focus of counseling. Counselors can encourage leaders to take an active role in asking employees what they need and how leadership can better support them, and to ask not just once, but on a regular basis because of continual changes in situations and needs. Furthermore, counselors can work with leaders to establish a working environment that encourages employees to voice their needs, desires, concerns, and ideas for change without fear of negative repercussions.

Helping leaders examine processes of teamwork and evaluation is another counseling application for organizational leaders. Exploring how team members interact, what contributions they make, and how best to manage change can ultimately help improve working relationships and productivity. When interpersonal or professional disagreements occur in the workplace, counselors can help leaders examine the issues and seek win-win solutions. Counselors can also help leaders develop skills in identifying and acknowledging concerns of individual team members, as well as skills in effective processing of concerns identified by the team as a group so that everyone is operating from the same knowledge base.

For the spirit-based leader, at the heart of all dealings with team and individual employee issues is the assumption that people want to contribute, desire to excel at work, and are doing the best they can. In other words, the foundation for responses in such leaders is trust and belief in the team and individuals on the team, resulting in giving the benefit of the doubt rather than automatically assuming the worst. One important role counselors can play is helping leaders determine what assumptions are being made, the basis for such assumptions, and the impact the assumptions are having. Related to this are assumptions regarding employee strengths and weaknesses. People vary in their attention to detail, organization of their workday, pacing of projects, need for interaction with colleagues, and so on. When an employee is performing poorly or "creating" difficulties in the workplace, counselors can help leaders examine organizational and leadership factors for contributions to the problem instead of assuming the problem resides solely with the employee. For example, someone who is perceived as taking too many breaks may not have adequate responsibilities or may have duties that are not sufficiently challenging. Likewise, excessive absences could suggest personal, alcohol, or substance abuse problems, but another possible explanation is an unreasonable level of stress resulting from responsibility overload, assignments that are too challenging, or a misfit between organizational and personal goals, values, or mission.

Counseling Applications for Employees

Although there is growing interest in nurturing the spirit of workers, widespread change has yet to be accomplished, and it is likely to be years, if not decades, before this type of organization is the norm. In the meantime, workers who wish to increase their satisfaction and nurture their spirit can undertake their own spiritual journey, examining purpose, values, assumptions, congruence between values and behavior, and congruence between employment and authentic self, all of which are appropriate fodder for counseling. Thus the counseling applications for organizational leaders also apply to employees.

There are many paths leading to connection with that which is spiritual; counselors can play a major role in helping employees identify the path or paths that work for them. Certainly the incorporation of journaling, reflection, or meditation into treatment is standard fare for counseling, facilitating connection with what therapists call one's inner voice or inner wisdom, or one's soul, and thus authentic self.

O'Hanlon (1998) listed six additional pathways to spirituality that counselors can help employees explore. First, physical or sensual activities, such as dancing, athletics, eating fine foods, and massages, offer the opportunity to move beyond oneself and the moment to a different dimension.

Another path to spirituality can be found in intimate relationships such as with one's partner or child. Connections with others in intimate relationship offer momentary glimpses of the eternal and flashes of understanding of pure love and the divine in all.

A third path to spirituality is through civic or community organizations or causes. Working with others for the betterment of society or the planet develops insight about the interrelatedness of all things.

Nature is yet another path to spirituality. Ocean, mountains, sunrise, sunset—these are a few aspects of nature that provide perspective as well as instill awe at the Great Mystery that created all.

Art, whether creating or enjoying it, is also a means of transcending self and nourishing the soul. Literature, painting, sculpture, acting/theater, movies, photography, music—all have the capacity to enlighten or expand awareness. Storytelling and reading/discussion groups, as encouraged by Wisely and Lynn (1994), are related to this path as well as others previously mentioned. These activities facilitate connection with others and discovery of commonalities.

O'Hanlon's sixth path to spirituality is through connection to God, the Universe, or a Higher Power. This method is most similar to religious activity but does not have to include religion.

Ultimately, nurturing one's spirituality is solitary work, although one may join with others on the journey and experience greater benefit through the connections formed. Moore (1997) stated that the soul is waiting to reveal itself; all that is needed is space or emptiness. This has not been my experience. Rather, for me, nurturing my spirit requires daily attention and large doses of self-discipline, which I sometimes exhibit and sometimes lack. I read, sing, journal, pray, reflect, attend worship services, and spend time in nature gardening, to name a few activities that nourish my soul. When I am consistent, the rewards are unlimited; when I sink into fear or approach daily living without reverence, the resulting fruit is bitter. I am just a novice at the beginning of my spiritual pilgrimage, and the path is jagged, undoubtedly due to my inconsistency. But I am finding that as I trust in the bounty and beneficence of the universe, open myself to the leading of spirit, and seek to love and serve others in ways true to my authentic self (which I am still discovering), I enjoy peace, contentment, and wonderful surprises that awe and thrill my soul.

Conclusion

Employees come to the workplace as whole beings, which includes a spiritual dimension. It is beneficial for both the organization and employees to acknowledge and address spirituality in the workplace because the results include teamwork, customer focus, diversity, and empowerment, among other positive outcomes. Counselors can help organizational leaders develop spirit-based leadership; they can also help employees develop their own spirituality.

Daily practice of spiritual principles such as truth, justice, trust, acceptance, openness, and connectedness, combined with large measures of communication and feedback, would undoubtedly create an environment in which souls are nourished and employees are engaged and passionate about their work. The words *spiritual or spirit-based leadership* would not require voicing; they would be evident through spirituality that would be integrated into the leader's daily living and working activities and would be inseparable from his or her identity or way of being in the world. So, too, would be the case for employees.

It would be marvelous if we could all work in organizations that operate on humanistic principles, but we cannot; there are not that many of them. It would be magnificent if we could all work for people whose leadership is based on spiritual principles, but we cannot; there are not that many of them. What we can do as counselors, however, is develop our own spirituality and acknowledge it as an important component of who we are, regardless of where we are, work included. We can also assist organizational leaders and employees to do likewise.

References

Briskin, A. (1996). *The stirring of soul in the workplace*. San Francisco: Jossey-Bass.

Conger, J. A., & Associates. (1994). (Eds.). *Spirit at work*. San Francisco: Jossey-Bass.

Cox, A. (1996). *Redefining corporate soul: Linking purpose and people*. Chicago: Irwin Professional.

Garfield, C., & Toms, M. (1997). The new story in business. In M. Toms (Ed.), *The soul of business* (pp. 1–26). Carlsbad, CA: Hay House.

Guillory, W. A. (2000). *The living organization: Spirituality in the workplace*. Salt Lake City, UT: Innovations International.

Herriot, P. (1992). *Management challenge: Balancing individual and organization needs*. London: Sage.

Hinterkopf, E. (1997). Defining the spiritual experience. *TCA Journal, 25*(2), 75–82.

Kanungo, R. N., & Menlonça, M. (1994). What leaders cannot do without: The spiritual dimensions of leadership. In J. A. Conger & Associates (Eds.), *Spirit at work* (pp. 162–198). San Francisco: Jossey-Bass.

McDermott, B. O. (1994). Partnering with God: Ignatian spirituality and leadership in groups. In J. A. Conger & Associates (Eds.), *Spirit at work* (pp. 132–161). San Francisco: Jossey-Bass.

Mitroff, I. I., & Denton, E. A. (1999). *A spiritual audit of corporate America: A hard look at spirituality, religion, and values in the workplace.* San Francisco: Jossey-Bass.

Moore, T. (1997, June). Spirituality and psychology: Care of spirit, soul, and world. Paper presetned at the New England Educational Institute Cape Cod Summer Symposium, Eastham, MA.

Nair, K., & Toms, M. (1997). The soul of business. In M. Toms (Ed.), *The soul of business* (pp. 123–146). Carlsbad, CA: Hay House.

O'Hanlon, W. (1998, July). *Spirituality and psychotherapy: Evoking soul and meaning in the service of change.* Paper presented at the New England Educational Institute Cape Cod Summer Symposium, Eastham, MA.

Orsborn, C., & Toms, M. (1997). Integrity in business. In M. Toms (Ed.), *The soul of business* (pp. 99–122). Carlsbad, CA: Hay House.

Palmer, P. J. (1994). Leading from within: Out of the shadow, into the light. In J. A. Conger & Associates (Eds.), *Spirit at work* (pp. 19–40). San Francisco: Jossey-Bass.

Rolbin, S. (1996). *Surviving organizational insanity: Keeping spirit alive at work.* Ottawa, Ontario, Canada: Lightkeeper.

Scott, K. T. (1994). Leadership and spirituality: A quest for reconciliation. In J. A. Conger & Associates (Eds.), *Spirit at work* (pp. 63–99). San Francisco: Jossey-Bass.

TAMU President's Executive Committee. (1992, December). *Quality of work life statement.* College Station: Texas A&M University. Retrieved July 3, 2001, from http://cis.tamu.edu/about/quality.work.php3

Trott, D. C., III. (1996). *Spiritual well-being of workers: An exploratory study of spirituality in the workplace.* Unpublished dissertation, University of Texas at Austin.

Wall, S. (1993). *Wisdom's daughters: Conversations with women elders of Native America.* New York: HarperCollins.

Webster's New World Dictionary. (3rd College ed.). (1994). New York: Prentice Hall.

Wisely, D., & Lynn, E. (1994). Spirited connections: Learning to tap the spiritual resources in our lives and work. In J. A. Conger & Associates (Eds.), *Spirit at work* (pp. 100–131). San Francisco: Jossey-Bass.

Job-Related Stress: Sources and Prevention Strategies

Don Pazaratz and William Morton

o survive in today's global economy, organizations and businesses have altered policies, workforce, product, and services. Work has become universally stressful. There are psychological and environmental determinants that create work-related stress. Clients often come into therapy because of stress at work, which affects the whole family. Rather than merely helping the individual adjust to the workplace, counselors should explore the client's values, choices, responsibilities, and challenges. This chapter discusses the need for organizations to reduce stress in the workplace.

Stress has been defined from a spectrum of conceptual frameworks and is reflected in two broad categories: person–environment constructs and stimulus–response. The following authors subscribe to the stimulus–response view. Selge (1974) explored the person–environment construct and focused on an individual's response to stress and concluded that any significant change in a person's life upsets his or her homeostasis, thus creating stress and requiring an adaptive response. Folkman (1984) supported this view and stated that individual stress is the result of external events or stimuli that trigger a maladaptive response in the individual. Pines and Aronson (1988) and Maslach and Leiter (1998) believed that burnout occurs because of prolonged excessive stress and reflects an inability on the part of the person to adequately adjust to highly emotional demands. However, stimulus and response definitions may be limiting, because a stimulus definition only looks at events in the environment, whereas a response focus is narrow and often only refers to a state of stress. This means that stress can be perceived as a process that is influenced by an individual's cognitive appraisal of stressful demands of the environment (Guidano & Liotti, 1983).

Stress as arising from environmental conditions are supported by a number of other researchers. Folkman (1984) stated that stress can be viewed as a transactional construct involving a misfit, based on a cognitive appraisal, between the environmental demands and the individual's capabilities. This means coping mechanisms account for individual differences in reaction to stressful situations. Brad (1984), in defining techno-stress, regarded it specifically as a disease of adaptation, based on the individual's inability to cope with new computer technologies. Raider (1989) viewed stress as a breakdown of personal defenses workers use to deal with and adapt to intense job stressors. For Robbins (1992), stress is a dynamic condition in which individuals are confronted with an opportunity, constraint, or demand related to what they desire and for which the outcome is perceived to be both uncertain and important. In summary, when stress is viewed dynamically, it occurs in interactions and in the context of a stressor and the ability of individuals to appraise their capacity to cope or the potential to experience distress. Therefore, stress is neither good nor bad in itself, but rather it can result from an interaction with a positive or negative stressor. Ultimately, the desire of the individual and the uncertainty of the outcome lead to distress.

Sources of Work-Related Stress

As society has shifted from an industrial base to an information age and global economy, a number of significant changes have and are occurring. The global economy has caused a downsizing and merging of corporations, in both the public and private sectors (Arthur, 1999). Trimming the fat in organizations has created job insecurity and increased employee anxiety about the future. Stability in all sectors of society has been replaced with constant change as information increases at a rapid rate and innovation becomes crucial to corporate existence. Changes have resulted in major increases in stress levels for companies, employees, and families (Maslach & Leiter, 1998). Corporations that once offered lifetime employment no longer offer such opportunities, thus upsetting the security of the North American workforce. Rapid technological advances have resulted in major changes in the way in which corporations do business. Hanson (1989) reported that almost half of today's workforce in the Western world is linked to electronic workstations. Arthur (1999) stated that the traditional concept of career is rooted in the stable conditions of the industrial model that has dominated the 20th century. Technological change has required new job descriptions, job retraining, downsizing the workforce, and new skills and competencies. For those workers who have resisted learning new technologies or are unable to improve their skill level, their lack of adaptation has resulted in increased stress levels (Bernstein, 1989).

Governments, experiencing decreased revenues, have reduced the workforce and redeployed civil servants. Social and educational programs have experienced budget cutbacks, yet the number of people seeking government assistance has remained constant, increasing worker stress levels. Clearly, some worker stress arises directly as a result of business or corporate practices such as role and task demands. Task demands are composed of expected activities and are usually defined in a job description.

Specific occupations have different levels of stress. Jobs that have high performance expectations and that require decision making can be highly stressful, particularly if the latitude of their decision-making powers have been limited by superiors. Quick and Quick (1984) suggested that it is not only the amount of stress a particular occupation causes but also the nature and source of stress of the occupation that cause problems. For example, law enforcement, air traffic controllers, physicians, dentists, and mental health professionals have been identified as high-stress positions.

Routine jobs with a high degree of repetition and minimal skill demands can be a source of high stress because of frustration and boredom (such as court stenographers). Worker overload, both quantitatively and qualitatively, can be stressful. Quantitative job overload is the result of too much work. Stress arises if the time limits for job completion are too constraining. Qualitative overload results when an employee is underqualified or unable to meet job expectations (Ganster, Mayers, Sime, & Tharp, 1983). Job insecurity is compounded when the prospects of future jobs are limited. Role conflict and role ambiguity can be a major source of stress for a worker, particularly when the expectations of superiors are not clearly communicated.

Poor interpersonal work relationships can contribute to employee stress with bosses, peers, and subordinates, creating the lack of a social support system. Poor working relationships have been characterized by low levels of trust, support, and interest in listening to or helping with problems confronting workers. Low levels of trust in working relationships have been related to role ambiguity and poor communication, resulting in low job satisfaction and the individual feeling a threat to his or her well-being (Braverman, 1999).

A tyrannical boss creates a tense working environment and can have employees operating in fear. If the boss is too permissive, or not definite with directives, workers can then be placed in a potentially conflictual dilemma of performing roles and task demands. Bennis and Nanus (1985) suggested that the effectiveness of organizational leaders rests on their ability to conceptualize and communicate a vision and to get people at all levels to buy into the vision. Tracey (1990) added that the future of an organization depends on how leaders use their power and influence with employees. Minden (1986) indicated that the variable that appears to determine the most amount of stress employees experience is in direct proportion to the interpersonal style of the boss.

The pressure of relationships or the lack of supportive others can be a source of employee stress. Factors such as office politics, rivalry, and lack of appropriate social support are potential sources of job-related stress. Social support by supervisors and by other workers, in the form of availability of a supportive other, is viewed as a balance to stress. Gadon (1988) reported the finding that supervisors were more willing to support workers with task-oriented problems and were reluctant to help them with emotional or personal problems. Robbins (1992) believed it is unethical for managers to intrude into an employee's personal life. Beck and Hillman (1986) stated that managers enter therapy to learn to manage their own stress but often keep their therapy confidential. When a manager suggests that an employee may require help outside the scope of supervisor–supervisee relationship, such an observation can place the relationship in a precarious position.

Impact of Workplace Stress

Freedman and Rosenman (1974) identified a personality type that has a greater risk of heart disease. Type A personalities are individuals who are highly competitive, time conscious, overscheduled, and exhibit superhuman behavior. These individuals avoid affect and tend to use denial of feelings as a defense mechanism. These individuals demonstrate a high relationship to heart disease and other stress-related illnesses (Chopra, 1993). Selge (1974) claimed that excessive occupational stress has an adverse physical effect on workers, such as cardiovascular disease, peptic ulcers, colitis, and skin disorders. Quick and Quick (1984) added there is a correlation between stressful demands and the physical and psychological well-being of the individual. For those individuals unable to cope with stress, stress may lead to excessive smoking, drug and alcohol abuse, violence, mental disorders, suicide, family problems, sleep disturbances, sexual dysfunction, and depression. Schradle and Dougher (1985) disputed this view, stating such conclusions are correlational in nature and do not precisely measure the causal relationship. Robbins (1992) also refuted the relationship between stress and physiological problems, stating that the symptoms are complex and present an objective measurement problem. But Robbins believed that psychological symptoms of tension, anxiety, irritability, boredom, and procrastination can be linked to job-related stress.

Prevention of Workplace Stress

Work life is where individuals spend most of their time, and it often becomes the setting that presents the highest challenge (Myers & Diener, 1995). Prevention of stress is preferred to maintain a productive, adaptive, and flexible work environment. Employees and organizations are interdependent, but organizations have a moral and legal responsibility for their employees' health. Central to stress prevention is the implementation of strategies to prevent stress for the individual and organization. Environmental stress reduction occurs and positive employee responses follow when employees' work-related goals are enhanced (Nichols, 1990). Therefore, primary prevention aims to maintain what Selge (1974) defined as individual *homeostasis*, or what Quick and Quick (1984) explained as the optimal individual stress level. This means that, to maintain job motivation, achieve goals, and ensure productive outcome, employees need some stress. However, stress that extends beyond optimal individual levels creates distress.

How does any organization or its employees reduce the impact of negative environmental conditions and maintain optimal stress levels? Howard (1998) believed that to survive personally in the new ruthless economy, individuals must be highly adaptable and communicate well. This requires the individual to be resourceful, to avoid the hazards of burnout and the loss of competitiveness. But this also means that employers must create opportunities favorable to employees' work-related goals and career development. Sternberg (1997) argued that success and failures in life, especially at work, stem from how people use the ability they have, or how they fit their thinking styles into the pattern demanded by the context in which they live and work. Work satisfaction is also viewed as occurring when there is a congruence of an individual's personality, values, and interests with the characteristics of one's circumstances (Oleski & Subich, 1996). Therefore, primary prevention on the individual level involves the employee assuming responsibility for maintaining optimum stress levels.

Secondary prevention is concerned with detecting or diagnosing distress. Tertiary prevention is aimed at providing physiological and psychological treatment of distress and the return of the individual to well-being. These treatment techniques include methods such as relaxation training (developing and maintaining a state of low tension), biofeedback (learning to control one's internal processes such as heart rate), meditation (a sustained effort at reducing strong emotions), and cognitive–behavioral skill training (learning to be goal directed in thinking and behaviors). This holistic approach means the individual develops stress control by being centered in the here and now, developing problem-solving strategies, and learning to accept uncertainty. These techniques have been shown to be successful in helping the individual (Billings & Moos, 1984; Maslach & Leiter, 1998) to manage stress. However, these methods do not reduce the sources of stress that occur in the work environment.

Interventions

Robbins (1992) stated that primary prevention begins with the selection of employees, that is, the person–job fit, and by maintaining improved communication to avoid ambiguity. Quick and Quick (1984) suggested that for organizational stress, management strategies should be directed toward altering the nature of job roles, tasks, work environment, and interpersonal relationships by changing the organizational structure. In discussing sexual harassment in organizations, Reese and Lindenberg (1998) believed there must be realistic and specific policies. Braverman (1999) illustrated how traditional tools for occupational health and safety, discipline, and employee relations are inadequate and inappropriate in responding to the problems of workplace violence. But, stress can be reduced when the work environment is structured to encourage freedom, challenge, meaning, and positive social atmosphere (Oleski & Subich, 1996). Managers can also maintain optimal stress levels by permitting employees to participate in goal setting by task clarification, role analysis, acceptance of demands, and conflict resolution. Menaghan (1983) concluded that a variety of stress management methods are effective in diminishing job stress but are limited when their focus is only on symptom reduction without trying specific methods to alleviate the causes of job stress.

Counseling Issues

There are various themes that are pertinent in counseling job-related stress; these include assessment career counseling, values clarification, coping strategies, and planning career changes. Patton and McMahon (1999) believed career counseling should not be driven by assessments but rather should utilize an active model based on the worker learning appraisal skills and cognitive strategies to meet future changes and contingency planning. Swanson and Fouad (1999) believed both career theories and assessment measures are relevant in practical counseling situations. They concluded that the effects of a stressful stimulus on an employee is lessened when the employee develops the ability to respond nonemotionally to work-related demands. Oleski and Subich (1996), in supporting the assessment approach to counseling, found that workers exhibit personal competence and strong work habits when they follow their interests and pursue what they enjoy.

In this new era of complexity and diversity, traditional career planning is practically useless, according to Popcorn and Marigold (1996), who believed that people are being constantly challenged to cope with rapid changes in their careers and personal lives. Therefore, counselors should teach learning strategies, social skills, and the advantages of focusing on future options or steps in planning transitions to deal with job and career changes. Seligman (1994) integrated career counseling into the life span of the individual. Seligman therefore believed the therapist is required to explore and support the emotional, physical, and mental development of clients.

In discussing disturbances, dissatisfaction, and disability that are often the reason for referral for counseling job-related stress, Axelrod (1999) concluded that the workplace is one more area in which disturbed individuals act out their problems and emotions. Thus, therapists are in a position to help individuals adjust to workplace stress, learn to connect with their internal self, develop their strengths (assets), and maximize their options. This inside-out approach should enable the individual to deal with a clash of values, where the economic and social world is managed on impersonal principles and people are expendable (Senge, 1990).

Turner (1996) determined that the greatest obstacle to an employee feeling successful and the cause for frustration with careers is society's devaluation of feelings. This means that many individuals do not trust their inner experiences and believe that only what is external is real, and what cannot be touched is not genuine. But in assisting clients, the counselor can show the client that what cannot be grasped physically can be acquired with the mind and soul. This may mean that clients reevaluate the assumptions and beliefs they hold about their perceived abilities (Allport, 1961).

For Menaghan (1983), the ability to cope means to be able to manage stress successfully and to show evidence of effectiveness in that task. Folkman (1984) supported this view but added that coping should be viewed as the regulation of emotions, dealing with distress, and the management of the problem situation.

Sternberg (1997) stated that thinking styles and behavior patterns are affected by a person's home life and work environment. Sternberg believed this explains why individuals experience success rather than failure when they use the same problem-solving strategies in both situations. Webb (1999), expanding on Sternberg, concluded that during counseling, when the therapist shifts from problem to purpose, this enables clients to develop competencies, potential, and progress. This means counselors can enhance a client's potential by helping the client to focus on opportunity seeking and teaching the client to think in terms of externalizing the problem as an opponent, teaming with other workers, and working toward a better future by setting goals. In essence, the worker has become empowered by shifting work strategies to plans and goals.

Conclusion

This chapter discusses some aspects of stress in the workplace and presents an analysis of the pertinent organizational issues and their effects on individual workers. One intent of this chapter is to present a proactive argument for organizational response to stress. Organizations should maintain a systematic process focused on corporate and individual adaptation to sustain the well-being of employees and their organizations. Prevention of stress for individual employees is based on the supposition that it is better to prevent stress than to deal with distress. Furthermore, the multiple roles and tasks people must handle in our rapidly changing society is a challenge for counselors. The sense of personal fragmentation and alienation occurs when individuals fail to successfully deal with the rapidly changing social order and do not learn new ways to integrate information and change in their lives.

In addition, it is necessary for individual employees to recognize and to take responsibility for managing their own stress levels in the workplace. Employees cannot assume organizations will adapt work expectations to accommodate individual stress levels even though such acts are highly preferable. Workers can, however, expect organizations to monitor and maintain optimal stress levels for all employees (Sullivan, 1987). Kraemer and Roberts (1996) believed collaborative rather than competitive relationships in the workplace reflect a philosophical consensus that, if practiced and sustained, will help dispel uncertainty and stress to the benefit of the worker. Finally, Cochran (1997) stated that when clients focus on personal identity in their careers, it provides for the essential subjective development or human purpose and passion.

References

Allport, G. W. (1961). *Pattern and growth in personality*. New York: Holt, Reinhart & Winston.

Arthur, M. (1999). *The new careers: Enacting the global economy*. Thousand Oaks, CA: Sage.

Axelrod, S. D. (1999). *Work and the evolving self: Theoretical and clinical considerations*. Hillsdale, NJ: Atlantic Press.

Beck, A. C., & Hillman, E. D., (1986). *Positive management practices*. San Francisco: Jossey-Bass.

Bennis, W., & Nanus, B. (1985). *Leaders: The strategies for taking charge*. New York: Harper & Row.

Bernstein, A. J. (1989). *Dinosaur brains*. New York: Wiley.

Billings, A. G., & Moos, R. H. (1984). Coping, stress, and social resources among adults with unipolar depression. *Journal of Personality and Social Psychology, 46*, 877–891.

Brad, C. (1984). *Technostress: The human cost of the computer revolution*. Boston: Addison-Wesley.

Braverman, M. (1999). *Preventing workplace violence: A guide for employers and practitioners.* Thousand Oaks, CA: Sage.

Chopra, D. (1993). *Ageless body, timeless mind: The quantum alternative to growing old.* New York: Harmony Books.

Cochran, L. (1997). *Career counseling: A narrative approach.* Thousand Oaks, CA: Sage.

Folkman, S. (1984). Personal control and stress and coping processes: A theoretical analysis. *Journal of Personality and Social Psychology, 46,* 479–492.

Freedman, M., & Rosenman, R. H. (1974). *Type A behavior and your heart.* Westport, CT: Fawcett.

Gadon, M. C. (1988). *Evaluation of an interpersonally oriented job stress management program.* Unpublished doctoral dissertation, University of Toronto, Toronto, Ontario, Canada.

Ganster, D. C., Mayers, B. T., Sime, W. E., & Tharp, G. D. (1983). Managing organizational stress: A field experiment. *Journal of Applied Psychology, 67,* 533–542.

Guidano, V. F., & Liotti, G. (1983). *Cognitive processes and emotional disorders: A structural approach to psychotherapy.* New York: Guilford Press.

Hanson, P. G. (1989). *Stress for success.* Toronto, Ontario, Canada: Collins.

Howard, V. A. (1998). *Seasons of learning: Talks to graduates on life after college.* Westport, CT: Praeger.

Kraemer, S., & Roberts, J. (1996). (Eds.). *The politics of attachment: Towards a secure society.* London: Free Association Books.

Maslach, C., & Leiter, M. P. (1998). *The truth about burnout: How organizations cause personal stress and what to do about it.* San Francisco: Jossey-Bass.

Menaghan, E. G. (1983). Individual coping efforts in psychological stress. In B. H. Kaplan (Ed.), *Trends in theory and research* (pp. 87–107). Toronto, Ontario, Canada: Academic Press.

Minden, M. M. (1986). *An experimental analysis of self-help instructional program for improving quality of working life.* Unpublished doctoral dissertation, University of Toronto. Toronto, Ontario, Canada.

Myers, D. G., & Diener, E. (1995). Who is happy? *Psychological Science, 6*(1), 10–19.

Nichols, C. W. (1990). *An analysis of the source of dissatisfaction at work.* Unpublished doctoral dissertation, Stanford University.

Oleski, D., & Subich, L. M. (1996). Congruence and career change in employed adults. *Journal of Vocational Behaviours, 49,* 221–229.

Patton, W., & McMahon, M. (1999). *Career development and systems theory: A new relationship.* Pacific Grove, CA: Brooks/Cole.

Pines, A., & Aronson, E. (1988). *Career burnout: Causes and cures.* New York: Free Press.

Popcorn, F., & Marigold, L. (1996). *Clicking: 16 trends to future fit your life, your work, and your business.* New York: HarperCollins.

Quick, J. C., & Quick, J. D. (1984). *Organizational stress and preventive management.* New York: McGraw-Hill.

Raider, M. C. (1989). Burnout in children's agencies: A clinical perspective. *American Association of Children's Residential Centers, 6,* 42–47.

Reese, L. A.,& Lindenberg, K. E. (1998). *Implementing sexual harassment policy: Challenge for the public sector workplace.* Thousand Oaks, CA: Sage.

Robbins, S. P. (1992). *Essentials of organizational behavior.* New York: Simon & Schuster.

Schradle, S. B., & Dougher, M. J. (1985). Social support as a mediator of stress: Theoretical and empirical issues. *Clinical Psychology Review, 5,* 641–661.

Selge, H. (1974). *Stress without distress.* Toronto, Ontario, Canada: McClelland & Stewart.

Seligman, L. (1994). *Developmental career counseling and assessment.* Thousand Oaks, CA: Sage.

Senge, M. (1990). *The fifth discipline.* New York: Doubleday.

Sternberg, R. J. (1997). *Thinking styles.* Cambridge, England: Cambridge University Press.

Sullivan, G. (1987). *Work smart, not hard.* New York: Facts on File Publication.

Swanson, J. L., & Fouad, N. (1999). *Career theory and practice: Learning through case studies.* Thousand Oaks, CA: Sage.

Tracey, W. M. (1990). *Leader skills.* New York: Amacon.

Turner, R. G. (1996). *The first and the rose: Human core needs and personal transformation.* New York: HarperCollins.

Webb, W. (1999). *Solutioning: Solution focused interventions for counselors.* Philadelphia: Accelerated Development.

Special Tools

Motivational Interviewing in the Workplace

John McCarthy and Patricia A. Cluss

otivational interviewing (MI) is a powerful style of brief counseling that assists clients in resolving ambivalence about potential behavior changes (Miller & Rollnick, 1991). MI has been supported in numerous studies, particularly in the substance abuse literature, and can be applied to diverse counseling situations, including those that involve helping clients in the workplace.

The applicability and practicality of MI have heightened its acceptance over the past decade by mental health professionals working with clients considering a behavioral change. MI encourages clients to express their own reasons for change and holds that confrontation of the client with counselor-determined reasons for change is countertherapeutic at best and, at worst, is likely to further steel the client against change. There is significant empirical support for the efficacy of MI in promoting change in various settings. As a short-term counseling method, MI may be adaptable for use in career counseling and workplace settings. This chapter summarizes the spirit and strategies of MI, discusses practical workforce-oriented applications, and illustrates the MI technique with fictitious client–counselor dialogues.

Motivational Interviewing: What Is It?

MI was first described by founder William Miller in a conversation with Norwegian psychologists who asked about his approach with clients with alcohol problems (Miller & Rollnick, 1991). Miller explained how the responsibility for treatment failure, in the traditional model of motivation as it applies to such disorders, is often assigned to clients. Clients are blamed for being unwilling to seek counseling, for failing to comply with and participate in counseling, and for failing to accomplish counseling goals. Commonly cited reasons for lack of positive counseling outcomes are client resistance and lack of motivation to change. According to Miller (1983), however, neither resistance nor motivation is a trait of clients but is "a product of the way in which counselors have chosen to interact" with clients (p. 150). He maintained that clients are not helped by direct confrontation but are aided instead through a process by which clients are encouraged to give voice to their own, not the counselor's, reasons for change. In MI, both motivation and resistance are seen as interactional variables that can increase or decrease depending on the client's experience with the counselor.

Defined by Miller and MI cofounder Stephen Rollnick as "a directive, client-centred counselling style for eliciting behaviour change by helping clients to explore and resolve ambivalence," MI is more goal-directed and focused than other person-centered approaches (Rollnick & Miller, 1995, p. 326). In MI, it is recognized that clients often have reservations about engaging in the change process as they enter counseling. It is the responsibility of counselors to aid clients in the motivational struggle that consideration of change often presents. Miller likened the client's experience of ambivalence to riding on a teeter-totter at the playground: on one side is the urge to do something about the presenting problem, and on the other side are many weighty reasons for avoiding change. According to Miller (1983), the counselor's most effective role is to help clients add weight to the positive change side while "gently removing weights and obstructions" from the avoidance side (p. 154).

Components of Brief Interventions and their Relationship to MI

Miller and colleagues (Miller & Rollnick, 1991; Miller & Sanchez, 1994) reviewed the literature on effective brief intervention strategies and identified six components that have been found to be effective. Using the acronym FRAMES to summarize these effective strategies, they list the components as follows:

- Feedback: in an objective and nonjudgmental style, offering clients personalized feedback about their personal risks and potential consequences of the problem behavior.
- Responsibility: emphasizing that clients are free to change or not change on the basis of their personal choice and that they, not the counselor, will decide whether to take any steps toward change.
- Advice: offering advice or recommendations in a supportive, non-coercive way.
- Menu: Providing multiple options of effective change strategies and encouraging client involvement in the choice of approach to change.
- Empathy: working with clients in a warm and nonjudgmental manner, communicating understanding of the clients' point of view about the problem.
- Self-efficacy: supporting clients' beliefs that they will be able to change successfully.

Out of these effective components of successful brief interventions come the following five basic principles of MI (Yahne & Miller, 1999).

Express empathy: The more the counseling atmosphere embraces and communicates acceptance, the more likely it is that clients will consider change. Listening closely to clients' experiences and responding empathically to promote the development of client–counselor rapport is the key skill in MI.

Develop discrepancy: Helping clients describe their most central goals, hopes, and dreams in life allows the counselor to underscore inconsistencies between who and where the client is now and how the problem behavior may be damaging the possibility of reaching desired goals in the future. Eliciting negative ramifications of their actions from clients can often help them begin to realize the need for change. In the MI style, motivational statements come from client, not from the counselor. Developing discrepancy between current behavior and future goals is a key motivator for clients' self-motivational statements.

The following questions are useful in the process of developing discrepancy (Miller, 1998, p. 127):

1. "What are the 'good things' about [the problem] for you?" Asking this question first and responding empathically to the client's responses increases the client's sense of the counselor as someone who understands and is interested in the problem from the client's point of view.
2. "What are the 'not-so-good things' about [the problem] for you?" This question is asked only after a full and comprehensive exploration of the good things. Clients often respond to the question by beginning to describe their reasons for wanting to change (self-motivational statements).
3. "What do you think might happen if you keep on [the problem behavior] as you have been?"
4. "Looking forward, where do you want to be in the future and how does [the problem behavior] fit into that?"
5. "Looking backward, how has [the problem behavior] affected how things used to be for you?"

Avoid argumentation: Counselors who create a confrontive atmosphere with clients as a strategy to promote change may find that opposition to change occurs instead, because a confrontive approach often sparks defensiveness and resistance to change on the part of the client (Miller, Benefield, & Tonigan, 1993). Arguing with clients about whether they have problems that require action is almost always counterproductive, raising obstacles rather than facilitating change. Another part of the MI approach to avoiding argumentation involves the avoidance of diagnostic labels. Entering into discussions or arguments about whether a client is an alcoholic, for example, is at best unnecessary and, at worst, likely to trigger defensiveness and further resistance (Miller & Rollnick, 1991).

Roll with resistance: According to Yahne and Miller (1999), the term resistance may be misleading. Ambivalence in the MI approach is seen as a completely normal response to the consideration of change, which often means giving up current well-practiced and, for that reason, comfortable behaviors. Instead of fighting or confronting resistance, an MI practitioner moves with it, using an empathic and reflective stance. When a client does not encounter the typical oppositional response from the counselor, he or she often is able to begin to consider the current situation from other perspectives.

Support self-efficacy: To be ready to change, people must not only feel the change is important but must also believe in their ability to be successful once they decide to change (Miller & Rollnick, 1991). Offering clients hope through realistic and optimistic affirmations of their abilities can help clients move toward taking steps toward change.

Phases of MI

MI proceeds in two phases. Phase 1 involves establishing rapport with the client, enhancing motivation to change, and dealing with resistance. Phase 1 opening strategies are designed to establish a relationship with the client that will set the tone for increased client self-knowledge and self-disclosure. Opening strategies include the use of open-ended questions, affirmations of client strengths, reflections or empathy, and summaries (the acronym OARS). Consistent with the notion that reasons for change should come from the client, the elicitation of self-motivational statements is an integral part of this phase. Ways to prompt such statements include exploring the pros and cons of the problem and of the possibility of changing, asking for elaboration, looking forward, looking backward, and amplified reflections. Additional strategies include decisional balance (e.g., "On the one hand you feel [the good things] about [the problem], but on the other hand you feel [the not-so-good things] about [the problem]") and rating importance and confidence (Miller & Rollnick, 1991; Rollnick, Mason, & Butler, 1999). Phase 2 is designed to help the client move toward action and to enhance commitment to a change plan. Phase 1 strategies are listed in italics in this chapter.

The use of Phase 1 strategies is reflected in the following brief physician interaction with a patient who firmly maintains that he has no drinking problem:

Physician:	I've really annoyed you by saying that there is a problem here. [*reflection*]
Patient:	Yes! I don't have a drinking problem!
Physician:	There really isn't any reason that you can see to be concerned about your drinking. [*amplified reflection*]

Patient: Well, maybe I overdo it sometimes [*client endorses the existence of a problem*], but I'm not an alcoholic.

Physician: I see. You think there are times when you drink too much, but you really don't want anyone to think of you as an alcoholic. [*reflection, avoidance of argumentation*]

Patient: Right.

Physician: Tell me about some of the times when you think you have had too much to drink. Give me a good example. [*open-ended prompt*]

Patient: Well, last Monday when I woke up I didn't feel too good, and . . . (Maher, 1998, p. 66)

By taking an empathic and open-ended approach with this patient, the physician avoids arguing about whether alcohol is a problem or not and helps the individual move toward willingness to explore the effects of drinking on his or her life. Experiencing this stance, clients may move from denial of the problem toward a more active consideration of the pros and cons of changing the drinking behavior.

MI and Stages of Change

MI is compatible with the transtheoretical model of change (Prochaska, Norcross, & DiClemente, 1994) that contends that readiness to change problem behaviors varies among individuals and that different interventions are needed for people in different stages of readiness. Individuals in the initial, or precontemplation, stage are not interested in changing and may deny the existence of a problem at all. The contemplation stage is marked both by an acknowledgment of a difficulty and by an active weighing of the pros and cons of changing. Ambivalence is the hallmark of this stage. Contemplators are thinking about change but are not ready to act on the problem or move toward solving it.

The third stage, preparation, is marked by an intention to take action on the problem in the near future, although some degree of ambivalence about doing so may still be present. Some initial steps in preparation for change may occur in this stage, such as a smoker cutting down the number of cigarettes smoked per day or setting a quit date. In the action stage, the person takes active steps toward change. The smoker throws away his or her cigarettes on the quit date, for example, cleans out the car, buys hard candy for use during urges to smoke, and sends all his or her clothes to the cleaners. In the maintenance stage, the individual works to preserve the action taken and to prevent relapse to the old behavior. This stage may last as long as 6 months, although the time frame varies from person to person.

Finally, people who have made a successful behavior change enter the termination stage, during which the problem becomes a former difficulty and is no longer an active threat. Even in this stage, however, the individual must always be prepared to manage triggers for relapse when they occur. Individuals rarely, if ever, move linearly from precontemplation through each of the stages in order without suffering setbacks in the process. Relapse to previous stages is common. Additionally, people can and often do remain in the earlier stages of the change process for very long periods of time.

MI can be used effectively with clients in any of the six stages. However, MI can be particularly effective with individuals in the stages of precontemplation and contemplation, because clients' ambivalence toward change is highest in these stages. The implementation of MI can vary in the first three stages of change (Noonan & Moyers, 1997). For clients in precontemplation who are not voicing any concern about a problem and are not even beginning to contemplate change, MI can create ambivalence by exploring the client's concerns about risks and likely consequences of the problem behavior. The contemplation stage is marked by clients' review of the pros and cons of changing. In this stage, MI can work to increase the discrepancy between the client's values and his or her current behavior, thus moving the client toward more active consideration of change. In the preparation stage, strengthening commitment to change and developing a change plan can further urge the client to action. In this vein, Miller (1983) sees MI as "a systemic series of strategies intended to help the person move from precontemplation to action" (p. 166).

Empirical Support for the Effectiveness of MI

As a prelude to addressing the uses of MI in workplace counseling, it is important to note that there is significant empirical support for the effectiveness of MI in many other settings. Given its development within the substance abuse field, many of the initial studies involved the use of MI with addictive behaviors. In his now classic investigation, Miller et al. (1993) tested the Drinker's Check-Up intervention. He advertised a "free check up for drinkers who would like to find out whether their drinking is causing them any harm" (Miller, Sovereign, & Krege, 1988, p. 255). Seventy-four percent of the resulting sample considered themselves to be only "social drinkers" but met criteria for alcohol dependence. Participants were randomly assigned to either an immediate or delayed (6 weeks) Drinker's Check-Up (DCU) group. The latter group served as a wait-list control. After completing the check-up—a comprehensive biological, psychological, and behavioral examination of drinking behavior and sequelae—participants were further randomized to either a 1-hour motivational feedback session or a 1-hour directive-confrontational Alcoholics Anonymous-type feedback session. Participants were followed up in 6 weeks and again 1 year later.

The motivational group showed a significant decrease in drinking days per week and a nonsignificant decrease in average weekly consumption of alcohol and peak blood alcohol levels compared with the wait-list control group at both follow-up points. An interesting finding of this investigation was that, overall, the best predictor of participants' drinking at 1 year was the number of resistance behaviors demonstrated by the participant during the interview. Even more interestingly, the best predictor of client resistance behavior during the interview was the number of confrontive statements made by the therapist during the interview, giving credence to Miller and Rollnick's (1991) contention that confrontation leads to resistance and that resistance leads to poorer outcome.

Another study investigating the efficacy of MI compared with other forms of treatment for alcoholism is known as Project MATCH, a multisite clinical trial that matched participants to alternative treatments on the basis of the specific needs and characteristics of the participants (Project MATCH Research Group, 1998). The project was the largest clinical trial of alternative psychotherapies at that time and enrolled over 1,700 participants. Three manualized treatments were tested: cognitive–behavioral therapy (CBT; 12 sessions over 12 weeks), a form of MI called motivational enhancement therapy (MET; 4 sessions over 12 weeks), and a 12-step facilitation group (12 sessions over 12 weeks). Participants were followed for 3 years. Results of this large project were mixed, with none of the three interventions emerging as clearly superior to the others. All modalities resulted in positive outcomes with a high rate of abstinence at 3-year follow-up. However, the MET condition produced essentially the same outcomes as the CBT and the 12-step intervention groups with only one third the number of sessions.

Similar findings were reported by Stephens and colleagues (Stephens, Roffman, & Curtin, 2000), who found that a 14-session CBT group and a 2-session MI group were equally effective compared with a control group for treatment of marijuana use. These outcomes are especially relevant to workplace counselors who, because of systemic limitations, may be able to see clients for only a few sessions. In their review of MI investigations on substance abuse and problem drinkers, Noonan and Moyers (1997) concluded that investigations "generally support the efficacy of MI with a variety of problematic behaviors (alcohol, marijuana, and opiate use) in a variety of settings (inpatient, outpatient, and primary care)" (pp. 13–14).

Effectiveness also has been demonstrated for MI in studies of smoking cessation with adolescents (Colby et al., 1998), pregnant drinkers (Handmaker, Miller, & Manicke, 1999), outpatient treatment entry for dual-diagnosis patients (Daley & Zuckoff, 1998; Swanson, Pantalon, & Cohen, 1999), diabetes self-care (Smith, Kratt, Heckemeyer, & Mason, 1997), primary care interventions for drinking and smoking (Butler et al., 1999; Senft, Freeborn, Polen, & Hollis, 1997), compliance with drug treatment for psychotic inpatients (Kemp, Hayward, Applewhaite, Everitt, & David, 1996), and HIV risk reduction (Carey et al., 2000).

The Use of MI in Workplace Counseling

The focus of MI on encouraging maximum change in the context of brief client–counselor interactions is a natural fit with the short-term counseling focus common to workforce Employee Assistance Programs (EAPs). EAPs typically work within a time-limited framework of two to eight sessions (Miller, Jackson, & Ward Kerr, 1994), allowing ample time from the MI standpoint to develop rapport, enhance client motivation and deal with resistance, strengthen commitment, and develop a change plan. MI in the workplace setting may be useful in helping employees deal with substance abuse, outplacement, and voluntary exit issues.

EAPs and Substance Abuse Issues

The concept of EAPs developed after the identification of the concept of occupational alcoholism. Because of the effect of substance abuse problems on workplace productivity, companies began to realize that it would be in their best interest to aid in the identification of alcoholism in their employees and provide assistance with employees' recovery process. In addition to encouraging employees to get help before reaching the point of job termination, supervisors were trained to understand alcohol-related issues to identify the problem earlier and to intervene before the point of termination.

In the 1960s, the focus of EAP counseling shifted to identifying and remediating impaired performance on the job as a result of alcoholism (Wrich, 1980). By the 1990s, over 85% of Fortune 500 companies offered some type of EAP service to employees (Shosh, 1996). At the end of the 20th century, EAPs were being designed "to provide a range of early intervention services to troubled employees and their families in order to improve the employee's on-the-job performance and productivity" (Hershenson, Power, & Waldo, 1996, p. 52).

In working with clients experiencing substance issues, EAP counselors may want to consider the use of MI. Miller et al. (1994) pointed out that the "less threatening nature of EAP consultation may make such intervention possible at much earlier stages" than with traditional therapies (p. 19). One study in Sweden found that brief MI counseling and monitoring with employees at risk for drinking problems—exactly the kind of assistance that an EAP can offer—correlated with decreased hospitalizations, sick days, and incidence of physical and mental disorders for the following 8 years when compared with a random sample informed of their alcohol risk by letter (cited by Miller et al., 1994).

Using an MI Approach in an EAP Counseling Session

The following is an example of how MI can be used in an EAP setting for a client with an alcohol problem (Miller & Rollnick, 1991, pp. 75–76):

Client:	I worry sometimes that I may be drinking too much for my own good.
Therapist:	You've been drinking quite a bit.
Client:	I don't really feel like it's that much. I can drink a lot and not feel it.
Therapist:	More than most people.
Client:	Yes. I can drink most people under the table.
Therapist:	And that's what worries you.
Client:	Well, that and how I feel. The next morning I'm usually in bad shape. I feel jittery and I can't think straight through most of the morning.
Therapist:	And that doesn't seem right to you.
Client:	No, I guess not. I haven't thought about it that much, but I don't think it's good to be hung over all the time. And sometimes I have trouble remembering things.
Therapist:	Things that happen while you're drinking.
Client:	That, too. Sometimes I just have a blank for a few hours.

Therapist:	But that isn't what you meant when you said you have trouble remembering things.
Client:	No. Even when I'm not drinking, it seems like I'm forgetting things more often, and I'm not thinking clearly.
Therapist:	And you wonder if it has something to do with your drinking.
Client:	I don't know what else it would be.
Therapist:	You haven't always been like that.
Client:	No! It's only the last few years. Maybe I'm just getting older.
Therapist:	It might just be what happens to everybody when they reach 45.
Client:	No, it's probably my drinking. I don't sleep well, either.
Therapist:	So maybe you're damaging your health and your sleep and your brain by drinking as much as you do.
Client:	Mind you, I'm not a drunk. Never was.
Therapist:	You're not that bad off. Still, you're worried.
Client:	I don't know about "worried," but I guess I'm thinking about it more.
Therapist:	And wondering if you should do something, so that's why you came here.
Client:	I guess so.
Therapist:	You're not sure.
Client:	I'm not sure what I want to do about it.
Therapist:	So if I understand you so far, you think that you've been drinking too much and you've been damaging your health, but you're not sure you want to change that.
Client:	Doesn't make much sense, does it?
Therapist:	I can see how you might feel confused at this point.

In this interaction, the counselor follows the client's lead, through empathic reflection, in identifying his concerns about his drinking habits. The counselor avoids arguing with the client about whether he is "a drunk" and uses reflection instead of confrontation in responding to the client's uncertainty about whether a problem exists. By the second half of the interchange, the client expresses growing certainty that a problem does exist ("I don't know what else it would be"). Using an amplified reflection, the counselor exaggerates the client's suggestion that his increased forgetfulness might be due to getting older ("It might just be what happens to everybody when they reach 45.") In a quintessential MI client response, the client rejects that notion and attempts to convince the counselor that a problem really does exist ("No, it's probably my drinking"). By the end of the interchange, the counselor summarizes the client's understanding that a problem exists and that there are serious health consequences that are occurring because of the problem. The counselor affirms the client's confusion as a reasonable feeling in this circumstance. The interaction is now poised to move toward strengthening commitment to change and development of a change plan.

Outplacement Services and Voluntary Exiters

Whether by layoffs, firings, retirement, transfers, or simply changing jobs, the departure of employees is a natural process within organizations. The use of MI strategies to assist departing employees resolve ambivalence about termination or resignation can be useful as well. Much attention in the workplace literature has focused on employees leaving employment involuntarily; for that reason, outplacement counseling has arisen in the past 30 years to aid those who have been terminated by industrial and governmental organizations. This area of workforce counseling is expected to grow at a rapid rate in the next decade (Zunker, 1998) because, in this period of spin-offs, mergers, and company takeovers, it is likely that involuntary job departures will continue to increase. Under these circumstances, terminated employees can be expected to have feelings of anger and resentment toward the company and supervisors. The use of counseling strategies to help employees manage such feelings and prepare to move ahead productively can be useful (Zunker, 1998).

Voluntary exiters—those who resign a position instead of being fired or laid off—exist as well. Though they choose to leave an organization, these employees may nonetheless experience ambivalence as part of the departure process. While the choice to leave may have several positive dimensions, it is not uncommon for job-related issues, such as positive relationships with colleagues, salary, or health care benefits, to make the decision difficult and not altogether clear for the employee who is in the process of deciding to leave.

Few studies exist on ambivalence of exiting employees in the workplace. In one study of 47 people exiting organizations, 25 of whom were part of a reduction in force, LaFarge (1994) found a high degree of ambivalence among both voluntary and involuntary exiters. Both groups expressed discomfort with what was perceived as an incompatibility between the two conflicting sides in the process of leaving. Only about 25% of individuals were able to acknowledge their ambivalence spontaneously.

Anger was an emotion that was often evident in the employees interviewed by LaFarge (1994). She noted that anger served two purposes.

Anger was a "distancing mechanism" that enabled further progress toward termination, separation, and change. In addition, the presence of anger confirmed the existence of a sense of connection to the organization, because it would be difficult to feel anger if no relationship with the organization existed at all (p. 189). LaFarge concluded that exiters appear to vacillate between their "desires to maintain their 'justifiable' and 'righteous' anger toward the organization and desires to put these uncomfortable and 'unproductive' feelings behind them" (p. 189).

Two other results from LaFarge's (1994) study are noteworthy. First, she found that exiters wavered between an attempt to comprehend the organization's or superiors' actions and being reproachful of them. Many expressed feelings of anger and hurt, yet also were intellectually able to empathize with the people who made the decision that caused their departure. Second, the most difficult aspect of the situation for people leaving an organization was ambivalence about themselves and their abilities. As one involuntary exiter commented, "I don't think I've ever felt so powerless and out of control of my life as I do now. They tell you you are out and there is nothing . . . that you can do about it" (p. 190). Many exiters had held a positive self-image of their competence and wanted to sustain this image on their departure but experienced difficulty doing so. As another involuntary exiter commented, "One time, I feel positive about stuff, the next I'm as negative as all get out. . . . All the tricks they teach you about how to find a job don't tell you anything about how to manage a split personality. . . . I don't know who I am anymore" (p. 191).

MI may be a helpful method of counseling both voluntary and involuntary exiters who are wrestling with departure ambivalence. The following counselor (Co) and client (Cl) interchange begins with a quote from one of the voluntary exiters in LaFarge's (1994, p. 188) study and demonstrates the possible use of MI. Some of the material has been condensed for the sake of this example.

Cl: I'm sure that I've sent out a lot of mixed messages to people about leaving [the company]. I'm angry about the way things have worked out here and I have a chip on my shoulder. I want to show them . . . that they screwed up by letting things get this far. But I also have a lot of affection for people here and for the company. It's been a great place to work. I'll miss it. So in the middle of this anger, there's affection and sadness. Depending on what I'm feeling at a particular moment, I act differently.

Co: I can certainly understand how those different feelings can be a part of a situation like this. On the one hand, you've really enjoyed working here, yet you're also mad about the way some things have been handled. [*a double-sided reflection*]

Cl: Yeah! If they hadn't let things get out of hand, I wouldn't be leaving here. That's for sure.

Co: In many respects it has been a good fit for you over the past 8 years, and it would feel both sad and frustrating to leave a work situation like this. [*reflection*]

Cl: It certainly is.

Co: You mentioned that you're angry [at them] for screwing things up. Tell me more about the other negatives over that time. [*asking for elaboration*]

[Negatives are explored in depth until the client "runs out of steam" for discussing the negative reasons for resigning.]

Co: And, as far as the good things about working there, you said that you cared a lot about the people.

Cl: The people . . . ah, I've made many friends here. The company's volleyball team made it to the finals of the league last year . . . so many of the people here have kids in the same school as mine. . . . It's been like a family. I'm the godfather to Joe's kids, for heaven's sake, and so many of us have been through the highs and lows of the company together and the highs and lows of our personal lives.

Co: It sounds as if there's been a nice community for you here. What other good things have there been about working there?

[Positives are explored in depth.]

Co: So there are a number of positives that you now have as a result of your time there, and those include [summarize]. As you look back over your time at the company, what have you gained that you'll be bringing to your next position? [*looking back, supporting self-efficacy*]

Cl: Uh, I haven't thought of that too much. I did get quite a bit of computer training along with good mentoring in sales. And contacts, too. I now know a lot of people in the area. They'll sure help me no matter what I do. I think the other thing that will be a key is I'll have some personal friendships. I'm sure I'll stay in touch with some people there.

Co: So it sounds as if there are some positive things that you'll be taking from here, and I'm wondering where you see yourself going in the future. Where do you see yourself occupationally 5 years from now? [*looking forward*]

Cl: In a much different place than I am now! You see, I'd really like to work with computer-based design that relates to the engineering industry. I've been reading a great deal about it for the past 3 years, and it's quite interesting. I think there's a big future in it, too.

Co: And that's not exactly what you were working toward with this company . . .

Cl: No! Heavens, no. I couldn't get into that kind of position with them, even if I stayed another 20 years. [Pause] Maybe, just maybe leaving is the right thing to do regardless of the when's or why's. Maybe this is the way for me to go to explore what I *really* want to do.

Four strategies reflective of MI are noted in this dialogue. First, the counselor utilizes reflections early in the dialogue as a way to develop rapport with the client. Through the counselor's use of empathy, the client comes to better understand his ambivalence about leaving the company and sees the counselor as a person who understands this conflict. Second, the counselor prompts a thorough discussion of the client's negative reactions to the job and empathizes with these thoughts before asking the client to talk about the positive things gained from working with the company. This strategy of thoroughly exploring one side of the ambivalence before describing the other is common to MI and often results in the client being better able to generate reasons to change (or, in this case, feel better about the change that is about to happen). Third, the client's sense of self-efficacy is supported by urging the client to describe the skills he now has available to take to a new position. Fourth, discrepancy is developed between the client's goals for himself (to work with computer-based design) and what he has been able to do in his present position, thus further reducing ambivalence about leaving and increasing motivation to move to another position.

Conclusion

Although empirical support for the use of MI in an EAP setting has yet to be demonstrated, MI may be an effective counseling style in the workplace setting, particularly in short-term circumstances and in situations in which occupational ambivalence is present. Its themes of soliciting reasons for change from the client and encouraging client responsibility for change are two characteristics that may provide useful assistance to employees experiencing workplace substance abuse problems and those experiencing ambivalent thoughts and emotions triggered by impending employment changes. EAP counselors may wish to seek out training in MI to test its effect on their counseling outcomes. Empirically driven studies investigating the benefits of MI in workplace settings are called for. Such investigations will increase our understanding of whether this brief intervention modality is as effective in the workplace as it has been shown to be in other counseling settings.

References

Butler, C. C., Rollnick, S., Cohen, D., Bachmann, M., Russell, I., & Stott, N. (1999). Motivational consulting versus brief advice for smokers in general practice: A randomized trial. *British Journal of General Practice, 49,* 611–616.

Carey, M. P., Braaten, L. S., Maisto, S. A., Gleason, J. R., Forsyth, A. D., Durant, L. E., & Jaworski, B. C. (2000). Using information, motivational enhancement, and skills training to reduce the risk of HIV infection for low-income urban women: A second randomized clinical trial. *Health Psychology, 19,* 3–11.

Colby, S. M., Monti, P. M., Barnett, N. P., Rohsenow, D. J., Weissman, K., Spirito, A., Woolard, R. H., & Lewander, W. J. (1998). Brief motivational interviewing in a hospital setting for adolescent smoking: A preliminary study. *Journal of Consulting and Clinical Psychology, 66,* 574–578.

Daley, D. C., & Zuckoff, A. (1998). Improving compliance with the initial outpatient session among discharged inpatient dual diagnosis patients. *Social Work, 43,* 470–473.

Handmaker, N. S., Miller, W. R., & Manicke, M. (1999). Findings of a pilot study of motivational interviewing with pregnant drinkers. *Journal of Studies on Alcohol, 60,* 285–287.

Hershenson, D. B., Power, P. W., & Waldo, M. (1996). Community counseling: *Contemporary theory and practice.* Needham Heights, MA: Simon & Schuster.

Kemp, R., Hayward, P., Applewhaite, G., Everitt, B., & David, A. (1996). *British Medical Journal, 312,* 345–349.

LaFarge, V. V. S. (1994). The ambivalence of departing employees: Reactions of involuntary and voluntary exiters. *Journal of Applied Behavioral Sciences, 30,* 175–197.

Maher, L. (1998, September 15). Motivational interviewing: What, when, and why. *Patient Care, 32,* 55–72.

Miller, W. R. (1983). Motivational interviewing with problem drinkers. *Behavioural Psychotherapy, 11,* 147–172.

Miller, W. R. (1998). Enhancing motivation for change. In W. R. Miller & N. Heather (Eds.), *Treating addictive behaviors* (pp. 121–132). New York: Plenum.

Miller, W. R., Benefield, G., & Tonigan, J. D. (1993). Enhancing motivation for change in problem drinking: A controlled comparison of two therapist styles. *Journal of Consulting and Clinical Psychology, 61,* 455–461.

Miller, W. R., Jackson, K. A., & Ward Kerr, K. (1994). Alcohol problems: There's a lot you can do in two or three sessions. *EAP Digest, 14,* 18–21, 35–36.

Miller, W. R., & Rollnick, S. (1991). *Motivational interviewing.* New York: Guilford Press.

Miller, W. R., & Sanchez, R. G. (1994). Motivating young adults for treatment and lifestyle change. In G. Howard & P. E. Nathan (Eds.), *Alcohol use and misuse by young adults* (pp. 55–81). Notre Dame, IN: University of Notre Dame Press.

Miller, W. R., Sovereign, R. G., & Krege, B. (1988). Motivational interviewing with problem drinkers: II. The Drinker's Check-Up as a preventive intervention. *Behavioural Psychotherapy, 16,* 251–268.

Noonan, W. C., & Moyers, T. B. (1997). Motivational interviewing. *Journal of Substance Misuse, 2,* 8–16.

Prochaska, J. O., Norcross, J. C., & DeClemente, C. C. (1994). *Changing for good.* New York: Avon Books.

Project MATCH Research Group. (1998). Matching alcoholism treatments to client heterogeneity: Project MATCH three-year drinking outcomes. *Alcoholism: Clinical and Experimental Research, 22,* 1300–1311.

Rollnick, S., Mason, P., & Butler, C. (1999). *Health behavior change: A guide for practitioners.* Edinburgh, Scotland: Churchill Livingstone.

Rollnick, S., & Miller, W. R. (1995). What is motivational interviewing? *Behavioural and Cognitive Psychotherapy, 23,* 325–334.

Senft, R. A., Freeborn, D. K., Polen, M. R., & Hollis, J. F. (1997). Brief intervention in a primary care setting for hazardous drinkers. *American Journal of Preventive Medicine, 13,* 464–470.

Shosh, M. (1996). Counseling in business and industry. In W. J. Weikel & A. J. Palmo (Eds.), *Foundations of mental health counseling* (2nd ed., pp. 232–241). Springfield, IL: Charles C Thomas.

Smith, D. E., Kratt, P. P., Heckmeyer, C. M., & Mason, D. A. (1997). Motivational interviewing to improve adherence to a behavioral weight-control program for older obese women with NIDDM. *Diabetes Care, 20*(1), 52–54.

Stephens, R. S., Roffman, R. A., & Curtin, L. (2000). Comparison of extended versus brief treatments for marijuana use. *Journal of Consulting and Clinical Psychology, 68,* 898–908.

Swanson, A. J., Pantalon, M. V., & Cohen, K. R. (1999). Motivational interviewing and treatment adherence among psychiatric and dually diagnosed patients. *Journal of Nervous and Mental Disease, 187,* 630–635.

Wrich, J. T. (1980). *The employee assistance program.* Center City, MN: Hazelden Foundation.

Yahne, C. E., & Miller, W. R. (1999). Enhancing motivation for treatment and change. In B. S. McCrady & E. E. Epstein (Eds.), *Addictions: A sourcebook for professionals* (pp. 235–249). Oxford, England: Oxford University Press.

Zunker, V. G. (1998). *Career counseling: Applied concepts of life planning.* Pacific Grove, CA: Brooks/Cole.

6

Using the Adlerian Lifestyle Construct as a Strengths Assessment Tool for Improving Employees' Success

Paul R. Peluso and Kevin B. Stoltz

ndividual Psychology, often referred to as Adlerian Psychology, was developed by Alfred Adler following his split from Sigmund Freud in 1911 over Freud's refusal to consider the influence of social interactions on the development of personality. Adler developed his ideas into a full working theory of human development and social interaction for clinical use. Adler's theory has also had a far-reaching impact on many subsequent theories of counseling, such as humanistic, existential, transactional analysis, and cognitive–behavioral (Dowd, 1997; Eckstein & Baruth, 1996; Freeman & Urschel, 1997; Watkins, 1997; Watts & Critelli, 1997). In its own right, Individual Psychology has been used primarily in clinical and educational settings and only recently has been used in organizational settings, despite the fact that Adler placed particular importance on work

(Dewey, 1991). However, many of these ideas have not been used by career counselors because they have traditionally been considered elements of mental health counseling and not career counseling. Niles and Pate (1989) described the schism between traditional career counseling and mental health counseling thus:

> Given the relationship between work and mental health, it is perplexing that there has been an artificial distinction between career counseling and mental health counseling on the part of many clients and counselors. Career counseling and personal counseling are often referred to as if they were completely separate entities. In fact, there are few things more personal than a career choice. (p. 64)

Rounds and Tracey (1990) proposed that career counseling is a subset of mental health counseling and that use of the psychotherapeutic process can generate better outcomes for career-related issues. At the same time, in the 1990s, there has been renewed interest in aspects of career counseling by mental health counselors, such as employee assistance, organizational consulting, and executive coaching, to name a few (Savickas, 1995). Adlerians, especially, have begun to put Adler's ideas to good use in the workplace as it has in the classroom with teachers and students, and to family interactions among parents and children (Kern & Peluso, 1999; Peluso & Kern, 1998). In fact, many of the elements of mental health counseling, and particularly those inspired by Individual Psychology, have become areas of focus for career counselors. In a review of the literature, Subich and Bilingsley (1995) found that career counselors and vocational psychologists are beginning to look at personality-driven factors, such as self-esteem, self-efficacy, and irrational beliefs. These have traditionally been avoided by career counselors in favor of focusing on career interest, aptitude, and skills training; however, there has been a shift toward embracing these concepts (Savickas, 1995). Blustein and Spengler (1995) argued that there is a wealth of information that can be obtained from understanding "noncareer domain" behaviors of the employee. One example they provide is the employee who wants to make career changes because of personality conflicts at work. According to Blustein and Spengler (1995), a central element of the career counseling process would be to understand the history of conflicts with parents or other authority figures.

Although there is growing interest in integrating elements of traditional mental health counseling (such as family-of-origin information) with career counseling, there are two primary obstacles: (a) Information about family-of-origin dynamics is often difficult to obtain systematically, and

(b) asking employees about areas of their personal life (particularly issues that do not directly relate to the workplace, such as childhood issues) has traditionally been seen as "off limits" at work (Blustein & Spengler, 1995; Levinson, 1991; Subich & Billingsley, 1995). Obtaining measures of systemic or process variables has been a challenge to the entire field of counseling for many years, but recent advances in measurement have begun to yield valuable information for counselors to use in multiple domains (Hackett & Watkins, 1995). The more difficult obstacle to overcome is the second, asking employees about their personal life. One reason for this is the diagnostic quality that comes from standardized testing and categorization. Often individuals are concerned with being "labeled" as problematic and either losing their jobs or upward mobility in the organization. Another reason for this difficulty is that traditionally, information about one's "private life" has been disallowed in the workplace, with employees being told not to bring their "problems at home" to work. Lastly, many people believe that it is not appropriate to be asked about personal information and see inquiries into this area as a "boundary violation" (Schnieder, 1991). As a result, employees are uncomfortable discussing noncareer domain elements of their life at work, thus making it difficult for counselors to obtain family-of-origin data (Levinson, 1991; Schneider, 1991). Yet, despite the "off limits" obstacle, these noncareer domains are still important for understanding the employee, and they provide critical information for the Employee Assistance Program (EAP) personnel, human resource officer, career counselor, or executive coach for the effective management of the workplace.

Individual Psychology has created a system that is both effective and respectful. One tenet of Individual Psychology is that the family unit is the fundamental source for development of one's lifestyle and, thus, an individual's concept and program for interacting with society on a larger scale. Lifestyle, in its most simple form, can be described as the consistent way in which one thinks, feels, and acts—formulated at an early age—to deal with the three tasks of social, work, and love relationships (Adler, 1964; Ferguson, 1989). This lifestyle is based on the experiences within the family (Dewey, 1991). Understanding the influence of family-of-origin on an employee is critical for gaining insight into the behaviors observed at work, because one's personal goals and behavior patterns are first formulated and established through one's experiences and interactions with the family system. That is, each individual brings to work a unique style of interacting with others and of completing assignments and responsibilities, which has been influenced by the family of origin. Once a career counselor, manager, supervisor, or EAP personnel gains an understanding of the family-of-origin dynamics underlying such actions, the set of behaviors an individual brings to bear on his or her work can be predicted and redirected. For the counselor, this provides a mechanism by which often complex organizational concepts of motivation, drive, and work style can be easily understood (Kern & Peluso, 1999).

The purpose of this chapter is to discuss the Adlerian construct of lifestyle as an effective tool to understand the behavior of individuals in the workplace. Information on the development of the lifestyle in the family of origin is presented, as well as a discussion of the impact of the lifestyle at work. In addition, instruments for measuring an individual's lifestyle are presented that can allow for counselors to easily overcome the obstacle of obtaining measures of family-of-origin dynamics. A description of common scenarios in which conflict disrupts the workplace as it relates to lifestyle dynamics follows. Lastly, an example of an intervention using the instruments in a work setting provides readers with specific ways to understand and resolve conflicts that are constructive for organizations and employees.

A Brief Primer on the Development of Lifestyle

Adler (1964) believed that the individual's subjective creation of reality is shaped from a very early age as a result of interactions within the family unit. According to Adler, it is from this subjective view of life (which he called the *schema of apperception*) that the individual constructs a "private logic," that is, the collection of attitudes and reactions the individual has about life and his or her place in it. Adler (1964) stated: "In considering the structure of a personality, the chief difficulty is that its unity, its particular style of life and goal, is not built upon objective reality, but upon the subjective view that the individual takes of the facts of life" (p. 183). The lifestyle is based on one's subjective perceptions about family relationships in the early years of life, which shapes the way a person relates to the environment, situations, and people. This process takes place by the age of 6. At this stage of development, individuals make decisions about their place in the world, what behaviors or strategies they will need to use to belong in a social group, and how this belonging to a social group will help them get basic physical and emotional needs met. The family, as the prototypical social group for the child, plays a crucial role related to the development of this private logic and eventual lifestyle. According to Adler, this lifestyle becomes the response set for life and is the common thread that weaves an individual's thoughts, feelings, and actions into a coherent pattern. Once set in place, this lifestyle remains relatively stable through adulthood; thus, from this perspective, lifestyle and personality are the same construct (Kern & Peluso, 1999; Miranda, 1994; Miranda, Kern, & Peluso, 1995).

However, a major difference in the Adlerian concept of lifestyle is that it is nonpathologizing, as many other theories of human behavior posit. Adler considered his theory a "psychology of use," meaning that an individual's choices about his or her behaviors, attitudes, and responses were the results of these early dynamic forces that continually influence his or her goals, decisions, and behaviors (Dewey, 1991). Thus, if the choices are destructive, they can be made to be constructive as well. Adlerians believe that lifestyle contains potential for both negative and positive behaviors and that it can takes us to our greatest successes but also to our greatest failures.

Lifestyle at Work

Adler (1964) believed that the purpose of lifestyle was to help an individual develop toward goals in life. He stated that, to be successful in life, all individuals had to accomplish three basic life tasks: love, friendship, and work. Adler was one of the first theorists to view work as important to both the psychological and the physical well-being of the individual. As a result, the clinical ideas incorporated in helping an individual with interpersonal problems in Adlerian therapy are easily adaptable for use with the employee in the workplace.

A more comprehensive understanding of lifestyle dynamics of employees could help supervisors negotiate the usually unavoidable personality clashes and work-related interpersonal conflicts (Kern & Peluso, 1999; Peluso & Kern, 1998). In today's society, we continually focus on quality, productivity, and work environment. Additionally, we are faced with more complex problems in the workplace, such as violence and terrorism. Applying a theory to understanding these dynamics in the workplace allows us to deal effectively with most employment situations. For example, one common scenario is that the person in charge may know that a particular employee becomes emotionally reactive if "pushed" to complete a work assignment. Given that the leader's goal is to keep the employee productive, he or she may avoid "pressing" the employee to perform for fear of causing unneeded disruption in the workplace. However, this avoidance by the leader in dealing with the emotionally reactive employee may not be possible when deadlines related to productivity surface. Thus, the person in charge, out of frustration, may see no other way than to confront the employee. If, however, the leader had some insight into the employee's lifestyle dynamics as well as his or her own, these tensions and conflicts may be avoided or mediated. Thus, for example, if the leader is trained to recognize lifestyle traits in oneself and others, then he or she may be able to identify potential conflicts early and effectively diffuse them (Kern & Peluso, 1999).

In addition, the concept of lifestyle brings an understanding of how the individual interacts with and perceives the environment. This can help managers, personnel professionals, and supervisors understand specific personality characteristics that are at play in an individual's approach to work and overall enjoyment in employment. Holland (1985) discussed the person–environment fit (also known as the P x E fit) as a prerequisite for career development. Adlerian theory sheds light into the interaction of the person and views of the environment. This becomes valuable to employers and managers in understanding the motivations of employees. If an individual prefers working in a small group setting and has a personality dynamic for that propensity but is asked to function in a large group activity, we know that the individual's stress level will increase. When stress levels increase in the individual, we understand that the individual's functioning becomes controlled by the parasympathetic nervous system (Selye, 1975). This automatic functioning not only is biologically based but is also tied into the psychological functioning. In short, lifestyle becomes more pronounced and the individual in the example may begin to withdraw from the group, increase barriers to communication, and cause distress among the other group members.

Employees and organizations under such stresses can begin to look chaotic and unpredictable. Productivity and individual achievement may start to suffer, and problems may seem unsolvable. However, armed with a powerful concept for understanding the employee, and an equally powerful tool for quickly understanding and measuring this concept, employers, managers, supervisors, team leaders, and many other leadership professionals can begin to understand why problems arise in the workplace and can take proactive steps to resolve issues before they affect productivity or break down into a complete catastrophe for the organization. In the following sections, we present tools for quickly and simply assessing these dynamics.

Measuring Lifestyle Quickly (BASIS-A)

Traditionally, Adlerian theorists used structured and detailed interview guides to elicit a person's lifestyle. This was a technique used by Adler himself in individual consultation and in public demonstrations and was expanded on by present-day Adlerians (Dinkmeyer, Dinkmeyer, & Sperry, 1987; Eckstein & Baruth, 1996). Although many Adlerians have created their own unique interview protocol, each follows a similar structure (Eckstein & Baruth, 1996; Kern, 1988; Mosak & Shulman, 1988; Walton, 1998). However, interview techniques can be time consuming and are often subjective appraisals of an individual's behavior, which makes a rapid intervention nearly impossible. Adlerians recognized this difficulty, and as a result of over 17 years of research, an objective measure of lifestyle was developed: the Basic Adlerian Scales for Interpersonal Success—Adult Form (BASIS-A; Wheeler, Kern, & Curlette, 1993).

The BASIS-A is a 65-item Likert-type questionnaire that is quick to administer (approximately 15 minutes) and easy to score and interpret. All of the items require respondents to answer questions from their memory of their childhood, which decreases the likelihood of response bias due to demand characteristics (Curlette, Wheeler, & Kern, 1997). In addition, the items of the BASIS-A rapidly obtains the family-of-origin information and provides a picture of the individual's lifestyle. The BASIS-A yields five dimensions (Belonging–Social Interest, Going Along, Taking Charge, Wanting Recognition, and Being Cautious) and has been validated with various personality assessment instruments such as the Minnesota Multiphasic Personality Inventory and the Millon Clinical Scales (Curlette et al., 1997). In addition, there are five minor or HELPS scales (Harshenss, Entitlement, Liked by All, Striving for Perfection, and Softness) that provide additional lifestyle information. Table 6.1 provides descriptions of each of the scales. Researchers have used the BASIS-A to study the lifestyles of varied groups of people, including corporate managers, teachers, prison inmates, batterers, and outpatient mental health clients (Miranda et al., 1995; Peluso & Kern, 2002; Slaton, Kern, & Curlette, 2000). Also, the BASIS-A has been used to assess the link between lifestyle and such variables as stress and coping, alcoholism, aggression, and medical adherence to treatment (Kern, Gfroerer, Summers, Curlette, & Matheny, 1996; Penick, 1997; Smith, Mullis, Brack, & Kern, 1999). Overall, the BASIS-A has proved to be a reliable measure for assessing the complex beliefs an individual holds about life and understanding the private logic that accompanies many of the behavioral choices that individuals make for themselves. In other words, the BASIS-A allows clinicians and consultants in the workplace to quickly and effectively tap into individuals' family-of-origin dynamics, assess the strengths they bring to the organization, and manage the potential conflicts and pitfalls that can hinder a company's functioning.

Table 6.1   Basic Adlerian Scales for Interpersonal Success–Adult Form (BASIS-A) Scales and Descriptions

BASIS-A Scale	No. of Items	Description
Belonging– Social Interest	9	High scores on this scale indicate a person with a high sense of belonging in a larger group setting, cooperative problem-solving styles, extroversion, and greater social skills.
Going Along	8	High scores on this scale indicate a person who prefers structure, likes to avoid conflict, and is rule-focused. Lower scores on this scale indicate a person who potentially has a more rebellious lifestyle and who can tolerate ambiguity well.
Taking Charge	8	High scores on this scale indicate that a person has leadership qualities and prefers to tell others what to do. People high on this scale may be seen as controlling.
Wanting Recognition	11	High scores on this scale indicate that a person enjoys and needs validation from others, tends to be success-driven, and is focused on personal achievement.

(continued)

Table 6.1 *(continued)*

BASIS-A Scale	No. of Items	Description
Being Cautious	8	High scores on this scale indicate a person who came from a confusing, unpredictable, and/or unsafe family-of-origin environment. Individuals with high scores will have adopted a cautious or suspicious approach toward problems and individuals. High scores on this scale also indicate sensitivity to the suffering of others.
Harshness	5	Individuals who score high tend to see their childhood in a negative manner, can be critical of others, and are less optimistic.
Entitlement	6	High scores reveal a belief that life should go one's way.
Liked by All	6	High scorers need the approval of others to feel good about themselves and do not like conflict with others.
Striving for Perfection	6	High scorers have standards for their actions and place themselves under great stress to achieve them. They have the ability to organize and problem-solve to achieve their goals.
Softness	5	High scorers view family as favorable and comfortable and are optimistic about themselves and the world.

Note. From *Basic Adlerian Scales for Interpersonal Success–Adult Form (BASIS-A) Interpretive Manual,* by R. M. Kern, M. S. Wheeler, and W. L. Curlette, 1993. Copyright 1993 by TRT Associates, Atlanta, GA. Adapted with permission.

Using Lifestyle (BASIS-A) to Counsel Employees

Used in organizational settings, the BASIS-A can facilitate effective team development, leadership and management styles training, employee performance appraisal, and organizational climate assessment. Table 6.2

offers information on how individuals with scores on each of the scales may behave in the workplace. In this section, we offer specific examples and problem scenarios in which the BASIS-A has helped organizations function more effectively.

A problem employee, from an Individual Psychology position, resembles a discouraged child who may exhibit poor work habits in the form of disregarding wishes of parents, performing poorly in school, having difficulty with teachers and classmates, and engaging in open or covert conflict with siblings and parents. The discouraged child in the family, like the problem employee, may surface because of sibling rivalry, inappropriate parenting skills, or unidentified physical or physiological impairments. This discouragement is usually manifested by actions and behaviors that seem to be destructive but that are actually strategies developed from the individual's lifestyle to find a place and feel a sense of belonging. In organizational terms, the dynamics of the problem employee may be described as a difficult personality type, an unmotivated worker, or one lacking certain work-related skills.

Identifying the discouraged employee and the underlying dynamics for the discouragement is the first (and possibly most important) step in resolving or preventing conflicts that disrupt the workplace. If discouraged employees are ignored or if their discouragement is not handled in a manner that communicates understanding and respect, they will continue to be discouraged, probably act out, and possibly discourage fellow employees. In terms of using the BASIS-A to identify and work with these individuals, some of the most common examples in which conflict in the workplace can result are the following dimensions: low Going Along, high Taking Charge (but not in a supervisory role), high Wanting Recognition, low Wanting Recognition, and high Being Cautious.

Employees with a low Going Along score may experience difficulty in the workplace because their free-spiritedness and independence may be seen as aggressive or insubordinate by supervisors. If they are properly motivated, these individuals can be valuable assets to organizations by helping to evaluate plans, disrupting "groupthink," and identifying weaknesses. However, if they are misunderstood or discouraged, they may be passively or actively defiant, be openly critical of the organization's flaws, and begin to "contaminate" or drag down other coworkers.

Similarly, individuals with high Taking Charge scores but who are not in a leadership position may feel discouraged that they are being underutilized. If this strength is recognized, they can be given responsibility for

Table 6.2 Basic Adlerian Scales for Interpersonal Success–Adult Form (BASIS-A) Themes in the Workplace

BASIS-A	Description at Work	
	High Scores	Low Scores
Belonging–Social Interest	Confident leader; works well in teams; visionary; extroverted; encouraging and supportive of others; good-listener; respected by others.	Self-directed; prefers to work alone, in high-structured, low-stress environments; may rely on self more than coworkers; may prefer close supervision; likes to work with ideas and abstract concepts.
Going Along	Prefers to know the rules; needs clarity in project requirements; avoids conflicts.	Independent; may be seen as critical or aggressive; good at spotting flaws in project plans; can be an asset when encouraged.
Taking Charge	Able to motivate others to perform tasks; enjoys delegating; may be seen as assertive or aggressive.	Can perform leadership tasks but prefers not to; may be seen as encouraging and sensitive.
Wanting Recognition	Agreeable and motivating to others; high need for validation of efforts; sensitive to discouragement; overemphasis on performance may lead to burnout.	Doesn't need validation for others; independent thinker; able to make decisions without concern for conflict; may be seen by others as cold or uncaring.

(continued)

Table 6.2 (continued)

BASIS-A	Description at Work	
	High Scores	Low Scores
Being Cautious	Sensitive to the needs of others; good at reading nonverbal cues from coworkers; dislikes change; conservative in decision making; often unsure of place in organization; avoids competition.	More at ease in the workplace; shows enthusiasm for change; good problem-solver; trusting and flexible; optimistic about future; may have difficulty with others who are questioning or pessimistic.
Harshness	Sees self in a more critical light than other coworkers.	Lower scores indicate less of this quality.
Entitlement	High need for validation as an important member of team; high sensitivity to discouragement.	Lower scores indicate less of this quality.
Liked by All	High need to please coworkers and win their acceptance; avoids conflicts.	Lower scores indicate less of this quality.
Striving for Perfection	High self-confidence in problem-solving skills; ability to finish tasks	Lower scores indicate less of this quality.
Softness	Optimistic view of one's abilities; can perform in stressful work setting.	Lower scores indicate less of this quality.

Note. From *BASIS-A Interpretive Guide for Leadership and Management*, by R. M. Kern and C. C. Rawlins, 1998. Copyright 1998 by TRT Associates, Atlanta, GA. Adapted with permission.

specific tasks within the organization that focuses this lifestyle dynamic in a positive, productive direction. It is important to note that their need for leadership can be evidenced either positively or negatively. If these individuals are not given some responsibility within the organization, this lifestyle dynamic will translate into open complaining. If a supervisor fails to recognize and address this, the individual's need for leadership can be used to foster open rebellion among coworkers.

Individuals with high Wanting Recognition scores require positive feedback about their job performance and have a high need for reassurance about their place in the organization related to their effectiveness. If the organization recognizes this lifestyle dynamic and provides this validation, these workers will be industrious and hard working. However, these individuals may be extremely sensitive to criticism and can burn out quickly. They are susceptible to being discouraged when there is a lack of feedback, and this can trigger irrational beliefs about their performance or job security. Conversely, individuals with low Wanting Recognition scores are self-assured and confident in their abilities and job performance. They do not need external feedback to maintain productivity. Guilt, intimidation, praise, manipulation, or other emotional tactics do not motivate them. Although these individuals are content to work under these conditions, they often have difficulty understanding the needs of others, particularly those with higher Wanting Recognition needs. Often these people seem aloof and unresponsive to others' concerns. This is a lifestyle dynamic that managers or supervisors need to be aware of in order to provide the optimal atmosphere for each employee to be productive.

Individuals with high Being Cautious scores are very sensitive to changes in the organization, are adept at reading the nonverbal cues of fellow employees, and are often the unofficial counselor for everyone else. This lifestyle dynamic is useful in the organization, because these individuals are often aware of the emotional climate of the workplace and can offer support to people. They can act as the proverbial "canary in the coal mine" about the toxicity of the organizational climate and can signal when change is needed. However, if the individual is discouraged, this ability can translate into oversensitivity to dangers that are not really there, or the quintessential "Chicken Little" response, which can unnecessarily disrupt the organization.

SuccessStyle Questionnaire

It becomes evident from the above examples that certain BASIS-A scores may translate into problems in the workplace, but not always. The critical element is whether the employee can be successful in fitting in the organization with his or her unique lifestyle. Many times in organizations, job responsibilities and activities are a poor fit for individuals. The poor $P \times E$ fit is usually thought to be caused by lack of training, skills, or, most damaging, lack of motivation on the employee's part. However, many times the incongruity of the $P \times E$ fit between employee and organization is the result of misunderstanding of the optimal work environment for the employee and can be easily resolved without disruption to the work group (Blustein & Spengler, 1995; Chartrand, Strong, & Weitzman, 1995; Hackett & Watkins, 1995). However, according to Chartrand et al. (1995), measuring the degree of congruence or incongruence of the individual with the work environment has been difficult at best. Although the BASIS-A provides lifestyle data, it alone cannot immediately give information about the goodness of an individual's $P \times E$ fit. The SuccessStyle Questionnaire (Peluso & Stoltz, 2001) is a 20-item instrument that has been developed to directly assess the employee's perception of the goodness of fit with the organization based on using the results of the BASIS-A assessment and Adlerian theory. Respondents indicate the level of agreement or disagreement with the statement based on a 5-point Likert scale. A sample of SuccessStyle items are shown in Table 6.3. The results of these responses are compared with the corresponding BASIS-A scale scores, with high discrepancies indicating potential areas of poor $P \times E$ fit and areas of congruence suggesting elements of the work environment in which the individual feels successful or in which the individual's lifestyle dynamics are in sync with the workgroup.

The focus of this instrument is concerned with the worldview of the employee, attempting to survey the employee's job experiences and framing them in the BASIS-A format. The SuccessStyle Questionnaire allows individuals to see the complex dynamics of lifestyle at the workplace, shedding light on the complex interaction of lifestyle, job performance, and employee perception. The advantage of this survey is that it allows the manager or supervisor to understand the employee's view of job duties and responsibilities. By framing the responses in the BASIS-A format, the employee, supervisor, and manager can then understand areas of difficulty and areas for development.

An Example Using the BASIS-A and the SuccessStyle Questionnaire

An example will assist in helping to understand the application of the SuccessStyle Survey and BASIS-A instruments. Bob manages Jim in a

Table 6.3   Samples of SuccessStyle Items

BASIS-A Scale	Sample SuccessStyle Items
Belonging–Social Interest	I often do my work individually.
Going Along	The rules or structure of the organization assists me in my ability to get my job done.
Taking Charge	I find myself taking a supervisory or leadership role in my job.
Wanting Recognition	I believe that my talents, skills, or abilities are being utilized to the *fullest* extent within the organization.
Being Cautious	I believe that I can rely on my coworkers to carry out their job tasks.

small work group for a large organization. Jim is a field technician whom Bob meets with occasionally during regional meetings, but they talk daily over the phone. Jim's work usually meets the minimum required, yet he seldom demonstrates performance beyond that of a beginning employee, even though he has been an employee of the company for 3 years. Bob has met with Jim occasionally for performance appraisals and has awarded Jim a rating of meeting standards, which states that Jim is meeting all the requirements of his job. Jim does demonstrate a skill for interacting well with customers but lacks the organizational follow-up skills that are required to satisfy the customer completely, which may be received as lip service. Bob recognizes that this is a fault in Jim and has tried to work with Jim in this area, but Jim continually does not perform to Bob's expectations. Bob is consistently called on to complete follow-up or assignments for Jim. This takes its toll on Bob's work schedule and is a continued source of irritation in their relationship.

Looking at Bob's lifestyle dynamics, as shown by his BASIS-A scores (see Table 6.4), one can see that his leadership style is characterized by his low Going Along score, high Taking Charge score, and high Wanting Recognition score. With this combination, a consultant can speculate that, as a leader, Bob may be more autocratic in his dealings with his subordinates (and Jim). As indicated by his low Going Along score, he is

---

Table 6.4   Examples of Basic Adlerian Scales for Interpersonal Success–Adult Form (BASIS-A) and SuccessStyle Questionnaire (SSQ) Scores

Bob's	Jim's	Jim's
BASIS-A Scores	BASIS-A Scores	SuccessStyle Scores
BSI-Moderate	BSI-high	SSQ1-low
GA-low	GA-moderate	SSQ2-high
TC-high	TC-moderate	SSQ3-high
WR-high	WR-high	SSQ4-moderate
BC-moderate	BC-low	SSQ5-moderate

Note. Bob is the manager and Jim is the employee. BSI = Belonging–Social Interest; GA = Going along; TC = Taking Charge; WR = Wanting Recognition; BC = Being Cautious.

---

probably very directive about what he wants done but does not like to give specific and detailed instructions, which can frustrate his employees and coworkers. He may have exacting standards and expectations that the assigned tasks will be carried out by his employees. In addition, he is not afraid to directly confront individuals when they are not performing to his expectations. However, the directness of his style may be softened a bit by his high Wanting Recognition score. Because he values validation from others, he is more likely to try to win subordinates over to his side. Another consequence of the high Wanting Recognition score is that he assesses his worth by what he has or has not done, which explains his tendency to "clean up" after Jim. This ultimately will lead to burnout in his job or a "blow out" with Jim.

A look at Jim's BASIS-A profile (also shown in Table 6.4) reveals that Jim is high on Belonging–Social Interest and Wanting Recognition and low on Being Cautious. In looking at this profile, one can quickly see that Jim is going to be a "people person" who is probably likable, charming, and outgoing. He is also probably fairly success driven, sensitive to the needs of others, and could get himself overcommitted by agreeing to too many things rather than saying no. He probably feels confident that whatever problems crop up, he can take care of them, but he dislikes having to do the mundane tasks that would proactively assure that problems would not exist because they take him away from doing what he feels he is best at: being with people.

In addition, Jim's SuccessStyle Questionnaire scores are presented (see Table 6.4), which allows a consultant or an EAP counselor to quickly assess the areas in which Jim perceives the most conflict between his lifestyle and the organization. At first glance, one can see that Jim feels fairly discouraged in the workplace, as evidenced by the high scores related to Going Along and Taking Charge. A consultant or counselor would then begin to explore whether Jim feels that he gets enough specific direction from Bob and whether he feels that the expectations are realistic. In addition, the moderate scores on Wanting Recognition and Being Cautious may indicate that Jim feels discouraged because others do not see or validate how well he interacts with the customers but criticize him for his lack of completed paperwork and adherence to procedures. Furthermore, Jim may have a hard time understanding or may just dislike the fact that Bob "gripes" about the things he does wrong and never "focuses on the positive." This could lead to more discouragement for Jim, and thus less effort on his part.

An intervention strategy for this scenario would be to educate Bob on his lifestyle dynamics and how he interacts with his employees in general, and Jim specifically. In particular, Bob could be encouraged to lower his high expectations of himself and others, as well as to be more specific in his directions. Another point to raise with Bob would be to sensitize him to his high need for validation, how this affects his ability to be direct with his employees, and how as a manager he will not always win the approval of his subordinates. For Jim, in educating him about his lifestyle, it will be important to reflect that working with people is a strength but that his overinvolvement with people tends to interfere with his ability and energy for paperwork and other routine tasks. If Jim can be encouraged to complete all of his work tasks and at the same time be recognized for both his accomplishments with customers and the internal procedures, it is probable that he can enjoy more success and satisfaction within the organization.

A final step in the intervention would be to bring Bob and Jim together to discuss their lifestyle dynamics in the working relationship. One aspect of this consultation would be to focus on the Belonging–Social Interest scale and how their differing scores translate into misunderstandings of specific work behaviors. For example, Bob's moderate score indicates that he may view Jim (with his high score) as oversocializing and ignoring other tasks that may look like a waste of time to Bob. However, for Jim, the social interaction is necessary for being successful in completing the job. This is his primary method for acquiring new task-related information and for maintaining his interest in the job. Thus, once both people learn to understand each other's strategies and viewpoints, they can then develop specific strategies for solving their relationship difficulties.

It is easy to see how the SuccessStyle Questionnaire provides a rapid understanding of the specific problems that an individual may have in the organization over and above the lifestyle information contained in the BASIS-A profile. This is particularly helpful for the consultant or the counselor, because he or she may not always have the BASIS-A profile of other coworkers or the supervisor. The SuccessStyle Questionnaire, in conjunction with the BASIS-A, can help to eliminate the guesswork in defining a specific area to work on, particularly with reticent, reluctant, or resistant clients. It allows for the counselor or consultant to establish immediate rapport with the client and move toward focusing on the difficulties that are confronting the employee.

Conclusion

We have presented Individual Psychology and the concept of lifestyle as a powerful tool for understanding the influence of family-of-origin issues on an employee's behavior. Through the objective measurement of lifestyle dynamics, certain patterns can emerge that, if the employee is discouraged or in the wrong environment, can create conflict and disruption at a cost to the organization. In particular, the BASIS-A and the SuccessStyle Questionnaire have been demonstrated to be useful tools for organizational consultants, career counselors, or EAP personnel to quickly assess an employee or a whole work setting and begin to make meaningful interventions. An additional advantage that the lifestyle construct, the BASIS-A, and the SuccessStyle Questionnaire have is that they are strengths-based and interactional. This provides the consultant or counselor with critical information related to these interactional dynamics in the workplace, which can be easily communicated to employees. The BASIS-A and the SuccessStyle Questionnaire can also be used to help consultants and EAP personnel in a variety of other ways, such as recognizing and developing leadership styles, team building and organizational cohesion, career coaching and development, and career pathing and selection. It is our hope that counselors will begin to use the principles and instruments to effectively understand individuals' behavior in the organization and provide successful interventions for them.

References

Adler, A. (1964). The individual psychology of Alfred Adler. In H. L. Ansbacher & R. R. Ansbacher (Eds.), *The individual psychology of Alfred Adler*. New York: Harper & Row.

Blustein, D. L., & Spengler, P. M. (1995). Personal adjustment: Career counseling and psychotherapy. In W. B. Walsh & S. H. Osipow (Eds.), *Handbook of vocational psychology: Theory, research, and practice* (2nd ed., pp. 295–330). Mahwah, NJ: Erlbaum.

Chartrand, J. M., Strong, S. R., & Weitzman, L. M. (1995). The interactional perspective in vocational psychology: Paradigms, theories, and research practices. In W. B. Walsh & S. H. Osipow (Eds.), *Handbook of vocational psychology: Theory, research, and practice* (2nd ed., pp. 35–66). Mahwah, NJ: Erlbaum.

Curlette, W. L, Wheeler, M. S., & Kern, R. M. (1997). *BASIS-A Inventory technical manual*. Highlands, NC: TRT Associates.

Dewey, E. A. (1991). *Basic applications of Adlerian psychology for self-understanding and human relationships*. Coral Springs, FL: CMTI Press.

Dinkmeyer, D., Dinkmeyer, D., Jr., & Sperry, L. (1987). *Adlerian counseling and psychotherapy* (2nd ed.). Columbus, OH: Merrill.

Dowd, E. T. (1997). A cognitive reaction: Adlerian psychology, cognitive (behavioral) therapy and constructivistic psychotherapy: Three approaches in search of a center *Journal of Cognitive Psychotherapy 11*, 215–219.

Eckstein, D., & Baruth, L. (1996). *The theory and practice of lifestyle assessment*. New York: Kendall/Hunt.

Ferguson, E. D. (1989). *Adlerian therapy: An introduction*. Vancouver, British Columbia, Canada: Adlerian Psychology Association of British Columbia.

Freeman, A., & Urschel, J. (1997). Individual psychology and cognitive therapy: A cognitive therapy approach. *Journal of Cognitive Psychotherapy 11*, 165–179.

Hackett, G., & Watkins, C. E. (1995). Research into career assessment: Abilities, interests, decision making, and career development. In W. B. Walsh & S. H. Osipow (Eds.), *Handbook of vocational psychology: Theory, research, and practice* (2nd ed., pp. 181–216). Mahwah, NJ: Erlbaum.

Holland, J. L. (1985). *Making vocational choices: A theory of vocational personalities and work environments* (2nd ed.). Englewood Cliffs, NJ: Prentice Hall.

Kern, R. M. (1988). *The Lifestyle Questionnaire Inventory (LSQI)*. Unpublished manuscript.

Kern, R. M., Gfroerer, K., Summers, Y., Curlette, W., & Matheny, K. (1996). Lifestyle, personality and stress-coping. *Journal of Individual Psychology, 52*(1), 42–53.

Kern, R. M., & Peluso, P. R. (1999). Using individual psychology concepts to compare family systems processes and organizational behavior. *The Family Journal, 7*, 236–244.

Kern, R. M., & Rawlins, C. C. (1998). *BASIS-A interpretive guide for leadership and management*. Highlands, NC : TRT Associates.

Kern, R. M., Wheeler, M. S., & Curlette, W. L. (1993). *Basic Adlerian Scales for Interpersonal Success–Adult Form (BASIS-A) interpretive manual*. Highlands, NC: TRT Associates.

Levinson, H. (1991). Diagnosing organizations systematically. In K. deVries (Ed.), *Organizations on the couch* (pp. 45–68). San Francisco: Jossey-Bass.

Miranda, A. O. (1994). *Adlerian lifestyle and acculturation as predictors of mental health of Hispanic adults*. Unpublished doctoral dissertation, Georgia State University, Atlanta.

Miranda, A. O., Kern, R. M., & Peluso, P. R. (1995). *Differences in leadership and lifestyle characteristics between transactional and transformational corporate leaders*. Unpublished manuscript.

Mosak, H., & Shulman, B. (1988). *Life Style Inventory*. Muncie, IN: Accelerated Development.

Niles, S. G., & Pate, R. H., Jr. (1989). Competency and training issues related to the integration of career counseling and mental health counseling. *Journal of Career Development, 16*(1), 63–71.

Peluso, P. R., & Kern, R. M. (1998). The seven habits of highly effective people and individual psychology. *Canadian Journal of Individual Psychology, 28*, 50–62.

Peluso, P. R., & Kern, R. M. (2002). An Adlerian model for assessing and treating the perpetrators of domestic violence. *Journal of Individual Psychology, 58*, 87–103.

Peluso, P. R., & Stoltz, K. B. (2001). *SuccessStyle Questionnaire*. Unpublished manuscript.

Penick, J. M. (1997). *Life style personality dynamics, health beliefs, and adherence with diabetic regimens*. Unpublished doctoral dissertation, Georgia State University, Atlanta.

Rounds, J. B., & Tracey, T. J. (1990). From trait-and-factor to person–environment fit counseling: Theory and process. In W. B. Walsh & S. H. Osipow (Eds.), *Career counseling: Contemporary topics in vocational psychology* (pp. 1–44). Hillsdale, NJ: Erlbaum.

Savickas, M. L. (1995). Current theoretical issues in vocational psychology: Convergence, divergence, and schism. In W. B. Walsh & S. H. Osipow (Eds.), *Handbook of vocational psychology: Theory, research, and practice* (2nd ed., pp. 1–34). Mahwah, NJ: Erlbaum.

Schneider, S. C. (1991). Managing boundaries in organizations. In K. deVries (Ed.), *Organizations on the couch* (pp. 169–190). San Francisco: Jossey Bass.

Selye, H. (1975). *The stress of life*. New York: McGraw-Hill.

Slaton, B. J., Kern, R. M., & Curlette, W. L. (2000). Personality profiles of inmates. *Journal of Individual Psychology, 56*(1), 88–109.

Smith, S., Mullis, F., Brack, G., & Kern, R. (1999). An Adlerian model for the etiology of aggression in adjudicated adolescents. *The Family Journal, 7*, 135–147.

Subich, L. M., & Bilingsley K. D. (1995). Integrating career assessment into counseling. In W. B. Walsh & S. H. Osipow (Eds.), *Handbook of vocational psychology: Theory, research, and practice* (2nd ed., pp. 262–294). Mahwah, NJ: Erlbaum.

Walton, F. X. (1998). Use of most memorable observation as a technique for understanding choice of parenting style. *Journal of Individual Psychology, 54,* 487–494.

Watkins, C. E. (1997). An Adlerian reaction in the spirit of social interest: Dialogue worth reckoning with. *Journal of Cognitive Psychotherapy, 11,* 211–214.

Watts, R. E., & Critelli, J. W. (1997). Roots of contemporary cognitive theories in the individual psychology of Alfred Adler. *Journal of Cognitive Psychotherapy 11,* 147–155.

Wheeler, M. S., Kern, R. M., & Curlette, W. L. (1993). *Basic Adlerian Scales for Interpersonal Success–Adult Form (BASIS-A) inventory.* Highlands, NC: TRT Associates.

7

Supervising the Problem Employee

Patrick H. Hardesty and Steven J. Morris

t would be easy if human systems could run like well-oiled machines. But if that were the case, there would be no need for supervisors in the workplace. Instead, it has to be recognized that trouble with people is going to be a common and natural occurrence when dealing with human relations. Therefore every supervisor will, at one time or another, need to solve people problems. Skill in working with people will make the difference between those who make good supervisors and those who do not. Good supervisors possess many interpersonal skills that help them succeed. They care about people, they can listen, they have empathy, they can encourage and motivate, they stay involved, they respect individuals, and they avoid demeaning others or damaging the self-esteem of fellow workers. These skills are valuable at all times. However, they become essential when dealing with the problem employee. This chapter examines the types of problems that supervisors can expect to encounter, ways to work through difficulties, and methods to avoid problems in the first place.

This chapter is based on three underlying premises. The first and perhaps most important premise is that all employees want to work and are capable of doing good work. From this perspective, when performance deficits become apparent, something is either wrong with the employee or with the employee's environment that is preventing success. The supervisor's job will be to identify the source of the difficulty or locate a professional who can identify the source of the difficulty. These other resources are usually available through the company's human resource or personnel department and in many companies through Employee Assistance Programs (EAPs).

A second premise is that people are able to modify their behavior. Skills can be learned and problems can be worked through. To be successful, good supervisors have an understanding of psychology that allows them to affect employee motivation, set realistic obtainable goals, and work with people in a cooperative manner. Good supervisors learn how to facilitate behavior change, which is essential for the problem employee. Good supervisors understand that learning anything new, including new interpersonal skills, will include setbacks along the way. One of the most important attributes of successful supervisors is that they have patience and they allow the time necessary for the desired behavior changes to occur.

The third premise is that the supervisor wants to see each employee succeed. Unfortunately, some supervisors would like problem employees to simply leave. Certainly this seems, on the surface, to be the quickest way to deal with a problem: make it go away. In some of these cases, supervisor interventions are often setups for failures. Situations are orchestrated so that the unwanted employee will be forced out of the organization. This chapter assumes that supervisors are willing to accept the challenge of working with each individual under their employ. In fact, having problems just go away may be a poor long-term strategy. Whatever conditions helped create the current problems may remain unchanged unless examined. These conditions may create problems in other employees. In addition, working through problems with the current employees can represent a long-term savings to the company. Many dollars are spent training people. It would be a shame to waste this investment. There is a cost associated with hiring and training replacements, but beyond that, there is no guarantee a replacement would be better or even as good as the previous employee.

Identifying Problems: The Supervisor Early Warning System

Working with problem employees is a bit like working with cancer—the earlier you intervene, the better the odds of success. Also, like a cancer, many problems do not spontaneously disappear. Indeed, if left alone, one problem employee could eventually affect others and maybe whole departments. To intervene early, supervisors must detect the problems early. So how can supervisors make sure their early warning systems are on and working? The most important asset to a supervisor is information, and the best way to gather information about employee successes and setbacks is through communication. Successful supervisors keep lines of communication open and possess good communication skills. Among the communication skills, there is none more important than the skill of listening. If a supervisor takes the time to listen to employees, many problems can be avoided or caught early.

Listening takes place in both formal and informal meetings. For listening to be effective, the supervisor has to see this time as valuable. The supervisor has to send the message that what employees say is valued. At the end of meetings, make sure there is time built in for employees to share concerns and issues. A supervisor who is available on the work site, such as walking through the warehouse, the office, or the factory floor, will have many opportunities to engage in informal conversations. Sometimes the supervisor initiates this, but important information is also obtained when a worker approaches the supervisor. At these times, it is important that the supervisor takes the time to have these conversations. If a supervisor is always in a hurry to get back to a project or meeting, employees will begin to feel as if they are not listened to. This will result in employees feeling as if communication with the supervisor is too much effort; they will not spontaneously approach the supervisor, and the supervisor will become starved for information. In other words, talking will stop. And one cannot be a good listener if no one is talking. When employees are talking, the supervisor has to be interested and indicate, through both verbal and nonverbal communication, that the information being shared is appreciated.

The second important aspect of the employee problem early warning system is performance monitoring. There is almost no type of problem that does not make itself known through drops in performance. This can be delay in production, reduced production, tardiness, and absenteeism.

Everybody has a bad day, but a number of bad days in a row is a sign that the supervisor needs to intervene.

People Problems in Business

Unfortunately, there are quite a number of people problems a supervisor needs to handle. Many of the issues are explored in more detail in other chapters of this book. Let us look at some of the issues that are common in today's work world.

Alcoholism and Other Substance Abuse

Substance abuse in the workplace accounts for days lost, lower production, and increased risks for accidents. Intoxicated employees present a danger to themselves and their coworkers. In 1990, the estimated cost to industry for chemical dependency was greater than $238 billion per year. By 1993, that had risen to over $400 billion per year (Hafer & Blume, 2000). Alcohol alone, the most abused drug, costs the United States $99 billion per year. Data reported by Hafer and Blume (2000) and by Strazewski (2001) find that chemically dependent employees:

- work at about 67% of capacity
- are late for work about 3 times as often as peers
- request early dismissal about twice as often
- are 16 times more likely to be absent from work
- are absent from work 7 or more days 2.2 times as much as peers
- will be involved in job-related accidents about 3.6 times more often
- are 5 times more likely to injure themselves
- are the cause of 40% of industrial accidents and fatalities
- will file a worker's compensation claim about 5 times more often
- will incur 300 times more medical cost than nonabusing peers
- will use medical benefits 8 times more often than nonabusers
- are more likely to engage in employee theft, accounting for 40% of all employee theft

The lowered productivity of an intoxicated or hung-over employee is sometimes covered up by increased production of coworkers. This, however, eventually leads to exhaustion, burnout, resentment, and lower morale of the coworkers. Coworkers can only cover up for so long. Interestingly, the resentment is not just felt toward the compromised colleague but to management as well for not recognizing and correcting the problem.

Workplace Violence

Violence is, of course, another serious problem in the modern workplace. The Centers for Disease Control declared violence in the workplace to be a national epidemic in 1992. In that year alone, 111,000 incidents of workplace violence were reported (Resnick, 1995). There are many variables associated with violence, including workplace violence. Among them are substance abuse, some psychological disorders, and some personality traits such as being a loner and having a history of problems with authority.

Most workplace violence is nonlethal. However, homicide cannot be ignored: It is becoming a workplace problem to be taken seriously. Homicide occurring at work was the third leading cause of occupational death for men and the leading cause for women in 1992. In 1990, homicide accounted for 42% of all workplace deaths among women and 11% of the workplace deaths for men. There are, of course, many circumstances that lead to homicide. Sometimes, people are murdered by spouses or intimate partners. Other times it is part of a robbery or other crime. The murders that usually make the news are those by disgruntled employees, often who have been demoted, denied promotion, or recently released from the company. In many of these cases, the supervisors and human relations personnel are targets, because they are experienced by the employee as insensitive, hateful, or evil.

Lynn McCLure has written extensively on the topic of violence in the workplace (e.g., McClure, 1996, 2000). In her books, she identified behaviors associated with potential violence. Because we have mentioned the importance of early detection in solving employee problems, it is useful to review the behaviors she identified as precipitants of violence. She recommended that supervisors look out for employees demonstrating the following behaviors:

- Employees who would rather act out their anger rather than work out their problems with others. These people will yell, slam doors, and throw things when frustrated or angry.
- Employees who put themselves first, doing whatever benefits them regardless of the impact their behavior may have on the team or company as a whole.

- Employees who will say one thing to a person but stab them in the back. These people are described as two-faced.
- Employees who are rigid. These people are inflexible and controlling in their dealings with coworkers and others.
- Employees who lie to escape responsibility or cover up mistakes.

There are other problems that could be connected to workplace violence. Substance abuse is connected to a multitude of problem behaviors, including violence, because of the lower inhibition often associated with substance abuse. Also, sudden changes in behavior should be attended to. These could be sudden changes in dress, hygiene, or social skills. Attention should be paid to someone who suddenly becomes withdrawn or who is observed talking to themselves.

Psychological Distress

Employees sometimes suffer from depression, anxiety disorders, and acute stress reactions, for which they need treatment. Greenberg and colleagues' (Greenberg, Stiglin, Finkelstein, & Berndt, 1993) study estimated the indirect cost of depression to be three times the cost of treatment. This included estimates of $11.7 billion as the cost of absenteeism and another $12.1 billion as the cost of reduced worker capacity. Suicide resulted in $7.5 billion in lost earnings (Greenberg et al., 1993).

Other psychological distress may be due to life circumstances outside of the workplace, but the effects are seen at work. This can happen when an employee is having trouble with family, is experiencing financial setbacks, or is dealing with legal difficulties. Although a supervisor is not a trained mental health professional, knowledge of human problems and sensitivity can be important assets for performing well as a supervisor. A modern supervisor knows the value of empathy or being able to see things from another's perspective (Fracaro, 2001).

Sexual Harassment

Sexual harassment has been a long-standing problem in the workplace. In 1980, the Equal Employment Opportunity Commission (EEOC) issued guidelines in which sexual harassment was considered a violation of Section 703 of Title VI. The 2001 EEOC Web page shows that 15,836 complaints were filed in the year 2000. Although not all cases were found to have merit, monetary benefits resulting from the conciliated cases totaled $54.6 million. Because of the liability the employer has for the quality of the work environment, supervisors must intervene quickly if a worker's behaviors are creating a hostile environment.

Employee Theft

Although not as dangerous to other people, employee theft accounts for many lost dollars to industry. Fraud and abuse of expenses and other sources of money cost the U.S. economy $400 billion a year (Zeune, 2001). In the year 2000, one half of large corporations experienced theft that amounted to an average of $500,000 each (Albrecht & Searcy, 2001).

Low Morale

Weiss (1998) reported that employees with low morale are unhappy and dissatisfied. The negative attitudes held and demonstrated by these employees promote negative attitudes and feelings among other employees. Therefore, low morale deserves immediate attention because it can quickly grow from an individual problem to a group problem.

According to Weiss (1998), morale is based on four feelings. First is satisfaction with the job itself. Employee satisfaction in all organizations tends to wax and wane. No one is more satisfied with their job than on their first day. Eventually, inevitable disappointments compromise satisfaction and morale. Second is pride in one's fellow employees. Everyone wants to play for a winning team. It is a good feeling to know that one's colleagues are highly competent and skilled. Third is acceptance of pay scales and promotion opportunities. Morale will quickly suffer if employees feel the company is unfair in these practices. Fourth are feelings of belonging to the company. People want to believe that they are part of a successful organization and that the group values their contributions.

Boredom

Boredom is different from low morale. It may be closer to depression. People forget to care about their job. Boredom leads to more errors in the workplace and can occur in any organization. Weiss (1998) suggested that boredom be addressed by allowing people to move to adjacent jobs. In this way, employees begin to understand the role their position plays in the larger functioning of the organization. In addition, the organization obtains personnel trained in more than one job. This is valuable in times of absenteeism.

Other Problems

Personality conflicts among coworkers present problems that can interfere with the smooth operation of a business. Other personality or social problems include general defiance of authority and intentional underproduction. It is difficult to establish a cost figure for these types of problems.

The Supervisory Role

Before tackling the problems of dealing with problem employees, we briefly examine the supervisory roles. White (1963) stated that people must master two worlds: the world of things and the world of people. Managers must also master these two worlds. First, they are responsible for the tasks of the organization. That is the product or service that defines the enterprise. This involves the organization of materials and physical resources. It includes bringing the necessary supplies to the assembly line or to the customer. The necessary resources, machines, tools, and raw materials that are needed to keep the employees functioning at their best have to be available when needed.

Managers who are supervisors of people must also ensure that the people the company employ carry out the enterprise, that they can and will do the job. The human resource is one of the most valuable resources of the company. Care and maintenance of this resource is worth much. The literature on supervision contains many metaphors to describe the roles or functions of the supervisor. They include such ideas as "supervisor as coach," "supervisor as cheerleader," "supervisor as trainer," "supervisor as teacher," "supervisor as mentor," and "supervisor as boss." An examination of this literature reveals five functions or responsibilities of supervisors, which we discuss below.

Company Oversight

This responsibility includes monitoring of process and product, making sure the rules are followed, and taking corrective or disciplinary actions. This function is becoming more complicated as there are concerns regarding employee privacy versus "snoopervision." However, as part of management, the supervisor is responsible for keeping company objectives in focus (Ramsey, 1999).

Trainer/Educator

This responsibility is to keep everyone up to date on innovations and changes in policy and procedure. Unfortunately, many supervisors are not trained in education. They do not know how to develop curriculum and build on existing knowledge structures. Employees have to be given feedback in helpful ways so that either good work is continued and expanded or errors can be corrected and the work put back on track. Good employee evaluation strengthens the company and the team as a whole.

Poorly handled evaluation kills morale. Evaluation has to be viewed as an educational and training tool, not a punishment tool. Unfortunately, because raises and promotion also depend on evaluation, it is difficult to not project the evaluation as simply a part of the punishment/reward system (Humphrey & Stokes, 2000).

Material Support

This function describes the supervisor's role as making sure material, services, and data are where they need to be when they need to be there. An employee just needs to reach for what is needed without appreciating how it got there. In this role, a supervisor has to be good at coordinating people, things, and data. But equally important is support of the person in the role of worker. This means taking care of the material needs of the worker. Included in this are adequacy of pay and health of the working environment.

Emotional Support

The supervisor has to attend to the motivational and psychological needs of the employees. It is the supervisor's job to keep the team alert, ready, and working at full potential. Supervisors are expected to keep company morale as high as possible. A good supervisor empowers the employees to take risks and reach for higher goals. Attempts at excellence are recognized and appreciated, even if they do not always lead to success. Scared employees are of only moderate value to the company. Lastly, the supervisor often has to serve as a dumping ground. There are times when employees have to get something off their chests or simply let out steam. An effective supervisor is tolerant and patient with this need. Often these events can be springboards to adjustments and improvements.

Team Leader

In this capacity, supervisors are expected to be savvy about group process and interpersonal dynamics. People have to work effectively together to accomplish higher goals. Work groups used to be homogeneous. Today's supervisors have to be skilled at getting a diverse group of employees to work together. Employees will be of different ethnic origins and of different generations. These differences, as well as differences in gender and educational background, are all potential areas of interpersonal conflict. Tensions created by these differences have the potential to negatively affect the performance of one or more individuals.

Work groups also used to consist of the same professionals. Accountants would work with accountants in the accounting department, whereas draftsmen would work with other draftsmen in the design department. Today, teams of professionals have to work together so that projects get executed effectively. People from diverse professional backgrounds will have to see the larger institutional picture to function as a valuable team member (Buhler, 2000; Humphrey & Stokes, 2000)

There are two things a supervisor is not. A supervisor is not a friend. It is important to be friendly but not to confuse the responsibility of supervision with friendship. It is probably impossible to avoid becoming friends with some workers and not with others. Many supervisors were promoted from a team of coworkers who were already their friends. However, on the job, the dual roles of friend and supervisor can create conflicts. The supervisor has to evaluate employees. Friendships can create the appearance of unfairness. Other workers can become bitter and harbor a grudge if the supervisor is seen as unfair (Seidenfeld, 1998).

A supervisor is not a psychologist. However, a good supervisor is best served by using sound psychological principles. A good supervisor knows about motivation, empathy, and how to facilitate excellence among employees. A supervisor is looking for ways to improve morale. Most importantly, and the focus of this chapter, a supervisor has to recognize when employees are suffering from stress or other psychological disturbances. Next, we review the psychological principles useful to supervisors.

Important Psychological Principles for Supervisors

Principle 1: Involvement in goal setting.   For employees to be motivated toward a goal, it is best if they have ownership in the goal. Ideally, the workers who are responsible for meeting the goal will have had input into its development and for the plan of action specified to meet the goal. Goals handed down from above will be less respected by employees. However, this cannot always be avoided. In these cases, it is important to communicate the role of the goal in the larger scheme of things. Even ideas with which people disagree will be more palatable if the rationale is explained and understood. The easiest way to lose team commitment is to simply have them do a task because the management said so. In this case, workers will work for the pay but may not give the extra 10% that could make a big difference in outcome. Because the problem employee already feels disenfranchised from the enterprise, involvement in developing corrective goals sets a positive tone.

Principle 2: Optimal challenge.   Goals cannot be too trivial or difficult. People are motivated by the correct amount of challenge. On the one hand, we are insulted by jobs that are too easy; we see them as menial. On the other hand, we do not even attempt to begin a challenge if it is too difficult. Why try if we know the odds are that we will fail anyway? Employees will sense that they are being set up if given unobtainable goals.

Principle 3: Goals must be measurable.   Vague goals are often unmet. With vague goals, it is easy for a supervisor to feel as if progress has not been sufficient while the employee could believe the goal was exceeded. An example of a vague goal is "we must increase production significantly or this division is in trouble." Supervisors who studied management certainly would have learned the importance of measurable goals. They add to accountability and let all team members monitor the group progress.

Principle 4: Timing of the reinforcement.   Near-term reinforcers are stronger than distant reinforcers. Therefore, long-term goals are best broken down into a series of short-term goals. Rewards should be continuous. People lose focus when rewards are spaced too far apart.

Principle 5: The right reinforcer.   It may take time to find the appropriate reinforcer. Everyone appreciates money as a bonus. But personal respect is also important to people. A "thank you" is inexpensive but valuable. It is surprising how difficult it can be for supervisors to remember to hand these out. Another powerful reinforcer is acknowledgment from a respected colleague. Later in this chapter, we examine the source of social influence available to supervisors and the power of the respected colleague.

Up to this point, we have been discussing reinforcers, but what about punishments? The type of work environment supervisors create is largely determined by the balance between the use of positive reinforcers and punishments. In a high punishment environment, people are afraid to take risks for fear of mistakes. This negatively affects morale and creates problem employee situations. We all know bosses who are a joy to work for and those for whom no one wants to work. Even successful but tough drill sergeants know when it is time to build morale and reward the troops. When the balance of discipline and reinforcement is correct, great productivity and loyalty can emerge.

How to Solve the Problem of the Problem Employee?

Regardless of the type of problem a supervisor is experiencing with an employee, we developed an eight-step approach to problem solving to provide a generic model of intervention (see Table 7.1).

The first three steps of the process are the preparation stage. These steps organize your actions. It is a mistake to try to intervene with a problem employee spontaneously. It is best to be organized and prepared. The next three steps are the action stage. This is a sequence of actions designed to enhance behavior change. The last two steps are the follow-up stage. Too many plans are wasted because there was no follow-up. We next examine each of these steps in more detail.

Step 1: Document the Behaviors

Getting the right information is essential to problem solving with the trouble employee. We have previously discussed the need for listening as part of the alert system for trouble. Listening is vital to getting the information about the problem. The first thing you need to understand is the actual behaviors being displayed by the employee. Is it tardiness? How often? How late? Is there a pattern? Is the problem absenteeism? If so, how

Table 7.1 Eight Steps to Solving Problems in Supervision

Stage	Step
Preparation	1. Document the behaviors
	2. Understand the situation
	3. Formulate a course of action—a plan
Action	4. Discuss the proposed course of action with the employee
	5. Get a commitment
	6. Engage in the plan
Follow-up	7. Monitor—document every meeting and every plan and every commitment
	8. Adjust the plan if needed or abandon the plan

many times and when? Again, is there a pattern? If there is a decline in the quality of work, make specific notes of exactly what has changed. If there have been arguments, document where and when. If a specific threat has been made, know the threat as accurately as possible. If there has been a charge of sexual harassment, get the facts.

Step 2: Understand the Situation

Once you understand the specifics of the problem, it is helpful to understand the context in which the problem behavior exists. This will help you see the problem from the employee's perspective. Maybe there are some job-related environmental problems that are exacerbating the problems seen in the employee. In deciding to intervene in a problem, you must exercise caution so as to not blame the victim. One of the biggest complaints about supervisors is that they are unfair (Seidenfeld, 1998). Is the employee under the impression that the company is unfair or that you, the supervisor, have been unfair? If so, this needs to be discussed directly. Otherwise, any corrective action you suggest will be seen as additional unfairness.

Another problem addressed in the literature is lack of employee development. In the ever-changing world in which businesses operate, the duties of many jobs are continually shifting. Changing work assignments or responsibilities can often tax the ability and training of an employee. Even supervisors suffer from lack of training, specifically in the art and science of supervision. Many supervisors are promoted from the ranks but are not trained to be effective supervision. As a result, there is an awkward adjustment period. Many learn the job from experience. But others, seemingly qualified supervisors, will fail from lack of training and not being able to pick it up on their own. Any worker can feel inadequate if they are not sure how to do the job (Friley, 1999).

Step 3: Formulate a Course of Action for Yourself and a Tentative Plan for the Employee

It is important to have a plan. The plan has to take into account company policy and resources. Some problems can be handled between the supervisor and the employee. Others have to use other resources such as an EAP. Although it is important that the supervisor have solutions before meeting with the employee, it is also important to remain open. In the course of talking with the employee, new ideas might emerge. Two heads might be better than one. In addition, we stated earlier that goals created by employees have the highest probability of success. Therefore, it is best if employees can help design solutions to their problems.

Step 4: Discuss the Proposed Course of Action With the Employee

At this step you are ready to meet with the troubled employee. All your people skills will be needed for this meeting. Although obvious to most supervisors, it needs to be emphasized that the location of the meeting should be private. Because the work or behavior of the employee is unsatisfactory, negative feedback will be necessary. This feedback is potentially embarrassing, and the employee has to feel he or she is in a safe place to hear it without undue defensiveness.

When meeting with the employee, confront appropriately. The focus should be the employee's performance on the job. Whether it is coworker relations or underproduction, the problems should be stated explicitly. Give behavioral feedback, not personality information. That is, identify the concerns without trying to psychoanalyze the employee. Most people do not even want their therapists to presume what they think or feel. Be willing to hear what the employee may wish to share about what is going on inside them, but do not offer opinions of your own in this regard. You have to keep the job as the focus of the discussion while showing care and support for the person.

As you offer your solutions or work cooperatively with the employee in designing a solution, you will need to understand your ability to influence the situation. Social psychologists have long studied social influence, and some of the results are valuable to understanding the supervisory relationship. We examine these below.

Social Power

French and Raven (1959) distinguished five types of social power: reward, coercive, legitimate, referent, and expert. A single powerful agent likely derives his or her power from more than one source. However, it is typical to examine each type separately.

Reward power and coercive power both involve social exchange. A person possesses reward power when he or she can influence the likelihood that reward will come or the person can influence the amount of reward. Coercive power is the power the person has to administer punishments or to remove expected positive reinforcers. Among the sources of rewards and punishments that can influence others are social reinforcers. Being liked or disliked are powerful motivators.

Legitimate power is contained within social roles that people are taught to respect. The teacher, policeman, president, elder, or supervisor possesses legitimate power inasmuch as one is socialized that these roles have the authority to govern and make decisions. The limitation, therefore, of legitimate power is the degree of socialization that has occurred. Another limitation is the degree to which a person perceives the powerful agent as representative of the class of people endowed with legitimate power. For instance, although an employee might feel that supervisors have legitimate authority, the employee might also feel a particular supervisor falls short of his or her expectations or definitions of a proper supervisor. In that case, the supervisor is no longer endowed with legitimate power.

Referent power stems from identification with the powerful agent. If one sees oneself as like the agent, then one is likely to feel that decisions and authority stemming from the agent are reasonable. If a person aspires to be an accountant, for instance, then other accountants have influence over him or her. Performing in accordance with their expectations will positively influence the person's self-esteem. Referent power comes from equals as well. A person may meet the expectations of his or her friends because the person wishes to be seen as a good, reliable friend. The friends are people he or she wishes to emulate, and therefore they have referent power to him or her.

Expert power exists when an agent possesses knowledge and skills one desires. Apprentices follow their master's wishes so that they can obtain the needed skills. The apprentice will follow most requests as long as it is felt the master is acting in good faith.

Social Power and Work Results

Supervisors working with problem employees present themselves as powerful agents. The source of power has some bearing on the success a supervisor has in influencing work improvement efforts from the employee. Results of this research were reviewed by Fedor and colleagues (Fedor, Davis, Maslyn, & Mathieson, 2001). First, we look at the results of influence attempts and employee responses to directives. Yukl and Falbe (1991) found there was a positive relationship between the use of expert and referent power and commitment to perform a task assigned by a manager. In this study, it was found that coercive power, which some supervisors use often, was negatively associated with commitment to perform the assigned task. Legitimate and reward power were not associated with commitment to complete the task. In a later study, Yukl, Kim, and Falbe (1996) found a positive relationship between the application of referent, expert, and legitimate basis of power and levels of commitment to follow a directive. Reward power was not predictive of commitment, and coercive power was not studied in this research.

Fedor et al. (2001) examined social power and its relationship to performance improvement efforts specifically. This is especially germane to this chapter because it is just such efforts that supervisors are asking of problem employees. Fedor et al. found that referent and expert power were positive predictors of performance improvement efforts, whereas coercive power was unrelated to such efforts. It is interesting that this study, consistent with previous work, did not find a relationship between reward power and effort to improve performance. Supervisors and managers often feel they can influence behavior by controlling rewards, but research continues to call this belief into question.

Next, we examine the research connecting social power with a broader range of work outcomes. For this, we review the results of meta-analyses. A meta-analysis is a method of research in which all or most of the previous studies on a topic are brought together and the results statistically combined. This allows a scientific method of discovering what the bottom line may be of the many studies conducted by social scientists on a topic. Podsakoff and Schriesheim (1985) showed that expert and referent power were generally related to positive organizational outcomes such as performance. When expert and referent power were high, there was a tendency for better organizational outcomes compared with situations when these were low. However, reward, coercive, and legitimate power were either negatively related or not related to positive organizational outcomes. The meta-analysis of Carson, Carson, and Roe (1993) found that expert and referent power were positively related to performance. In addition, the use of expert and referent power was also positively correlated to the satisfaction employees had with supervisors and to overall job satisfaction.

Employee Self-Esteem and Improvement Efforts

Dealing with the problem employee usually means giving negative feedback. There is research to help us understand the way in which negative feedback is given and received. Most of this research demonstrates that receiving negative feedback lowers self-esteem. If negative feedback is provided to an employee whose self-esteem is low to begin with, there is a negative effect on self-efficacy. Interestingly, the deleterious effect of negative feedback on self-efficacy is not observed when negative feedback is provided to employees who have high self-esteem (McFarlin &

Blascovich, 1981; Tang & Sarsfield-Baldwin, 1991). Employees with high self-esteem may be resistant to external feedback, including negative feedback. It appears these employees make more stable internal positive evaluations (Artkinhead, 1980; Brockner, 1988; Campbell, 1990; Robinson & Smith-Lovin, 1992; Shrauger, 1975; Sweeney & Wells, 1990).

Unfortunately, the troubled employee may be someone of low self-esteem. Low self-esteem is associated with many problems. Therefore, the negative feedback provided to these employees is likely to reduce self-efficacy beliefs. This presents a conundrum in that performance expectations and one's beliefs in personal efficacy are often related to efforts to improve performance (Bandura & Cervone, 1983). It is these efforts that supervisors are hoping to encourage by providing the feedback. The reason for intervening is to facilitate positive change in the performance of the employee. So the supervisor is put in an interesting double bind. Whereas the person with high self-esteem may respond to negative feedback by trying to improve, the person with low self-esteem may simply quit (Brockner, Derr, & Laing, 1987; McFarlin, Baumeister, & Blascovich, 1984).

Combined Effects of Social Power and Self-Esteem

Fedor et al. (2001) investigated the relationship between self-esteem and source of power. Because people with high self-esteem make more positive internal attributions, response to negative feedback will be partially based on the perceived credibility of the feedback. Therefore, feedback from people high in referent and expert power is expected to have a greater influence on effort among workers with high self-esteem. If the person providing the feedback is viewed as low in referent and expert power, then the quality of the feedback is minimized or rejected by workers with high self-esteem, and there may be the perception that there is no need to respond. Fedor et al.'s study did not find that expert power moderated the connection between self-esteem and response to negative feedback. However, referent power was found to have a significant effect with workers of high self-esteem. As expected, high self-esteem employees are more likely to respond to feedback if the source of the feedback is perceived as high in referent power. In the case of employees with low self-esteem, the type of power of the source of the negative feedback did not seem to affect the relationship between self-esteem and efforts to improve.

These studies indicate that a supervisor will be most influential when approaching the employee as someone who is an example of the proper employee. The discussions will also be more productive if the employee sees the supervisor as an expert in the area of work. However, if a supervisor hopes to buy improvement efforts with rewards or to coerce improvement with threats, research indicates that the chances of success will be diminished. Therefore, the supervisor should approach the employee with genuine concern as one worker to another. The supervisor should indicate that this is could be a win-win situation that is beneficial to the supervisor, the employee, and the organization as whole if all workers perform at their best. The problems noted by the supervisor are best presented as obstacles to best performance, not as indications that the person is bad and needs to be punished. The following advice for approaching an employee and giving performance feedback is compiled from the works of Peters (2000) and Weiss (1988). Some of these points were also discussed in other parts of this chapter.

- Criticize without being emotional. Sarcasm, anger, or other demeaning emotions prevent your message from getting through. Remaining calm and using a helping tone increase the probability that negative feedback will be used appropriately.
- Always discuss negative feedback in private. Embarrassing an employee will not only reduce the chances that positive change will occur now but will also create long-term morale problems.
- Make the meeting important, without interruptions. Supervisors need to value the privacy of employees, and interruptions feel like violations of privacy.
- Communicate expectations clearly and address performance problems honestly and directly. It is necessary to point out the unacceptable behaviors specifically so both parties are aware of what is being discussed. Supervisors who are not direct lose respect.
- Point out what can be better. We discuss planning in the next section. One important aspect of planning is that telling someone to stop a behavior is insufficient. It is important to identify corrective behaviors.
- Be positive with your statements and advice. Include the positive contributions of the employee. Indicate confidence in the person's ability to do to right thing and also point out the value to the employee and to the company of doing things right.
- After discussing negative behaviors and outcomes, and probably being critical of someone's behavior, say something positive and

uplifting. Leave the person feeling as if he or she is still valued and has an important contribution to make.

- Use self-feedback. Allow the employee to summarize his or her own work and evaluate whether he or she has been successful at meeting his or her goals. Two advantages stem from this approach. First, employees can be tougher on themselves than a supervisor can be. Second, the employee will own the evaluation and therefore work harder to correct the self-identified shortcomings or weaknesses.
- Make feedback frequent and informal.

Planning

Nobody plans to fail, but many fail to plan. In the previous step, we indicated that the supervisor should have a plan of action for his or her own process and a tentative plan for the employee's necessary change. Now that the supervisor is at the stage of discussing the problem with the employee, it is important that, together, a workable plan is formulated. There are some basics to planning that therapists use with clients to enhance helpful change. Applegate (1980) outlined a number of important aspects of good planning.

The first is that the plan should focus on behavior that the individual can perform. This is the concept of independence. Of course we are concerned with outcome, but for most businesses, any outcome depends on the efforts of many people. There are still some jobs such as piece work where the outcome (e.g., number of units assembled) is a direct measure of an individual's performance, but this is not true for the majority of positions. This principle of planning is *independence*.

A good plan should be able to begin *immediately*. It is beneficial if the first step in the improvement process can begin that day or the next. The longer the wait to begin something, the more the enthusiasm diminishes.

A good plan includes *repetitive* activities. It is best if there is some activity that can be practiced. However, there is a danger in expecting too much. For instance, if an employee is expected to improve the time specific reports are completed, it would be too big a jump to go all the way to the goal that all reports will be on time. Instead, set the goal that perhaps 5 of the next 10 reports, then 7 of the next 10 reports, will be completed on time. Of course it seems that a supervisor should just be able to tell an employee to shape up and expect results because of the power of the paycheck. This does indeed work sometimes. Often though, smaller, accomplishable goals build to a powerful outcome. This is the method of behavioral change taught to psychotherapists. Small gains are appreciated, because they lead to the agreed-upon goal.

Start plans are more successful than stop plans. That is why diets never work. The expression "nature abhors a vacuum" is correct in this case. If the plan is to help stop an employee from doing something, then a better idea is to think of something to do instead—and start doing that.

Step 5: Get a Commitment

Once the plan is created, it must be worked on. A commitment to proceed with the plan must not be vague. "I think I can do that" is not a commitment. "I will" is the only acceptable response. If the employee is unable to make the commitment, then the reason has to be known. Perhaps the plan came from the supervisor and not the employee, and the employee does not think it can really be done.

Step 6: Engage in the Plan

It is up to the employee to make the effort to improve performance. At this point, the supervisor can serve as water boy and coach, making sure that there is the correct emotional and tangible support to enhance success.

Step 7: Monitor—Document Every Meeting and Every Plan and Every Commitment

While the supervisor is supporting the efforts for improvement, the successes and setbacks, the meetings, discussions, and commitments need to be documented. Should there come a need for disciplinary action, these documents testify to the due process that was accorded the employee.

Step 8: Adjust the Plan If Needed or Abandon the Plan

All plans have kinks that need to be worked out. Be aware that if a plan is not followed precisely, this may be an indication of adjustments needed to the plan instead of an indictment of the employee's motivation, effort, and ability. There are always ways to make plans better once they are seen in action. Mistakes and setbacks are expected along the way to improvement. But these can also be teaching and learning opportunities. If a mistake is made, do not jump to conclusions. Investigate the circumstance completely. Supervisors who help employees learn from mistakes increase the effectiveness of their team. If handled correctly, it is possible to turn lemons into lemonade without blaming or criticism (Bielous, 2000).

Equally important is analyzing success. Too much focus on failures and shortcomings can lead to an atmosphere of critical supervision and leave employees feeling unappreciated. It is also important to recognize strengths (Pollack, 1999).

Prevention

Finally, it is important to look at the best way to deal with problem employees, and that is to prevent problems in the first place. There are some behaviors that supervisors engage in that create problem employees. Some have been mentioned previously, but it is worth reviewing these points again. Many of these were reviewed by Seidenfeld (1998) and Pollack (1999).

- Playing favorites will be the quickest way to lower morale and create problem employees. It is important to be vigilant in being fair and even-handed in dealing with employees.
- Not caring will be quickly picked up by employees. If the supervisor does not care, the employees will not see the value in their contribution.
- Not being involved or aware puts a supervisor at a great disadvantage. A supervisor has to spend time with the employees. Employees have no respect for supervisors who do not know what is going on. Give regular feedback and get regular feedback.
- Supervisors invite problems by not being direct. It is important to learn to effectively and dispassionately discipline employees when necessary. It is equally important to be direct in compliments. Not being direct leads to loss of respect of supervisor.
- Be honest when talking with employees, and do not keep secrets. Explain things thoroughly. Tell your employees what you know. If you do not know something, be honest and say you don't know. If you know something that is confidential or is not ready to be revealed, simply say this is the case. Employees will respect this forthright approach. Know in advance what you want to say, and organize your thoughts. Chance remarks can backfire and negatively affect people. An unintended inflection of voice or a few inappropriately chosen words can be misunderstood, hurt people's feelings, and lead to hostility.
- Empower employees by allowing them to make decisions that affect the way they do their jobs. Empowerment shows that you

trust their skills and builds trust in the employee that the company and supervisor are concerned and involved.

- Treat employees equitably. If people give to the company and get nothing in return, they will try to make the relationship more equal by doing only what is necessary to hold their jobs.
- Keep the company and unit goals known and in focus. People will tend to drift from the organizational goals without reminders. Help employees see how their work contributes to larger goals. Periodically review the mission and goals of the position, unit, and organization.
- Display confidence in the skills and abilities of your employees. Doubts should be reviewed privately or with the correct management personnel. A supervisor's lack of confidence can quickly lower morale.

Conclusion

Professionals working with employees today have to be aware of the effects of human problems on the individual worker, fellow coworkers, and the organization as a whole. To reduce problems in the workplace, the supervisor or human resource person has to know how to recognize difficulties when they occur and how to intervene. There are many types of problems that employees experience, and it is unreasonable to assume that supervisors can be expert in each area. Instead, in this chapter, we suggest an eight-step process that focuses on work-related behavior that results in a plan of action for improvement. Our procedures also advocate a collaborative problem-solving style to enhance the probability of success. Lastly, the best way to solve the problem of troubled employees is to prevent them from arising. The last part of this chapter reviews the type of management behaviors that can inhibit or promote problems among employees.

References

Albrecht, W. S., & Searcy, D. J. (2001). The top 10 reasons why fraud is increasing in the U.S. *Strategic Finance, 82*(11), 58–61.

Applegate, G. (1980). If only my spouse would change. In N. Glasser (Ed.), *What are you doing?* (pp. 34–47). New York: Harper & Row.

Artkinhead, M. (1980). An empirical test of a new theory of human needs. *Organizational Behavior and Human Performance, 4*, 142–175.

Bandura, A., & Cervone, D. (1983). Self-evaluations and self-efficacy mechanisms governing the motivational effects of goal systems. *Journal of Personality and Social Psychology, 45*, 1017–1028.

Bielous, G. A. (2000). Create an atmosphere of blameless error (Employee supervision). *Supervision, 60*(4), 13.

Brockner, J. (1988). *Self-esteem at work: Research, theory, and practice.* Lexington, MA: Lexington Books.

Brockner, J., Derr, W., & Laing, W. (1987). Self-esteem and reactions to negative feedback: Towards greater generalizability. *Journal of Research in Personality, 21*, 318–333.

Buhler, P. M. (2000). Managing in the new millennium. *Supervision, 61*(6), 6.

Campbell, J. D. (1990). Self-esteem and clarity of the self-concept. *Journal of Personality and Social Psychology, 59*, 538–549.

Carson, P. P., Carson, K. D., & Roe, C. W. (1993). Social power bases: A meta-analytic examination of interrelationships and outcomes. *Journal of Applied Social Psychology, 23*, 1150–1169.

Equal Employment Opportunity Commission (2001). *Sexual harassment charges EEOC and FEPAs combined: FY 1992–FY 2000.* Retrieved from www.eeoc.gov/stats/harass.html

Fedor, D. B., Davis, W. D., Maslyn, H. M., & Mathieson, K. (2001). Performance improvement efforts in response to negative feedback: The roles of source power and recipient self-esteem. *Journal of Management, 27*, 79.

Fracaro, K. (2001). Empathy: A potent management tool. *Supervision, 62*(3), 10.

Frank, E., & Thase, M. E. (1999). Natural history and preventative treatment of recurrent mood disorders. *Annual Review of Medicine, 50*, 453–468.

French, J. R. P., & Raven, B. H. (1959). The bases of social power. In D. Cartwright (Ed.), *Studies in social power* (pp. 150–167). Ann Arbor: University of Michigan Press.

Friley, E. (1999). Silent antagonism: Silence of workers who feel inadequate because they are not properly trained by their supervisor. *Supervision, 60*(6), 14.

Greenberg, P. E., Stiglin, L. E., Finkelstein, S. N., & Berndt, E. R. (1993). The economic burden of depression in 1990. *Journal of Clinical Psychiatry, 54*, 405–418.

Hafer, F. D., & Blume, E. R. (2000). The growing cost of doing nothing. *Electric Perspectives, 25*, 36–43.

Humphrey, B., & Stokes, J. (2000). The 21st century supervisor. *HR Magazine, 45*, 185.

McClure, L. F. (1996). *Risky business: Managing employee violence in the workplace.* New York: Haworth Press.

McClure, L. F. (2000). *Anger and conflict in the workplace: Spot the signs, avoid the trauma.* Manassas Park, VA: Impact.

McFarlin, D. B., Baumeister, R. F., & Blascovich, J (1984). On knowing when to quit: Task failure, self-esteem, advice, and nonproductive persistence. *Journal of Personality, 52*, 138–155.

McFarlin D. B., & Blascovich, J. (1981). Effects of self-esteem and performance feedback on future affective preferences and cognitive expectations. *Journal of Personality and Social Psychology, 40*, 521–531.

Peters, P. (2000). 7 tips for delivering performance feedback. *Supervision, 61*(5),12.

Podsakoff, P. M., & Schriesheim, C. A. (1985). Field studies of French and Raven's bases of power: Critique, reanalysis, and suggestions for future research. *Psychological Bulletin, 97*, 387–411.

Pollack, T. (1999). Cash in on success: Supervisors should focus on strengths of subordinates. *Supervision, 60*(4), 24.

Ramsey, R. D. (1999). The "snoopervision" debate: Employer interests vs. employee privacy. *Supervision, 60*(18), 3.

Resnick, P. (1995, March). *The clinical prediction of violence.* Training presented by Solutions Training Institute, Columbus, IN.

Robinson D., & Smith-Lovin, L. (1992). Selective interaction as a strategy for identity maintenance: An affect control model. *Social Psychology Quarterly, 55*, 12–28.

Seidenfeld, M. (1998). The art of supervision. *Supervision, 59*(4), 14.

Shrauger, J. S. (1975). Responses to evaluation as a function of initial self-perceptions. *Psychological Bulletin, 82*, 581–596.

Strazewski, L. (2001). Facing facts about workplace substance abuse. *Rough Notes, 144*, 114–118.

Sweeney, P. D., & Wells, L. E. (1990). Reactions to feedback about performance: A test of three competing models. *Journal of Applied Social Psychology, 20*, 818–834.

Tang, T., & Sarsfield-Baldwin, L. (1991). The effects of self-esteem, task label, and performance feedback on goal setting, certainty, and attribution. *Journal of Psychology, 125*, 413–418.

Weiss, W. H. (1988). *Supervisor's standard reference handbook* (2nd ed.). Englewood Cliffs, NJ: Prentice Hall.

Weiss, W. H. (1998). Employee involvement, commitment and cooperation: Keys to successful supervision. *Supervision, 59*(11), 12.

White, R. W. (1963). Ego and reality in psychoanalytic theory. *Psychological Issues, 3*(Whole No. 11), 3.

Yukl, G., & Falbe, C. M. (1991). The importance of different power sources in downward and lateral relations. *Journal of Applied Psychology, 76*, 416–423.

Yukl, G., Kim, H., & Falbe, C. M. (1996). Antecedents of influence outcomes. *Journal of Applied Psychology, 81*, 309–317.

Zeune, G. D. (2001). Are you teaching your employees to steal? *Business Credit, 103*(4), 16–21.

3

Special Populations

8

....

Working With Ethnic Minority Employees in the Workplace

John M. Dillard and Debra A. Harley

he workforce in the United States is becoming increasingly culturally diverse, and ethnic minorities constitute a significant source of needed employment skills and talents (Osipow & Fitzgerald, 1996). As the ethnic minority population continues to increase, more information is needed about them for professionals to work more effectively with them. Many studies have been reported regarding the career behaviors of ethnic minorities, but there is a paucity of professional literature that deals with specific ethnic groups such as African Americans, Hispanic Americans, Asian Americans, and American Indians as employees. Except for scant pieces of data referring to them in comparison with Caucasians, little is known about career behaviors of ethnic minorities as employees in the American workplace.

This chapter explores the career development of ethnic minorities in the workplace. The primary focus of the discussions is on ethnic minority workers who have contributed significantly to the building of the U.S. economy. The chapter begins with a brief examination of the career development among ethnic minorities. Then we present discussions on social conflicts in the workplace, personal problems and concerns affecting ethnic minorities' work performance, an assessment of the types of employee assistance models, and special counseling considerations for professionals working with ethnic minorities in the workplace.

Brief Overview: Career Development of Ethnic Minorities

The United States is composed of various ethnic groups. African Americans, Hispanic Americans, Asian Americans, and American Indians constitute the largest ethnic minorities in the United States (Osipow & Fitzgerald, 1996). Individuals from these groups are part of the American workforce. The success of the American workforce is dependent not only on Caucasian American workers but on ethnic minority workers as well.

Although each group makes significant work contributions annually to the U.S. economy, the career development of ethnic minority workers compared with Caucasian American workers appears disproportionately distributed (Herr & Cramer, 1996). For example, Herr and Cramer (1996) contended that the careers African Americans select or those careers that are available to them are somewhat skewed. According to Holland's classification system, African Americans appear underrepresented in the Enterprising (i.e., realty and law positions) and Investigative (computer programmer and architect positions) categories and overrepresented in the Realistic (i.e., barber and truck driver positions) and Social (i.e., social worker and teaching positions) categories. Herr and Cramer speculated whether these employees cluster in these overrepresented categories and less in others by personal choice or the workplace's social barrier. In a similar study using Holland's classifications, Place and Payne (1996) reported that a group of 230 African American college students responded quite high to the Social and Enterprising categories. Income levels are higher for many careers in other categories, but many African Americans tend to choose an overrepresented category, such as social career fields.

As another example, there are African Americans trained to work in the computer and information technology (I.T.) field, but few Silicon Valley firms are recruiting ethnic minorities (Roach, 2001). Jacoby (1999) maintained that African Americans are

> underrepresented not just in I.T. but, far more broadly and fatefully, in science—in the research, teaching, and commercial uses of every scientific discipline. [African Americans] account for roughly twelve percent of the U.S. workforce but only four percent of the doctors and five percent of the jobs in engineering, computer science, and scientific research. (p. 24)

The *San Francisco Chronicle* newspaper reported a 1998 study of 33 leading Silicon Valley firms employing 146,000 employees, where only 4% of these workers were African Americans and 7% were Hispanic. Eight percent of African Americans and 14% of Hispanics make up the workforce in the San Francisco Bay area (Roach, 2001).

Another part of ethnic minorities' career development can be delineated through their employment patterns and individual and family income. For example, White and Rogers (2000) reported that Caucasian unemployment reached a low of 4% in 1998, African American rates were 9%, and Hispanic rates were 7%. Approximately 20% of African American men ages 20 to 24 were unsuccessful in securing employment during this period of high employment. White and Rogers (2000) suggested that people unable to attain work during a period of high employment demand reflect a "multiple-problem population" (p. 1036). In 1994, for those couples in which the husband was employed, wives were also employed in 61% of Hispanic, 79% of African American, and 75% of Caucasian couples. Wives' earnings made significant contributions to family resources.

Conclusively, career development and careers of ethnic minorities are indeed affected by many external as well as internal variables, and ethnicity adversely affects these groups in the manner in which they participate in the workforce. However, there are commonalities in their career development and career adjustment process. Some ethnic minorities are overrepresented in some career fields and less represented in others. There are several related factors contributing to their performance in the workplace, and these factors are discussed in the following sections.

Ethnic and Cultural Issues

Given the effects of advanced technology, corporate mergers, trends toward later retirement, and changing demographics of the workplace, the view of workers held by business and industry is undergoing change (Herr, 1999). The dynamics of business are reflected in the work environment and in the behaviors required of employees (e.g., complexity, speed, and mobility; Oblinger & Verville, 1998). Oblinger and Verville emphasized that as the workplace changes, so will behaviors sought in employees. Because people's lives are constantly changing, employees also experience changes in behavior that may be inconsistent with the work environment. Unfortunately, employees' personal and work issues frequently overlap and may present difficulties in the workplace. Because workers do not leave their personal problems at the door when they enter the workplace or leave their work problems at work when they go home, employers find that they must address both employees' work and personal issues in relation to work activity. As a result, the vocabulary of business and industry is rapidly changing to include terms such as Employee Assistance Programs (EAPs), human resource development, stress control centers, career management, and career services (Herr, 1999; Schmidt, Riggar, Crimando, & Bordieri, 1992).

Ethnocentrism and Acculturation in the Workplace

In workplace settings, two concepts that offer insight into a lack of culturally inclusive modalities are ethnocentrism and acculturation. Ethnocentrism refers to the belief in the inherent superiority of one's own ethnic group or culture and should be "uncritically and unquestioningly accepted" (Stopsky & Lee, 1994, p. 429). In addition to the belief of inherent superiority of one's own cultural ways, other key concepts define ethnocentrism. According to Baruth and Manning (1992), ethnocentrism means the belief that one's cultural ways are "universally applicable in evaluating and judging human behavior" (p. 156). Tiedt and Tiedt (1990) summarized ethnocentrism to mean "the centrality of dominance of the national group identity that may limit an individual's perspective"(p. 11). Gollnick and Chinn (1994) interpreted ethnocentrism as the "inability to view other cultures as viable alternatives for organizing reality" (p. 9). Nieto (1996) explained ethnocentrism as "discriminatory belief and behaviors based on ethnic differences" (p. 306). Adler (1993) expressed ethnocentrism to be "a dangerous form of provincial naivete" (p. 41). To understand ethnocentrism, four points are important in this process. First, ethnocentrism operates on the closed-minded belief that one's own culturally learned norms are valid and superior and should be the standard for other cultures. Second, ethnocentrism encompasses the belief that other cultures or ethnic groups are inferior if they do not meet the norms of one's own cultural or ethnic group. Third, ethnocentrism is a worldview that limits one's ability to perceive other ethnic groups without bias or to relate to other cultures respectfully. Fourth, ethnocentrism includes the belief that other cultures or ethnic groups, being inferior, should at best be changed by education or coercion to adopt the norms of one's own culture and at worst should be denigrated, segregated, discriminated against, and oppressed (Grant & Ladson-Billings, 1997).

Acculturation is defined as a process by which racial and ethnic minority groups come into contact with the mainstream culture, resulting in subsequent changes in their original cultural patterns (Berry & Sam, 1997). While integrating values, beliefs, and patterns of behavior of the mainstream, these groups maintain many of their own ethnic beliefs and traditions (Dillard, 1987). However, the key difference in the process of socialization into accepting the cultural values of the larger society is that "acculturation is not so much identification as it is internalization" (Robinson & Howard-Hamilton, 2000, p. 11). Berry and Sam examined four acculturation strategies: assimilation, traditionality, integration, and marginality. Assimilation refers to people who do not desire to maintain their cultural identities. Traditionality identifies people who choose to maintain their cultural connections and avoid interaction with others. Integration describes those with interest in maintaining their original culture while simultaneously seeking interactions with other cultures. Marginality encompasses little interest in cultural maintenance and limited desire to interact with others from different cultures. The rate of acculturation of groups is influenced by several factors, including the degree of isolation from the native culture, and by societal prejudice and discrimination (Grant & Ladson-Billings, 1997).

In addition to various stressors of job duties, racial and ethnic minority employees confront adversities related to a host of factors that are internal and external to the workplace that serve to affect and influence their job performance. Racial and ethnic minority employees are frequently confronted by a number of devices designed to marginalize them in the workplace (e.g., token representation, devaluation, and verbal abuse; Harrison & Shariff, 1996). For example, racial discrimination, cultural insensitivity, and backlash against affirmative action are factors that minority groups experience in addition to job-related stress.

Cultural diversity is one important term that is receiving more attention in business and industry. Diversity represents, at least on a very basic level, the recognition by business and industry that the workforce is changing in composition in relation to the demographic shift in the United States. However, the attitudes, beliefs, and practices of employers with regard to diversity-specific responses to employees from minority groups are not changing. According to Hughes (1993), "for all the good they do, diversity programs have yet to make a dent in what most experts consider to be the number-one impediment to advancement of [women] and minorities: lingering and deep-seated prejudice" (p. 30). Because racial minorities are expected to "fit in" to existing modes of functioning and ignore, eliminate, or suppress their cultural frame of reference, employers tend to focus primarily on organizational culture and ignore individual diversity. Anderson (1993) posed numerous questions for consideration for organizations regarding diversity. A sample of these questions include the following: How does a company's conceptualization of diversity mesh with existing values about quality and productivity? Do existing structures support only male, Caucasian, Eurocentric values? Are organizational systems flexible enough so that diverse employees can adapt to them, and vice versa? The answers to these questions have been and continue to be elusive.

It is clear that ethnic and cultural issues pervade workplace settings. "The dynamics of race, discrimination, and the experience of one's identity are always present and can play a major role in symptom formation" (Grossmark, 1999, p. 75). Cultural differences may affect the expectations of both employees and employers. However, research addressing strategies to help mitigate the effects of work and personal stressors of racial and ethnic minority employees in business and industry is limited.

Research on Ethnic Minority Employees in Business and Industry

The cultural landscape of the United States is changing, and this change has implications for the labor market. Although the number of racial and ethnic minority groups is increasing, "American Caucasian males will continue to be the single largest gender/race identity group in the U.S. workforce for many years" (Cox, 1991, p. 39). However, Cox questioned the viability of what he termed the traditionally Caucasian male "monolithic organization" (Kikoski & Kikoski, 1996). Given this fact, changes occurring in the racial and ethnic composition of the U.S. workforce present major challenges to organizations (Wooldridge, 1996). An examination by ethnic category reveals that little change is expected for African Americans in the labor force, who comprise approximately 11% of both the 1992 and 2005 labor forces and about 12% of labor entrants. In contrast, Hispanics/Latinos are projected to increase from 8% in 1992 to 11% in 2005 and will make up 15% of entrants. Asian Americans will comprise almost 8% of workforce entrants during this period (Fullerton, 1993). Collectively, racial and ethnic minorities are forecast to represent 35% of the workforce entrants (Kikoski & Kikoski, 1996). Given this realization, the issue of cultural diversity is in every aspect of the U.S. workforce and is a constant presence for the EAP professional (Grossmark, 1999).

In 1976, Dunnette expressed the need for research on racial minorities in the field of organizational psychology. In spite of the increasing diversity of the workforce, research in this area is still negligible (Wooldridge, 1996). According to Cox and Nkomo (1990), research on the organizational behavior of racial minorities in the workforce has been hindered by (a) a general lack of attention, (b) research questions that are too simplistic, (c) an absence of theories of race effects, and (d) the types of research designs used. Collective results of earlier studies found that African American female and male managers placed a greater emphasis on extrinsic work values than did Caucasian female or male managers (Blazini & Greenhaus, 1988, as cited in Dance, 1993); Hispanics/Latinos were more satisfied with personnel policies and less satisfied with supervision, job task, rewards, coworkers, and employee competence (Rubaii-Barrett, Beck, & Lillibrige, 1991); and Asian American men exhibited less need for dominance, aggressiveness, exhibitionism, autonomy, and heterosexuality, whereas Asian American women were more deferent, nurturing, and achievement oriented than their Caucasian counterparts (Sue & Wagner, 1973).

A diverse workforce exists in the United States across race and ethnicity as well as gender, age, disability, and sexual orientation. Whether increased diversity of the workforce leads to increased stress and lower organizational performance or high performance and morale will depend largely on the skills of managers and EAP personnel (Wooldridge, 1996). EAP personnel need to have adequate knowledge and skills levels regarding diversity of employees. In the absence of limited research and literature about the influence of cultural attitudes, beliefs, and values on work performance, EAP personnel need to engage in self-awareness and self-education to curtail deficits. Clearly, a theory of inclusive management is the most appropriate for a diverse workforce.

Salient Personal Problems Affecting Performance in the Workplace

Most employees perform their duties and responsibilities well, with little or no difficulties. For some employees, their personal concerns are rarely visible to others. There are employees, however, whose work performance is affected by many factors, such as job dissatisfaction, family problems, drug and alcohol abuse, and discrimination (Hutri, 1996). Bohland and Fleming (1999), for example, stated that many Colorado employers are not cognizant that some of their employees with on-the-job performance problems abuse alcohol and drugs. They further stated that a 1998 report by the state's Alcohol and Drug Abuse Division found 8% of the state's general population had been dependent on drugs or alcohol within 18 months of the survey.

These kinds of employee behaviors can and often do affect others. For instance, Reynes (1998) reported: "Six years ago, John Hyland, president of Hyland Brothers Lumber Co. in Lincoln, Nebraska, noticed that lots of employees' problems on the job seemed to reflect back to personal difficulties, financial, legal, alcohol, drugs, or whatever" (p. 73).

Frequently, alcohol and drug abuse problems are manifestations of other problems with employees (Royce & Scratchley, 1996). Other kinds of problem behaviors an employee sometimes might exhibit are patterns of tardiness and absenteeism or they might convey a hostile uncooperative attitude toward supervisors, coworkers, or even customers (Reynes, 1998). For example, because Hispanic/Latino workers place the family above work priorities, they may not be as responsive (or respond differently than supervisors expect) when a family member is experiencing a crisis. Thus, employers should expect occasional absences (Kikoski & Kikoski, 1996). In addition, employees' behavior may be influenced by cumulative effects of stress on the body and mental state and loss of control over a basic physiological function (the sleep cycle; Denenberg & Braverman, 1999). Denenberg and Braverman observed that "although alcohol and drugs have been prominently targeted as threats to work performance, research in human physiology is calling attention to what may well be a more imminent hazard: pervasive fatigue" (p. 25).

Nevertheless, one of the major concerns among many employees is sub-stance use and abuse. Lapham, Chang, and Gregory (2000) stated:

> Substance abuse is increasingly recognized as a significant cause of workplace problems. Most illicit drug abusers and heavy drinkers are employed. Alcohol and other drug abuse are associated with job-related absenteeism, turnover, injury rates, and increased medical care costs. Reduced productivity among employees with substance abuse disorders is also caused by social and family problems and off-the-job substance abuse. For each employee who abuses alcohol or drugs, companies lose an estimated $7,261 per year. (p. 134)

Gregg (1998) reported that a 1996 work–family survey conducted by *Business Week* and the Center on Work and Family at Boston University found that 42% of employees perceive their work has a negative effect on their personal lives. Of those employees, 22% also felt they cannot have a satisfying family life and still vocationally advance in their companies.

There are some employees whose behavior seems unpredictable when they respond to certain work-related conditions (change in work sched-ule) with sudden explosive behavior (McClure, 1996). Employees who become highly emotionally charged often can and do have a dangerous impact on coworkers as well as themselves. National statistics indicate that murder is the leading cause of death for women at work and the second leading cause for men at work (McClure, 1996). Furthermore, workplace violence is increasing at an alarming rate. The U.S. Justice Department reports, for example, that almost 1 million violent crimes occur in the workplace annually. McClure (1996) stated that there are certain types of employees who are likely to become violent in a stressful situation. For example, individuals with patterns of aggression and violence are more likely to continue to engage in violent behavior (Loeber & Stouthamer-Loeber, 1998).

In fact, workplaces are microcosms of society, and the diversification of the workplace has unfortunately been accompanied by an increase in aggressive and violent behavior among employees (Clay, 2000), including hate crimes, religious discrimination, and racism (Tate, 1999). A negative outcome of diversification in the workplace is conflict between employees or conflict between employees and supervisors due to anger with one another as a result of individual differences (Solomon, 1992). Because of increased violence in the workplace, EAPs need to develop programs that increase awareness of and celebrate coworkers' individual strengths while promoting open lines of communication.

In short, there are several factors that can affect an individual emotionally and physically. How a person will react, given the psychological makeup to handle his or her circumstances, is often unpredictable. The greater problem is, however, that other people, such as family members, coworkers, or the worker himself or herself, can become negatively affected. EAP professionals are often associated with large corporations to provide needed assistance to employees experiencing personal problems.

Types of Employee Assistance Models in Industry

EAPs were originally established to assist employees who demonstrated problems with alcoholism or substance abuse. However, attention has broadened to include issues that might influence job performance (e.g., family problems, financial problems, or mental health concerns; Kinney, 2000; Schmidt et al., 1992). Given this expansion, employers not only vary the types of services provided by their EAPs but also administer their programs in a variety of different ways (Kinney, 2000; Monroe, 1988). Typically, EAPs offer direct services (e.g., counseling and referral) and indirect services (e.g., lectures and workshops; Lewis, Lewis, Packard, & Souflee, 2001). EAPs deliver services to both individual employees and the work organization. As a service to organizations, EAPs can be designed to deliver services with an aim toward productivity restoration and productivity enhancement (Cagney, 1999).

Some employers use in-house/internal or on-site counselors who meet individually with employees and who may also make referrals to external specialists in the community. Other employers retain external consultants who come to the employer's location for specified periods of time to counsel employees. Alternatively, some employers make arrangements for employees to meet with independent EAP counselors/consultants at off-site locations. These last two approaches are referred to as out-of-house/external models (Darick, 1999; Masi & Friedland, 1988). Masi and Friedland identified two additional models of EAPs: the consortium model and the affiliate model. In the consortium model, several companies pool their resources to develop a collaborative program to maximize individual resources. Generally, this model works best for companies with fewer than 2,000 employees. Services may be delivered on-site or off-site. With the affiliate model, a vendor subcontracts to a local professional rather than use its salaried staff. Using this model allows the vendor to reach employees in any location (Masi & Friedland, 1988). According to Dickens (1999), "vendor management and benefits coordination may become the focus of the EAP as the shift of tertiary interventions moves more to the 'outsourced' management care system" (p. 424).

Another model of an EAP is a member assistance program (MAP). A MAP is the labor organization corollary of an internal EAP. Some MAPs are totally union operated (e.g., the Teamsters and the Longshoreman) and deliver services to union members and their families. MAPs are highly efficient and effective for employees who are hired by the type of job or who are mobile (Cagney, 1999).

Many larger companies are also becoming involved in behavioral health managed care organizations (MCO; e.g., health maintenance organization [HMO]) that provide whatever medical care is needed or the required prior approval for a treatment referral, if the insurance is to cover the costs (Kinney, 2000). The rationale for utilization of HMOs is that it is cost-effective. However, a major concern related to HMO systems is that payment is often based on a per capita formula with an established reimbursement paid for a diagnostic category, rather than reimbursements being made on the basis of actual costs incurred (Alston & Harley, 1999). One valuable lesson that MCOs have learned is that contracting employers value highly the work-site-focused services offered by EAPs; in fact, EAP enrollment has increased 45% since 1994 (Cagney, 1999).

When EAPs are not available, employers can facilitate the employee's understanding of company benefits as related to the necessary professional assistance. Employers are in a position to make referrals to appropriate services and programs. In addition, employers can help the employee identify potential community resources (Schmidt et al., 1992).

Assessment of Current Employee Assistance Models

Regardless of the type of EAP used, each type has advantages and disadvantages. Some advantages of in-house/internal EAPs include service at lower cost, increased control over the quality as well as the types of services offered, increased supervision and referrals, more positive acceptance by unions, quicker response time to the needs of employees, internal links to other parts of the organization, and integrated knowledge of the organizational structure (Cagney, 1999; Masi & Friedland, 1988; Monroe, 1988). Disadvantages of in-house/internal programs include more difficulty ensuring confidentiality and substantial start-up cost, especially for a small employer (Darick, 1999; Monroe, 1988). Conversely, out-of-house/external programs are advantageous because they are viewed as providing better accountability, ease of start-up and implementation, a greater breadth of expertise, decreased potential conflicts of interest, and lowered legal liability (Cagney, 1999). From a disadvantageous viewpoint, out-of-house/external programs are seen as more complex to run, may have a more difficult decision-making process, and may offer less accountability and decreased responsiveness (Masi & Friedland, 1988). However, both internal and external programs offer the advantage of offering a 24-hours-a-day toll-free service line allowing employees flexibility in seeking assistance at any hour of the day or evening (Darick, 1999).

Use of affiliates requires that they have specialized training in EAP and be well-versed in the structural functions of work organizations, human resource management issues, labor law, and legislative and regulatory mandates that affect the workplace. Moreover, it is essential that affiliates differentiate between EAP services that include the interests of the organization and those that offer a private treatment relationship with the employee (Cagney, 1999). For ethnic minority workers, the EAP is urged to put effort into knowing the organization and to considering the possible dynamics of individual referral situations because they contain information that can enhance the intervention process as well as information that can be deleterious (Grossmark, 1999). The EAP must have the flexibility to meet the organization's needs (e.g., productivity) and the individual needs of the employee. In other words, EAP workers might make an effort to be alert to the possibility that individual concerns (e.g., family, community, or religious) may provide explanation for behavior they do not understand (Kikoski & Kikoski, 1996).

The selection of one type of EAP over another is usually decided on the basis of the needs and resources of the organization. EAP product/service line allows an organization flexibility to choose a mode of access to the program that the employee desires (Darick, 1999). Overall, EAPs have been shown to improve productivity and to lower cost (Van Den Bergh, 1995).

Current EAP practice seems to indicate a preference for the broad-brush approach (Royce & Scratchy, 1996). In other words, the roles and functions of EAP professionals have evolved from a focus on an individual to a more systemic view. The resulting conceptual change is identified as *organizational counseling* (Ginsberg, Kilburg, & Gomes, 1999, p. 440).

Dickens (1999) emphasized that collaboration sets the stage for developing and promoting a holistic approach to EAP service delivery. Increasingly, the delivery of integrated human services in the workplace is an evolving model for employee assistance theory and practice (Ginsberg et al., 1999). Ginsberg et al. stressed that the traditional model of assessment, triage, and referral is antiquated with respect to scope. The application of the broad-brush approach, if handled knowledgeably, offers positive potential for ethic minority groups. According to Kikoski and Kikoski (1996), the differences between the more task-oriented Caucasian male cultural paradigm and the more person-oriented Latino cultural paradigm frequently establish expectations about behavior and approaches to problem solving. Kikoski and Kikoski explained that it is not that one cultural style is superior or another is deficient but rather that mutual expectations are not met in their interaction. It would be useful, whenever possible, to use multidisciplinary teams to assist employees and organizations confronting multidimensional obstacles. In an era when strategic choices need to be made about the allocation and deployment of limited corporate resources, EAPs are poised to take advantage of opportunities to elevate or solidify their importance in the organization. According to Ginsberg et al. (1999), the provision of "integrated human services, collaboration among a multidisciplinary team, and the application of the principles of an organizational counseling framework positions the employee assistance professional differently within the organization and adds value for the employee assistance field" (p. 454).

Special Considerations for Working With Ethnic Minority Employees

Meeting the needs of a diverse workforce is not only beneficial from the standpoint of harmonious working relationships but also makes good business sense because of the mix of workers that exists and the ability to maintain a competitive edge in a global economy. Because EAPs are charged with the relevancy of guiding the employee into the new space of intervention or therapeutic endeavor, their practice with racial and ethnic minority employees needs to encompass two concepts: credibility and giving (Grossmark, 1999). Credibility refers to employees' perception that the EAP professional or program is offering effective and trustworthy help. Giving refers to employees' experiences of bringing something away from the encounter with the EAP. Although these concepts apply to any employee, they are particularly relevant to racial minorities because they might be skeptical about services owing to the historical lack of provision of culturally responsive services, which results in EAP's lack of credibility (Grossmark, 1999).

Another important consideration for working with ethnic minority employees is the psychodynamics of referral and matching. For example, a referral of an African American employee to a Caucasian service provider who would seek to make the intervention situation an isolated experience and avoid consideration of race or ethnicity in the intervention situation would indicate a poor match. Although being the same race between client and EAP professional is not necessarily the most important factor, it is important to avoid mismatches based on culture, ethnicity, and language (Grossmark, 1999). This requires the interventionist to be aware of his or her own identity issues. In addition, Grossmark emphasized that simple ethnic matching may be an attempt by the EAP professional to find a short cut to feeling culturally competent and good. Any attempt of this nature is to be avoided.

Furthermore, EAPs need to consider their relationship to the culturally diverse providers that will constitute the provider network. The EAP professional is "urged to put effort into knowing the providers and to considering the possible dynamics of every referral situation as it arises" (Grossmark, 1999, p. 82). Given that services are individualized to meet the specific needs of the employee, EAP professionals are to respond to this requirement. The responsibilities of EAPs, both internal and external to the organization, are paramount to the employee's and employer's success and productivity. Therefore, as a final implication of working with racial and ethnic minority employees, EAPs must examine the cultural competence of their services and providers.

Some Counseling Considerations for Working With Ethnic Minority Employees

Career counseling is being challenged to meet the needs of ethnic minority employees in the United States (Peterson & Gonzalez, 1999; Zunker, 1998). Assisting ethnic minority employees is often not a simplistic task, because many of their concerns or problems in the workplace hinge on, as stated earlier, alcohol and substance abuse, family problems, and racial/ethnic and gender discrimination (Walsh, Bingham, Brown, & Ward, 2001). For career counseling practitioners to effectively deal with these and other concerns, clients' concerns must be resolved in the context of employees' role in and out of the workplace and society in general (Brown & Pinterits, 2001).

Professionals must consider their preparation for working with racial and ethnic minorities who have career concerns or problems. Professionals must establish culturally appropriate relationships with ethnic minority employees to ensure positive outcomes. They should consider their understanding of the impact of their own ethnic development, worldviews, cultural experiences, and their effect on the counseling encounter with ethnic minority employees (Ward & Bingham, 2001). Professionals dealing with employees' problems sometimes become closed-minded as ethnic minority or women employees convey to them their real or perceived feelings of being discriminated against in the workplace by supervisors and coworkers. However, professionals must understand the importance of assisting these employees in exploring the issues thoroughly so that they will reach satisfying conclusions and learn how to effectively deal with this issue now and in the future. To help employees to become or to continue as productive workers, professionals must consider the whole person (the employee), which will enable them to resolve other problems, such as drugs and alcohol.

In dealing with substance abuse issues, for instance, Galvin (2000) contended that in more traditional settings, behavioral health care practitioners have provided early intervention, treatment, follow-up for substance-abusing members, including employees and their families, along with counseling services for families with substance abusers. Galvin concluded that it is difficult to measure how much and the types of substance abuse prevention that were available. However, a substantial number of prevention programs adopted in the workplace are now linked to broader health care services, including wellness, health promotion and education, and behavioral health services.

In a study to determine the belief, social support, and background predictors of employee likelihood to use an EAP for drinking problems among predominantly male Caucasian, African American, and Latino employees ages 22 to 69, Galvin (2000) found several supportive responses from the employee participants. The employees believed that they would secure professional assistance, such as EAP, if they believed they had a drinking problem; greater social support and supervisor encouragement also increased the stated likelihood of their going to an EAP; and the increased belief in EAP effectiveness was related to increased stated likelihood of going to an EAP. African Americans and hourly workers were more likely to say they would use an EAP. However, male employees and those who reported drinking during working hours were less likely to say they would use an EAP for a drinking problem (Galvin, 2000).

Conclusion

Ethnic and racial minorities in the United States have played and continue to play a major role in the American workforce. Their overrepresentation in some lower paying career fields and underrepresentation in some of the higher paying fields is a condition that must be changed. We should note, however, that ethnic minorities are positioned in most careers fields, however small or large. Although discrimination in the workplace appears to have a significantly greater impact on African Americans than other groups, other variables affecting their career adjustment, roles, and patterns also impact other minority groups as well. Employees' personal problems could indeed be associated with their job performance and interactions with coworkers as well as family members.

The quality and effectiveness of EAP professionals can play an important part in helping workers identify and resolve their problems and to be productive employees. Professionals should consider the importance of understanding the backgrounds of these ethnic minority groups to ensure that they provide them with the best available options for succeeding in their career field, increasing productivity, and maintaining employment.

References

Adler, S. (1993). *Multicultural communications skills in the classroom.* Boston: Allyn & Bacon.

Alston, R. J., & Harley, D. A. (1999). Managed care and privatization in counseling and rehabilitation. In C. G. Dixon & W. G. Emener (Eds.), *Professional counseling: Transitioning into the next millennium* (pp. 14–33). Springfield, IL: Charles C Thomas.

Anderson, J. A. (1993). Thinking about diversity. *Training and Development, 47*(4), 59–60.

Baruth, L. G., & Manning, M. L. (1992). *Multicultural education and children and adolescents.* Needham Heights, MA: Allyn & Bacon.

Berry, J. W., & Sam, D. L. (1997). Acculturation and adaptation. In J. Berry, M. Segall, & C. Kagitcibasi (Eds.), *Cross-cultural psychology* (Vol. 3, pp. 291–326). Boston: Allyn & Bacon.

Bohland, K., & Fleming, G. (1999, November, 1). Under the influence. *Colorado Business Magazine, 26*, 38–40, 42.

Brown, M. T., & Pinterits, E. J. (2001). Basic issues in the career counseling of African Americans. In W. B. Walsh, R. P. Bingham, M. T. Brown, & C. M. Ward (Eds.), *Career counseling for African Americans* (pp. 1–25). Mahwah, NJ: Erlbaum.

Cagney, T. (1999). Models of service delivery. In J. M. Oher (Ed.), *The employee assistance handbook* (pp. 59–69). New York: Wiley.

Clay, R. A. (2000). Securing the workplace: Are our fears misplaced? *Monitor in Psychology, 31*(9), 46–49.

Cox, T. (1991). The multicultural organization. *Academy of Management Executives, 5*(2), 39.

Cox, T., & Nkomo, S. (1990). Invisible men and women: A status report on race as a variable in organizational behavior research. *Journal of Organizational Behavior, 11*, 419–431.

Dance, R. A. (1993). *African American women: How do they rate as managers.* Unpublished doctoral dissertation, Virginia Commonwealth University, Richmond.

Darick, A. A. (1999). Clinical practices and procedures. In J. M. Oger (Ed.), *The employee assistance handbook* (pp. 3–13). New York: Wiley.

Denenberg, R. V., & Braverman, M. (1999). *The violence-prone workplace.* Ithaca, NY: Cornell University Press.

Dickens, R. S. (1999). The alignment of EAP and business unit goals. In J. M. Oher (Ed.), *The employee assistance handbook* (pp. 421–438). New York: Wiley.

Dillard, J. M. (1987). *Multicultural counseling: Toward ethnic and cultural relevance in human encounters.* Chicago: Nelson-Hall.

Dunnette, M. D. (Ed.). (1976). *Handbook of industrial and organizational psychology.* Chicago: Rand McNally College Publishing.

Fullerton, H. N. (1993, November). The American work force, 1992–2005: Another look at the labor force. *Monthly Labor Review,* p. 36.

Galvin, D. M. (2000). Workplace managed care: Collaboration for substance abuse prevention. *Journal of Behavioral Health Services and Research, 27,* 125–130.

Ginsberg, M. R., Kilburg, R. R., & Gomes, P. G. (1999). Organizational counseling and delivery of integrated human services in the workplace: An evolving model for employee assistance theory and practice. In J. M. Oher (Ed.), *The employee assistance handbook* (pp. 439–456). New York: Wiley.

Gollnick, D. M., & Chinn, P. C. (1994). *Multicultural education in a pluralistic society* (4th ed.). New York: Macmillan College.

Grant, C. A., & Ladson-Billings, G. (Eds.). (1997). *Dictionary of multicultural education.* Phoenix, AZ: Oryx.

Gregg, L. (1998, September 1). Humanity in the workplace: When work/family becomes an HR issue. *Credit Union Executive,* p. 32.

Grossmark, R. (1999). Cultural diversity and employee assistance programs. In J. M. Oher (Ed.), *The employee assistance handbook* (pp. 71–89). New York: Wiley.

Harrison, L., & Shariff, Z. (1996). Race, diversity and public administration: A literature analysis. In M. F. Rice (Ed.), *Diversity and public organizations: Theory, issues, and perspectives* (pp. 15–34). Dubuque, IA: Kendall/Hunt.

Herr, E. L. (1999). *Counseling in a dynamic society: Contexts and practices for the 21st century.* Alexandria, VA: American Counseling Association.

Herr, E. L., & Cramer, S. H. (1996). *Career guidance and counseling through the life span: Systematic approaches* (5th ed.). New York: Harper Collins.

Hughes, R. (1993). Navigating the differences. *Training and Development, 47*(4), 29–33.

Hutri, M. (1996). When careers reach a dead end: Identification of occupational crisis states. *Journal of Psychology, 130,* 383–400.

Jacoby, T. (1999). Color blind: The African American absence in high tech. *New Republic, 220*(13), 23–27.

Kikoski, J. F., & Kikoski, C. K. (1996). *Reflexive communication in the culturally diverse workplace.* Westport, CT: Quorum Books.

Kinney, J. (2000). *Loosening the grip: A handbook of alcohol information* (6th ed.). Boston: McGraw-Hill.

Lapham, S. C., Chang, L., & Gregory, C. (2000). Substance abuse intervention for health care workers: A preliminary report. *Journal of Behavioral Health Services and Research, 27,* 131–143.

Lewis, J. A., Lewis, M. D., Packard, T., & Souflee, F. (2001). *Management of human service programs.* Belmont, CA: Brooks/Cole.

Loeber, R., & Stouthamer-Loeber, M. (1998). Development of juvenile aggression and violence. Some common misconceptions and controversies. *American Psychologist, 53,* 242–259.

Masi, D. A., & Friedland, S. J. (1988). EAP actions and options. *Personnel Journal, 67*(6), 61–67.

McClure, L. F. (1996). Risky business: Managing employee violence in the workplace. New York: Haworth Press.

Monroe, J. L. (1988). Employee assistance programs: Legal issues. *Employment Relations Today, 15,* 239–243.

Nieto, S. (1996). *Affirming diversity: The sociopolitical context of multicultural education* (2nd ed.). White Plains, NY: Longman.

Oblinger, D. G., & Verville, A. L. (1998). *What business wants from higher education.* Phoenix, AZ: Oryx Press.

Osipow, S. H., & Fitzgerald, L. F. (1996). *Theories of career development* (4th ed.). Boston: Allyn & Bacon.

Peterson, N., & Gonzalez, R. C. (1999). *The role of work in people's lives: Applied career counseling and vocational psychology.* Belmont, CA: Brooks/Cole.

Place, A., & Payne, C. (1996). An investigation of reasons for professional career choice among African-American college students. *Education, 117*(1), 43–51.

Reynes, R. (1998). Programs that aid troubled workers. *Nation's Business, 86*(6), 73–74.

Roach, R. (2001). Silicon Valley under fire for weak minority recruitment efforts. *Black Issues in Higher Education, 18*(2), 38–39.

Robinson, T. L., & Howard-Hamilton, M. F. (2000). *The convergence of race, ethnicity, and gender: Multiple identities in counseling.* Upper Saddle River, NJ: Merrill.

Royce, J. E., & Scratchley, D. (1996). *Alcoholism and other drug problems.* New York: Free Press.

Rubaii-Barrett, N., Beck, A., & Lillibridge, C. (1991). Minorities in the majority: Implications for managing cultural diversity. *Public Personnel Management, 22,* 503–521.

Schmidt, M. J., Riggar, T. F., Crimando, W., & Bordieri, J. E. (1992). *Staffing for success: A guide for health and human service professionals*. Newbury Park, CA: Sage.

Solomon, C. M. (1992). Keeping hate out of the workplace. *Personnel Journal, 71*(7), 30–36.

Stopsky, F., & Lee, S. S. (1994). *Social studies in a global society*. Albany, NY: Delmar.

Sue, S., & Wagner, N. N. (1973). *Asian Americans: Psychological perspectives*. Palo Alto, CA: Science and Behavior Books.

Tate, G. A. (1999). Structured racism, sexism, and elitism: A hound that sure can hurt. *Journal of Counseling and Development, 77*, 18–20, 52.

Tiedt, P. L., & Tiedt, I. M. (1990). *Multicultural teaching: A handbook of activities, information, and resources*. Needham Height, MA: Allyn & Bacon.

Van Den Bergh, N. (1995). Employee assistance programs. In R. Edwards (Ed.), *The encyclopedia of social work* (19th ed., pp. 842–849). San Francisco: Jossey-Bass.

Walsh, W. B., Bingham, R. P., Brown, M. T., & Ward, C. M. (2001). *Career counseling African Americans*. Mahwah, NJ: Erlbaum.

Ward, C. M., & Bingham, R. P. (2001). Career assessment for African Americans. In W. B. Walsh, R. P. Bingham, M. T. Brown, & C. M. Ward (Eds.), *Career counseling for African Americans* (pp. 27–48). Mahwah, NJ: Erlbaum.

White, L., & Rogers, S. (2000). Economic circumstances and family outcomes: A review of the 1990s. *Journal of Marriage and the Family, 62*, 1035–1051.

Wooldridge, B. (1996). Workforce diversity, identity groups and management theory. In M. F. Rice (Ed.), *Diversity and public organizations: Theory, issues, and perspectives* (pp. 35–49). Dubuque, IA: Kendall/Hunt.

Zunker, V. G. (1998). *Career counseling: Applied concepts of life planning*. Pacific Grove, CA: Brooks/Cole.

9

Counseling Employees With Disabilities

Kimberly K. Asner-Self and Pamela J. Leconte

ince the concept of employment began, workers have qualified as an essential, if not the most essential, component of the work world. One might even consider the employee as "human capital investment," a valuable commodity to be trained, retained, and supported to provide the most effective and efficient short-term and long-term overall productivity. The corporate world understands the need for employee retention and investment. In 1993, employers invested $55.3 billion on employee training. By 1997, it was estimated that an average of 4.39% of payroll at the leading-edge Fortune 500 companies was being invested in training (Bassi & Van Buren, 1999). To protect their investment, many employers use Employee Assistance Program (EAP) counselors to help with the identification, prevention, intervention, and resolution of personal and other difficulties, which can adversely affect employee productivity.

EAP counselors, whether they are internal to the organization or part of contractually retained external services, design work-site-based programs to promote overall employee health and productivity. Common programs include awareness and sensitivity training, short-term counseling, and conflict resolution. In addition, EAP counselors develop and maintain a network of referral resources in the community to help them promote a healthy, productive work environment. Common employee issues that can adversely affect workplace productivity include substance abuse, untreated mental health problems, violence in the workplace, unresolved family problems, and conflicts related to miscommunication and perceived hostility among a diverse workforce. Employees with disabilities are part of that diverse workforce and, like all employees, face any or all of the same stressors. In addition, employees with disabilities face real and perceived adverse attitudes and acts in the workplace, discrimination, and adjustment to disability. EAP counselors need to be able to recognize some of the unique issues faced by employees with disabilities to assist efficiently.

In this chapter, we explore who employees with disabilities are, what factors affect their employment, and what resources (particularly in the areas of assessment and accommodations) exist for the EAP counselor working both to create and maintain a disability-friendly work environment and to counsel the employee with a disability.

Employees With Disabilities

People with disabilities are all around us, in everyone's family, in everyone's social milieu, in everyone's workplace. In fact, those of us who do not currently have a disability may find this to be a temporary condition as aging and accidents quickly change each of our perspectives. Certainly, a disability can be considered a dynamic state of being in that impairment today is not indicative of impairment tomorrow (Zola, 1993). A recovering substance abuser, for example, is always in recovery, yet there may be times when, perhaps, a flex-time accommodation for attendance at a recovery support group during normal working hours is necessary and other times when it is not. Someone with a diagnosis of bipolar disorder (American Psychiatric Association, 2000) may need time to adjust to medication early in the diagnosis process, during times of comorbid illness, or unusually high life stress (e.g., death of a parent or child), yet may need no overt, subsequent accommodation under normal working conditions.

Some people have apparent disabilities that are readily recognizable, sometimes by their accommodations (e.g., using prosthetics; devices for assisted mobility such as a cane, a walker, or a wheelchair; assistive audio, visual, or computer software devices; or animal assistants). Others have disabilities that are nonapparent or invisible such as epilepsy; learning disorders such as dyslexia and dysnumeria; chronic diseases such as diabetes, cancer, asthma, and HIV/AIDS; and emotional difficulties manifested in depression, anxiety, and long-term mental illnesses such as recurrent depression and anxiety, bipolar disorder, and schizophrenia; still others are recovering substance abusers.

Disability is a natural part of life. Yet how does one define disability for the purposes of employment? Most employers are familiar with the Americans With Disabilities Act of 1990 (ADA; P.L. 101-336), thus the most useful definition of a disability for EAP counselors is the three-part definition from the ADA: A person with a disability

- Has a physical or mental impairment that substantially limits one or more major life activities
- Has a record of such an impairment, or
- Is regarded as having such an impairment.

Specific interpretations of this definition can be found at the Department of Justice Web site at www.usdoj.gov/crt/ada or by contacting a Disability and Business Technical Assistance Center (800-949-4232).

People with disabilities become employees with disabilities in three ways: through hiring practices inclusive of people with disabilities, through posthire injury or illness, and through job task changes resulting in the appearance of a hitherto irrelevant work-related disability. There are an estimated 54 million people with disabilities in the United States (Ogle et al., 1998), of whom approximately 30 million are between 15 and 65 years of age, the traditional working years. Of those, almost 60% or 18.5 million have disability-related employment problems, including difficulty obtaining and retaining employment (U.S. Bureau of the Census, 1997). How many potential employees exist? The U.S. Bureau of the Census (1997) estimates that 23% of the U.S. population 15 years and older has one or more disabilities, including, but not limited to, difficulty with sight (3.7%), hearing (3.8%), speech (1.1%), walking (9.4%), using stairs (9.5%), lifting and other physical tasks (8.7%), learning (1.7%), mental retardation or developmental delay (0.7%), and depression or anxiety (3.3%). In addition, the ADA definition includes people living with long-term, chronic, debilitating illnesses such as diabetes (5.9%; American Diabetes Association, 1996) and HIV/AIDS (0.5%; Centers for Disease Control and Prevention, 2000) as well as recovering substance abusers.

A Louis Harris and Associates poll in 1994, commissioned by the National Organization on Disability, found that over three quarters (79%) of Americans with disabilities want to be an integral component of the productive workforce. Those who did not want employment cited a variety of structural barriers such as loss of Social Security income and health coverage (Stoddard, Jans, Ripple, & Kraus, 1998). In a global market economy, the spoils go not just to the individual worker or industry but to the society as a whole that is capable of effectively utilizing its natural resources, whether they be oil or an educated workforce (Scotch & Berkowitz, 1990). If one quarter of the United States' potential worker pool has disabilities, coupled with low unemployment rates, and with employers' complaints that they cannot find enough qualified employees, actively expanding the applicant pool to hire qualified workers with disabilities and actively working to retain valued employees who acquire disabilities is simply good business sense. In fact, "many employers, especially larger ones, have concluded that increasing the employment and the employability of persons with disabilities is good business" (Hearne, 1991, p. 116). EAP counselors consulting on hiring can be particularly helpful to the organization either by working with human resources personnel on job analyses, the development of job descriptions, assessment, and a comprehensive recruitment plan or by maintaining a network of qualified vocational specialists and evaluators to assist in the hiring process.

Employees with disabilities do not merely come from a diverse applicant pool. Many employees become employees with disabilities while on the job. The number of workers disabled on the job has declined slightly since 1972, from 10.9 occupational injuries or illnesses per 100 workers to 8.4 per 100 workers in 1994; however, the loss of workdays per 100 workers has increased from 47.9 to 86.5 (Stoddard et al., 1998).

Finally, the last category of employees with disabilities is one that is often overlooked: employees whose job tasks have changed with technological advances requiring a different set of skills and potentially highlighting a hitherto accommodated disability. For example, the computerization of a flexible manufacturing line requires an earlier successful and productive machinist to work with a computer interface, yet the employee has a learning disability that requires accommodation to allow for the transition and to read the screen. The needs of this category of employees are not being met, and they have filed the most complaints to the Equal Employment Opportunity Commission (EEOC) since the 1990 ADA was enacted (Casper, 1995).

Employees, employers, and families may need EAP assistance in vocational evaluation, job reanalysis, workplace accommodation, and emotional acceptance of and adjustment to disability. Recognition of some of the factors affecting employees with disabilities, myths and misconceptions about said employees, and costs related to accommodation and what resources are available can enhance the EAP counselor's overall effectiveness.

Factors Affecting Employees With Disabilities

Many people with disabilities, especially those with nonapparent or hidden disabilities, resist informing potential employers or current employers about their disabilities for fear of losing their jobs or being discriminated against in other ways. This not an unwarranted fear. The history of discrimination against people with disabilities has been long and complicated (Zola, 1993), from the outright destruction of those deemed a burden to the more recent and subtle forms of discrimination based on attitudes of ignorance and fear (Szymanski, Ryan, Merz, Trevino, & Johnston-Rodriguez, 1996). Until recently, physical barriers unintentionally limited access for many people with disabilities. For example, stairs, curbs, poor lighting, and traditional voice phones meant otherwise qualified people with disabilities could not access work. Legislation has helped to address physical barriers and blatant forms of discrimination, and employers and coworkers have noted that providing accommodations for employees with disabilities often benefits all in the workplace; for example, ramps, improved lighting, and job sharing enhance working conditions for employees and increase overall productivity (Hearne, 1991).

Now, however, most people involved in the disability policy world and those with disabilities themselves believe that discrimination emanates more from the subtler, more intangible aspects of social attitudes. These attitudes rise from a number of factors: lack of awareness or understanding of disabilities and how they are manifested in the workplace, a fear of hiring or working with people with disabilities because of lack of experience doing so, a fear that persons with disabilities will be nonproductive or costly employees (because of absences and insurance costs), and concern about how nondisabled workers may react (Kiernan, Marrone, & Butterworth, 1999). These attitudes can be changed if EAP counselors in collaboration with disability experts provide sensitivity training and disability awareness to employers and employees (U.S. Department of Labor, 1995).

Employer Concerns About Hiring and Retaining Employees With Disabilities

Employers are, as are we all, products of the greater societal environment where the aforementioned attitudes based on lack of awareness or understanding of disabilities, their costs, and how they are manifested in the workplace exist. Cost is, of course, an evident, tangible concern for most employers. Not only are employers concerned about the potential of lost productivity, but they are also concerned about the cost of expensive accommodations as well as costs resulting from potentially expensive litigious interactions with employees resulting from miscommunication, misunderstandings, and unmediated work-related conflict (Kiernan et al., 1999).

In a study of calls made to the Office of Disability Employment Policy's Job Accommodation Network (JAN), a federal toll-free service designed to offer advice to businesses and employees about workplace disability issues, only approximately 16% of calls were related to concerns about accommodation and costs. Almost 70% of these accommodations cost under $500, with an average reported return in benefits on their investment of $28.69 to the dollar. In 20% of the cases, no accommodations at all were required (Bruyere, 2000b; U.S. Department of Labor, 1996). A 1998 telephone survey of 1,900 nonfederal and federal employer human resources managers conducted by Cornell University supported previous studies and found that costs of accommodations (as well as cost of training and supervision) were not viewed as problems or barriers (Bruyere, 2000a). Examples of low-cost or no-cost accommodations include the following:

- changing the placement of a computer screen (CRT) so that an employee with use of only his or her left eye can increase productivity
- enlarging the print on a work schedule so that a warehouse worker with a visual perception learning disability will know when he or she is to work
- installing a tall stool for a cashier to lean against to prevent pain from a chronic back injury

Almost 70% of people with disabilities do not need special equipment or technology to perform their jobs effectively (Stoddard et al., 1998). Thus, it is not the costs of accommodations that present a barrier for employees with disabilities; it is the employer's perception of expense and lack of resources and expertise that constitute an obstacle of note.

The Americans With Disabilities Act of 1990 (ADA)

Employers are also concerned about complying with the ADA and the cost of potential lawsuits in regard to unintentional noncompliance. In fact, over a third of calls to JAN's hotline over one year in the mid-1990s were related to understanding the ADA (U.S. Department of Labor, 1996). The ADA (Public Law 101-336) represents a major piece of civil rights legislation that was deemed necessary by the U.S. Congress and the 54 million persons with disabilities and their advocates, because of the historically dismal employment rates. In 1997, the Current Population Survey found that for civilians of working age, 20% of men and 11% of women with disabilities were working full time compared with 80% men and 54% women without disabilities who were working full time (Bruyere, 2000b). In brief, the ADA offers a legal blueprint for private employers, state and local governments, employment agencies, labor organizations, and joint labor-management committees with 15 or more employees with regard to hiring, firing, and retention policies.

Most surveys, reports, editorials, and articles about the ADA and its implementation have been positive; however, fear of litigation remains (Waters & Johanson, 2001). Waters and Johanson (2001) also found that awareness of the ADA by human resource professionals in larger communities was not greater than those in small communities, but that "awareness and impact" of the law was greater in larger organizations than small ones (p. 47). Although many human resource professionals know about ADA, they are not aware of relevant judicial decisions that apply to their work. EAP counselors can help.

Title I, in particular, addresses equal access to employment opportunities regardless of disability by requiring equal opportunity in selection, testing, hiring, and promotion of qualified applicants with disabilities and prohibiting discrimination against employees with disabilities. In addition, Title I of the ADA protects a qualified person with a disability from discrimination. A qualified person refers to someone who meets the prerequisites for employment and who can perform the essential functions of the job with or without reasonable accommodation (ADA, 1990). Reasonable accommodations refer to any adaptations, adjustments, or modifications to a particular job, "employment practice, or the work environment that makes it possible for a qualified individual with a disability to participate in the job application process, perform the essential functions of the job, and/or enjoy the benefits and privileges of employment equal to those enjoyed by employees without disabilities" (Bruyere, 2000b, p. 19). This is determined on a case-by-case basis.

Of particular interest to EAP counselors is that since ADA passed into law most of the initial questions posed to JAN and the Department of Justice originated from employed persons with disabilities (Casper, 1995). Many of these employees had been struggling with accommodations with their current employers. This was a surprise to policy makers, who assumed most questions and complaints would come from people trying to gain access to employment. Employers are, understandably, concerned about ADA lawsuits, yet from 1990 through 1995, there were only 650 lawsuits out of the 6 million business and over 600,000 public and private employees covered by the ADA (U.S. Department of Labor, 1996). Those lawsuits are hardly frivolous, as the employers and employees involved must first go through an internal mediation process to seek resolution to the conflict. Should resolution remain elusive, the U.S. EEOC, in search of mediation, reviews the case. It is only when the conflict cannot be resolved at this juncture that lawsuits are cleared for the courts. Efforts are made all throughout the process to find a common ground, and help is available. In fact, 13% of the calls to JAN from 1994 to 1995 represented concerns related to managing workplace conflict regarding employers and employees with disabilities.

How EAP Counselors Can Help

EAP counselors can become involved in a multipronged manner: (a) consulting in the process of recruiting and hiring qualified employees, (b) conducting (or arranging for a state vocational rehabilitation or ADA specialist to conduct) sensitivity and awareness training, (c) mediating conflict between employers and employees, and (d) counseling employees adjusting to disability and offering referral sources and services to employers and employees alike.

Hiring Employees With Disabilities

Counselors may begin by consulting with recruiters and human resources personnel trained to seek out and attract the most qualified candidates for a position. Consultation may include collaborating on the development of disability-friendly position descriptions enumerating the job tasks, expectations, and the skills, knowledge, and ability needed to complete the job requirements successfully. Most importantly, job descriptions should be written for every position in a company; they should include essential functions of the job and functions that could be assigned, if necessary, to someone else in the event that an employee with a disability could perform the essential functions only. Requiring the ability to perform "essential functions" assures that an individual will not be considered unqualified simply because of inability to perform marginal or incidental job functions (Cornell University, 2000). If a job description is written prior to advertising or interviewing applicants, the descriptions are considered evidence of essential functions. Rehabilitation job placement and vocational evaluation personnel have found that many of the nonessential functions of a job can be distributed to others without creating a hardship or any additional costs to other employees or the employer. This "job carving" accommodation accounts for a commonsense approach to meeting the needs of the employer and the worker with a disability.

Once a job position description is designed, EAP counselors may aid in the development of a recruitment plan that includes disability-friendly position advertising and publications targeting employment fairs for people with disabilities, state and local vocational rehabilitation agencies, and schools and colleges with students with disabilities (such as Gallaudet University in Washington, DC, for the hearing impaired). Most community colleges and 4-year universities provide disability support services to their students with disabilities, so the professionals who work in those offices could serve as a resource as well. As a part of the plan, recruiters can be encouraged to check disability-related Web sites that routinely post resumes and resources. Some employers even offer incentive bonuses to recruiters who refer qualified applicants who have disabilities (U.S. Department of Labor, 2000). Finally, employers can use a tax incentives packet on the ADA, designed to help offset some of the costs of improving accessibility (U.S. Department of Justice, 1998).

Disability Awareness and Sensitivity Training

Creating an effective workplace means developing a good working team. New hires, newly promoted employees, and others whose job responsibilities have changed often participate in team-building exercises in orientation and subsequent training throughout their work tenure. EAP counselors can be instrumental by integrating disability awareness into orientations and subsequent personnel training or contacting their state vocational rehabilitation specialist to conduct such training. Such training should include the recognition, exploration, and normalization of attitudinal barriers along with the workplace-appropriate tools to address attitudinal change. For example, it is not unusual for people to avoid a fellow employee who happens to have a disability for fear of inadvertently being insensitive by saying or doing something offensive. Communication skills training can help all involved. Learning about affirmative and negative phrases, practicing active listening skills, and being introduced to good feedback technique should be an integral part of the training. Employers and other employees can learn to see the individual before the disability by using affirmative phrases such as "person who uses a wheelchair" instead of such negative phrases as "confined or restricted to a wheelchair." The latter can evoke feelings of pity potentially leading all to believe the person with a disability is somehow less capable than those without a disability (U.S. Department of Labor, 1995, 1999). Such training will not change the workplace overnight; however, it does represent a good faith effort toward healthy societal change and has had a positive effect on promoting more positive and inclusive attitudes toward employees with disabilities (Antonak & Livneh, 1995).

Helping Employees and Employers Negotiate Accommodations

Just as EAP counselors may consult with personnel regarding hiring practices, they may be invaluable resources to the organization when positions need to be redesigned or accommodations need to be obtained. Every year, workers become injured on the job while others sustain non-work-related injuries or illnesses that interfere with their ability to fulfill their job requirements without accommodation. The employees often need help returning to work productively and negotiating accommodations. In addition, there are employees who may have disabilities, usually hidden ones, that did not interfere or present barriers to their work until they received a promotion, their work assignments changed, or technological change in the workplace demanded skills that were compromised by their learning disabilities, emotional problems, or technological changes in work. This phenomenon is increasing as jobs of the 21st century require more flexibility, more use of computers, or higher level skills such as trouble shooting, problem-solving, and abstract thinking (21st Century Workforce Commission, 2001).

Many EAP counselors may have had experience working with rehabilitation professionals from the worker's compensation system in assisting employees to return to work. Most employees can qualify for worker's compensation assistance, insurance company support, or state vocational rehabilitation help. Such help may include vocational assessment and evaluation to determine current and future employment capabilities and interests, a systematic job analysis and redesigned position description along with appropriate accommodations, and counseling to address the employee's adjustment to disability in the workplace. Vocational assessment is also helpful in identifying physical capacities, appropriate job matches, and employee preferences as a risk management strategy. For instance, some worker's compensation claims and subsequent payments could be reduced if employee-job matches were made as part of a preemployment assessment process. Worker's compensation disability payments more than doubled between 1983 and 1993 to the point that payments were estimated at $23.4 million (Stoddard et al., 1998). This lesson is illustrated by the types of chronic conditions that cause work limitations: back disorders (21%), heart disease (11%), arthritis (8%), respiratory disease (5%), mental disorders (4%), lower extremity impairments (4%), and diabetes (3%; Stoddard et al., 1998).

Vocational assessment or evaluation is not necessary in all cases. However, where an employee can no longer perform his or her duties as defined prior to acquiring a disability, assessing the employee's skills and, perhaps hitherto untapped, capabilities can lead to reassignment to duties that continue to advance corporate productivity or agency goals. A few EAP counselors may be qualified to administer vocational assessments to evaluate an employee's current abilities and predict future performance. Others might request such evaluation from a professional "certified in vocational evaluation" (CVE); these evaluators may be employed by a variety of insurance companies, worker's compensation systems, and rehabilitation agencies and programs or may be independently employed. CVE refers to the national certification that these professionals gain through specific training, education, and experience approved by the national accrediting body, the Commission on Certification of Work Adjustment and Vocational Evaluation Specialists (2001).

Vocational assessment resources that are readily available to EAP counselors might be similar to those used in preemployment screening and placement decisions made by human resource or personnel managers. These resources commonly include interest inventories (e.g., the Holland Self-Directed Search Inventory and the Strong Interest Inventory), aptitude tests (e.g., the Differential Aptitudes Test), and temperament or personality surveys (e.g., the Myers–Briggs Type Indicator and the Keirsey

Temperaments Sorter). However, more in-depth and specialized assessment and evaluation can be conducted by a vocational evaluator to assist in identifying new interests, physical capacities and limitations, altered aptitudes, and so on postinjury. These individualized employee characteristics can then be matched to the job requirements and rigors of their previous or new jobs.

Adjusting to Disability

Finally, EAP counselors can work with employees and employers in adjusting to working with a disability. Common issues in counseling might include grief over the change in one's sense of work identity and the working relationships established based on performance as an employee (Szymanski et al., 1996). The counseling relationship may consist of exploring the evolution of a healthy productive work identity inclusive of disability. To do so, the employee with a disability must address attitudes of denial, anger, fear, pity, jealousy, patronization, and even hatred emanating not only from able-bodied employees but also from his or her own internalized sense of self (Vargo, 1989). EAP counselors, depending on expertise, may be able to address such work-related identity over a short solution-focused manner while referring employees to rehabilitation counselors in the community whose specialization may be counseling individuals adjusting to the long-term implications of their particular circumstances.

Resources Available to the EAP Counselor

Throughout this chapter, we have suggested that EAP counselors maintain and avail themselves of a vast array of rehabilitation and disability resources to promote a disability-friendly workplace while working with employees with disabilities. In this section, we briefly describe resource availability and accessibility for EAP counselors.

Many rehabilitation personnel are anxious to improve the employment opportunities of people with disabilities and to assist employers and companies who employ them. Rehabilitation counselors, vocational evaluators, job development and placement specialists, and rehabilitation technologists are all available from state rehabilitation agencies, rehabilitation hospitals, and one-stop shops to assist employers and EAP counselors. As noted earlier, rehabilitation counselors can provide resources for or participate in sensitivity training for employers and their employees.

They can refer EAP counselors to other rehabilitation personnel or may provide direct services for those employees who qualify for state agency services (they can explain the eligibility process for the state). Job development and placement specialists are trained to match people with disabilities to occupations for which they have high interest and adequate skills or training. Job placement functions may also be provided by employment specialists or supported employment specialists, who often work with individuals with more severe cognitive (e.g., mental retardation or acquired brain injury) or sensory disabilities (e.g., blindness or those without speech). Employment specialists are prepared to spend more time working with the employee with a disability to help train him or her and to develop natural supports within the work setting. Natural supports are strategies that other, experienced employees can use to assist the employee with a disability; these are used only if there is no loss of productivity, time, or money to the nondisabled employee.

Vocational evaluators, as noted previously, are professionals who work within rehabilitation settings (e.g., state vocational rehabilitation agencies, hospitals, and insurance companies), school systems, community colleges, and industry. They are trained to conduct job analyses and to analyze essential functions of specific jobs and task analyses (i.e., step-by-step sequencing and descriptions of each task that comprises a specific job). They assist employers to develop current job descriptions, recommend ergonomic arrangements of work sites for maximum productivity, and suggest work site accommodations. Vocational evaluators are knowledgeable of work and work requirements as well as performances, abilities, and capabilities of people with disabilities. They can be called on to assess a work environment and make recommendations to accommodate the employee with a disability. A national directory of vocational evaluators is available from the national Vocational Evaluation and Work Adjustment Association at www.vewaa.org.

Rehabilitation technologists and engineers can provide some of the same work site assessment and accommodation recommendations, but they typically have more technical expertise for developing low-technology (jigs and rearrangements of work) assistance and high-technology assistive services and devices. EAP counselors can access their services through the state rehabilitation agency or the Rehabilitation Engineering and Assistive Technology Society of North America (RESNA) at www.resna.org. RESNA provides a directory of certified assistive technology practitioners as well as assistive technology suppliers.

Every region (10) of the nation has a Disability and Business Technical Assistance Center that provides free information and referral services, technical assistance to employers, and training on all aspects of the ADA and other topics related to disability. The toll-free number for these centers is (800) 949-4232 (V/TTY); calls are automatically routed to the caller's region. Also, every state has a rehabilitation agency that can provide sensitivity training to employers who request it. The outcomes of such training can result in the integration of more qualified employees in the workplace, where research over the years shows that workers with disabilities demonstrate better-than-average attendance, remain loyal to their companies, and do not cause insurance costs to rise (Du Pont, 1990).

The U.S. Department of Labor's Office of Disability Employment Policy (ODEP) was approved by Congress in 2001, comprises the former President's Committee on Employment of People With Disabilities, and was formed to focus specifically on increasing employment of people with disabilities using a multipronged, long-term, sustained approach. To achieve this goal, the Office provides services that are available via the Internet or by contacting the Department of Labor, including policy analysis, technical assistance and outreach, constituent services, and the provision of competitive grants to support One-Stop Career Centers.

One-Stop Career Centers are designed to offer assistance both to people with disabilities accessing the economic mainstream and businesses and organizations creating a disability-friendly workplace (U.S. Department of Labor, 2001). The ODEP's Web site, www.dol.gov/dol/odep/public/sitemap.htm, lists a number of available programs, services, technical assistance materials, and additional resources to businesses. Resources include guidelines for developing a culturally diverse workplace inclusive of employees with disabilities, mentoring and developing employees for promotion and leadership roles, and conducting a job analysis, creating a position description, and designing a recruitment strategy to cast the broadest net possible to attract the best qualified employees. Information regarding the laws and legal rights of employers and employees as well as incentives for hiring people with disabilities is available.

The Job Accommodation Network (JAN), also on the ODEP Web site, offers the EAP counselor technical information on economical job accommodations for people with disabilities and Title I of the ADA. JAN provides information on statistical trends related to the employment of people with disabilities as well as resources available to the EAP counselor for technical assistance, funding, education, and services. JAN is readily available toll-free at (800) 526-7234 or via their Web site at www.jan. wvu.edu/english/homeus.htm. In addition, the ODEP Web site features reports and updates from the Presidential Task Force on Employment of Adults With Disabilities, which monitors policy, recommends policy changes, and keeps the administrative branch of government informed of the needs and progress of employment for people with disabilities.

Other federal-level programs include the U.S. Department of Education's funded source for accommodations and recommendations for purchases of assistive technology titled ABLEDATA. This resource can be reached through www.abledata.com. Finally, the EEOC (800) 669–400 (voice) or (800) 669–6820 (TTY for people who are hearing impaired), or www.eeoc.gov, also offers information on the creation of a disability-friendly workplace as well as mediation procedures and legal recourse available for employees and employers involved in a dispute.

On the state level, the Rehabilitation Act of 1973 (P.L. 93-112) and subsequent amendments provides for a state–federal vocational rehabilitation service system. These agencies are usually housed under the state department of education and provide services such as counseling, transportation, vocational assessment, job development and placement assistance, employment specialists (i.e., job coaches), funding for assistive technology, skill and awareness training, and accommodations (Berry, Price-Ellingstad, Halloran, & Finch, 2000). They can provide a valuable alliance and resource for the EAP counselor working with an employee with a disability. In fact, of the 13 categories of services they offer, counseling and assessment are used the most (Berry et al., 2000). As mentioned earlier, they can be reached toll free at (800) 949-4232 (V/TTY).

Finally, there are state liaison committees or commissions and governmental agencies designed specifically to aid in the employment and retention of people with disabilities, such as the Governor's Office on Employment of People With Disabilities. These committees vary in their missions from state to state; however, they are generally set up to promote self-reliance among people with disabilities with employment as an essential component. A listing of state liaison committees is available on the ODEP Web site listed earlier.

Conclusion

In summary, EAP counselors are perfectly positioned to include and provide support to employees with disabilities whether they are job candidates, employees who acquire disabilities during their work tenure through injury or illness, or people whose hitherto irrelevant disabilities become apparent because of technological change. Resources abound on both the national and state levels to aid the EAP counselor in working with both employers and employees in relation to disability. In addition, by assisting in the development of a disability-friendly workplace, EAP counselors aid in the creation of a productive workplace for all.

References

American Diabetes Association. (1996). The impact of diabetes *Facts and Figures*. Retrieved February 8, 2002 from http://www.diabetes.org

American Psychiatric Association. (2000). *Diagnostic and statistical manual of mental disorders—Text revision* (4th ed.). Washington, DC: Author.

Americans With Disabilities Act of 1990, Pub. L. No. 101-336, § 2, 104 Stat. 328 (1991).

Antonak, R. F., & Livneh, H. (1995). Direct and indirect methods to measure attitudes toward persons with disabilities, with an exegesis of the error-choice test method. *Rehabilitation Psychology, 40*, 3–24.

Bassi, L. J., & Van Buren, M. E. (1999). Valuing investments in intellectual capital. *International Journal of Technology Management, 8*, 414–432.

Berry, H. G., Price-Ellingstad, D., Halloran, W., & Finch, T. (2000). Supplemental security income and vocational rehabilitation. *Journal of Disability Policy Studies, 10*, 151–165.

Bruyere, S. M. (2000a). The Americans With Disabilities Act: Where we stand ten years later. *New Directions in Rehabilitation Counseling* (Vol. 11, Lesson 3). New York: Hatherleigh.

Bruyere, S. M. (2000b). Civil rights and employment issues of disability policy. *Journal of Disability Policy Studies, 11*(1), 18–28.

Casper, M. W. (1995). Transition educators: Instrumental personnel in fulfilling the promise of ADA. *Journal for Vocational Special Needs Education, 17*, 112–115.

Centers for Disease Control and Prevention. (2000, December 6). Persons reported to be living with HIV infection and with AIDS, by state and age group, reported through June 2000. *Surveillance Report, 12*(1). Retrieved from http://www.cdc.gov/hiv/stats/hasr1201/table1.htm

Commission on Certification of Work Adjustment and Vocational Evaluation Specialists. (2001). Retrieved February 11, 2002 from http://www.ccwaves.org

Cornell University. (2000). *Employment support representative training: Module IV. Orientation to vocational rehabilitation*. Ithaca, NY: Program on Employment and Disability, Cornell University.

Du Pont, E. I. de Nemours and Company. (1990). *Equal to the task* (2nd ed.). Wilmington, DE: Author.

Hearne, P. G. (1991). Employment strategies for people with disabilities: A pre-scription for change. In J. West (Ed.), *The Americans With Disabilities* (pp. 111–128). New York: Milbank Memorial Fund.

Kiernan, W. E., Marrone, J., & Butterworth, J. (1999). Beyond demographics: Strategic responses to a changing workforce . Boston: Institute for Community Inclusion/UAP, Children's Hospital.

Ogle, R. L., Moses, H., Peterson, L., Coleman, K. M., Cooper, R., Goldstraw, R., Kontnier, L. D., McKinnon, W. R., & Wang, L. L. (1998). *Re-charting the course: First report of the Presidential Task Force on Employment of Adults with Disabilities*. Retrieved February 11, 2002 from http://www.dol.gov/dol/_sec/public/programs/ptfead/rechart/index.htm

Rehabilitation Act of 1973, 29 U.S.C. § 701 et seq.

Scotch, R. K., & Berkowitz, E. D. (1990). One comprehensive system? A histor-ical perspective on federal disability policy. *Journal of Disability Policy Studies, 3*, 1–20.

Stoddard, S., Jans, L., Ripple, J., & Kraus, L. (1998). *Chart book on work and dis-ability in the United States: An info use report* . Washington, DC: U.S. National Institute of Disability and Rehabilitation Research. Retrieved from http://www.infouse.com/disabilitydata/workdisability/html

Szymanski, E. M., Ryan, C., Merz, M. A., Trevino, B., & Johnston-Rodriguez, S. (1996). Psychosocial and economic aspects of work: Implications for people with disabilities. In E. M. Syzmanski & R. M. Parker (Eds.), *Work and disabil-ity: Issues and strategies in career development and job placement* (pp. 9–39) Austin, TX: Pro-Ed.

21st Century Workforce Commission. (2001). *A nation of opportunity: Strategies for building America's 21st century workforce*. Washington, DC: U.S. Depart-ment of Labor.

U.S. Bureau of the Census. (1997). *Americans with disabilities—Table A*. Retrieved from://www.census.gov/hhes/www/disable/sipp/disab97/ds97ta.html.

U.S. Department of Justice. (September, 1998). *Tax incentives packet on the Americans With Disabilities Act*. Retrieved from://www.usdoj.gov/crt/ada/taxpack.htm

U.S. Department of Labor. (1995, October). *Communicating with and about peo-ple with disabilities*. Retrieved from://www.dol.gov/dol/odep/public/pubs/fact/comucate.htm

U.S. Department of Labor. (1996, July). *Cost and benefits of accommodations* [ODEP Education Kit 1996]. Retrieved from http://www.dol.gov/dol/odep/public/pubs/ek96/benefits.htm

U.S. Department of Labor. (1999). *Attitudinal barriers* [ODEP Education Kit 1999]. Retrieved from http://www.dol.gov/dol/odep/public/pubs/ek99/barriers.htm

U.S. Department of Labor. (2000, July). *Disability friendly strategies for the workplace*. Retrieved from http://www.dol.gov/dol/odep/public/pubs/ek00/friendlystrat.htm

U.S. Department of Labor. (2001, July). *Presidential task force on employment of adults with disabilities.* Retrieved from http://www.dol.gov/dol/_sec/public/programs/ptfead/main.htm

Vargo, J. W. (1989). In the house of my friend: Dealing with disability. *International Journal for the Advancement of Counselling, 12,* 281–287.

Waters, K. M., & Johanson, J. C. (2001). Awareness and perceived impact of the Americans With Disabilities Act among human resources professionals in three Minnesota cities. *Journal of Disability Policy Studies, 12,* 47–54.

Zola, I. K. (1993). Disability statistics, what we count and what it tells us: A personal and political analysis. *Journal of Disability Policy Studies, 4,* 9–39.

10

Gay, Lesbian, and Bisexual Employee Issues in the Workplace

Kathleen M. Kirby

merican society is becoming more comfortable, in general, discussing sexuality and sharing personal sexual issues. Although sexualized statements within advertisements are still used to titillate, tease, and sell products, the subject of sex and sexuality is also being discussed between individuals in relation to personal choice and lifestyle. The general cultural norm or bias has become more accepting of sex outside of marriage, but it remains basically heterosexual, ranging from the conservative declaration of deviance for nonheterosexual affection to sexual experimentation to romance and life-long commitment to a general sanctioning and assumption of heterosexual pairing. As the norm has become broader and more diverse, many individuals who once hid their divergence from the norm are now revealing their sexual preferences for specific sexual performance and acts and, also, sexual orientation for same-sex rather than opposite-sex romantic attachments.

The fact that gay, lesbian, and bisexual (GLB) individuals are now more likely to share their identity at work may cause difficulty for heterosexual individuals who do not understand or approve of a lifestyle different from their own. Sharing personal sexual identity may also prove anxiety provoking for GLB individuals who sometimes are unaware of the difficulty others may have in accepting their sexuality or who may be unprepared to discuss or explain this aspect of their selves.

GLBs face many problems in the workplace, ranging from criticism and nonacceptance to personal or physical attacks, discrimination, and potential job loss (Bernat, Calhoun, Adams, & Zeichner, 2001; Van Den Bergh, 1999). Given general societal bias, the vast majority of coworkers and employers assume all workforce members to be heterosexual. Deviating from this norm by "coming out"—letting others know of one's true sexuality—is a bold step and a sometimes disquieting course of action for many reasons. This chapter discusses general issues of GLB individuals, homophobia, identity development, career and workplace issues, and effective corporate response to the likelihood of harassment.

Homophobia or Fear of Homosexuality

Homophobia, the fear of homosexuality and homosexuals, is often driven by the general cultural acceptance of same-sex attraction as deviant and wrong. Homophobia has been evoked to reinforce general gender roles. For example, girls are sometimes teased about being "queer" or "lesbos" because they demonstrate interest in sports, are assertive, dress in masculine-oriented attire, or wear short boylike hair. Boys may be coerced into traditionally masculine behavior by being called a "faggot" or "homo" because they show tender emotion, are not interested in sports, are not aggressive, or enjoy girl-like activities and hobbies such as reading or mutual non-competitive play. Lesbian bating—calling individuals lesbian to damage their reputation—was used as one way to discredit the Women's Movement (Pharr, 1988) and has been used to bring into disrepute women who may make other men and women uncomfortable because of their nontraditional attitudes or beliefs. Because cultural norms are strong and homophobia is often used as a tool of control, everyone is affected to some degree by it—even those individuals with same-sex orientation. In fact, internalized homophobia often drives doubts and contributes to low self-esteem in GLB individuals as they struggle to accept their sexuality and integrate it into their self-concept. One young man described his own homophobia as an internal voice telling him that he was not "good enough" to be respected and loved.

Although same-sex sexual behavior has existed across cultures through-out history (Fukuyama & Ferguson, 2000), many are unaware that homosexuality has been and is accepted as natural in numerous past and present cultures. The concept of same-sex romantic and sexual attraction is affected by the social structures in place in each culture (Broido, 2000). Generally, in American culture, most heterosexual and many homosexual individuals are not cognizant of the history of homosexuality and base their awareness of same-sex attraction on innuendo and stereotypes with-out seeking personal knowledge. Untrue and often hurtful stereotypes abound. These include the belief that homosexuals recruit heterosexual individuals to the "cause" rather than attempt to seek friends and roman-tic interests; that gay males are always feminine and likely to be hair dressers, floral designers, artists, and actors rather than truck drivers, con-struction workers, accountants, engineers, and other more "masculine" occupations; and that lesbians, who innately lack femininity, are more likely found in the masculine jobs mentioned previously.

Homophobia affects attitudes and acceptance of individuals seen as dif-ferent from the gender norm whether or not they are "out" (declared to have same-sex attraction). It helps to put pressure on GLBs to be closeted by subtly underscoring the likelihood of nonacceptance and possible retal-iation, including potential professional discrimination, loss of job, and targeted violence. It also creates anxiety about revealing personal details to others because there may be a fear that others "can't understand" same-sex attraction (Blumenfeld & Raymond, 1988; Szymanski, Chung, & Balsam, 2001).

Identity Development

GLBs' acceptance of self is an extremely important factor in facilitating healthy relationships in personal and work arenas. Many theorists have posited the stages of identity formation for GLB individuals. Cass (1979) believed that because of the cultural bias toward heterosexism, GLBs, like other minorities, must come to accept their self, learn to see themselves in a positive light, deflect negative attitudes of others, and integrate sexual identity into total self-concept. In other words, GLBs must struggle to envision themselves as multidimensional and accept their sexual orienta-tion and concomitant choices as reflections of their inner being but not a definition of their total selves. They must come to know, accept, and affirm all of their selves.

Cass (1979) put forward a six-stage linear model of homosexual identity formation: (a) identity confusion (I'm not sure who I am), (b) identity comparison (Am I really like other people?), (c) identity tolerance (I'm different; I'm probably gay/lesbian/bisexual), (d) identity acceptance (I am gay/lesbian/bisexual), (e) identity pride (Gay/lesbian/bisexual people are good people; I am a good person), and (f) identity synthesis (I am many things and have many interests and I am gay/lesbian/bisexual).

Similar theories target specific same-sex orientation and accentuate different issues. Ponse (1978) saw lesbian development encompassing five interactive tasks achieved in any order: a subjective feeling of being different, coming to believe that this feeling may be lesbian, accepting a lesbian identity, developing a lesbian network, and involvement in a lesbian relationship. Faderman (1984) and Ettore (1980) added various aspects of sociopolitical context to these theories. Sophie (1986) integrated existing theories into stages of awareness, testing and explanation, identity acceptance, and identity exploration.

Troiden (1993) suggested that although a linear, sequential progression was assumed in most male-oriented theories of gay development, the research indicates a spiral or progressive circular repeating pattern. Troiden noted that society has given males more latitude in forming sexual relationships, and gay males are sexually active much earlier than lesbians and, also, their heterosexual counterparts. Finnegan and McNally (1987) advocated a model in which individuals move back and forth frequently between all stages, whereas Fassinger and Miller (1996) proposed two parallel, catalytic and interactive paths of identity development: an internal individual sexual identity development process and a contextual group-membership identity development process.

Bisexuality is acknowledged as more difficult to integrate into self-identity because of pressure to form one sexual identity from both heterosexual and homosexual communities (Udis-Kessler, 1995). De Cecco and Shively (1984) asserted that same-sex sexual behavior was not restricted to a minority of the population but appeared to be a fundamental aspect of human sexuality. Theoretically, the development of a bisexual identity has not been adequately explained and is most often referred to as a behavior rather than a sexual orientation (Rust, 1992). Bisexual individuals and people of color, as well as others who belong to more than one marginalized group, appear to have more difficulty integrating their identities (Greene, 1997).

No matter the theory used, there appears to be a stage of self-acceptance that may sometimes be expressed as interest in GLBs of note and, perhaps, a need to ask for affirmation verbally or through what may appear to be militant actions. At times, the need for affirmation is the primary social interaction between GLB individuals and those around them. It is often difficult for individuals who are approached by others to react affirmatively, especially if they are uncertain of the meaning and reason for displays such as symbols (rainbow flag, pink triangle), telling actions (limp wrists, lisps, extremely short or spiked hair), unfamiliar language (dyke, butching it up, lipstick lesbian, seeking bears [hairy men]), or unusual dress (men in bustiers and bead necklaces, women in jockey shorts). Through these experiences, negative stereotypes are often reinforced and homophobia is also justified.

Human resources and career development counselors should be aware of identity development theory so they may understand and approach GLB individuals in a supportive fashion. The tasks to be undertaken and the needs of the GLB individuals vary depending on where they fall along the developmental continuum or tasks of GLB identity development.

Coming Out/Revealing Sexual Orientation

All individuals decide how much of their personal life they are willing to share with others in their workplace. GLB individuals must make decisions about how much to share and in what way they will reveal important aspects of their selves. They may choose to assume a false heterosexual identity, avoid the issue of sexuality, or share their sexual orientation and integrate it into their work persona. If coming out is elected, then the manner in which GLBs reveal their sexual orientation is another issue. All strategies have rewards and consequences and may require ongoing attention to detail or education of others (Day & Schoenrade, 1997; Friskopp & Silverstein, 1995; Triandis, Kurowski, & Gelfand, 1994). Because of the heterosexist bias of American society, coming out is a constant process as employees are placed in different contexts and new workers join the workplace (Woods & Lucas, 1993), but it may have positive physical as well as emotional benefits. It has been found that gay men who conceal their homosexual identity experience increased risk of cancer, pneumonia, bronchitis, sinusitis, and tuberculosis than their "out" counterparts (Cole, Kemeny, Taylor, & Visscher, 1996), and lesbians who reveal their sexual orientation experience less physical and mental health problems than their closeted friends (Morris, Waldo, & Rothblum, 2001; Rosario, Hunter, Maguen, Gwadz, & Smith, 2001; Saari, 2001; Selvidge, 2001).

In their study of Harvard Business School graduates, Friskopp and Silverstein (1995) discovered that lesbians were more likely to be out in the beginning of their career and become more closeted as their career progressed, whereas gay men were more likely to be closeted in the beginning of their career and become progressively more open about their personal life as their career advanced. Their data suggested that lesbians suffered more discrimination because of their sexual orientation, and the fact they were female, they also more easily "passed" as heterosexual than gay men. Friskopp and Silverstein's study also provides a glimpse of who comes out at work. The researchers found that gay and lesbian professionals who decided to come out at work to one or more individuals were comfortable with their own sexual orientation, were out to heterosexual friends and family, had a partner or GLB friends who encouraged them to come out at work, and did not consider the workplace a hostile environment. Those who endorsed the most items suggesting happiness and contentment at work also had developed and used a coming-out plan. In general, those who were most satisfied with their current out status had experienced many coming outs with heterosexual friends and relatives before revealing their sexual orientation at work.

Friskopp and Silverstein (1995) discovered that the gay and lesbian professionals they studied who remain closeted at work experienced personal and professional losses. These included vulnerability to blackmail and other forms of harassment, discomfort with socializing, lack of a strong support system, inability to experience more intense and supportive relationships with heterosexuals, fewer networking opportunities with other GLBs, more problems within personal relationships, lowered self-esteem, and diminished legal grounds in discrimination suits. They also noted that individuals who expressed a wish to be closeted at work reported they experienced more overt discrimination and homophobia than those who were more out. Friskopp and Silverstein also found that there was often a stratified acceptance of GLBs in many companies. GLB sexual orientation might not be tolerated in management but was sought after in company divisions such as the art department or within marketing, especially when the GLB community was targeted as consumers.

Providing an atmosphere in which employees and potential employees are in "the closet" can prove detrimental to companies. It may rob them of special talent or the best person for the job, create situations in which teamwork is challenged, negatively affect morale and productivity, decrease personal loyalty to the company, and provide impetus for employees to seek work elsewhere in companies with a more affirming environment.

Career Issues

Career choice and decisions are often affected by internal heterosexism or homophobia. The GLB individual may be directed or diverted from career exploration or choice to express or suppress their sexuality. Depending on the stage of identity development, an individual may choose to investigate careers and job settings to protect themselves, explore options, be able to work in geographical locations that are known to be more GLB friendly, signal heterosexuality to others, offer dating opportunities, or provide privacy and solitude for personal contemplation and protection from discovery (Nauta, Saucier, & Woodard, 2001). Friskopp and Silverstein (1995) found that one third of the GLB Harvard Business School graduates they surveyed stated that their sexual orientation had hurt their career. In the Out/Look survey (Woods, 1992), 32% of respondents stated that their sexual orientation issues had influenced their choice of application to companies for employment, 30% stated that sexual orientation issues had probably or definitely influenced their choice of careers, and over 50% predicted that it would affect their future decision making regarding careers.

Griffin (1992) developed a model for career counseling with GLB individuals. It consists of helping individuals explore the force or pressure that occurs as the fear of discrimination is countered by the individual's personal integrity or need to be genuine. The model includes the exploration of such factors as the extent of general sociability and required socialization in a work setting, the dating or coupled status of the client, the longevity of the partnered relationship, interaction of sexual identity management within the partnered relationship, and the presence of children. It stands to reason that juggling multiple identities such as being African American, low income, and lesbian needs to be handled differently by the counselor than interventions with European-origin White, upper-middle-class, gay males. Identity development and degree of "outness" are concepts that also are important for the career counselor to assess and use to modify counseling approaches appropriately to assure the efficacy of the individual interventions (Kirby, 2000).

Some industries and jobs are more accepting of minority sexual orientation than others. For example, Woods and Lucas (1993) described the "ghettoization" of minorities as the relegation of minorities to the peripheral or support positions within a company rather than to the central decision-making positions. Power positions are off limits; to access these decision-making positions, one must be noncontroversial and nonthreatening to the status quo. Examples of "support positions" include human resources, secretarial and other support staff positions, and sales staff. These positions tend to be more predictable and safe because they are performance-based. Success in the position is based on concrete and objective facts and figures.

Although marginalization of job choice may protect individuals, it may also limit them. Many jobs on the periphery have limited career ladders. Because there tends to be a more tolerant attitude toward difference and a more diverse workforce within the perimeters of many companies, individuals who spend more than a modicum of time within the folds of this frontier may lack the experience to handle the edgier and less tolerant land of the power elite. Career aspirations may suffer, and opportunities for advancement may be limited. It has been established that individuals who work in areas of limited opportunity for career advancement show less motivation to seek advancement even though it may exist elsewhere (Cross, 2000). Opportunities may be lost because of the perceived difficulty in "fighting one's way out of the ghetto," lack of exposure or example, deficiency in vision, unresolved career goals, or from the self-defeating behavior of negativism (i.e., not trying).

Mentoring Issues

Mentoring programs have been an important part of grooming the workforce. Having a mentor was extremely important for 53% of GLB individuals interviewed by Friskopp and Silverstein (1995). Many of the 47% without mentors mentioned that they wished they had one in order to receive advice, encouragement, insight, and leadership on both personal and professional issues.

Both GLB and heterosexual individuals are able to provide mentorship for GLBs. Such mentors could be successful individuals in other companies, although commonly they are senior individuals in the same company. Having a mentor means that the nuances of the company or industry are interpreted for the person mentored. Social gatherings not normally available to the mentored individual now may become accessible. Methods and strategies for fast-tracking or achieving promotion and success are shared. There is often someone available for advice about ideas and decisions.

Most GLBs express interest in mentoring others even if they have not been mentored themselves. Although many companies and organizations have mentoring programs, individuals also are able to informally ask others to act as mentors. Regularly, more than one individual with different expertise as mentors are sought, thereby increasing the breadth of political, personal, and career advice available.

It is frequently difficult for any individual to find a mentor. GLBs may discover that they are hesitant or unprepared to approach potential mentors. They may be concerned about coming-out issues, homophobia, or becoming more visible within a company—both as the mentored individual becomes a potential "fast tracker" and as a target for those who do not approve of those with a minority sexual identity. Those who are in the closet have made a practice of withholding intimate details from others in the workplace. The mentor–mentee relationship is built on a foundation of candor, integrity, and openness. If an individual is closeted, the issues of coming out to a mentor are paramount. At what point in the relationship this occurs often affects the quality, loyalty, and enthusiasm generated within the relationship. Closeted GLBs are less likely to seek GLB mentors in part because of fear of detection of their sexual orientation by association with a GLB individual, whether out or closeted. If GLBs remain closeted to their mentors, the revelation of their sexual orientation may negatively affect the mentoring relationship. Depending on how widely recognized the mentor–mentee relationship is within the workplace, a decline within this relationship may affect both mentor's and mentee's career path. Ramifications and risk should be clearly explored before committing to a mentoring relationship. Those who suggest or broker such relationships should also be aware of the possible risks to both parties.

GLB Affirmative Policies

Organizational researchers have found that companies with clear affirmative policies regarding diversity and minority worker protection had sexual minority workers with more positive attitudes toward their jobs and their employers (Button, 2001). It is likely that these companies retained workers longer. Written statements of nondiscrimination may be the only way GLBs have of knowing or being reassured that their job is not contingent on majority culture approval. As such, to be most effective, a nondiscrimination policy should be prominently displayed in company manuals, highlighted in training and orientation sessions, and posted prominently.

There are several other ways that organizations may signal acceptance of GLBs. Providing diversity workshops presenting accurate knowledge about homosexuality and bisexuality, contradicting common misperceptions and stereotypes, and helping heterosexual employees understand their own sexuality as well as that of others may lower the anxiety of workers (Cross, 2000; McNaught, 1993; Mickens, 1994). Facilitating informal GLB networks within the workplace may signal support and provide social encouragement, particularly when dealing with diversity. Some organizations may formalize this group to signal stronger report for GLBs. Companies may provide an even stronger signal of message by providing identical benefit coverage to same-sex domestic partners as that provided for spouses (Baker, Strub, & Henning, 1995; McNaught, 1993; Mickens, 1994). In addition, company policies extending bereavement and sick-care leave policies to domestic partner benefits also provide an accommodating environment for sexual minorities. Corporate sponsorship of HIV/AIDS benefits also indicates an accepting environment for GLBs.

The provision of antiharassment and domestic partner policies may serve to enhance a company's ability to attract highly qualified sexual minorities, women, and racial and ethnic minorities. Although the benefits of providing a safe and accepting environment for sexual minority members and others have generated positive outcomes in many instances, there have been negative internal and external consequences for some companies (Mickens, 1994). For example, there were no problems when Microsoft and Xerox instituted coverage for domestic partnerships, but when plans to enact such policies were announced by the U.S. Forest Service, some employees objected. Walt Disney World faced objections, organized boycotts, and legal actions when they instituted insurance coverage for domestic partners.

The manner in which company policies are introduced to an organization's workforce and the general development of the institution may influence the level of internal acceptance of and lack of resistance to these policies. For instance, nondiscrimination policies for GLBs were the first harassment/discrimination policies introduced at Microsoft. The existence of multiple policies of nondiscrimination, affirming such guidelines to the workforce through multiple listing and emphases, and a serious enforcement of these policies in multiple locations and geographical areas may influence external reactions. Button (2001) noted that further research is needed to establish the potential costs and benefits of affirming sexual diversity so that they may be more appreciated by organizational decision makers.

Friskopp and Silverstein (1995), who studied graduates of the Harvard Business School, recommended that any study of company antidiscrimination policies for GLBs include the "bottom line," for example, the cost–benefit afforded the company. To do so, it is necessary to estimate the size of the reference group. In general, research has estimated that GLBs comprise 10% of the population. As most GLBs are self-supporting, there may be a slightly higher percentage in the workforce.

In 2000, the U.S. Bureau of the Census began collecting some figures relating to the GLB population. The Census Bureau did not collect data that addressed sexual orientation but did ask individuals about the nature of their cohabitation of households. They found that 2% of U.S. households reported being same-sex couples (U.S. Bureau of the Census, 2001). This figure may be underreported because of the circular and indirect manner in which it was collected and derived.

Diversity Workshops

Brian McNaught (1993) noted in his book, *Gay Issues in the Workplace*, that GLBs are present in the workplace, homophobia exists in the work world, homophobia affects productivity, ignorance is the adversary, and behavior, not beliefs, is the issue because corporations are not in the business of dictating personal values. He called for diversity training as a remedy and noted that tolerance does not require acceptance, and challenging people's beliefs does not necessarily change them. His advice to diversity educators is to acknowledge the limits of their expertise; to stick to discussing general factual information and behavior rather than philosophy, morality, and religious issues; and to not become side-tracked.

All trainings must have specific goals. A diversity workshop emphasizing GLB issues should, at minimum, address the following: (a) the corporate commitment to and policy of nondiscrimination; (b) factual information about homosexuality; (c) employees' understanding of and feelings toward homosexuality, heterosexism, and homophobia; (d) the effects of homophobia on employees and the corporation; and (e) and collaborative strategies to address homophobia in the workplace (McNaught, 1993).

Diversity educators must be familiar with the subject and be able to handle a sometimes angry, hostile, and possibly embarrassed, bewildered audience. They must be able to defuse hostility, deal firmly but lightly with antagonism and animosity, reframe hatred and loathing, and remain positive and informative while nurturing the participants and creating an atmosphere of tolerance and acceptance.

One of the most important issues to be aware of is the sometimes naïve or unrealistic sense of safety that can be communicated to GLBs during these workshops. As with everything else in life, tolerance and respect grow as a process rather than a reaction to information or a single group experience. The purpose of addressing homophobia within a workshop setting is not to encourage premature coming out but to initiate the process of creating a safe workplace for all employees. Diversity educators should be capable of short-circuiting a coming-out proclamation that might be offered during or shortly after a workshop. Not only is coming out an important process for the individual, but it is also an act that should be contemplated, rehearsed, and thoughtfully planned. As noted previously, the most successful out individuals in the workplace appear to be those who have practiced coming out, are out to their families, have extensive support systems, and are realistically aware of the possible effect of this revelation on personal and work relationships (Day & Schoenrade, 1997; Kirby, 2000).

Workshops tend to be more effective if there is interaction between participants, and exercises include opportunities to evaluate the work atmosphere, temporarily take on the role of the individuals oppressed, and brainstorm possible solutions and interventions that may help to improve the workplace in regard to the tolerance of marginalized groups and comfort of all employees. McNaught (1993) offered specific suggestions in his book for workshops specifically designed for the GLB issues in the workplace, and Blumenfeld and Raymond (1988) provided extensive suggestions for workshops for the general public that could easily be modified for use within the workplace. It is not only essential that the workplace leader is both extremely familiar with and knowledgeable about GLB issues but also important that the leader have exceptional ability in handling critical group processes, in particular, and multicultural issues, in general. It is not enough to be gay, lesbian, or bisexual; the workshop leader must be experienced in the group process and capable of diffusing hostility and gently reinforcing tolerance, creating a comfortable atmosphere while recognizing the limits of individual belief.

Although one specific workshop may be helpful in raising awareness within a company, and policy is essential to reinforce workplace compliance, a targeted program that creates a series of experiences and allows time for discussion and reaction is generally more effective. Collaboration with experts will help a company create the most effective and successful intervention strategies.

Conclusion

This chapter introduced issues affecting GLB individuals in the workplace. It underscored the importance of irradiating homophobia to improve workplace morale, productivity, and interpersonal effectiveness.

Issues surrounding self-concept and identity for the GLB individual were discussed. Important topics include the toll that secrecy exerts on the GLB employees during their work hours and also within their personal and social lives. This chapter noted that individuals who are out in the workplace have been shown to generally be mentally and physically healthier, more positive and optimistic, and more productive than their closeted peers. They are less likely to feel discriminated against and more likely to set boundaries within their workplace relationships.

Also discussed was the idea that tolerance within the workplace does not mean personal acceptance of homosexuality; however, beliefs are not an excuse for discriminatory, prejudiced, or disrespectful behavior. A lack of factual knowledge and exposure is often the impetus for inappropriate and unacceptable behavior. Diversity training was recommended as a partial remedy for dealing with harassment and discrimination. GLB issues should be addressed within a company's diversity program. The knowledge and training skills of the workshop leader is necessary to ensure the efficacy of the interventions needed to allow individuals to face their fears, uncover their prejudices and false knowledge, and participate in creating a tolerant and genial workplace environment.

This chapter noted that an understanding of GLB identity development was essential for the manager, career counselor, and human resources administrator. The interaction of self-concept, identity, and career choice was highlighted. This chapter referenced the fact that certain stages of identity development and management may impact GLB behavior and confuse as well as frustrate coworkers.

The importance of a support system to facilitate personal and professional growth was affirmed. Mentoring issues for the GLB were discussed; the importance of match between GLB and mentor was highlighted, and it was noted that a mismatch could be detrimental to both parties. Factors of identity development and coming-out status were maintained to be the most important elements of the early mentoring relationship and contribute highly to its longevity and effectiveness. It was also noted that a number of GLBs wished for mentors but did not have them. Many of those individuals recognized the importance of mentoring and were willing to mentor others in the future.

Institutional response to, attitude toward, and policies about discrimination were discussed. It was noted that multiple strategies were best for signaling acceptance of GLBs and diversity within the workplace, including the following: (a) prominent placement of institutional policies of nondiscrimination in company handbooks, employee contracts, employee orientation, and employee training; (b) encouragement of GLB support groups; (b) formal or informal mentoring programs including GLB individuals; (d) instituting employee benefits for domestic partners equal to that of heterosexual mates; (e) extending family leave to include domestic partners; and (f) corporate sponsorship of HIV/AIDS benefits. It was emphasized that within a company, corporate leadership including modeling tolerance and acceptance was the most significant factor in signaling the importance of modifying the workplace environment.

References

Baker, D. B., Strub, S. O., & Henning, R. R. (1995). *Cracking the corporate closet: The 200 best (and worst) companies to work for, buy from and invest in if you're gay or lesbian—and even if you aren't.* New York: HarperCollins.

Bernat, J. A., Calhoun, K. S., Adams, H. E., & Zeichner, A. (2001). Homophobia and physical aggression toward homosexual and heterosexual individuals. *Journal of Abnormal Psychology, 110,* 179–187.

Blumenfeld, W. J., & Raymond, K. (1988). *Looking at gay and lesbian life.* New York: Philosophical Library.

Broido, E. M. (2000). Constructing identity: The nature and meaning of lesbianism, gay and bisexual identities. In R. M. Perez, K. A. DeBord, & K. J. Bieschke (Eds.), *Handbook of counseling and psychotherapy with lesbian, gay, and bisexual clients* (pp. 13–33). Washington, DC: American Psychological Association.

Button, S. B. (2001). Organizational efforts to affirm sexual diversity: A cross-level examination. *Journal of Applied Psychology, 86*, 17–28.

Cass, V. C. (1979). Homosexual identity formation: A theoretical model. *Journal of Homosexuality, 4*, 219–235.

Cole, S. W., Kemeny, M. E., Taylor, S. E., & Visscher, B. R. (1996). Elevated physical health risk among gay men who conceal their homosexual identity. *Health Psychology, 15*, 243–251.

Cross, E. Y. (2000). *Managing diversity: The courage to lead.* Westport, CT: Quorum Books

Day, N. E., & Schoenrade, P. (1997). Staying in the closet versus coming out: Relationships between communication about sexual orientation and work attitudes. *Personnel Psychology, 50*, 147–163.

De Cecco, J. P., & Shively, M. G. (1984). From sexual identity to sexual relationships: A contextual shift. *Journal of Homosexuality, 9*(2/3), 1–26.

Ettore, E. M. (1980). *Lesbians, women and society.* London: Routledge & Kegan Paul.

Faderman, L. (1984). The "new" gay lesbians. *Journal of Homosexuality, 10*(3/4), 85–95.

Fassinger, R. E., & Miller, B. A. (1996). Validation of an inclusive model of sexual minority identity formation on a sample of gay men. *Journal of Homosexuality, 32*(2), 53–79.

Finnegan, D. G., & McNally, E. B. (1987). Dual identities: Counseling chemically dependent gay men and lesbians. Center City, MN: Hazelden.

Friskopp, A., & Silverstein, S. (1995). *Straight jobs; gay lives.* New York: Scribner's.

Fukuyama, M. A., & Ferguson, A. D. (2000). Lesbian, gay and bisexual people of color: Understanding cultural complexity and managing multiple oppressions. In R. M. Perez, K. A. DeBord, & K. J. Bieschke, (Eds.), *Handbook of counseling and psychotherapy with lesbian, gay, and bisexual clients* (pp. 81–106). Washington, DC: American Psychological Association.

Greene, B. (1997). *Ethnic and cultural diversity among lesbians and gay men.* Newbury Park, CA: Sage.

Griffin, P. (1992). From hiding out to coming out: Empowering lesbian and gay educators. In K. M. Harbeck (Ed.), *Coming out of the classroom closet* (pp. 167–196). Binghamton, NY: Harrington Park Press.

Kirby, K. M. (2000). *Multiple identities and differing needs of the not-yet-out gay, lesbian and bisexual client.* Unpublished manuscript.

McNaught, B. (1993). *Gay issues in the workplace.* New York: Pocket Books.

Mickens, E. (1994). *The 100 best companies for gay men and lesbians.* New York: Pocket Books.

Morris, J. F., Waldo, C. R., & Rothblum, E. D. (2001). A model of predictors and outcomes of outness among lesbian and bisexual women. *American Journal of Orthopsychiatry, 71*(1), 61–71.

Nauta, M. M., Saucier, A. M., & Woodard, L. E. (2001). Interpersonal influences on students' academic and career decisions: The impact of sexual orientation. *Career Development Quarterly, 49*, 352–362.

Pharr, S. (1988). *Homophobia: A weapon of sexism.* Berkeley, CA: Chardon.

Ponse, B. (1978). *Identities in the lesbian world: Social constructions of the self.* Westport, CT: Greenwood Press.

Rosario, M., Hunter, J., Maguen, S., Gwadz, M., & Smith, R. (2001). The coming-out process and its adaptational and health-related associations among gay, lesbian, and bisexual youths: Stipulation and exploration of a model. *American Journal of Community Psychology, 29,* 352–362.

Rust, P. C. (1992). The politics of sexual identity: Sexual attraction and behavior among lesbian and bisexual women. *Social Problems, 39,* 366–386.

Saari, C. (2001). Counteracting the effects of invisibility in work with lesbian patients. *Journal of Clinical Psychology, 57*(5), 10–33.

Selvidge, M. M. D. (2001). The relationship of sexist events, heterosexist events, self-concealment and self-monitoring to psychological well-being in lesbian and bisexual women. *Dissertation Abstracts International: Section B: The Sciences and Engineering, 61*(7-B), 3861.

Sophie, J. (1986). A critical examination of stage theories of lesbian development. *Journal of Homosexuality, 12*(2), 39–51.

Szymanski, D. M., Chung, Y. B., & Balsam, K. F. (2001). Psychosocial correlates of internalized homophobia in lesbians. *Measurement and Evaluation in Counseling and Development, 34*(1), 27–38.

Triandis, H. C., Kurowski, L. L., & Gelfand, M. J. (1994). Workplace diversity. In H. C. Triandis, M. D. Dunnett, & L. M. Hough (Eds.), *Handbook of industrial and organizational psychology* (2nd ed., Vol. 4, pp. 769–827). Palo Alto, CA: Consulting Psychologists Press.

Troiden, R. R. (1993). The formation of homosexual identities. In L. D. Garnets & D. C. Kimmel (Eds.), *Psychological perspectives on lesbian and gay male experiences* (pp. 191–217). New York: Columbia University Press.

Udis-Kessler, A. (1995). Identity/politics: A history of the bisexual movement. In N. Tucker, L. Highleyman, & R. Kaplan (Eds.), *Bisexual politics: Theories, queries and visions* (pp. 17–30). New York: Harrington Park Press.

U.S. Bureau of the Census. (2001). *Profiles of general demographic characteristics 2000: 2000 census of population and housing United States.* Washington, DC: U.S. Government Printing Office.

Van Den Bergh, N. (1999). Workplace problems and needs for lesbian and gay male employees: Implications for EAPs. *Employee Assistance Quarterly, 15*(1), 21–60.

Woods, J. D. (1992). Self-disclosure at work. *Out/Look, 16,* 87–88.

Woods, J. D., & Lucas, J. H. (1993). *The corporate closet: The professional lives of gay men in America.* New York: Free Press.

11

....

Issues of the Delayed
or Reentry Worker

Mary H. Guindon

he concerns of delayed or reentry workers as they learn about and adjust to today's changing workplace climate need special attention from counselors. This chapter discusses delayed or reentry workers of both genders whose major life-role identity has been that of homemaker and who have shifted that identity to that of worker. The chapter uses a gendered context perspective to discuss expectations of the delayed and reentry worker. It applies Astin's (1984) model of career choice and work behavior and offers a meaningful framework by which to understand the delayed or reentry worker of either gender. It discusses the implications of sex role socialization, perceived structure of opportunity, and motivation for the delayed or reentry worker and presents possible assets and issues in the workplace. Implications for counselors are framed within the principles of corporate management.

The last three decades of the 20th century saw unprecedented changes in society and the workplace. The Civil Rights Movement of the 1960s and the Women's Movement of the 1970s led to antidiscrimination and affirmative action legislation that contributed to increasing numbers of women and diverse populations entering the workforce. Some were delayed entrants. Shifts in the way people view work and its meaning, changes in the economic climate, and variations of political realities have meant that workers have voluntarily or involuntarily left the workplace at various times in their lives. Most of these workers eventually reenter the workforce. Much attention in the career counseling literature is either focused on methods by which people can enter or reenter the workforce and find meaningful careers or focused on adults at the point of career transitions or in career crises. Less attention is paid to delayed-entry or reentering workers once they have found employment. Although a preponderance of career development literature focuses on work adjustment or adaptation to the work environment and on the effect of the work environment on the individual (Dawis & Lofquist, 1984; Hershenson, 1996), the concerns of the delayed or reentry worker can be overlooked. Yet they are a population that may need special attention from counselors, supervisors, and managers as they learn about and adjust to today's changing workplace climate. Role conflict, unrealistic self-concept, low self-esteem, lack of understanding of workplace culture, and naivete about such issues as effective communications, career pathing, and organizational expectations can be common issues. In addition, many delayed or reentry workers are women, and research suggests that they continue to hold different kinds of jobs than their male counterparts, are paid less, and have fewer opportunities for advancement (Sharf, 2002). Consequently, meeting the needs of delayed or reentry workers is an important function of counselors working in organizational settings.

Who Is the Delayed or Reentry Worker?

The *delayed worker* is any person who has not held a full-time position for pay and whose major life-role identity has been other than that of worker. The *reentry worker* is one whose major life-role identity has been that of worker but who has been out of the paid workforce for an extended period of time. For the purposes of this chapter, they are discussed together. Both groups face similar issues upon their entry into the workforce because they lack knowledge about the contemporary world of work and may tend not to have appropriate or current occupational skills. Although some of their expectations are the same as those of any new employee, they differ in their life experiences from others in the workforce, and their expectations can be quite different in some important ways.

Delayed or reentry workers fall in many categories: immigrants, prior offenders, mid-life career changers, older workers, former military person-nel, and full-time homemakers (see Isaacson & Brown, 2000). Students, of course, are often delayed entry or reentry workers. This chapter con-centrates on those whose major life-role identity has been homemaker and who have shifted that identity to that of worker. Although other delayed or reentry workers face many of the same challenges presented here, they have needs that are so individualized and specific that they warrant specialized treatment beyond the scope of this chapter and are not addressed here.

Full-Time Mothers/Homemakers

At the end of the 20th century, women held over one third of the more than 14 million executive, administrative, and management jobs, and as the beginning of the 21st century unfolds, approximately half the work-force will be female (Aburdene & Naisbitt, 1992). The working woman of today is assumed to enter the workforce upon completion of her educa-tion and is expected to stay in the workforce until retirement. Stereo-typical ideas of the contemporary female worker may invoke images of the young, educated, upwardly mobile woman who devotes herself to a career patterned on the traditional masculine model; or she is assumed to be the young working mother equally concerned with job, day care, and family. However, many women enter the paid workforce for a short period of time and leave it for an extended time to fulfill the mother/homemaker role. Although less of a factor for contemporary women, some still elect to assume the role of full-time mother and homemaker after completion of their education rather than enter the workforce.

Studies that distinguish between different types of women (i.e., career-oriented, family-focused, etc.) yield few definitive results and often indi-cate conflicting or simplistic conclusions (Herr & Cramer, 1992). The majority of women fall into one of three basic labor force groups: regular entry, returning worker, or delayed/late-entry worker (Isaacson & Brown, 2000). The first group of women can expect to enter the workforce after their schooling and to work for the majority of their adult lives. Although they may leave the workforce for short periods of time to undertake homemaking and mothering duties, they are predominantly part of the regular entry group. Our concern in this chapter is with the latter two groups. Returning workers are those who also enter the workforce after their schooling but leave it for a sustained period of time. Delayed and late-entry workers are those who have not had any meaningful work expe-rience outside of the home. In both cases, this is the woman who is perceived of by herself and others as more traditionally oriented. She centers on her identity as a full-time career homemaker who has either never entered the workforce in any substantive way or has withdrawn from the workplace for a significant period of time. She has either only minimally worked outside the home or her work history ended 5, 10, or more years ago. Although she makes up a significant population in higher education, her occupational skills were never developed or, if previously developed, have become obsolete. She fits the traditional, societal expectations of gender roles for women. These stereotypical ideas endorse nurturance, affiliation, connection, and personal fulfillment through facilitating fulfillment in others (Basow, 1992; Miller, 1986).

Full-Time Fathers/Homemakers

As women have increasingly taken on the role of full-time worker and more couples are concerned equally with issues of child rearing and dual careers, the role of fathering in men's lives has begun to come to the attention of researchers and counselors. Although as yet few in number and less well documented, some men choose the role of full-time father/homemaker. Few researchers have turned their attention to fathers who take on this identity. Because of societal expectations and norms, it may be that they are more likely to have spent some of their adult lives in the paid workforce before undertaking the role of full-time parent and homemaker. What we can surmise is that in many ways they are similar to their female counterparts but that because they are seen as unusual they face issues that are at the same time like and unlike their male colleagues. Gender roles for men have been less fluid and more strictly defined than for women. Stereotypical images of males endorse strength, control, power, and restricted emotional involvement and range (O'Neil & Egan, 1992). Male workers are seen to be independent of, even disconnected from, their relational roles as fathers, husbands, and homemakers. Gender roles involve standards, expectations, and norms that any given male fits (or does not fit) in varying degrees (Levant & Pollack, 1995). The societal expectation for men is that they be full-time workers throughout their adult lives and that they should strive to succeed at all costs in a hierarchical structure (Levant & Pollack, 1995; Miller, 1986; Peterson & Gonzalez, 2000). Masculinity means providing financial support for their families as the good provider (Peterson & Gonzalez, 2000) as well as providing care and emotional support (Doherty, Kouneski, & Erickson, 1996; Levant & Pollack, 1995; Levine & Pitt, 1995). For men who are "stay-at-home dads," the first expectation is not realized in service to the latter two expectations. These men do not fit the traditional male reference group identity and may be see themselves as members of more than one reference group (Eisler, 1998). Consequently, when these men return to the workplace, they may have issues more closely aligned with female homemakers yet face challenges to their gender role identity because of the societal norms of what it means to be a man.

Expectations of the Delayed or Reentry Worker

Generally accepted is the concept of the gendered context of life in which males and females experience their worlds differently because of learned gender differences and societal expectations (Cook, 1993; Gysbers, Heppner, & Johnston, 1998; Matlin, 1996; Unger & Crawford, 1992). Sex role socialization in childhood and adolescence, and later in the workplace, determines internalized perceptions of male and female roles. Consequently, women's expectations of work may differ from men's. Despite advances toward workplace equity, perceptions of what types of work are available and what kinds of work will satisfy their needs are distinct for men and women. According to Astin (1984), this is a result of differences in expectations. Astin delineated a model of career choice and work behavior that is needs based. It offers a meaningful framework by which to understand the delayed or reentry worker of either gender and is applied here with this worker in mind.

Astin's Sociopsychological Model of Career Choice and Work Behavior

Astin's (1984) model suggests that one's expectations as workers are a function of three important factors: sex role socialization, the perceived structure of opportunity, and motivation. Each of these factors is explained in this section, and the impact on delayed and reentry workers is discussed in the section that follows it.

Sex Role Socialization

An impressive amount of literature suggests that women's reality in the workplace is different from men's (Gysbers et al., 1998). People begin to develop expectations about work in childhood through the process of socialization. Just as with other areas of life, individuals internalize the values of their society, their community, and their family about the meaning of work in their lives. In the case of work values, women and men learn sex-typed activities early. Gender role socialization can lead women and men to have different hierarchies of core personal values (Eccles, 1994). Girls tend to favor activities that involve nurturing others and engage in cooperative play. Socialization for boys, in contrast, means acquiring resources and engaging in competitive sports (Cosse, 1995). Although this has been changing in recent times, these messages were internalized in many delayed or reentry workers when they were young. Consequently, the traditional view is that women's early lessons and resultant values tend to be translated into sublimation of the self and direct service to others (Gilligan, 1982; Miller, 1986), whereas many men translate their lessons and values into tangible results such as money, power, and prestige through the vehicle of the world of work (Levant & Pollack, 1995).

Perceived Structure of Opportunity

The perceived structure of opportunity determines one's expectations and plays an integral and important role in one's work choices. Social change occurs as a result of major historical events and technological advances. This tends to account for the differences in generational and idiosyncratic expectations of career choice and work behavior. It may at least partially explain the wide variety of women's and men's attitudes and behaviors surrounding decisions about work itself. Astin (1984) described seven determinants of work expectations and behavior that constitute the structure of opportunity: (a) the distribution of jobs, (b) sex typing of jobs, (c) discrimination, (d) job requirements, (e) family structure, (f) advances in reproductive technology, and (g) the economy

Motivation

Three basic and interactive needs are motivators of work behavior. These are survival needs, pleasure needs, and contribution needs. "Survival needs are satisfied by means of the money earned through employment; pleasure comes from engaging in the work activity; and contribution needs are satisfied through the knowledge that [one's] work benefits others" (Astin, 1984, p. 120). McClelland (1961, 1965) identified three needs that act as motivators within organizational settings: need for achievement, need for power, and need for affiliation. Workers high in need for achievement prefer tasks of moderate difficulty and risk, want frequent and concrete feedback, and prefer pay that is contingent on their job performance. Workers high in need for power want control over others, visibility, status and prestige, and recognition. Workers high in need for affiliation want close interpersonal relationships and are especially sensitive to hostility and rejection. They avoid conflict and confrontation.

Implications of Astin's Model for Delayed and Reentry Workers

With the above explanations in mind, let us investigate how Astin's (1984) model might impact on delayed and reentry workers.

Sex Role Socialization

The implications for more traditional and quite often mature women are evident. They were socialized in a time when homemaking was viewed as the main and sometimes only meaningful area for need fulfillment. They learned to value home over work. Until recent times, women had few role models in the world of work. Research on cohorts who grew up before the influx of women into the workplace suggested that, although some career-oriented women tend to have been exposed to maternal models of work competence, most successful career women saw men, often their fathers, as their role models (Greenfield, Greiner, & Wood, 1980; Hackett, Esposito, & O'Halloran, 1989). Women who consider homemaking and child rearing as their main or only major work role view their role models as homemakers, usually their mothers. Consequently, they may have little understanding of the demands of the work world and possess little experience in how to negotiate the workplace culture. Reentry men, on the other hand, do not meet the traditional male model because they chose to stay home rather than work outside the home for pay. How they came to value home over work is not yet clearly researched. What is clear is that they have few if any same-sex role models in the home. Their sex role socialization suggests that by taking on the role and identity of full-time homemaker, they have not met their traditional "obligation" as men. They may face issues of shame and guilt associated with the male sex role (see Levant & Pollack, 1995). When returning to work, they may have an understanding of the demands of work through previous work experiences and because their role models were their working fathers. However, they may have incomplete knowledge of the major changes in workplace culture that have so quickly taken place in the global and information era.

Perceived Structure of Opportunity

The implications of the gendered context of life may have the greatest impact here. For the delayed or reentry woman, the structure of opportunity becomes particularly salient. Hers was the era when the inequitable distribution of jobs was a given, sex typing of jobs was assumed, discrimination may have gone unchallenged, and job requirements were more rigidly categorized by gender. Traditional men were beneficiaries of this system. However, many contemporary men believe that they are now as disadvantaged as women and discriminated against as much as women (Farrell, 1993; Kimmel, 1996). For the nontraditional male, this can contribute to gender role conflict.

For both men and women, the family structure, of course, might have been unique to his or her special circumstances, but the societal messages encouraged adherence to the two-parent, two-to-four-child household where father alone held a job and mother alone assumed the duties of the home. Today the structure of opportunity surrounding family issues has meant more choices and more freedom to create family structures with no one set standard being perceived as more important, necessary, or desirable than another. Work opportunities, therefore, are less dependent on the family structure.

The sociological impact of advances in reproductive technology cannot be overemphasized. When women were freed from nonvoluntary childbearing, the structure of opportunity changed for women, who no longer had to stay home to bear and rear children, and for men, who no longer had the sole responsibility to support those children through the single income they could generate.

The economy has had a varying impact on the lives of women and men. To some extent, this is age and life-stage dependent. Because the economy tends to be cyclical, whether or not either a man or woman can choose to leave or reenter the world of work depends on the availability or scarcity of jobs. For example, layoffs or downsizings could encourage some men to make the choice to be a full-time homemaker or propel some full-time female homemakers to seek full-time employment outside the home. In any case, before the worker is at the point of reentering the workplace, the economy most relevant to her or his life may have been the economy most directly related to being a consumer rather than a producer of goods and services

Motivation

For delayed or reentry workers, needs as motivators have relevance. Survival needs may motivate them to enter or reenter the workplace. Expectations may initially concern monetary rewards, whereas other needs may be viewed as having peripheral significance. As the delayed or reentry worker adjusts to the work environment, needs related to achievement, power, and affiliation may grow in significance. Pleasure and contribution needs may replace basic survival needs as primary motivators. Or, especially in the case of those for whom survival needs are not an initial issue, pleasure and contribution needs may be the important motivators initially, and money (survival) needs only later gain significance. For this delayed or reentry worker, need for recognition, power, or affiliation has primary significance. In each case, motivators change and needs expectations within the work world shift quickly.

Achievement needs may be significant for women who choose to enter or return to the workforce. Reentry women have been shown to score significantly higher on measures of achievement motivation than married career women (Erdwins, Tyler, & Mellinger, 1982). In a large-scale study of women's lives (Baruch, Barnett, & Rivers, 1983), themes of work and achievement dominated women's interviews. Close to half of those surveyed reported the most rewarding part of their lives was related to work and educational achievement. In fact, women viewed their work roles as a source of well-being and their nonwork roles as a source of stress and high strain (Barnett & Baruch, 1987), although there were marital status differences. In one study, compatibility between work and life roles was a concern for married women, whereas formerly married women valued autonomy and achievement (Erdwins & Mellinger, 1985). The need for achievement means that the delayed or reentry woman expects to perform tasks of moderate difficulty and risk, to receive concrete feedback for tasks undertaken, and to be paid contingent on her job performance.

One reason the work role provides a sense of well-being for women is that the organizational setting provides the means by which affiliation needs can be met. Full-time female homemakers report feelings of isolation and lack of meaningful relationships. Need for affiliation means that the delayed or reentry woman expects to form interpersonal relationships on her job. For women with affiliation needs, however, many may have difficulty distinguishing between social and professional relationships. Because relationship and connection play a primary part in many women's sense of well-being and sense of identity (Gilligan, 1982; Miller, 1986), some women typically avoid conflict and confrontation. They may be particularly sensitive to perceived or actual hostility and rejection.

No parallel studies on reentry men were found, and it may be that their motivators are more like those of traditional men once they make the transition to the workplace. If this is the case, they may not value affiliation needs as highly as traditional women. We could expect that the reentry man may place greater value on need for power. This means that they may be more likely than reentry women to seek power, visibility, status, prestige, and recognition. It may also be that they are more like delayed or reentry women. If this is the case, then reentry men may equally value need for achievement and may also value need for affiliation. Because research on returning men is scant in the counseling literature, no definitive conclusions can be drawn.

Whether man or woman, when one returns to the workforce after a lengthy hiatus or enters it for the first time at a mature age, he or she comes into the workplace setting with high expectations about affiliation and recognition or about power, achievement, and monetary reward. Regardless of which motivators are of most significance, the delayed or reentry worker has expectations of a chance to make a contribution in an area he or she may not have previously considered because of the structure of opportunity and his or her own sex role socialization.

Assets and Issues

With high expectations, many delayed or reentry workers come into the organizational world manifesting the enthusiasm usually exhibited by their younger colleagues, possessing the life experience generally considered the domain of the mature, and exhibiting the vitality and intensity of the "This is my last chance to make a difference" mid-life career changer. Yet for the person who is reentering the workplace after a lengthy absence or for the person who has never worked outside the home, insecurity, stress, and other emotions and uncertainties may be present. Changes have occurred in homes and family structures.

Delayed and reentry workers begin their careers for varied reasons. Although some fit neatly into the category of "empty nester" working for personal and professional fulfillment (Herr & Cramer, 1992), many return to work for other reasons. Financial reasons are common. In today's economy, it is usually necessary for both spouses to work. Some work to supplement their spouse's income or to pay for their children's college education; others to take over for their involuntarily unemployed spouses; and others, to increase revenues for their spouse's retirement income. Some may be coping with the ripple effect of spousal job loss with emotional responses such as depression, anger, and fear. Divorce and widowhood cause some people, usually women, to go unprepared into the world of work. These displaced homemakers experience ambivalence, role conflict, career indecision, or guilt. Social and psychological barriers can be real.

Workers in the labor force face constraints caused by the gendered context. Discrimination against working women, for example, still exists in subtle and indirect ways (Cook, 1993). Sexual harassment is faced by one third to half of women in the workplace (Aburdene & Naisbitt, 1992) and is becoming more common for men. There are, of course, tangible strides in workplace equity. Many women experience discernible indications of dignity, respect, and value in today's workplace climate. Nevertheless, the issue of comparable worth is still unresolved.

Returning employees' understanding of corporate culture may be fragmented, and they may have no realistic sense of how to assess their worth. Delayed and reentry workers, by virtue of the fact that they have been out of the workforce for a number of years, may tend to either devalue the contribution they can make to the workplace or to overvalue their past education and life experiences. Some may tend to seek and accept employment below their ability levels. They may not attempt salary negotiations. Some may accept first (and low) offers; others may demand unrealistically high figures and effectively shut themselves out of any offers. They may accept whatever offer they get, be happy to be working at all, and only later begin to be concerned about possible inequities in relation to other employees. Or, they may not understand that time at home does not directly translate into comparable time within the corporate structure and that innate ability does not equal skills honed over years in the world of work. They may perceive their age-related cohorts, both male and female, who have worked throughout the years as direct competitors. Resentments may surface.

The delayed and reentry worker may exhibit symptoms of low self-esteem (Brockner, 1988). Those with low self-esteem report a sense of powerlessness, a lack of authentic identity, and a fear in trust of self-direction (Wells & Marwell, 1976). Some are people of talent who until recently may not have seen themselves as achievers. This career "undershooting" highlights the low level of aspiration of some returning workers. Although there are no simple causes, at least in the case of women, this appears to be a combination of early childhood conditioning, occupational stereotyping, fear of failure, fear of success, and discriminatory hiring practices (Herr & Cramer, 1992).

Additional issues may surface. Feeling like the new and early-career worker that he or she is, the delayed or reentry worker will nonetheless face the bias and judgments facing the older worker. Although age discrimination in employment hiring practices has been reduced by federal mandate, career problems are heightened for the older worker. Hostility toward older workers may not be overt or common, but passive–aggressive policies and acts such as limited promotion opportunities are not unusual (Herr & Cramer, 1992). It is not uncommon for the views of older workers to be discounted and for their opinions to be ignored; they may have to work especially hard to have their point of view heard. For early-career older workers, this may be particularly difficult because they have not had years in the organizational structure to build up credibility.

Bias against older workers indicates a belief in a lack of flexibility, obsolescence of skills, and inability to retrain successfully (Peterson & Gonzalez, 2000). These biases seem to contradict the facts for older workers (Brewington & Nassar-McMillan, 2000). Many mature reentry workers may tend to be more flexible by virtue of their willingness to begin new lifestyles later in life. Many enter the workforce with updated skills as a result of their own retraining efforts. It is well documented that one of the fastest growing populations in educational institutions is the mature, returning woman. On the positive side, age has been found to be related to overall job satisfaction, job involvement, internal work motivation, and organizational commitment. It also is negatively related to job turnover (Rhodes, 1983).

Implications for Counselors

Counselors are in an ideal position to provide vehicles through which understanding and sensitivity can be enhanced for all employees. They should be aware of the special needs and issues of delayed and reentry workers and offer ways by which these employees can make a successful transition into the workplace setting. The following principles of good corporate management provide suggestions by which counselors can assist these workers.

1. In today's global economy, corporations have a responsibility to promote understanding about diversity in their own workplace. Employees need to have opportunities to be sensitized and made of aware of differences and similarities of various kinds. In the

case of the delayed and reentry worker, this principle can be of help in two ways:

    a. The delayed and reentry worker can learn about the nature of today's diverse workforce.

    b. Other workers can be provided with the opportunity to understand the issues involved in being a delayed or reentry worker.

2. Corporations and their managers bear the responsibility of orienting their workers to the corporate culture. Counselors in organizational settings are experts in discerning culture (processes, procedures, informal systems, mores, etc.) and educating their clients through career management processes. How much of corporate culture is clearly spelled out? How much is based on unspoken assumptions rather than on easily accessible policies? What may seem obvious to seasoned employees may not be to delayed and reentry workers.

3. Corporations and their managers need to teach all their employees what options are available to them for upward and lateral career progress. Whether through training seminars or through formal and informal communications lines, counselors can provide straightforward and clear information about career paths, career ladders, and so on. They can inform their clients about the mechanics by which upward mobility may be achieved. Although delayed and reentry workers may have had the benefit of career counseling that led to their employment, these nontraditional workers may be left to their own devices when it comes to career planning once they have secured employment. Because they may tend to devalue or overvalue their skills and abilities, they may not be in a position to understand what they qualify for or how they may position themselves to qualify in the future.

4. Corporations must take leading roles in training and retraining their workers to meet the needs of the global information age. New technologies demand new knowledge and new training. Counselors can play a role in internal and external communications. Training and education have been shown to be major vehicles for late entry and reentry into the world of work. Reentry workers should be trained to understand the impact of the work revolution. The past employment system has broken down, and there has been a major change in the nature of the

psychological contract between the individual and the organization (Watts, 1996). In this new era of the "boundaryless career"
(see Arthur & Rousseau, 1996) in which workers are in business
for themselves as free agents, manage their own career success,
and owe no loyalty to their employers, increased commitment
to in-house training either in classrooms or via the Internet
and other distance education formats could mean the opportunity to train reentry workers who are committed and loyal to
the employer.

5. Corporations must take a new look at older workers. The gray-
ing of America will continue. Although health care costs are a
concern, today's employees are capable of working longer and in
better health than those of earlier decades. Counselors as experts
in human development can provide leadership in disseminating
information about the relative health, commitment, and expertise of these older workers. For delayed and reentry workers, this
will create opportunities to have fuller careers in terms of years
of service and increased responsibilities.

6. Corporations must lead the way in eliminating the inequitable
distribution of jobs, sex stereotyping of jobs, and covert discrimination that still exists in society. To compete at the world-class
level, corporations must give each worker regardless of gender,
race, ethnicity, or age opportunities to contribute and succeed.
Counselors, with their humanistic orientation, multicultural
expertise, and knowledge of interpersonal relationships, can do
much to alleviate mistrust and conflict. They can diffuse appre-
hensions about the meaning of work and who is qualified to
do it and assist in preparing reentry workers for a more equi-
table workforce.

7. Humanistic models of corporate management are being implemented more often as the quest for quality continues. There is a
greater realization that the well-being of employees affects short-
and long-range corporate health. For example, work/life balance
programs have mushroomed as more women have gained positions of leadership in the workplace. Counselors can play a role
in translating new paradigms across the organizational structure.
Specifically, in reference to delayed and reentry workers, counselors can ensure that channels of communication are open and

running smoothly so that these employees may access whatever help they need in making a successful transition to full-time employee. Organizational socialization is important to work adjustment and can be facilitated by counselors (Swanson & Parcover, 1998). Counselors are well versed in communications styles, effective verbal communications, the meaning of nonverbals, and interpersonal relationships. They can offer orientation sessions on organizational culture and training sessions to those among the delayed and reentry population who are naive about such communications issues. Counselors in organizational settings also can offer career counseling and personal counseling to reentry workers who desire or need it. Special attention should be paid to motivators of these new employees. Other resources such as referrals to full-service Employee Assistance Programs (EAPs), as appropriate, should also be offered.

8. Corporations have begun to address mentoring relationships as viable means to employees' success and productivity. Increasingly, people in organizations recognize the benefits of mentoring relationships. Mentors are those with advanced experience and knowledge who provide support and facilitate the upward mobility of less experienced organizational members. Benefits include increased self-esteem, decreased alienation, increased job satisfaction, and career commitment (Soski & Godshalk, 2000). Mentoring has been shown to be important for men but essential for women (Ragins, 1989). For reentry workers of both genders, this may be especially important. Counselors can be instrumental in facilitating mentoring relationships.

Conclusion

Although sociological changes and historical realities indicate that few people will initially delay entry into the world of work, the trend toward stopping out of the workplace is likely to continue. Consequently, reentry workers of both genders, all races, ethnicities, and ages will increase. New theoretical models of adult development and transition may be needed to address the diversity of men's and women's experiences. Until such a time as new paradigms supplement existing ones, counselors are advised to individualize their counseling approaches to the diverse needs of returning workers.

References

Aburdene, P., & Naisbitt, J. (1992). *Megatrends for women.* New York: Villard Books.

Arthur, M. B., & Rousseau, D. M. (1996). *The boundaryless career: A new employment principle for a new organizational era.* New York: Oxford University Press.

Astin, H. S. (1984). The meaning of work in women's lives: A sociopsychological model of career choice and work behavior. *Counseling Psychologist, 12,* 117–126.

Barnett, R. C., & Baruch, G. K. (1987). Social roles, gender, and psychological distress. In R. C. Barnett, L. Beiner, & G. K. Baruch (Eds.), *Gender and stress* (pp. 122–143). New York: Free Press.

Baruch, G., Barnett, R. C., & Rivers, C. (1983). *Lifeprints: New patterns of love and work for today's woman.* New York: New American Library.

Basow, S. A. (1992). *Gender: Stereotypes and roles* (3rd ed.). Pacific Grove, CA: Brooks/Cole.

Brewington, J. O., & Nassar-McMillan, S. C. (2000). Older workers: Work-related issues and implications for counseling. *Career Development Quarterly, 49,* 2–15.

Brockner, J. (1988). *Self-esteem at work: Research, theory, and practice.* Lexington, MA: Lexington Books.

Cook, E. P. (1993). The gendered context of life: Implications for women's and men's career-life plans. *Career Development Quarterly, 41,* 227–237.

Cosse, W. J. (1995). Who's who and what's what? The effects of gender on development in adolescence. In B. R. Wainrib (Ed.), *Gender issues across the life cycle* (pp. 5–16). New York: Springer.

Dawis, R. V., & Lofquist, L. (1984). *A psychological theory of work adjustment: An individual differences model and its application.* Minneapolis: University of Minnesota Press.

Doherty, W. J., Kouneski, E. F., & Erickson, M. F. (1996). *Responsible fathering: An overview and conceptual framework.* Washington, DC: U.S. Department of Health and Human Services.

Eccles, J. S. (1994). Understanding women's educational and occupational choices: Applying the Eccles et al. model of achievement-related choices. *Psychology of Women Quarterly, 18,* 585–609.

Eisler, R. M. (1998). Male reference group identity dependence: Another concept of masculine identity to understand men? *Counseling Psychologist, 26,* 422–426.

Erdwins, C. J., & Mellinger, J. C. (1985). Reentry women after graduation. *Journal of Genetic Psychology, 147,* 437–446.

Erdwins, C. J., Tyler, Z. E., & Mellinger, J. C. (1982). Achievement and affiliation needs of young adult women and middle-aged women. *Journal of Genetic Psychology, 141,* 219–224.

Farrell, W. (1993). *The myth of male power.* New York: Berkely Publishing Group.

Gilligan, C. (1982). *In a different voice.* Cambridge, MA: Harvard University Press.

Greenfield, S., Greiner, L., & Wood, M. M. (1980). The "feminine mystique" in male-dominated jobs: A comparison of attitudes and background factors of women in male-dominated versus female dominated jobs. *Journal of Vocational Behavior, 17,* 291–309.

Gysbers, N. C., Heppner, M. J., & Johnston, J. A. (1998). *Career counseling: Process, issues, and techniques.* Boston: Allyn & Bacon.

Hackett, G., Esposito, D., & O'Halloran, M. S. (1989). The relationship of role model influences to the career salience of educational and career plans of college women. *Journal of Vocational Behavior, 35,* 164–180.

Herr, E. L., & Cramer, S. H. (1992). *Career guidance and counseling through the lifespan: Systematic approaches* (4th ed.). New York: HarperCollins.

Hershenson, D. B. (1996). Work adjustment: A neglected area in career counseling. *Journal of Counseling and Development, 74,* 442–446.

Isaacson, L. E., & Brown, D. (2000). *Career information, career counseling, and career development* (7th ed.). Boston: Allyn & Bacon.

Kimmel, M. (1996). *Manhood in America: A cultural history.* New York: Free Press.

Levant, R. F., & Pollack, W. S. (Eds.). (1995). *A new psychology of men.* New York: Basic Books.

Levine, J. A., & Pitt, E. W. (1995). *New expectations: Community strategies for responsible fatherhood.* New York: Families and Work Institute.

Matlin, M. (1996). *The psychology of women.* New York: Holt, Rinehart & Winston.

McClelland, D. C. (1961). *The achieving society.* New York: VanNostrand.

McClelland, D. C. (1965). N-achievement and entrepreneurship: A longitudinal study. *Journal of Personality and Social Psychology, 1,* 389–392.

Miller, J. B. (1986). *Toward a new psychology of women.* Boston: Beacon.

O'Neil, J. M., & Egan, J. (1992). Men's and women's gender role journeys: A metaphor for healing, transition, and transformation. In B. R. Wainrib (Ed.), *Gender issues across the life cycle* (pp. 107–123). New York: Springer.

Peterson, N., & Gonzalez, R. C. (2000). *The role of work in people's lives: Applied career counseling and vocational psychology.* Belmont, CA: Wadsworth/Thomson Learning.

Ragins, B. R. (1989). Barriers to mentoring: The female manager's dilemma. *Human Relations, 42,* 1–22.

Rhodes, S. R. (1983). Age-related differences in work attitudes and behavior: A review and conceptual analysis. *Psychological Bulletin, 93,* 328–367.

Sharf, R. S. (2002). *Applying career development theory to counseling* (3rd ed.). Pacific Grove, CA: Brooks/Cole.

Soski, J. J., & Godshalk, V. M. (2000). The role of gender in mentoring: Implications for diversified and homogenous mentoring relationships. *Journal of Vocational Behavior, 57,* 102–122.

Swanson, J. L., & Parcover, J. A. (1998). Annual review: Practice and research in career counseling and development—1997. *Career Development Quarterly, 47,* 98–134.

Unger, R., & Crawford, M. (1992). *Women and gender.* New York: McGraw-Hill.

Watts, A. G. (1996). Toward a policy for lifelong career development: A transatlantic perspective. *Career Development Quarterly, 45,* 41–53.

Wells, L. E., & Marwell, G. (1976). *Self-esteem: Its conceptualization and measurement.* Beverly Hills, CA: Sage.

12

....

Counseling Displaced Homemakers

Eugenie Joan Looby

isplaced homemakers are a population whose numbers have been steadily increasing since the 1970s. According to Benokraitis (1987), this population has been a concern of researchers, legislators, women's groups, and even journalists. Minimal mention of displaced homemakers has been made in the career counseling literature. Therefore, it is imperative that career counselors become aware of this special needs population and devise specific career information, counseling tools, and techniques that will help to maximize this population's career effectiveness.

The term *displaced homemakers* refers to women who have considered themselves primarily homemakers but now have to enter the labor market because of unexpected changes in their status or circumstances (Isaacson & Brown, 2000; Zunker, 2002). While the number of displaced homemakers is estimated between 7 and 30 million, it is difficult to predict accurate figures. Although they may range from 25 years to 65 years and older, the majority of displaced homemakers are between 35 and 64 years of age (Benokraitis, 1987), with the largest numbers consisting of middle-aged women. The crucial aspect of displaced homemakers is that they lack appropriate marketable and career-seeking skills (Benokraitis, 1987; But-ler & Weatherley, 1992; Castro, Dickstein, & Kane, 1990; Isaacson & Brown, 2000; Zunker, 2002).

This chapter focuses on the career development needs of displaced homemakers and explores ways in which career counselors can facilitate this population's transition into the workplace. The chapter is divided into five sections: (a) demographic profile and general characteristics, (b) Hopson and Adams's (1977) model of adult transitions, (c) workforce transition issues of displaced homemakers, (d) addressing the special career needs of displaced homemakers, and (e) practice implications.

A Demographic Profile of Displaced Homemakers

Displaced homemakers consist primarily of women who have marginal experience in the paid labor force because they have chosen to make a home and to care for their families. They become displaced from their career as homemakers with the loss of financial support through divorce, abandonment, disability, or death of the family breadwinner or through loss of government benefits (Benokraitis, 1987; Butler & Weatherley, 1992; Castro et al., 1990; Isaacson & Brown, 2000; New York State Association of Displaced Homemaker Center Directors, 2000). Although the numbers vary, there are an estimated 7 to 16 million displaced homemak-ers in the United States (Castro et al., 1990; New York State Association of Displaced Homemaker Center Directors, 2000), and these figures may be underestimated. Benokraitis (1987) classified a displaced homemaker as (a) an individual between 35 and 64 years who has worked in the home providing unpaid services to family members, (b) does not have a job, (c) has experienced or would find difficulty getting employment, and (d) relied exclusively on another family member's income but no longer receives it because of separation, death, or divorce.

Castro et al. (1990) contended that nearly 60% of displaced homemak-ers live below the poverty level and that many more American women are likely to experience the same fate. According to Castro et al. (1990), "about 22 million married women are out of the labor force, dependent on their husband's income. And many of these, asserts the Displaced Homemakers Network, based in Washington, 'are just a man away from poverty'" (p. 80). Additionally, rising midlife divorce rates and no-fault divorce laws, coupled with lack of eligibility for unemployment insurance, old age benefits, and Aid to Families With Dependent Children (AFDC), have placed many displaced homemakers in financially precarious circumstances (Benokraitis, 1987; Butler & Weatherley, 1992; Castro et al., 1990).

The most vulnerable of displaced homemakers are middle-aged women between the ages of 45 and 65 years, who are without male partners and have to assume the financial responsibilities. These women experience significantly higher poverty rates (U.S Bureau of Census, 1989). Additionally, with the aging of the baby boomers, the population of middle-aged women is predicted to grow to 31.5 million, with another 15% increase by 2010 (Butler & Weatherley, 1992; U.S Bureau of the Census, 1990). Furthermore, middle-aged women's financial futures are undoubtedly shaped by their circumstances in early and young adult life (Berlin & Jones, 1983; Elder, 1985; Gee & Kimball, 1987). One may therefore expect that the ranks of displaced homemakers will swell to alarming proportions. And these numbers do not include all the other classes of individuals such as single mothers, widows, and others who qualify as displaced homemakers.

Society conditions women to remain dependent on their husbands. Therefore, there are harsh financial penalties doled out to middle-aged women without male partners (Butler & Weatherley, 1992). Divorce and widowhood, for example, have a profound impact on displaced homemakers. Not only do they lack marketable skills but also they lose a substantial portion of income. Butler and Weatherley (1992) asserted:

> In the first year after divorce, a woman, on average, experiences a 73-percent decline in her standard of living, whereas an ex-husband experiences a 42-percent increase. Women who have been married longer—middle aged women—suffer the greatest financial loss after divorce. Divorce courts generally expect a woman without dependent children to support herself and will often consider a man's income to be his own, despite the sacrifices a woman may have made in helping her husband build his career and the fact that she may not be able to earn a livable wage. (p. 512)

Another factor is that displaced homemakers may have received AFDC benefits while raising children. With the loss of these benefits when children reach the age of 18, these women may have to find gainful employment. This is not a task that is accomplished easily. Displaced homemakers may have no skills and may have to accept menial jobs to sustain an income. Furthermore, many employers may be reluctant to hire middle-aged displaced homemakers because of their age and the perceived difficulties that these women may experience, such as health concerns, absenteeism, and lack of dependability.

According to Butler and Weatherley (1992), the Social Security Act ignores the plight of the middle-aged displaced homemakers because it is designed for dependent children and elderly people. Displaced homemakers have worked all their lives in the home and, when they lose their source of support, find it difficult to enter an unfriendly and unfamiliar labor market. The authors contended that a displaced homemaker, for example, will not receive social security disability insurance if she is injured while working in the home. Additionally, if she has received AFDC, she will not be eligible for such benefits when her children reach 18. Furthermore, a childless widow will not get benefits until she is 60, and Supplementary Security Income (SSI) and Disability Income (DI) are restricted to people with severe disabilities in the preretirement age group (Lopata & Brehm, 1986). The average age of widowhood is 56 (Block, Davidson, & Grambs, 1981); however, many AFDC mothers are still in their 40s when their children are grown. Thus, they are left financially vulnerable.

Castro et al. (1990, p. 80) concurred that Social Security and pensions are of little help because "A woman married for more than ten years typically collects no more than two-thirds the Social Security that she and her husband would have received. Ex-wives and widows rarely get more than half their spouse's pension." Tyson (1998) felt that many late-entering women pay severe consequences for delaying entrance into the workforce. Some of these consequences include occupying traditional female occupations that pay less, being less likely than men to receive pensions, having less savings than men, and having lower Social Security benefits than men because of less time spent in the workforce. Tyson also cautioned that today's liberal divorce laws place women at greater risk for financial difficulty in later life.

It is evident that loss of financial support through marital dissolution, death, abandonment, disability of the family breadwinner, or the loss of government benefits are among the most compelling reasons why displaced homemakers are thrust into the workforce. Displaced homemakers are at an additional disadvantage because they may have little or no employment history, possess obsolete training or skills, suffer from low levels of self-esteem, and function from an external locus of control (Kerka, 1988). Furthermore, this period of traumatic changes can be extremely stressful for these women. The next section presents a model for coping with adult transitions and stress that has utility for displaced homemakers.

Hopson and Adams's Model of Adult Transitions

Hopson and Adams (1977) presented a seven-stage model of coping with adult transitions. Although the model has been adapted to career transitions, it is extremely well suited to other adult crises. In Stage 1, called Immobilization, the individual suffers a loss, such as being fired from a job, losing a mate, or losing an important support system. This loss produces emotions such as shock, disbelief, incredulity, numbness, and immobilization. Depending on the individual's coping style, this stage may extend from 1 day to several months. Displaced homemakers may experience similar emotions when they are confronted with loss of financial support, divorce, abandonment, widowhood, or entering the workforce.

In Stage 2, referred to as Minimization, the individual attempts to trivialize, minimize, or deny the impact of the loss and convince himself or herself that all is well. Displaced homemakers may also deny the reality of their particular circumstances and continue to act in ways that reinforce the "way things were" or their previous lifestyle. In Stage 3, referred to as Self-Doubt, reality sets in and doubts about providing for oneself and others, doubts about assuming new responsibilities and tasks, and much anxiety about the future are evident. Displaced homemakers also experience insecurity about their marketability, concern about being responsible for others, and fear about their financial future.

Stage 4, called Letting Go, focuses on increased awareness of the situational realities and a recognition that decisions must be made about the future. The individual is less emotional and more pragmatic and begins to set goals and develop realistic plans. In this particular stage, displaced homemakers must set goals and make plans for the future that include employment, caretaking responsibilities, acquiring more educational and technical skills, and becoming a viable member of the workforce.

Stage 5 is referred to as Testing-Out. Here, the individual develops an increased sense of confidence and attempts to test out new skills, options, and behaviors. Similarly, with displaced homemakers, this is the juncture at which they may "test out" a number of options, especially those designed to facilitate successful integration into the workforce. Stage 6, Search for Meaning, involves understanding the present changes precipitated by the crisis and why these changes have occurred. Displaced homemakers may finally realize that they are indeed the sole providers and attempt to enhance specific skills that will help them meet their new role responsibilities more effectively. Finally, in Stage 7, Internalization, the individual has developed new coping mechanisms and has learned to manage the transitions effectively.

Hopson and Adams's (1977) model may alert career counselors about behaviors expected from adults who are in crisis; however, many displaced homemakers' financial crises and workplace transitions are not resolved neatly, especially those that are unanticipated and involuntary. Sharf (2002) agreed by indicating that "for some women, entry or reentry into the workforce can be traumatic. Particularly if reentry is due to divorce or death of a husband, a woman can find herself in an uncomfortable and unfamiliar position with sole responsibility for her income and survival, as well as the survival of her family" (p. 265). The next section discusses unanticipated crises that displaced homemakers may experience as they enter into the workforce.

Workforce Issues for Displaced Homemakers

Research has suggested that displaced homemakers are more likely to be unemployed longer, lose jobs instead of leaving them, have larger salary differentials when compared with males in similar jobs, are discouraged with work, and hold multiple jobs (Batten & Kestenbaum, 1976; Benokraitis, 1987; Klein, 1975; McEaddy, 1976). These and other employment problems continue to persist for displaced homemakers. Among the more frequent are the following: (a) lack of vocational preparation and skills, (b) caregiving and child-care difficulties, (c) inadequate education, (d) maintaining job stability, (e) age and sexual discrimination, (f) psychological concerns, (g) unfamiliarity with workplace laws, (h) salary inequities, and (i) inadequate support systems.

Displaced homemakers lack vocational preparation and current marketable skills (Benokraitis, 1987; Castro et al., 1990; Isaacson & Brown, 2000). Many displaced homemakers never intended to work. Furthermore, for the women who worked previously, their skills may be rendered obsolete in today's workplace. Additionally, many displaced homemakers may not have the requisite skills and expertise to acquire the kinds of jobs that will provide substantial income. Displaced homemakers frequently occupy menial, clerical, service, low-paying, and female-dominated occupations (Benokraitis, 1987; Tyson, 1998). And this cuts across displaced homemakers of all educational levels. Although many of these women are overqualified for these service positions, their economic circumstance often leaves them little choice of jobs.

Care-giving roles and responsibilities provide additional challenges. Displaced homemakers may have to juggle taking care of children, parents, or a sick relative in addition to working. The low-paying jobs in which they may engage usually do not offer the flexibility, ability, and mechanisms to balance their additional responsibilities, for example, compensatory time, personal and sick leave, and flexible work schedules. This presents additional dilemmas, particularly with making choices about going to work or taking care of a sick child or family member.

Displaced homemakers may not have the requisite educational preparation to secure suitable, well-paying jobs. Because they have been absent from the workforce, knowledge relating to job-seeking skills, interviewing skills, resume preparation, and dressing for success may be additional things for which these woman are totally unprepared (Castro et al., 1990). Furthermore, they may be competing with younger, more educated, career-minded employees. If immediate financial compensation is necessary, displaced homemakers may not have the luxury of obtaining additional training or job preparation skills. Therefore, service and clerical occupations that do not require special skills or educational qualifications may be the easiest, quickest jobs available. Benokraitis (1987) contended that some displaced homemakers may have unrealistic job expectations. This may be due to lack of sophistication with the labor market and the unwillingness of more educated displaced homemakers to accept entry-level positions.

Benokraitis (1987) indicated that frequent job changes are common among displaced homemakers. Reasons for this phenomenon include unfamiliarity with the work environment, caregiving responsibilities, lack of skills, lack of education, health problems, and job dissatisfaction. Benokraitis argued that because displaced homemakers change jobs frequently, it is difficult for them to establish seniority and job stability, they are usually the first to get laid off, and they are poorly paid. Not having a credible work history may be a stumbling block to displaced homemakers obtaining suitable employment.

It is not uncommon for displaced homemakers to experience age and gender employment discrimination (Benokraitis, 1987; Butler & Weatherley, 1992; Tyson, 1998). Employers may prefer to hire younger women because of their productivity, longevity, and quicker cognitive abilities.

Additionally, some employers may not want to invest in retraining older individuals. Younger women may not experience as many health problems as older women, and it may be more cost-effective to hire younger individuals. Also, because displaced homemakers usually occupy female-dominated jobs, employers may not consider hiring them for non-traditional occupations.

The multiple unanticipated traumas in displaced homemakers' lives may result in mental health issues such as low self-esteem, stress, poor coping skills, lack of assertiveness, and unanticipated grief and loss. These difficulties can affect their transition into the workplace (Hanna, 2002; Isaacson & Brown, 2000; Sharf, 2001). For example, displaced home-makers may feel inadequate in the workplace because of a lack of transfer-able skills, and their lack of self-esteem may disable them from seeking employment comparable with their skills. They may also have unrealistic job expectations fostered by misinformation about the job market, and they may not know how to be assertive in the workplace, especially in cases of sexual harassment or discrimination or when other rights have been violated. Each of these situations may adversely impact displaced homemakers' self-esteem and self-efficacy.

Similarly, displaced homemakers may not be familiar with workplace laws pertaining to job discrimination and sexual harassment. Protecting their financial livelihood may prevent them from speaking out. They may feel that such action will result in job loss, retaliation, ostracism, being taken advantage of, and exploitation.

Displaced homemakers usually seek immediate employment and accept the first job that can allow them to meet their financial obligations. These jobs are often menial, and the decision to pursue them is usually made quickly. Such jobs provide few benefits such as health coverage and flexible work schedules, offer no pension, allow little opportunity for saving assets, and will not increase the women's social security benefits (Tyson, 1998). In addition to the wide salary inequities between com-parable male and female occupations, displaced homemakers will often accept jobs that men will not pursue. Therefore, economic compensation is often inadequate to meet displaced homemakers' financial needs.

Finally, although the loss of their major financial support system is traumatic, displaced homemakers must also contend with finding addi-tional support systems, which will enable them to balance work and changing role responsibilities. For example, support systems that address displaced homemakers' physical, emotional, and financial needs, along with child care, housing, skills training, and self-enhancement issues, will help these women to normalize their situation. The next section addresses ways in which career counselors can intervene in addressing the special needs of displaced homemakers to facilitate their transition into the workplace

Addressing the Special Career Needs of Displaced Homemakers

Displaced homemakers have special needs that must be addressed before they can effectively participate in the labor market. The needs will depend on whether these women are seeking immediate employment, are willing to enter training programs, or are willing to engage in career exploration. While this discussion is specifically tailored to displaced homemakers, it may be equally relevant to all women in the workforce.

Zunker (2002) claimed that many women place internal restrictions on themselves when they consider reentering the labor force. Women who have considered nontraditional careers place internal restrictions on themselves by believing that they are not qualified for such careers. Displaced homemakers who have had little exposure to career exploration activities frequently select traditional, female-dominated, low-paying, clerical, and service occupations. They may have limited options and lack the necessary confidence and assertiveness to pursue other career alternatives. Career counselors can help to educate displaced homemakers about nontraditional employment options and offer options more suited to their talents and skills.

The prospect of entering the workforce can be a daunting one for displaced homemakers who have never worked. These women may question their skills, abilities, and self-efficacy surrounding workplace success (Sharf, 2001). Bandura's (1986) self-efficacy theory focuses on people's judgments about their own abilities to manage or accomplish tasks. Several authors (Hackett & Betz, 1981; Lent, Brown & Hackett, 1994) have proposed that people's perceptions about themselves prevent them from choosing particular careers or even advancing in those that they presently occupy. These authors used the example of women who have been conditioned not to study math and science because they are expected to do poorly. Displaced homemakers with low levels of self-esteem and poor career preparation skills may doubt their ability to succeed in the workplace, become discouraged and overwhelmed with their responsibilities, and leave tasks incomplete. Lack of familiarity with the workplace engenders self-doubt, low levels of self-efficacy, and failure to sustain employment. Career counselors should help displaced homemakers identify goals and tasks that can increase their self-efficacy. If this does not occur, then displaced homemakers will continue to question their abilities and career potential.

Displaced homemakers have found their identities with their husbands and families. Losing these systems that were critical to their financial security and self-identity can be devastating. Such crises may force displaced homemakers to engage in new behaviors such as becoming independent and assertive. Learning independence includes making decisions about career and personal responsibilities, establishing new roles, and adopting tasks that were the purview of the breadwinner. These roles can be disconcerting for displaced homemakers, both in the home and in the workplace. For example, engaging in tasks that require independent work and quick decision-making skills and adopting leadership roles may be difficult. Displaced homemakers may also lack the assertiveness to allow their voices to be heard, especially if they are being treated unfairly in the workplace. They may believe that being assertive may mean losing their jobs, especially in cases of sexual harassment or discrimination. It is therefore imperative that career counselors provide opportunities for displaced homemakers to work on leadership, assertiveness, decision-making skills, and developing independence. These skills are invaluable in the workplace.

Sharf (2001) reiterated the impact of outcome expectations and goal setting on workplace success. When working with displaced homemakers, it is important that career counselors identify their strengths and weaknesses and help them to set realistic and attainable occupational goals. Literature (e.g., Benokraitis, 1987) suggests that displaced homemakers select jobs for which they may be overqualified or those that are unattainable. It is important that these women have a realistic appraisal of their potential to maximize successful career outcomes. Setting realistic goals and engaging in tasks that portend success, increase displaced homemakers' self-efficacy and work satisfaction.

Displaced homemakers are unfamiliar with the work environment. Therefore, programs that educate these women about workplace expectations are critical to their success. Zunker (2002) felt that such programs should include topics that address workplace expectations, communication skills, promotions, and job benefits, among others. Additionally, displaced homemakers reentering the workforce should be educated about career options other than the ones in which many find themselves (clerical, service, and menial). They should be given ample information to pursue a wide range of career options. Displaced homemakers should also be educated about relevant workplace federal laws, such as those under Title VII of the Civil Rights Act of 1964 and Title IX of the Educational Amendments of 1972. These laws address issues such as discrimination, adequate compensation, and educational opportunities (Zunker, 2002). Displaced homemakers should be aware that in the workplace, they are provided protections under federal law.

Locus of control, a concept developed by Rotter (1975), measures the degree to which individuals feel that they control their lives (internal locus of control) as opposed to others, luck, chance, or fate (external locus of control). Displaced homemakers will probably rate low on internal locus of control and high on external locus of control. Individuals who function with an internal locus of control take charge of their environment, have a desire to succeed, believe in themselves and their skills, are motivated to do well in their jobs, accept responsibility for decisions, and make better employees (Hanna, 2002). Displaced homemakers reentering the workforce have to develop an internal locus of control in which they feel that they are competent and responsible for their performance and their own lives. Developing an internal locus of control can empower displaced homemakers to practice new behaviors and set and achieve individual goals. Instead of waiting for things to happen, they can make things happen. Developing an internal locus of control can also increase displaced homemakers' self-esteem and self-efficacy, thus leading to better career choices and outcomes.

Low levels of self-confidence and self-esteem may also plague displaced homemakers (Benokraitis; 1987; Isaacson & Brown, 2000; Kerka, 1988) caused by a variety of reasons. For example, those who are divorced may blame themselves for the divorce. Their lack of marketable skills may engender feelings of inadequacy in the workplace. These women devalue their strengths because they have not been equipped to enter the workforce; they feel at a disadvantage with other coworkers; they may doubt their skills and feel that nothing they learned previously is transferable. Additionally, coworkers and even the boss may cause them to doubt their abilities. If displaced homemakers attempt tasks and are unsuccessful, such failure may diminish their confidence as individuals and competent workers. Efforts should be made to modify these women's self-concept and self-esteem through counseling and other avenues. Career counselors must assess displaced homemakers' strengths and weaknesses and encourage them to work on tasks that involve success building. Successful completion of such tasks helps build self-esteem and improves confidence and competence. Displaced homemakers must acquire high levels of self-confidence and self-esteem if they are to succeed in the workplace.

Displaced homemakers enter the labor market lacking occupational information and job search/seeking skills. What skills and information they do possess are obsolete, and they have unrealistic expectations about the world of work. It is important that they are provided with the most current career information, including job-seeking techniques, how to use occupational information, exploring a wide range of career options, and information about potential problems in the workplace (Zunker, 2002). Further programs should be put into place for displaced homemakers that cover topics such as basic interviewing skills, dressing for success, communication patterns, assertiveness training, developing self-esteem, and other skills that may prove invaluable in the workplace. If the displaced homemaker has time to enter a training program, this would be to her benefit. However, if she must find employment immediately, then she may not be afforded the opportunity to participate in such a program.

Isaacson and Brown (2000) emphasized the importance of identifying support systems that displaced homemakers can utilize as their roles shift. For example, displaced homemakers may need support with child care or caregiving if there is a sick or disabled spouse in the home. They may need support with housing and taking care of basic survival needs. Social service agencies, employment centers, professional counselors, and other entities may provide invaluable economic, emotional, and social support. In addition, displaced homemakers may seek support from family, friends, the church, and ministers. Displaced homemakers also have to struggle with grief and loss issues, especially in the case of death of a spouse. Career counselors should familiarize themselves with these women's needs and with resources that can help them. If these needs are not met, then the displaced homemaker's productivity and employment outcomes may be compromised.

Displaced homemakers may experience significant amounts of trauma and stress as they attempt new roles. Many may have to work and balance child rearing and caregiving, take care of the household, and assume new responsibilities. Additionally, they may be confronted with personal issues such as grief and loss, lack of assertiveness, and low levels of self-esteem, and they may be overwhelmed with the crisis in which they find themselves. They may have no support systems and feel totally overwhelmed.

These stressors may build to crisis proportions and can lead to unhealthy consequences, such as substance abuse, burnout, and many physical and psychological problems. If the stress is not alleviated, it can spill over into the workplace and may be manifested in tardiness, absenteeism, carelessness, missed days, incomplete tasks, poor disposition, violence, lack of concentration, and unclear thinking. Because of these internal and external stressors experienced by displaced homemakers, career counselors must intervene and help these women devise effective ways of handling stress. For example, identifying community support systems and referring these women to support groups may prove beneficial. Additionally, teaching displaced homemakers skills such as prioritizing, eliminating self-defeating thoughts, time management, decision making, and encouraging them to engage in hobbies, maintain healthy lifestyles, exercise, and develop a sense of humor may help to relieve stress (Hanna, 2002).

Sexual harassment in the workplace continues to plague women and affects them physically, emotionally, and financially (Hanna, 2002; Isaacson & Brown, 2000; Sharf, 2002; Zunker, 2002). Individuals disagree about what constitutes sexual harassment; however, according to Hanna (2002, p. 245) the legal definition of sexual harassment given by the Equal Employment Opportunity Commission (EEOC) in 1980 is as follows:

> Harassment behaviors are unwelcome sexual advances, requests for sexual favors, and other verbal or physical conduct of a sexual nature. Sexual harassment is present when submission or rejection of such behavior is made a term or condition of employment; is used in employment decisions; or creates an intimidating, hostile or offensive working environment. The conduct may be verbal or physical and may also include the circulation of sexually explicit photographs or literature.

Displaced homemakers may be particularly vulnerable to sexual harassment. Unfortunately, instances of sexual harassment can pose painful challenges and dilemmas. For example, because the job may be these women's only source of income, reporting the harassment may result in job loss and not reporting it may result in devastating emotional and physical consequences. They may feel powerless to do anything about the harassment and fear being ostracized, not believed, or blamed for causing the harassment. Career counselors should educate women about their legal remedies if they are targets of sexual abuse. Moreover, every woman should be familiar with how the company in which she works or plans to work handles sexual harassment complaints before she accepts a position. A potential problem still exists if the company does not have a sexual harassment policy; however, the woman can still contact the EEOC if there is no company remedy for her grievance.

Discrimination in the workplace is an issue that displaced homemakers may face. With midlife women, this may be particularly evident in areas such as age, race, and financial compensation (Benokraitis, 1987; Butler & Weatherley, 1992). Employees may prefer to hire younger workers because they may be perceived as more productive, reliable, stable, and skilled. Furthermore, employers may not want to invest resources into training older employees whose longevity with the company may be questionable. The salary patterns for women and minorities differ, as do the hiring patterns (Sharf, 2001; Tyson, 1998). Women may move in and out of the workforce more frequently than men and make less money than men because they tend to occupy lesser paying jobs (Sharf, 2001). Even though it is illegal, gender, race, religious, and age discrimination continue to exist in the workplace, as well as awarding privileges and promotions unfairly. Career counselors should educate displaced homemakers about avenues for remedying discrimination, such as filing a complaint with the EEOC. Although protections such as the 1964 Civil Rights Act and the Americans With Disabilities Act exist, redressing injustices in the workplace is one of the most effective means of ensuring that everyone has equal career opportunities.

Displaced homemakers face many challenges as they move from the security of being a homemaker to the world of work. The next section includes specific recommendations and practice implications for career counselors who work with displaced homemakers.

Practice Implications

The following are suggestions gleaned from the career development literature for facilitating displaced homemakers' reentry or entry into the workforce (Benokraitis, 1987; Butler & Weatherley, 1992; Castro et al., 1990; New York State Association of Displaced Homemaker Center Directors, 2000; Isaacson & Brown, 2000; Kerka, 1988; Sharf, 2001, 2002, Tyson 1998; Zunker, 2002).

- Career counselors should assess the displaced homemaker's knowledge and skills and secure career placements that provide maximum utilization of these skills.

- Career counselors should be familiar with employment trends and employment agencies and use these resources to secure employment for displaced homemakers.
- Career counselors should be familiar with training and educational programs that address the mental, physical, and career needs of displaced homemakers and encourage them to participate in such programs. For example, programs might include career preparation skills, self-enhancement skills, and addressing mental health issues such as stress, coping, developing self-esteem and assertiveness, and health and wellness, among others.
- Career counselors should identify and refer displaced homemakers to support groups that address many of the issues that they have to confront.
- Career counselors should be familiar with federal and state job-training programs and encourage displaced homemakers to take advantage of these programs.
- Career counselors should be aware of the barriers that displaced homemakers face, such as harassment, discrimination, and lack of support services. They should be able to devise solutions that may reduce or eliminate such barriers.
- Career counselors should help displaced homemakers to set realistic career goals that are congruent with their specific life circumstances and skills.
- Career counselors should be familiar with social service and other agencies and resources that can provide displaced homemakers with assistance such as daycare, housing, caregiving, health concerns, and legal issues.
- Career counselors should be familiar with organizations and agencies that can provide financial assistance to displaced homemakers who are transitioning from home to work.
- Career counselors should be familiar with specific federal laws that deal with sexual harassment, discrimination, and any other policies that affect displaced homemakers' employment.
- Career counselors should encourage displaced homemakers to participate in individual, family, and group counseling.
- Career counselors should utilize the resources of the church and family to enhance their work with displaced homemakers.
- Career counselors should help displaced homemakers build new sources of support to replace ones that were lost.

- Career counselors should encourage displaced homemakers to address grief and loss and other mental health concerns they may be experiencing before they enter the workplace.
- Career counselors should serve as advocates for displaced homemakers and support policies created to address their needs.
- Career counselors should be familiar with federally funded programs that are specifically designed to meet the needs of displaced homemakers.

Conclusion

The population of displaced homemakers has grown tremendously since the early 1970s, and the numbers will steadily increase. Displaced homemakers did not plan to enter the workforce but have been thrust into it because of loss of their financial support system. They lack the career sophistication of individuals who have deliberately charted their occupational futures. Therefore, they have very different needs. In addition to addressing occupational concerns, career counselors must ensure that the psychological, social, emotional, and survival needs of displaced homemakers are met to enable their occupational success.

References

Bandura, A. (1986). *Social foundations of thought and action: A social cognitive theory*. Englewood Cliffs, NJ: Prentice Hall.

Batten, M. D., & Kestenbaum, S. (1976). Older people, work, and full employment. *Social Policy, 7*, 30–35.

Benokraitis, N. (1987). Older women and reentry problems: The case of displaced homemakers. *Journal of Gerontological Social Work, 10*, 75–92.

Berlin, S., & Jones, L. E. (1983). Life after welfare: AFDC termination among long-term recipients. *Social Service Review, 57*, 378–402.

Block, M. R., Davidson, J. L., & Grambs, J. D. (1981). *Women over forty*. New York: Springer.

Butler, S. S., & Weatherley, R. A. (1992). Poor women at midlife and categories of neglect. *Social Work, 37*, 510–516.

Castro, J., Dickstein, L., & Kane, J. (1990, Fall). Caution: Hazardous work. *Time, 136*, 79–80.

Elder, G. (1985). *Life course dynamics: Trajectories and transitions, 1968–1980*. Ithaca, NY: Cornell University Press.

Gee, E. M., & Kimball, M. M. (1987). *Women and aging*. Toronto, Ontario, Canada: Butterworths.

Hackett, G., & Betz, N. (1981). A self-efficacy approach to the career development of women. *Journal of Vocational Behavior, 18*, 326–339.

Hanna, S. (2002). *Career by design: Communicating your way to success* (2nd ed.). Englewood Cliffs, NJ: Prentice Hall.

Hopson, B., & Adams, J. D. (1977). Towards an understanding of transitions: Defining some boundaries of transition. In J. Adams, J. Hayes, & B. Hopson (Eds.), *Transition: Understanding and managing personal change* (pp. 1–19). Montclair, NJ: Allenheld & Osmun.

Isaacson, L. E., & Brown, D. (2000). *Career information, career counseling, and career development* (7th ed.). Needham Heights, MA: Allyn & Bacon.

Kerka, S. (1988). Single parents: Career-related issues and needs. *ERIC Digest, 75*, 1–3.

Klein, D. P. (1975). Women in the labor force: The middle years. *Monthly Labor Review, 11*, 10–16.

Lent, R. W., Brown, S. D., & Hackett, G. (1994). Toward a unified social cognitive theory of career and academic interest, choice, and performance. *Journal of Vocational Behavior, 45*, 79–122.

Lopata, H. Z., & Brehm, H. P. (1986). *Widows and dependent wives: From social problem to federal program.* New York: Praeger.

McEaddy, B. J. (1976). Women who head families: A socioeconomic analysis. *Monthly Labor Review, 6*, 3–9.

New York State Association of Displaced Homemaker Center Directors. (2000, March). *Displaced homemaker program of New York State Association of Displaced Homemaker Center Directors.* Retrieved from http://www.wdsny.org

Rotter, J. (1975). Some problems and misconceptions related to the construct of internal versus external control of reinforcement. *Journal of Consulting and Clinical Psychology, 43*, 56–67.

Sharf, R. (2001). *Life's choices: Problems and solutions.* Pacific Grove, CA: Brooks/Cole

Sharf, R. (2002). *Applying career development theory to counseling* (3rd ed.). Pacific Grove, CA: Brooks/Cole.

Tyson, A. S. (1998). For many older women, retirement is a luxury they can't afford. *Christian Science Monitor, 90*, 9–11.

U.S. Bureau of the Census. (1989). Poverty in the United States: 1987. *Current Population Reports, Series P-60, No. 163.* Washington, DC: U.S. Government Printing Office.

U.S. Bureau of the Census. (1990). *Statistical abstract of the United States* (10th ed.). Washington, DC: U.S. Government Printing Office.

Zunker, V. G. (2002). *Career counseling: Applied concepts of life planning* (6th ed.). Pacific Grove, CA: Brooks/Cole.

13

The Storied Approach: A Constructivist Perspective on Counseling Dual-Career Couples

Michael E. Hall and Nancy E. Huenefeld

This chapter presents the Employee Assistance Program (EAP) counselor with a pragmatic approach for assisting dual-career couples with their unique career and relationship dilemmas. Highlighted are critical elements from selected dual-career couple and career development theories, research, and counseling practices. Constructivist career theory is overviewed as an introduction to contemporary career theory. A narrative or storied approach is presented as a constructivist strategy for the practice of employment or career counseling because of its face validity for the counselor with limited training in the methodologies of career, marital, and relationship counseling. The storied approach is then applied to three dual-career couples; each case illustrates one of the three aspects of the

We gratefully acknowledge the useful comments received from Pamelia E. Brott and Doug Scheaffer.

constructivist approach (i.e., co-construction, deconstruction, and reconstruction) and a different category of the major types of dual-career couple challenges. The chapter concludes with a summary of the limitations of dual-career couple theory, research, and practice implications.

Dual-Career Couple Issues

Rapoport and Rapoport (1971) are credited with introducing the term *dual-career couple*. Although 30 years have passed, little research and theory development have focused on the issues of dual-career couples. As a result, the literature is composed mostly of anecdotal rationales for how to assist dual-career couples. This section overviews the extant literature on theory, research, and counseling methods for dual-career couples.

If dual-earner couples are defined as where both partners are members of the paid workforce, yet at least one person works for nonmaterial or other motivational reasons, then dual-career couples is "where both partners are highly career-committed, and view employment as an essential part of their self-definition" (Stoltz-Loike, 1992, p. xxi). The dual-earner couples are also distinguished by one partner's job being viewed as more important, which can allow the subordinate career partner to work part time (McDonald, 1999). By contrast, in dual-career couples, both partners take great professional and personal pride in their careers (Maples, 1981). (For further delineation of working couples [e.g., entrepreneurial, co-entrepreneurial couples], see Marshack, 1998.)

With its genesis in the sociopolitical context of the 1970s to 1980s, the early dual-career couple literature reflected interest in women's growing participation in the workforce, in general, and, in particular, their entrance into the "professional" (i.e., "careers" versus "jobs") ranks. As is customary with new lines of knowledge, early dual-career couple research began with definitions and descriptions of lifestyle (e.g., marital quality/satisfaction and mother–child relationship issues). This professional interest contributed to the popularization of such terms as *role strain, male privilege, backlash*, and *mommy track*.

While the aforementioned view of the early dual-career couple literature may cast a somewhat negative valence (i.e., focus on the negative consequences) on the lifestyle, the benefits of the dual-career couple lifestyle have not gone unreported. For example, Argyle (1989) observed that preliminary research indicated that married women with careers made for a "more satisfied wife" (p. 69) and that multiple roles (i.e., shifting roles between home and work) recharged women, in counter distinction to draining them (Wilcox-Matthew & Minor, 1989). Moreso, men reported being very satisfied with their dual-career relationship (Stevens, Kiger, & Riley, 2001).

Specific relationship benefits have also been identified. In dual-career couples, the commonality of roles between spouses or partners—both being involved in "home" and work—gives them numerous elements to talk about and increases the quality and solidarity of the marriage. By having a balance, and feeling accomplished and fulfilled through a career, women tend to value and look forward to family time more than when women do not work. Positive effects are perceived in the mother–child relationship when both parents are employed, even while no direct negative effects on the children are reported. Also, in dual-career families, parents serve as role models that help expand their children's career and relationship/lifestyle options (Easterbrooks & Goldberg, 1985; Wilcox-Matthew & Minor, 1989).

Arguably, the most significant nonrelational benefit of the dual-career couple lifestyle is in the financial realm. Although dual-career couples have financial issues, having two incomes increases their standard of living and thus decreases the potential of large-scale problems that other couples experience. For example, having two high-paying incomes reduces the fear of a partner losing a job.

Being a dual-career couple means that both individuals are committed to developing a meaningful career (i.e., extensive formal education, developmental or progressive career path), while also pursuing the pleasure of a nuclear family (whether with or without children) that presents a unique constellation of challenges. Most of what is written about these issues is anecdotal and based on clinical work; however, some preliminary research exists. (An overview of these issues is presented, yet the reader is encouraged to use the references to explore these issues further.)

There are five main issue areas that are prominent in the dual-career couple literature: equity, housework, synchronicity, social support, and parenting. The first issue, equity, is not a dual-career couple issue exclusively, yet it is prominent among dual-career couples because of limited resources (e.g., energy, time, and support systems). Work and family can be competing demands, often leading to role overload and little time for intimacy (Farber, 1988). Balancing individual and couple needs and maintaining a personal identity are very challenging (Goldenberg & Goldenberg, 1984). For most couples, balancing is still seen as the woman's responsibility. Research by Becker and Moen (1999) has shown that scaling back activities (such as work, community work, social activities) has helped couples adjust, however, again with "women disproportion[ately] do [ing] the scaling back" (p. 995).

Equity issues are more prevalent when both members of the couple value the same things, which can include activities, life roles, recognition, and support from a partner. In comparison with more traditional types of couples, marriage appears to be central to both men and women's identities in dual-career couples. In addition, work was found to be important for both women's and men's health and well-being. More exclusive to dual-career couples is the expression that competition and selfishness are significant relational issues. These competitive and selfishness issues include: competition for time, time with each other, same resources, and perceiving one partner as getting ahead in her or his career (see Barnett & Rivers, 1996; Glickauf-Hughes, Hughes, & Wells, 1986; Thomas, 1990).

Another common issue for dual-career couples is housework. Even in the 21st century, women still do most of the housework, and this includes in dual-career couples. This imbalance of responsibility at home is a major source of marital dissatisfaction for women (Thomas, 1990). In fact, satisfaction of task division at home was a significant predictor for both men and women's marital satisfaction (see Stevens et al., 2001, for further research information). Time spent on housework takes away valuable family and social time (see Stevens et al., 2001; Thomas, 1990).

Synchronicity is the coordination or timing of education/training, level, or trajectory within a career for a dual-career couple. Specific issues of asynchronicity include differences in when partners begin their career, when levels of advancement occur, and when a partner pursues more education. For example, how does the launching of one's career prior to becoming a couple affect how most career decision making occurs after they become a couple? Another example is the decision about who will (and when to) quit or cut back work hours to assume primary child-care/parenting roles. By adjusting for children, the couple's chances to advance, seniority, and earning power can be affected negatively (Barnett & Rivers, 1996; Sekaran & Hall, 1989, as cited in Sperry, 1993).

Although there is no clear line of research in this area, dual-career couples may be expected to have support system issues, consistent with other relational populations. Because dual-career couples are still a new lifestyle phenomena, there is a lack of role models from whom to learn. Changing geographic locations, for example, to accommodate their careers, dual-career couples may lose good external support (e.g., not being able to access family members who live nearby). Similarly, with very busy schedules, dual careerists may experience real constraints on their availability to develop and maintain new relationships with families and friends (Farber, 1988).

Children can be an enriching part of a dual-career couple's lives. In dual-career couples, both partners appear very invested in their families. For example, fatherhood is critical for emotional health for men, and men view fatherhood as central to their lives. Although children are valued in dual-career couples, the realities of filled calendars means frequent life adjustments (e.g., finding daycare, nurturing couple intimacy).

Increased father participation, when to have or adopt children, and which partner "flexes" for emergencies are all parenting issues requiring negotiation. These issues are particularly demanding of support systems during preschool ages (see Barnett & Rivers, 1996; Thomas, 1990).

Career Development Theory and Counseling Practice

In this section, traditional and contemporary approaches to career development and counseling are briefly described. We then review an intervention based on the constructivist perspective. Following the intervention model are case examples illustrating the application of the constructive framework to counseling dual-career couples. Our hope is to provide counselors with a strategy and techniques for working with dual-career couples, a variation of the individual employee presenting for career counseling in the organizational or private setting.

Summarizing the status of career development scholarship, Brown (1996) observed that among the traditional theories, trait-oriented, learning-based, and developmental theories continue to be most influential on both career practice and research. However, challenging logical positivism, the philosophical root system of traditional theories, is the postmodern worldview that emerged in the 1990s. This epistemological view has been translated into contemporary career [meta]theories such as contextualism and constructivism.

Contemporary Career Development Theory

Brown and Brooks (1996) noted that while the traditional theories of career development are rooted in the philosophical position of logical positivism, there is a growing interest among social scientists in a contemporary approach: constructivism. Constructivism departs from positivism's assumption that the contexts or environments in which career development occurs are neutral or relatively unimportant. Taking issue with this assumption, constructivism holds that context is most important and that instead of passively accepting an existing reality, individuals are indeed active in constructing their own reality. The main assumptions of constructivism can be summarized as follows:

1. All aspects of the universe are interconnected; it is impossible to separate figure from ground, subject from object, people from their environments.
2. There are no absolutes; thus human functioning cannot be reduced to laws or principles, and cause and effect cannot be inferred.
3. Human behavior can only be understood in the context in which it occurs.
4. The subjective frame of reference of human beings is the only legitimate source of knowledge. Events occur outside human beings. As individuals understand their environments and participate in these events, they define themselves and their environments. (Brown & Brooks, 1996, p. 10)

Constructivist Career Counseling

The logical positivist worldview, which dominated the first half of the 20th century, resulted in the practice of career counseling adopting a problem-solving approach; one characterized by assessment and diagnosis, counselor-directed process, and decision making being a process of matching such personal attributes as abilities, interest, personality, and values with information about the world of work (e.g., occupational classification, workforce needs). By contrast to this oversimplified, matching process (Crites, 1981; Patton & McMahon, 1999), Brott (2001) portended that the complexity of the 21st century work world, not to mention nonwork life, has resulted in a movement toward a view that career counseling "is no longer a singular process that is focused on making a job choice; it is, instead, a range of interventions to deal with psychological issues that accompany the client's career concerns" (Herr, 1997, as cited in Brott, 2001, p. 305).

Young and associates (Young, Valach, & Collin, 1996; Young, Valach, Dillabough, Dover, & Matthes, 1994; Young et al., 1997) were among the earliest in the career field to posit how the constructionist theory and research are applied to the practice of career counseling. Originally begun as a research methodology, they studied the career-related conversations that occur between parents and adolescents. Actual parent–adolescent conversations were recorded, then analyzed not only for career content but especially for how the dyads constructed conversations and assigned meaning to personal goals and the intentions of others (i.e., family members and the counselor).

Brott (2001) advanced the application of the constructivist perspective to career counseling through use of a narrative technique called the *storied approach*. At the center of the storied approach is exploration of the client's world through the three phases of story development: co-construction, deconstruction, and construction (or reconstruction, according to Savickas, 2000). The co-construction process involves the client and counselor revealing the client's life stories, whereas the deconstruction entails disassembling or "unpacking" the stories for the purpose of examining various perspectives. [Re]construction, on the other hand, focuses on the client reauthoring stories with a future orientation.

We elected to focus on the constructivist tradition for four reasons: (a) because of its established usefulness "for counselors to understand how their clients make sense of their immediate experience" (Brown, 1996, p. 515), (b) its potential utility to career practitioners (e.g., Patton & McMahon, 1999; Peavy, 1997; Richardson, 1993; Savickas, 1993), (c) its compatibility with "many of the systems-based theories of marriage and family counseling" (Brown, 1996, p. 515), and (d) its perceived relevance to the lives of women and people with non-Eurocentric worldviews (Brott, 2001).

Young et al.'s (1996) review of their contextualist approach implies four additional reasons why a constructivist approach can be particularly attractive to practitioners: (a) The everyday language, characteristic of the approach's constructs, increases the credibility of counseling with clients; (b) the techniques make it unnecessary for the counselor to be steeped in formal testing methodology; (c) possession of in-depth knowledge of various industries or a referring company's career paths is minimized; and (d) there is little need for counselor familiarity with intricate couples or family counseling techniques.

The Storied Approach Applied to Counseling Dual-Career Couples

Described next is the application of the storied strategy to counseling dual-career couples. As an overview, the counseling process and the counselor's stance and tools are delineated. Then case examples are presented, each case depicting a different issue frequently identified in the dual-career couple literature. A separate phase of the storied approach is illustrated in each of the three case examples.

Counseling Process, Stance, and Tools

The *process of counseling*, from a storied approach, is composed of exploration of the couple's world through story development: co-construction (i.e., to reveal), deconstruction (i.e., to unpack), and reconstruction (i.e., to reauthor). Consequently, the *counselor's stance* is to facilitate or aid the couple's resolution of a career dilemma by clarification of purpose and meaning. This requires the counselor to switch from use of information-gathering techniques to directly solve a problem to a posture that generates a shared experience for the couple. In essence, the counselor structures the storytelling to serve as a template for viewing the couple's past, present, and future life.

The primary *counseling tools* are language and dialogue: the use of active listening and clarifying questions to establish a collaborative counselor–client relationship (versus the "expert" to "novice"); the assessment and identification of patterns between clients' needs, hopes, dreams, and so on; and, ultimately, defining the meaning and actions the couple elects to achieve in their "new" reality (Brott, 2001).

The secondary counseling tools are Brott's (2001) seven *influence questions*, used to map the client's stories. These questions may be classified as follows:

1. defining moments (i.e., elicit distinctive memories)
2. sparkling moments (i.e., identify high points)
3. peopled (i.e., recognize others who have a relationship with the stories)
4. opening space (i.e., note limitations and explore others' perceptions)
5. preferences (i.e., selection of desired outcomes)
6. themes (i.e., relationships between events and people in the stories)
7. name the story (i.e., ascribed meanings).

Pat and Jan: Case Example of Relocation Issues

A review of the extant dual-career couple literature indicates that relocation issues are a frequently reported experience (Hall, 1999). The case of

Pat and Jan is presented as an example of how counselors may apply the storied approach in dual-career couple's counseling. The counselor's stance and the counseling tools are confined to the *co-construction* segment of the counseling process. The career counseling technique of lifeline development is also used.

Pat, a senior accountant, has finally done it. With the award of CPA, scheduled for the end of next month, there is increased discussion between the department supervisor and the executives about reassigning Pat to the divisional headquarters where there is a need for a leader of the newly established "auditing team." This would represent Pat's second promotion and would result in positioning for entrance into the organization's managerial track, especially if it were combined with attainment of the coveted MBA degree.

The reassignment would require relocating from Iowa, where Pat has been on staff for 5 years, to Baltimore, Maryland. This is attractive to Pat, who has often talked of the desirability of living near aging parents (in eastern Pennsylvania). Also, strong consideration has been given to accepting Pat's undergraduate alma mater's repeated invitation to apply to their renowned business school's weekend MBA program.

Jan, who has been married to Pat for 8 years, is a junior staff attorney with a prestigious firm that has a history of rewarding senior staff with an offer of "partner." Jan is "on track" to reach senior attorney status early next year and is being wooed by a competitor's promise of partner. Jan has been aware of Pat's increased pining for the mid-Atlantic area but attributed it to the romanticizing of one's childhood home and alma mater. Pat is bewildered by Jan's lack of enthusiasm for this imminent birth of a long-held dream. Jan is irritated that Pat "goes ballistic" when their discussions hint at passing on this "golden opportunity."

The couple presents for conjoint career counseling. After completing the standard EAP intake and screening procedures, the partners share their individual perspective. They both describe their marriage as "good" to "very good," until the relocation issue sprang up 2 months ago. After the counselor conveys content and empathic listening, the storied approach may be introduced with the following.

Counselor: I want to suggest a way of us working together called "the storied approach." It will allow me to get to know you by being exposed to your life story. It will probably take us a few sessions (three to six), but it can enable you to build a plan that resolves this career relocation dilemma in a way that both honors your career aspirations while preserving your relationship.

Counselor: [Proceed after the couple consents and other general questions answered.] The storied approach has three phases to it: co-construction, deconstruction, and reconstruction. Today, I want to lead into the first phase, co-construction. The goal is for you to describe and depict your career life as a couple. I'll ask questions to help bring out potentially useful details and personal meanings.

[Place in front of the couple a large, poster-size piece of paper (newsprint works well) with a box of colored pencils (pen and pencil can be substituted for colored pencils or markers).]

Counselor: I want you to draw and verbally describe a lifeline of your past and present life together. Each of you takes a turn and mark what you perceive as significant events and people that depict your individual career-life story since becoming a couple. Don't discuss or comment on each other's offerings; that will come later.

[If more structure is needed, suggest drawing a horizontal line through the middle of the page with a vertical mark at the left end, designating the couple's beginning date and a vertical mark on the right end representing the present date. Observe who goes first. Do they discuss this or is it negotiated? How is it negotiated? Or is there resignation of which one goes first based on gender, or on whose career has the most social prestige, most financially profitable, and so on?]

Process Questions. The following are examples of each of the influence questions that the counselor asks to facilitate the co-construction process. (Have the clients verbalize a response and portray it on the lifeline with words or a symbol of their choosing.)

Counselor: What are your earliest memories of work, your career, and your relationship when you first became a "couple?" [or] Tell me about your life in eastern Pennsylvania right after undergraduate school, before moving to Iowa. Where did you live and what do you recall about the key people and events?

Counselor: [Probing for *defining moments* (i.e., distinctive memories) and *sparkling moments* (i.e., high points)] What do you remember about the most significant events and people of that era? What was a major accomplishment from this chapter of your career–life?

Pat: When I left that public accounting firm that I joined right out of college and accepted the corporate accounting position in Iowa—after only one year, I felt like I could make anything happen in my career!

Jan: Being positioned for senior staff attorney and possibly partner— even though I stepped out of my career for three years to be home with our daughter—said to me, "I *can* make up for lost time!" And Millie—as my mentor and the firm's only female partner—played the critical role of interpreter of the male-cultured traditional firm. What a God-send!!

To conclude the co-construction process, the counselor uses reflective questions to elicit identification of the people and secondary events that add texture or "detail" to this chapter in the couple's career–life. To summarize and prepare the clients for the deconstruction phase that is to follow, highlight client awareness of personal meaning by asking the clients to identify themes and, ultimately, to title this chapter in their career–life.

Pat and Jan were asked the following wrap-up questions: "As you look at your lifeline, can you identify the main themes?" and "Based on these career-life themes, what would you title this chapter of your life?" "The Thrill of Victory," was Jan's response, "I've pulled it off and I'm on my way to the gold!" Pat said, "I'd call it. . . . 'The Tortoise and the Hare' because it shows that even though I started my law career later than most, I can make up for lost time with steady, strategic effort."

[The counselor ends and transitions to the next session by stating that the identified events, people, themes, and chapter heading will be examined for core meanings in the deconstruction phase.]

Elena and Marco: Case Example of Parenting Issues

The case of Elena and Marco is here presented as an illustration of the application of the storied approach, during the *deconstruction* segment of dual-career counseling. The counselor's stance is that of disassembler (i.e., guiding the couple through the unpacking of their stories for meaning). The primary tools used by the counselor are, again, reflection and inquiry, to clarify affect, but also the use of confrontation to uncover alternative perspectives of the same events. This can be achieved by use of the following influence questions as secondary tools: (a) opening space (i.e., locate exceptions to life themes, generate different viewpoints, identify various life roles) and (b) peopled (i.e., identify the role of others in the stories). The goal of the deconstruction segment of counseling is to prepare for or introduce a future orientation to the couple.

Elena and Marco initially presented for EAP counseling because of their conflicted relationship. The presenting issue was whether now was the time for them to become parents, because their employer had concluded a 3-year history of running an award-winning on-site child-care program. During the last 3 months, they have been avoiding the topic because previous discussions about the impact of parenthood on their careers ended with mutual feelings of exasperation. They freely admitted to the EAP counselor that how they were handling this frightened them because, heretofore, "we agreed on just about everything!" Their goal was to examine parenthood without sacrificing their relationship or careers.

In the co-construction segment, Elena and Marco's lifelines revealed three critical events (i.e., defining moments and sparkling moments): (a) the postponement of marriage until the completion of their graduate education, (b) their graduation with "his-n-her's" PhDs in physics, and (c) gainful employment for both within the R & D (research and development) division of a nuclear energy think-tank. They seemed pleasantly surprised to learn that they had anything in common, as it appeared that of late they could not see eye to eye on anything.

Process Questions. The following are examples of each of two types of influence questions (i.e., peopled and opening space) that the counselor makes use of to facilitate the deconstruction or unpacking process.

Counselor: Elena and Marco, as you think about your lifeline chapter titled, "The Lucy and Ricardo Years," what and who do you recall influenced your decision to postpone marriage and parenthood?

Elena: Well, certainly Marco's parents. They're *very* much traditionalist from Cuba.

Marco: And Elena's [parents] are definitely Catholic. So we were not about to live together and start having kids right away. The families wouldn't have any of that!

Elena: To be fair, Marco, we too felt that this part of our faith—not starting a family outside of marriage—was something we wanted to hold on to, right?

Counselor: [After reflecting the content and inferred meaning to the couple, the counselor extends the peopled task.] Besides family members, how has your marriage and parenting roles been impacted by colleagues in R & D?

[The couple remarked about the significance of coworkers' subtle hints (and examples) about the 5-years-of-marriage mark being the "smart" time for dual-career science marriages to begin their families. Several follow-up questions probed the who, what, and how of each specific coworker to ascertain their influence on Marco and Elena.]

Counselor: [As a bridge to "open spaces," the counselor asks the following question] How have you coped with family, cultural, and religious expectations that you enter parenthood sooner rather than later?

[Marco commented that, while not conscious of it before now, he could see that they were on the fast-track with respect to their careers in science; so they could indeed "get on with the mommy/daddy-track part," as their cultural heritage dictated. Elena admitted, sheepishly, that early in her graduate school years, she overachieved academically so that it would be "crazy" for Marco to suggest that they marry and she stop at the master's-degree level to start a family while he pursued his terminal degree.]

Counselor: What would Lucy and Ricardo do if they were in your shoes? [Another open-space question]

Elena: I remember this episode on the "Lucy Show," before they had Little Ricky. As the bandleader, Ricky received an out-of-state offer to become the permanent house-band at a new club in another state. I don't know, it could have even been in Cuba. And while initially all for it, Ricky soon chilled on the idea when he started to think about Lucy wanting to have a baby soon, the neighbors they would lose, and the effect of relocation on the other band members.

Marco: Yeah, I think he'd [Ricardo] look at what's best for everyone; what's good for other parts of his and Lucy's life, not just his career.

Counselor: [At the session's end, the counselor asks the couple this question] Is there a way you can talk about parenting that embraces the reality of your dual-career science marriage?

Counselor: [The transition to the final segment, reconstruction (i.e., develop a positive future orientation), is achieved with the following statement:] In our final segment, I'll invite you to build upon your life story; one that is not driven by the fear of failing to meet others' expectations, but instead one of a successful dual-career couple who creatively plans for how parenthood will fit within their dual-career science marriage.

Xia and Kim: Case Example of Equity Issues

When they first came in for counseling, Xia complained that Kim was no longer interested in sex and that it seemed as though they were losing their connection to Kim's family. Xia is a consultant to import businesses and developed an independent consulting practice over the past 5 years. Working as one of two accountants at a small company, Kim found it overwhelming keeping up with all of the housework and attending Xia's regular business dinners. Both are first-generation Americans, and their families immigrated to the United States from mainland China.

Through co-construction and deconstruction, it became clear that Xia made most of the decisions at home. Although initially supportive of Kim becoming an accountant, Xia still expected Kim to be available for Xia's business dinners and to keep house. Kim, poised to take the CPA exam, was experiencing role overload. Kim said, "I've struggled to maintain some personal identity through my career while still being a 'good' partner."

Xia and Kim realized that they were trying to live the American dream as their families had wanted for them. They were also trying to honor more traditional roles from their Chinese heritage. They wanted to have a "better life" because their families had worked so hard to finance their educations. The unanticipated relational cost, however, was little intimacy between them and minimal time with their families and friends.

In the reconstruction phase, the counselor works with clients to recreate their story or to write a new chapter for their lives. With couples, as opposed to individual clients, this means collaborating yet still honoring each partner's desires. In this phase of the storied approach, the counselor emphasizes use of the three influence questions: preferences, themes, and naming (ascribing meaning). Using the reconstruction phase of the storied approach, the counselor may present the following.

Counselor: You have shared some personal struggles and hopes of your families. You have also sorted out some of the causes for your issues. Now we are going to shift our focus to your hopes and goals both personally and as a couple. We will explore your preferences for your life together and how to support each of you in your individual career goals.

[Hands each person a large pad of lined paper and pen or pencil.]

Counselor: On this paper, I want you to write the five ways you most want to spend your time. Then, please put them in order of importance. Also, out of the activities you do in your day, write the three things you least want to spend time doing. Please order the three things in order of disinterest.

[Process note: Let them know that five and three items are just guidelines and encourage them to write more if they wish.]

After the clients complete the listing and prioritization tasks, Kim is asked to share first, because Xia is used to making most of the decisions. (Exceptions to this would be made if cultural issues make it an insult or not acceptable if the man does not share first.)

Counselor: Kim, would you please share the things you least want to spend time doing and explain why.

[When Kim is finished, have Xia share. Then, bring out large sheets of paper, crayons, pens and pencils.]

Counselor: Based on what you have each shared, write, draw, or tell me a story together about where you want to go on your journey as a couple. Use these tools [point to paper, crayons, etc.] to redesign your lives. Think of creative ways to have outside support and help to balance the activities you do not enjoy doing. Feel free to be messy and change or start over on your project.

[Process note: Note if they go back into old patterns that, in the deconstruction segment, they said they did not like. If self-defeating patterns are manifest, say something like "I see that Kim is supporting Xia's career—how is Xia going to support Kim's?" or "It looks like Kim is doing all the housework again—what are some other options?" Encourage them to brainstorm ideas, start over on a new piece of paper, write down or explore two or more options, and keep humor in the process.]

The next steps in the reconstruction process would be to set goals as a couple based on their new "vision" and to list their ideas of how to accomplish their goals and activate or enlarge their support system. Potential obstacles also need to be identified so the couple can plan how to handle those predictable and unpredictable issues. The counselor may identify further counseling needs such as time management skills. Finally, clients can be asked to share with each other what they have learned through this process (about themselves, their partner, and their relationship) and their gratitude for the other's risk taking and openness. Discuss choosing an annual or biannual time to sit down to assess how things are going, recontract for how they want things to be, and finally predict future challenges both personally and professionally.

Conclusion

Dual-career couples are increasingly common and introduce new challenges to career counseling. Juggling two careers and a relationship/family can be very rewarding yet requires strong communication and time management skills. Common issues arise for dual-career couples, such as relationship and career equity, synchronicity in career trajectory, housework responsibility, adequate social support, and child-rearing issues. Because these issues vary and shift throughout the life span, in this chapter we presented a brief overview of these key issue areas and also a career counseling theory that can be adapted to various issues in the dual-career couple lifestyle.

The constructivist theory was presented using a storied approach, validating that it is not only the issues couples are working through but also the perceptions and experience they have of these issues. By structuring a way for clients to tell their stories, the counselor can help them make sense of and share their struggles with their partner. Case examples were used to illustrate the counseling process of co-construction (i.e., to reveal), deconstruction (i.e., to unpack), and reconstruction (i.e., to reauthor) to address common dual-career couple issues. Not only is the theory flexible for multiple dual-career couple issues, but it is also flexible in use with all types of couples, including those from diverse cultural and sexual orientation backgrounds.

In discussing dual-career couples, we would be remiss not to mention the critical gap missing in the literature of cultural issues. Cultural issues are the paper on which dual-career couples lives are written. Because the literature barely includes anything about a dual-career couple's culture, we encourage you to explore cultural issues within your counseling with all clients. Moral, spiritual, and religious values and sexual orientation are areas void in the dual-career couple literature (Russo, 1987).

Racial and ethnic issues need more research. Thomas's (1990) work was the only article on dual-career couples addressing race directly. She researched problems of Black dual-career couples. She found issues specific to being a person of color in a predominantly White work environment and guilt for doing better than other Black friends and family. Working in a predominantly White work environment, Thomas found social isolation, (perceived) racial discrimination, and difficulty instilling Black values and appreciation for Black culture. Her article demonstrates the value of exploring how cultural issues affect dual-career couples.

In summary, the dual-career couples literature suggests there are many issues specific to dual-career couples that EAP or career counselors may encounter. Five main categories of issues are equity, housework, synchronicity, social support, and parenting. The storied approach, based on constructivist theory, is a flexible way to work with dual-career couple issues in time-limited career counseling. The three stages (i.e., co-construction, deconstruction, and reconstruction) help couples express their individual and couple perspectives, make sense of their lives, and create a vision for their future career and relationship.

References

Argyle, M. (1989). *The social psychology of work*. London: Penguin Press.

Barnett, R. C., & Rivers, C. (1996). *She works, he works: How two-income families are happy, healthy, and thriving*. Cambridge, MA: Harvard University Press.

Becker, P. E., & Moen, P. (1999). Scaling back: Dual-earner couples' work–family strategies. *Journal of Marriage and the Family, 61*, 995–1007.

Brott, P. E. (2001). The storied approach: A postmodern perspective for career counseling. *Career Development Quarterly, 49*, 304–313.

Brown, D. (1996). Status of career development theories. In D. Brown, L. Brooks, & Associates (Eds.), *Career choice and development* (3rd ed., pp. 513–525). San Francisco: Jossey-Bass.

Brown, D., & Brooks, L. (1996). Introduction to theories of career development and choice: Origins, evolution, and current efforts. In D. Brown, L. Brooks, & Associates (Eds.), *Career choice and development* (3rd ed., pp. 1–13). San Francisco: Jossey-Bass.

Crites, J. O. (1981). *Career counseling: Models, methods, and materials*. New York: McGraw-Hill.

Easterbrooks, M. A., & Goldberg, W. A. (1985). Effects of early maternal employment on toddlers, mothers and fathers. *Developmental Psychology, 21*, 774–783.

Farber, R. S. (1988). Integrated treatment of the dual career couple. *American Journal of Family Therapy, 16*, 46–57.

Glickauf-Hughes, C. L., Hughes, G. B., & Wells, M. C. (1986). A developmental approach to treating dual career couples. *American Journal of Family Therapy, 14*, 254–263.

Goldenberg, I., & Goldenberg, H. (1984). Treating the dual career couple. *American Journal of Family Therapy, 12*, 29–37.

Hall, M. E. (1999, Fall). *Challenges for dual career couples: The career planning news*. State College, PA: Penn State University-Career Services.

Maples, M. F. (1981). Dual career marriages' elements for potential success. *Personnel and Guidance Journal, 60*, 19–23.

Marshack, K. (1998). *Entrepreneurial couples: Making it work at work and at home*. Palo Alto, CA: Davies-Black.

McDonald, K. A. (1999). Study reveals dilemmas of dual-earner couples. *Chronicle of Higher Education, 45*(22), A21.

Patton, W., & McMahon, M. (1999). *Career development and systems theory: A new relationship*. Pacific Grove, CA: Brooks/Cole.

Peavy, R. V. (1997). A constructive framework for career counseling. In T. L. Sexton & B. L. Griffin (Eds.), *Constructivist thinking in counseling practice, research and training* (pp. 122–140). New York: Teachers College Press.

Rapoport, R., & Rapoport, R. N. (1971). Further considerations of the dual career family. *Human Relations, 24*, 519–533.

Richardson, M. S. (1993). Work in people's lives: A location for counseling psychologists. *Journal of Counseling Psychology, 40*, 425–433.

Russo, N. F. (1987). Dual career couples: Research, assessment, and public policy issues. *Counseling Psychologist, 15*, 140–145.

Savickas, M. L. (1993). Vocational psychology in the postmodern era: Comment on Richardson (1993). *Journal of Counseling Psychology, 41*, 105–107.

Savickas, M. L. (2000, June). *Career choice as biographical bricolage.* Paper presented at the Ninth Global National Career Development Association Conference, Pittsburgh, PA.

Sperry, L. (1993). Tailoring treatment with dual career couples. *American Journal of Family Therapy, 21*, 51–59.

Stevens, D., Kiger, G., & Riley, P. J. (2001). Working hard and hardly working: Domestic labor and marital satisfaction among dual-earner couples. *Journal of Marriage and the Family, 63*, 514–526.

Stoltz-Loike, M. (1992). *Dual career couples: New perspectives in counseling.* Alexandria, VA: American Counseling Association.

Thomas, V. G. (1990). Problems of dual career Black couples: Identification and implications for family interventions. *Journal of Multicultural Counseling & Development, 18*, 58–67.

Wilcox-Matthew, L., & Minor, C. W. (1989). The dual career couple: Concerns, benefits and counseling implications. *Journal of Counseling & Development, 28*, 194–198.

Young, R. A., Valach, L., & Collins, A. (1996). *A contextual explanation of career* In D. Brown, L. Brooks, & Associates (Eds.), *Career choice and development* (3rd ed., pp. 477–512). San Francisco: Jossey-Bass.

Young, R. A., Valach, L., Dillabough, J., Dover, C., & Matthes, G. (1994). Career research from an action perspective: The self-confrontation procedure. *Career Development Quarterly, 43*, 185–196.

Young, R. A., Valach, L., Paseluikho, M. A., Dover, C., Matthes, G. E., Paproski, D. L., & Sankey, A. M. (1997). The joint action of parents and adolescents in conversation about career. *Career Development Quarterly, 46*, 72–86.

14

Adaptation and the Foreign Assignment: Counseling Expatriates

Joseph A. Lippincott and Ruth B. Lippincott

International business travelers, particularly those who are on extended assignments in another country, are faced with considerable cultural conflicts and inconsistencies. The present literature describes the effects of acculturative stress among expatriates (Aycan, 1997; Kraimer, Wayne, & Jaworski, 2001) as well as mitigating factors that may lead to stress reactions (Shaffer & Harrison, 1998; Ward, 1997). There appears to be a need, however, for palliative treatment approaches for expatriates experiencing acculturative stress responses. This chapter identifies acculturative stress phenomena among expatriates and describes an adaptation of a treatment protocol for mediating acculturative stress among international sojourners, with specific applications for international businesspersons.

Expatriates and Acculturative Stress

An expatriate is an individual who lives and works in another country. Terms such as *foreign assignment* and *overseas assignment* have traditionally been used to describe employees who reside in another country for business or commercial reasons. The National Foreign Trade Council estimates that more than 250,000 American businesspersons are presently on foreign assignments, with relocation costs averaging $60,000 U.S. dollars per person (Kraimer et al., 2001). Between 20% and 40% of expatriates prematurely terminate their international assignment because of adjustment issues, and more than 50% do not achieve optimal job performance (Kealey & Protheroe, 1996). Revenues lost by U.S. businesses that are due to failed foreign assignments are estimated at over $2 billion per year (Giacalone & Beard, 1994).

Often, the urgency of an international deal causes companies to make the mistake of sending their personnel off on foreign assignments without the benefit of prior training or ongoing support to deal with the challenges of cross-cultural adjustment. While these personnel may have met the selection criteria for technical competency and business acumen, these qualities cannot compensate for insufficient preparation and support to deal with the transition to a different culture. Without such preparation and support, personnel are forced to adjust through trial and error, often to the detriment of both the company's and the individual's reputation and ultimate success, as well as the individual's psychological well-being (Giacalone & Beard, 1994).

Adaptation to a different culture, also referred to as *acculturation* (Ward, 1996), is required, to some degree, of all individuals who do business internationally. Programs of cross-cultural training and support, preferably tailored for participants to take into account factors such as length and type of assignment, magnitude of cultural differences, and prior cross-cultural experience, need to be provided to expatriates to help them make that adjustment. An effective program will minimize the negative impact of the acculturative process on both the expatriate's job performance and personal well-being. Expatriates who fail to become personally acclimated to their new cultural environment find it virtually impossible to be effective professionally (Kealey, 1996).

The process of acculturation involves both *sociocultural adaptation*, which is defined in terms of behavioral competence, and *psychological adjustment*, which is defined in terms of physical and psychological well-being (Ward, 1996, 1997). Sociocultural adaptation is influenced by the development of cultural awareness and the quality of the expatriate's social skills. Psychological adjustment involves coping with the stress that emanates from the acculturation process. Unsuccessful sociocultural adaptation and psychological maladjustment produce *acculturative stress*.

To be effective, cross-cultural training and support programs need to address both sociocultural and psychological adjustment issues. Historically, typical corporate programs had an occasional lecture or seminar on the "Do's and Don'ts" of business etiquette around the world. Such programs are not enough to prepare the expatriate even for the sociocultural component of his or her adjustment. Moreover, training programs that are insufficiently comprehensive can actually be counterproductive (Black & Gregersen, 1991).

An effective program provides thorough predeparture training and, for extended assignment, continued training and support services after arrival. Predeparture training helps the expatriate arrive with realistic expectations and goals, as well as with the skills to understand the new culture and to communicate and interact effectively. If an employee's spouse and family are relocating with the employee, the training should also include these individuals. Studies show that a large percentage of spouses experience serious adjustment problems, resulting in a negative impact on the success of the employees in their foreign assignments (Kealey, 1996; Shaffer & Harrison, 1998). In addition to teaching cultural values and norms and language skills, the program should enable the expatriates and their families to identify support systems and encourage them to reserve time for stress-diminishing activities.

The cross-cultural literature suggests that expatriates should be taught adaptation to, but not adoption of, the new culture (Anderson, 1994; Brake, Walker, & Walker, 1995; Giacalone & Beard, 1994). The expatriate should not be compelled to change his or her own value system. Giacalone and Beard's (1994) model, utilizing impression management theory, teaches expatriates appropriate behaviors for a specific culture and then coaches them on how to activate these behaviors at appropriate times—a technique not unlike acting. Brake et al. (1995) developed a cultural orientations framework that categorizes key value orientations that shape and motivate behavior in various parts of the world and associates those values with specific cultures. The program encourages participants to be conscious of their own values and those of other cultures, and to recognize the potential impact of these value differences on their cross-cultural encounters (including such key events, from a businessperson's perspective, as presentations and negotiations). Similarly, Gudykunst, Guzley, and Hammer (1996) described a program based on anxiety/uncertainty management theory that teaches sojourners, such as expatriates, to manage uncertainty by understanding relevant cultural variables to interpret host nationals' behavior. Informational texts, such as

Engholm's book on Asian business etiquette, *When Business East Meets Business West* (1991), and Training Management Corporation's *Doing Business Internationally: The Resource Book to Business and Social Etiquette* (1997), are both culture-specific and business-specific. They can be useful reference sources for international business travelers.

Terms like *ecoshock*, and the more common term *culture shock*, are attempts to describe more vividly the reaction of sojourners, including expatriates, to acculturative stress. These terms refer to the impact on both the mental and physical health of the individual (Anderson, 1994; Ward, 1996; Winkelman, 1994). Cross-cultural programs that provide comprehensive training in sociocultural issues should help in minimizing acculturative stress. Nevertheless, while the severity of these stress reactions may vary among individuals, acculturative stress affects all expatriates in some way, and preventative measures will not forestall all reactions. Normal problems and typical life changes, for example, are often exacerbated in a foreign environment (Ward, 1997). Businesses and other commercial enterprises employing expatriates need to recognize the critical role played by their support services. Substantial predeparture training is a good start, but that training is frequently inadequate for effective expatriate adjustment. The predeparture training must be followed by on-site counseling services that provide coping assistance and actual interventions, if indicated. The benefits of such support services are economic as well as interpersonal. The impact of an effective support program can mean the difference between the success and failure of the foreign assignment (Giacalone & Beard, 1994).

The Role of the Counselor

The primary role of the counselor who works with expatriates is education regarding cultural norms and expectancies and minimization of acculturative stress responses. As previously noted, although solid predeparture preparation serves to ameliorate acculturative stress reactions, all expatriates will react to their new culture in some way.

Ideally, the cultural acclimation of expatriates occurs slowly and steadily. The role of the counselor, as Winkleman (1994) noted, is to stabilize the individual and then to facilitate his or her cultural adjustment. To be effective, the acculturative stress treatment model employed must be comprehensive and adaptable and should address the acculturation process variables of culture learning, social skills, psychological stress, and (more rarely) psychopathological symptoms (Berry & Kim, 1988; Ward, 1997).

Counseling for expatriates can take place in a number of ways. The counselor can be an expatriate or a native counselor. In either case, however, such individual needs to have extensive knowledge of both the host culture and the employee's culture of origin, with particular emphasis on business interactions.

The treatment interventions described herein for expatriate acculturative stress responses have multiple goals. As stated previously, an important consideration is to foster adaptation to the new culture but not to promote adoption of the new culture. Unlike some immigrants who may choose to embrace their new chosen culture and become assimilated, expatriates are "extended visitors" who will ultimately return to their culture of origin. Repatriation efforts are often difficult for expatriates who have become too immersed in another culture. Black and Gregersen (1991) used the term *going native* to describe expatriates who form such a strong identification to the new culture that a reverse acculturation of sorts occurs upon their return home.

The counselor's role begins as a clinical consultant who provides an initial assessment of the newly arrived expatriate. In addition to assessing cultural knowledge, comfort, and expectations, which will be a measure of the effectiveness of any predeparture training, the counselor at this juncture will also assess any personal, family, or developmental stressors.

Treatment Model

Initial Assessment

Although the counselor's role may primarily be culturally informative and psychoeducational, there needs to exist a respectful and trusting relationship. To establish this connection, the counselor should promote a "getting-to-know-one-another" process with the client in which cultural experiences and expectations are shared. Some self-disclosure is appropriate here, particularly regarding the counselor's encounters with, and suggestions about, the present culture. The counselor should be neither too formal nor too distant. Establishment of the therapeutic relationship begins during this initial contact. The goal here is to assess the expatriate's cultural experiences and reactions. At this point in the counseling relationship, an insight-oriented therapeutic approach is not necessarily warranted.

The counselor needs to learn as much as possible about the expatriate: personality factors, approaches to problem solving, interpersonal relationships, and career and professional goals, among others. Particular emphasis should be paid to the present job assignment. Issues to be examined include the expatriate's expectations about the assignment and the reasonableness of those expectations. Specific workplace issues and tasks should be discussed as they relate to the present culture.

Cultural Psychoeducation

As the counselor becomes more aware of the expatriate's value system and interpersonal style, he or she should look for potential inconsistencies or conflicts as the expatriate begins to navigate in the new culture. A solid understanding and appreciation of the present culture by the counselor is vital, as the counselor increasingly becomes a "cultural consultant."

The expatriate needs to be aware of what to expect, not only in the business culture but also socially and politically. Invitations by host country businesspersons to dine at their homes or attend parties are often extended. The counselor may now reinforce cultural expectations and norms that were described in predeparture training. The counselor may also consider sharing information about personal experiences within the culture. This is particularly germane if the counselor is also an expatriate. Anecdotes and stories of new foods, customs, and expectations can be quite normalizing and therapeutic for the new expatriate.

Other Assessment Areas

Language and Communication

Language proficiency is often a very significant stressor for expatriates (Brake et al., 1995; Deshpande & Viswesvaran, 1992). The counselor as cultural consultant needs to compare the expatriate's speaking and writing ability with his or her ability genuinely to comprehend spoken words, in formal and informal settings. A practical consideration for expatriates who lack confidence in their language skills is tutoring. Language tutors are usually readily available, and fees are nominal. The company may wish to consider hiring a language expert, particularly one with experience in business terminology.

Formal spoken language is not the only source of miscommunication. Often, what is not said may be as important as what is said. International employees need to understand, relatively speaking, the effects of body language, intonations, and other subtle forms of communication. As Giacalone and Beard (1994) pointed out, "even individuals who are conversant in another language may suffer enormous difficulties, for style of communication may produce a variety of confusing and misguided signals" (p. 623).

Cultural Differences

Although the expatriate may initially find the cultural differences in the host country exciting, the more novel these customs, norms, and values are in relation to the expatriate's own, the more difficult it will tend to be for the expatriate to adapt. For example, there may be significant differences in the way people regard matters such as personal space, formality, hierarchy, directness, respectfulness, aggressiveness, emotional responses, eye contact, dress, and punctuality. Some of the differences may be so extreme as to be counterintuitive to the expatriate, and others can be so subtle that they go unrecognized. Although the expatriate may have been informed of these differences in predeparture training, it can be difficult to identify them outside of the classroom. The counselor needs to help the expatriate develop sensitivity and adaptation to these differences.

Family Issues

The relative comfort and adjustment of spouses and children is a primary factor in staying, versus returning home, for many expatriates (Black & Gregersen, 1991; Karpati, Dagley, & Shahnasarian, 1994; Shaffer & Harrison, 1998). Counselors need to include spouses, or significant others, and family members in the same assessment and cultural psychoeducational issues as the expatriates themselves. Issues such as language fluency and cultural novelty can lead to social isolation, anxiety, and boredom for the spouses and children. Because spouses are often not allowed to work in the host country, many are concerned about the interruption of their own careers. Spouses and children may also react to inferior living conditions and may be homesick for the friends, family, and routine of home.

Assessment should occur regarding the depth and dimensions of the couple's relationship predeparture. The changes, anxieties, and frustrations experienced in cross-cultural relocation can exacerbate problems in a previously strained marriage. A parallel counseling process is therefore indicated in which the integrity of the couple's relationship is explored, as well as the impact of the new cultural experiences on all of the family members. Counselors who do not feel comfortable or competent in providing couples' counseling should consider making a referral.

Social Network

A telling question to ask expatriates, especially those who are newly arrived, is "What do you do after work?" Many businesspersons spend months, and even years, on assignment yet remain totally uninvolved in local events and unaware of local establishments. As is the case with any counseling client, it is important to explore recreational and leisure interests. It is neither necessary nor advisable for expatriates to become totally immersed in their new culture. However, a certain level of involvement is healthy and growth promoting. Exploration of the expatriate's predeparture social and leisure activities provides for comparisons with present outlets.

Gender Issues

Counselors need to assess the expatriate's understanding of culture-specific gender expectations and roles and counsel accordingly. This may be particularly pertinent for businesswomen. Although these women may have had difficulty being treated equally in their home country, they may find gender inequities even more profound in the new culture. The movements in the United States to combat sexual harassment and to promote respect for diversity, equal opportunity, and political correctness are not shared, or are not as prominent, in many other parts of the world.

In some countries, particularly in Asia, a female expatriate may be associated more with her training, skills, and job position than with being a woman. Nevertheless, that same woman may need to deal with her reactions to seeing the local women, even in professional positions, not being treated with the same respect as men and not being allowed to participate as peers with the men. The female expatriate must decide if and how to repress her reactions, and to what extent she wants to try or should try to effect change. Counselors may need to help the expatriates wrestle with the feasibility and appropriateness of attempting to change culturally condoned, gender-specific attitudes and practices, particularly if business transactions are to be conducted successfully.

Racial and Ethnic Issues

Counselors need to be aware of the overt and covert sentiments toward expatriates' cultures of origin. People in some countries have long-standing histories of hostility or ill will toward people of certain other countries. In addition, particularly during times of political unrest, people from countries considered unsympathetic toward a particular cause may be viewed antagonistically. An expatriate with a particular national origin or family surname may be subject to discriminatory treatment for reasons that may or may not be readily apparent. Although expatriates cannot expect to change strong national sentiments, they can, with the counselor's assistance, understand and adapt, learning appropriate precautions and avoiding behaviors that may be viewed as negative stereotypes of the expatriate's culture of origin.

Esoteric Issues

It is important to explore the meaning of the present assignment to the expatriate on a practical as well as philosophical plane. Many businesspersons view their foreign assignment as a means of advancement and attainment of more professional autonomy. In some companies, however, expatriates are concerned that they will be "forgotten" by the parent company while they work in obscurity at a foreign affiliate. They may also be concerned about being excluded from important decisions and from the home office political scene. Counselors need to strategize with expatriates so that a balance may be achieved between their involvement in both local and parent company issues. Counselors should explore the personal meaning of the expatriate's overall job as well as the present assignment. This allows the employee to perceive a balance of sorts between the present, limited foreign assignment and his or her career as a whole.

Acculturative Stress: Treatment Considerations

Counselors need to be aware that not all acculturative stress reactions, indeed not even most, are pathological responses. A certain degree of excitement and anxiety, and even a modicum of discomfort, is part of the normal acculturative process. Sandhu, Portes, and McPhee (1996) introduced the term *cultural adaptation pain* to describe the normal, expected, and even growth-promoting phenomena experienced by sojourners living in a culture substantially different from their own.

There are those individuals, however, who will invariably develop acculturative stress symptoms that go beyond discomfort and become debilitating in some manner. Counselors need to pay particular attention to any premorbid behaviors experienced by the expatriate predeparture that may influence or exacerbate an acculturative stress response. Employees with histories of substance abuse, clinical depression, or other psychopathological syndromes, or those with impaired interpersonal relationships, may be particularly susceptible to adjustment difficulties.

One group of researchers has identified certain preexisting traits as significant predictors for expatriate adjustment difficulties (Fukunishi, Berger, Wogan, & Kuboki, 1999). In their study of 56 expatriates being seen for outpatient counseling in Tokyo, Fukunishi et al. described a constellation of traits among the more poorly adjusted individuals. The term *alexithymic traits* was used to describe a premorbid syndrome that included psychosomatic traits, difficulty in self-identification and description of feelings, and poor stress-coping abilities. Any one of these factors could negatively influence adjustment to a new culture. When these features appear in aggregate, however, counselors need to be particularly alert.

Counselors should be aware of any previous psychological issues or interpersonal stressors experienced by the expatriate. Most of these preexisting phenomena will already be familiar to the counselors through their work with their other clients. Depression, impairment of self-esteem, couples' conflicts, and many other presenting issues can be treated by the counselor using his or her usual clinical approach. The additional factors with respect to the expatriate, though, are the influences of abrupt change and cultural differences.

Anxiety, in its many forms, is one of the most common experiences of cross-cultural sojourners (Kirmayer, Young, & Hayton, 1995). Walton (1990) described "cognitive inconsistencies" experienced by these sojourners, including generalized worry, self-doubt, an exaggerated sense of pressure and demands (internally as well as externally), and other cognitive anxiety. He recommended stress management training or stress reduction exercises to mediate the anxiety experienced as part of cross-cultural adaptation.

In treating acculturative stress reactions among expatriates, counselors can use cognitive interventions as a vital therapeutic adjunct, an important element of the treatment as a whole. Again, the approach chosen in treating such cognitive inconsistencies may be that with which the counselor is comfortable, an approach that has been effective with other clients.

The cognitive restructuring approach described by Aaron Beck (1979) and Judith Beck (1995) has been used in part to treat acculturative stress-induced anxiety (Lippincott, 1999). The use of cognitive technique, although potent in and of itself, may prove even stronger therapeutically when included with other approaches previously employed successfully by the counselor. Such integration of different psychotherapeutic theories and techniques has proved helpful in ameliorating a variety of clinical concerns (Goldfried, 1995).

Conclusion

The variables that affect the adjustment—cultural as well as career—of international businesspersons are numerous and intimately interconnected. A potentially potent prophylactic intervention for minimizing acculturative stress reactions is comprehensive predeparture training. In order for such training to be effective and to retain potency, however, it needs to be thorough, sufficiently tailored for the specific individuals, and occur longitudinally, over time (Hites, 1996). The timeworn notion of providing one-size-fits-all training needs to be abandoned.

It is inevitable, however, that even with the solid predeparture preparation, expatriates will experience acculturative stress reactions. Although present expatriate literature contains numerous references for the preparation and acculturation of international business travelers, there do not appear to be strategies regarding the use of counseling during the foreign assignment to minimize the occurrence of acculturative stress reactions, nor do there appear to be strategies regarding the treatment of acculturative stress reactions once they occur.

The focus and intent of this chapter is to provide counselors with suggestions for understanding the etiology of acculturative stress, to identify stress-induced symptoms and responses and, most importantly, to consider treatment approaches for mediating these symptoms and responses.

References

Anderson, L. E. (1994). A new look at an old construct: Cross-cultural adaptation. *International Journal of Intercultural Relations, 18*, 293–328.

Aycan, Z. (1997). Acculturation of expatriate managers: A process model of adjustment and performance. In Z. Aycan (Ed.), *New approaches to employee management: Vol. 4. Expatriate management: Theory and research* (pp. 1–40). Greenwich, CT: JAI Press.

Beck, A. T. (1979). *Cognitive therapy of depression.* New York: Guilford Press.

Beck, J. S. (1995). *Cognitive therapy: Basics and beyond.* New York: Guilford Press.

Berry, J. W., & Kim, U. (1988). Acculturation and mental health. In P. R. Dasen, J. W. Berry, & N. Sartorius (Eds.), *Health and cross-cultural psychology* (pp. 207–236). Newbury Park, CA: Sage.

Black, J. S., & Gregersen, H. B. (1991). The other half of the picture: Antecedents of spouse cross-cultural adjustment. *Journal of International Business Studies, 22*, 461–477.

Brake, T., Walker, D. M., & Walker, T. (1995). *Doing business internationally: The guide to cross-cultural success.* Burr Ridge, IL: Irwin.

Deshpande, S. P., & Viswesvaran, C. (1992). Is cross-cultural training of expatriate managers effective: A meta analysis. *International Journal of Intercultural Relations, 16,* 295–310.

Engholm, C. (1991). *When business east meets business west.* New York: Wiley.

Fukunishi, I., Berger, D., Wogan, J., & Kuboki, T. (1999). Alexithymic traits as predictors of difficulties with adjustment in an outpatient cohort of expatriates in Tokyo, Japan. *Psychological Reports, 85,* 67–77.

Giacalone, R. A., & Beard, J. W. (1994). Impression management, diversity, and international management. *American Behavioral Scientist, 37,* 621–636.

Goldfried, M. R. (1995). *From cognitive–behavior therapy to psychotherapy integration.* New York: Springer.

Gudykunst, W. B., Guzley, R. M., & Hammer, M. R. (1996). Designing intercultural training. In D. Landis & R. S. Bhagat (Eds.), *Handbook of intercultural training* (2nd ed., pp. 61–80). Thousand Oaks, CA: Sage.

Hites, J. M. (1996). Design and delivery of training for international trainees: A case study. *Performance and Improvement Quarterly, 9,* 57–74.

Karpati, F. S., Dagley, J., & Shahnasarian, M. (1994, April). *Facilitating the cross-cultural transfer and adjustment of global managers and their families.* Paper presented at the annual convention of the American Counseling Association, Minneapolis, MN.

Kealey, D. J. (1996). The challenge of international personnel selection. In D. Landis & R. S. Bhagat (Eds.), *Handbook of intercultural training* (2nd ed., pp. 81–105). Thousand Oaks, CA: Sage.

Kealey, D. J., & Protheroe, D. R. (1996). The effectiveness of cross-cultural training for the expatriates: An assessment of the literature on the issue. *International Journal of Intercultural Relations, 20,* 141–165.

Kirmayer, L. J., Young, A., & Hayton, B. C. (1995). The cultural context of anxiety disorders. *Psychiatric Clinics of North America, 18,* 503–521.

Kraimer, M. L., Wayne, S. J., & Jaworski, R. A. (2001). Sources of support and expatriate performance: The mediating role of expatriate adjustment. *Personnel Psychology, 54,* 71–99.

Lippincott, J. A. (1999). Acculturative stress among Asians: Assessment and treatment issues. In D. S. Sandhu (Ed.), *Asian and Pacific Islander Americans: Issues and concerns for counseling and psychotherapy* (pp. 43–55). Commack, NY: Nova Science.

Sandhu, D. S., Portes, P. R., & McPhee, S. A. (1996). Assessing cultural adaptation: Psychometric properties of the Cultural Adaptation Pain Scale. *Journal of Multicultural Counseling and Development, 24,* 15–25.

Shaffer, M. A., & Harrison, D. A. (1998). Expatriates' psychological withdrawal from international assignments: Work, nonwork, and family influences. *Personnel Psychology, 51,* 87–118.

Training Management Corporation. (1997). *Doing business internationally: The resource book to business and social etiquette.* Princeton, NJ: Princeton Training Press.

Walton, S. (1990). Stress management training for overseas effectiveness. *International Journal of Intercultural Relations, 14*, 507–527.

Ward, C. (1996). Acculturation. In D. Landis & R. S. Bhagat (Eds.), *Handbook of intercultural training* (2nd ed., pp. 124–147). Thousand Oaks, CA: Sage.

Ward, C. (1997). Culture learning, acculturative stress, and psychopathology: Three perspectives on acculturation. *Applied Psychology, 46*, 58–62.

Winkelman, M. (1994). Cultural shock and adaptation. *Journal of Counseling & Development, 73*, 121–126.

Temporary Employees: A Primer for Counselors

Debra S. Preston

estructuring, downsizing, rightsizing, trimming the fat—these terms became buzz words in the 1990s. Whatever the euphemism, the bottom line was that millions of people were out of work. The U.S. Department of Labor's Bureau of Labor Statistics (BLS; 1992) reported that, in the recession of 1990, over 9 million people became unemployed. Only a small number of those who lost jobs in the recession were rehired by their former employers (Gardner, 1994). The majority of the remaining workers initiated job searches and actively sought reemployment in permanent jobs but met a great obstacle. Not only was the American private sector not employing as many workers, but also the United States military services began a reduction in forces that released at least 548,000 veterans into the civilian labor-seeking market (Thompson, 1992).

Consider these two scenarios of modern employment:

> I have two college degrees and a good track record. I was really secure.
> Then my company started trimming the fat—and I was considered

excess baggage. I ended up temping for almost a year, and eventually accepted a position offered to me while on a temporary assignment.

My wife accepted a promotion, which made it necessary for us to move to another state. My wife is an executive, and I'm a factory worker. I temped at industrial jobs for eight months until I finally found another job. (Mendenhall, 1993, p. 15)

Both of these workers are in what Schlossberg (1984) called a *career transition*. Career transitions are either planned, as in the case of job security, or unplanned, as in the case of a job transfer. Many individuals adapt to job transitions by entering the temporary workforce. Temporary workers, also known as temporaries or contingent workers, have a relationship with their employer that is contingent on the employer's need for labor on a specified project (Hipple, 2001). The BLS defines contingent work as "Any job in which an individual does not have an explicit or implicit contract for long-term employment or one in which the minimum hours worked can vary in a nonsystematic manner" (Polivka, 1996c, p. 4). Thus, temporary workers hold assignments that generally last for a specified time period rather than ongoing, permanent positions.

Some temporary workers report more job satisfaction with their employment choices than others. For example, consider the following two statements:

I never, ever dreamed I would resign from a very well paying, secure job with great benefits simply because I didn't want to work there anymore and I wanted to do something different. But at the age of thirty-nine that is exactly what I did . . . I turned in my resignation, tightened my belt, made some adjustments and went through with my plans. (Mendenhall, 1993, p. 14)

I'm the type of person that if I do a job, I want to do it. And I want to be challenged. So all of these assignments have been really sort of easy for me. But I try not to let that bother me because I know it's not something I'm going to stay with. (Henson, 1993, p. 180)

Current job satisfaction is likely to be an influence on career decisions made during transitions. Job satisfaction is defined as the difference between the reality of the job and the worker's expectations of the job based on a variety of factors such as pay and work environment. Dissatisfaction with a job may lead to disengagement from the job or the occupation as a whole (Clemons, 1988; Hoppock, 1935). Individuals who enter temporary work with perceptions that are not realized once they are in the field may meet with dissatisfaction. Temporary workers with low levels of job satisfaction may quit their jobs precipitously and without adequate planning for career transitions. Furthermore, job dissatisfaction can have devastating effects on individuals (DeCotis & Summers, 1987; Hendrix, Steel, & Schultz, 1987; Kesler, 1990). For example, O'Toole (1973) found multiple consequences of job dissatisfaction, which include mental and physical health problems. Kornhauser (1965) associated low self-esteem, anxiety, depression, and psychosomatic illness with job dissatisfaction. In contrast, Schultz (1982) found that job satisfaction influences the quality of one's work activities; specifically, high levels of satisfaction have been correlated with high performance, low turnover, and low absenteeism.

So, has temporary work become a permanent industry? If so, who chooses this occupation and why? Do temporary workers find job satisfaction? Finally, is it possible to use an assessment tool to help individuals who are experiencing career transitions determine if temporary work will be a satisfying job choice? This chapter contains a description of a typical temporary worker, a description of the temporary work industry, an examination of the reasons individuals choose temporary work, an examination of job satisfaction theories related to temporary work, and a description of suggestions for counseling individuals considering temporary employment.

Profile of Typical Temporary Workers

Temporary workers have been considered in the same context as those who engage in part-time, leased, contract, or seasonal work. Historically, the lack of an established definition of temporary workers has hindered exact estimates of this segment of the labor force. For example, the BLS uses three different formulas to estimate the contingent workforce and thus reported that the actual number of individuals in the temporary workforce in 1995 may have been as few as 2.7 million workers or as many as 6 million workers (Polivka, 1996a). The first formula defines temporary workers as workers who have been placed in their assignments for less than 1 year and expect to leave it within 1 year. The second formula uses the same time requirement as the first formula but also includes self-employed workers and independent contractors to the first formula. The third estimate expands the second formula by removing the time requirement (Polivka, 1996c).

The BLS began tracking contingent workers in 1995 with a national survey (Polivka, 1996b). In the first survey, it was found that typical temporary workers were female, Black, and between the ages of 16 and 24 years. On the average, temporary workers were enrolled in school and were three to four times more likely to be enrolled in an educational program than permanent workers. Perhaps surprisingly, temporary workers were more likely to be found in professional occupations such as university teaching rather than in lower skilled occupations such as sales. These findings cast shadows on the image of temporaries as low-skilled workers. The study was replicated in 1997, and results indicated that the total percentage of temporary workers increased slightly from 9.8% of the total labor force in 1995 to 9.9% of the labor force in 1997 (DiNatale, 2001). Other findings such as demographic data were similar to the first survey (Hipple, 1998). In 1999, the survey was again replicated, and the proportion of the labor force in temporary work decreased slightly to 9.3% . Temporary workers were again found to be young, Black or Hispanic, and female. However, in comparison with earlier reports, more temporary workers stated a preference for temporary work rather than for permanent employment. The reasons that temporary workers have reported for selecting temporary employment include the flexibility of the work arrangements so as to tend to family obligations or attend school (DiNatale, 2001).

Historically, temporary workers on an average earned 15%–20% less than permanent employees (Moreau, 1994). In 1997, wages for workers in the temporary workforce averaged $329 per week, whereas permanent workers earned an average of $510 (Cohany, 1998). Benefits for temporary workers have been available once the worker met specific criteria, usually an accumulation of over 1,500 hours of service in 1 year (Moreau, 1994), and about one fourth of temp workers were eligible for health insurance in 1997 as compared with two thirds of permanent workers (Cohany, 1998).

The Rise of Temporary Work as an Industry

Brokering agencies for temporary workers became commonplace during World War II. As 17 million men left the civilian workforce for military service, women took their places in factory jobs. There was an increase of job openings in the lower paying clerical jobs that had been abandoned by the women. Temporary positions were created to fill this void. This phenomenon was noted as the foundation of women in the workforce (Belous, 1989). Women have continued to comprise the largest segment of the temp workforce, although the percentage of male temporary workers has increased from 20% in 1989 to 28% in 1994 (Lawlor, 1994). After the end of World War II, men returned to their past jobs; however, temporary workers were still used to replace permanent workers who were either ill or on vacation.

Contributing to the growth of the temporary work industry was an increase in the use of temporary employees as adjunct workers by companies who sought to reduce personnel costs, gauge personnel needs, and screen potential new employees (Steinberg, 1993). Naisbitt (1984) projected that from the 1980s to the year 2000, there would be a social reevaluation of the contributions of permanent employees to their organizations. Although Naisbitt and Aburdene's (1990) prediction that this reevaluation would result in 10 million workers serving as leased employees by the year 2000, even the most liberal of the BLS estimates places the number as closer to 6 million workers (Hipple, 2001).

Belous (1989) stated that during the 1980s, the temporary labor force grew 40%–50% faster than the entire labor force, with a 33%–50% increase in the number of jobs created for temporary workers. Between 1982 and 1994, the total temping industry grew by more than 360%. The number of individuals employed as temporaries in 1993 alone grew by 21% over 1992's participants. Almost 17% of all jobs added during the economic recovery of 1982–1987 were temporary positions. The same situation occurred with the 1990 recession and subsequent recovery. For example, service and temporary positions accounted for 153,000 new jobs in 1994 alone (Greenwald, 1994).

The emergence of information occupations, such as those that involved computer specialties, has been a trend that explains some of the growth of the temporary help industry. The National Association of Temporary Services (1994) stated that 63% of temporary workers served in clerical capacities. Additionally, 50% of growth in the temporary industry during the 1990s was forecast to be in office services (Moore, 1992). However, today's temporary workers often possess advanced computer skills. The National Association of Temporary Services found that specialty temporaries are part of the fastest growing segment of the temporary industry. Today's temporary workers are likely to perform more sophisticated tasks and more likely come to the assignment with advanced skills than their predecessors (Melchinno, 1999).

The totality of the contributing factors has led to the rise of the temporary work industry, which has produced an annual $67.5 billion trade with at least 3 million workers participating daily (National Association of Temporary Services, 2001). This trend is expected to last well into the 21st century, which may see an increase in workers who perform specific duties for a company but who do not hold traditional, permanent positions (Judy & D'Amico, 1997). For example, the BLS projects that the occupation of college and university faculty will be among the largest growing occupations (Bureau of Labor Statistics, 2000). Positions for temporary workers in university teaching positions have also been on the rise (Hipple, 2001). Thus, it is likely that temping will continue to have a stronghold on the labor force.

Reason for Choosing Temporary Work

The inability to secure a permanent position may be one reason that individuals find themselves in temporary work. Another reason for selecting temporary work may be that individuals choose temporary work as a primary occupation. Individuals may also choose temporary work as a solution to a career transition. These three areas are explored independently.

Temporary Work as the Only Option

On average, the temporary help industry has experienced a 15.7% annual growth despite four recessions over the last 20 years. The fundamental basis for this growth has been the reshaping of the corporate workforce. The temporary work industry has been closely aligned with the strategic staffing approach to hiring that gained popularity in the 1990s (Collins, 1994). Increasingly, the focus in the organization has been on core employees in internal departments that maintain the organization (Sacco, 1989). Other duties such as mail, payroll, and personnel have often been outsourced to contract agencies (Stanley, 1994). Personnel needs have been assessed and controlled through flexible staffing, thus saving the corporation money. Using temporary workers has served as a way to handle shifting work loads while screening for possible permanent hires (Messmer, 1993). Allan and Sienko (1998) found that contingent workers displayed higher motivation than permanent workers perhaps in an attempt to gain a permanent spot. In summary, it has appeared that the increased use of temporaries suggests a permanency of temporary positions (Bridges, 1994; Feldman & Doerpinghaus, 1992; Grossman & Magnus, 1989; Millner, 1989).

Temporary Work as a Career Choice

Besides the changing corporation, personal choice has explained some of the rise in the temporary work industry. The National Association of Temporary Services (1994) reported that 40% of temporary employees have been offered permanent positions. Of this percentage, 38% have refused the offer for reasons such as not liking the environment, not liking the pay, and preferring to remain in temporary work.

One reason individuals have chosen to work as temporaries has been the opportunity to enhance career opportunities by building skills that improve permanent employment prospects. The National Association of Temporary Services (1994) identified the opportunity to update or build skills as a primary reason for seeking temporary work. In the same survey of temporary workers, the National Association of Temporary Services found that 80% of temporary workers agreed with the statement that temporary work provides experience and training that enhanced career opportunities. In 1994, 30% of temps received over 20 hours of free training. Over 80% of today's temporaries have word-processing skills and 20% have desktop publishing competencies (Barrance, 1994; Olsen Temporaries, 1994; Richman, 1994).

The need for basic literacy skills as well as more advanced computer skills has been intensifying as workplaces undergo restructuring. For example, the loss of highly skilled workers due to early retirement or lay-off has not been replaced by entry-level workers. More than one tenth of job applicants have been rejected because they lacked basic workplace literacy skills. Temporary workers have often come to the employer with advanced workplace skills (Richman, 1994). Temporaries have often received training in the latest technology from the brokering agency, and they have often trained current core employees (Sacco, 1993). Also, there have been times when the available staff did not have the necessary skills for a project. Losey (1991) stated that the need for specialized services has increased the use of temporaries with specialized skills, such as accountants, nurses, and engineers. Thus, temporary work has often enhanced an individual's permanent job prospects by providing training opportunities for the updated skills needed in today's workplace.

Another possible reason for choosing temporary work has been the flexibility in scheduling work time limits so that workers can meet other commitments, such as family obligations. The workplace and family have been the two central institutions in most American's lives (Zedeck & Moiser, 1990). Changes in work environments, social values, and family structures have occurred at a rapid rate (McDaniels, 1989). For example, only 20% of families are traditional nuclear families, and almost 60% of today's families are headed by single mothers (Burge, 1987; Friedman, 1987). There has also been a significant increase in dual-career families (Rosin, 1990; Zedeck & Moiser, 1990). The changing family structure has created career-work conflicts for many workers.

Greenhaus (1988) described the basis of most conflicts that produce stress for working families as being time based, strain based, and behavior based. The strain has been particularly harsh on women as many of them have been in a position whereupon they serve as primary caretakers to both their children and their parents. Temporary work has provided flexibility for individuals, especially women, to work while still attending to family needs (Rothausen, 1994).

Another possible reason for choosing temporary work has been related to the aging workforce. The older worker has been expected to be one of the fastest growing segments of the workforce (Bureau of Labor Statistics, 2000). Between 1989 and 1994, the proportion of temporaries age 35–64 rose from 40% to 50% (Lewis, 1994). Corporate restructuring has created a phenomenon of early retirement and employee contract buyout. Many of these workers possess the same skills that are sought in the temporary workers hired to fill the employment gaps. The American Association of Retired Persons conducted a poll that found that 51% of these retired workers wanted to work beyond age 65, and they desired to enter the company pool of temporary workers. Besides the benefit to the company of retaining highly skilled, committed, and motivated employees, working may have a positive impact on individuals (Hanisch & Hulin, 1990). Working retirees have reported fewer health problems and financial problems than those not returning to work (Brown & Gray, 1991). Temporary agencies have responded to the need for employment of these workers by creating special recruitment programs aimed at the older worker (Lexington, 1990).

Temporary Work as a Career Transition Solution

The choice to enter temporary work may be for the purpose of adjusting to a career transition. Career transitions may be anticipated, such as job promotion, or they may be unanticipated, such as job termination. The concept of career transitions has been studied by career theorists such as Donald Super and Nancy Schlossberg.

Super's Life-Span/Life-Space Approach to Career Development

In his work, Super (1976, 1980) addressed the definition of a career, a transition, and job satisfaction. Super (1976) defined a career as follows:

> The sequence of major positions occupied by a person throughout [his or her] pre-occupational, occupational, and post-occupational life; includes work-related roles such as those of student, employee, pensioner, together with complementary vocational and familial and civic roles. Careers exist only as people pursue them; they are person centered. (p. 20)

Career development occurs in stages that Super defined as growth, exploration, establishment, maintenance, and decline. Transitions occur as individuals move from stage to stage and as individuals confront external forces, such as restructuring of the work environment, or internal forces, such as illness. As individuals transition through stages, they are expected to occupy nine different roles. In the approximate order of occurance, they are son/daughter, learner, worker, spouse, parent, homemaker, citizen, leisurite, and pensioner. Throughout the lifecycle, work is a primary focus for most individuals, although for some individuals this focus is peripheral, incidental, or even nonexistent. Other foci, such as leisure activities and homemaking, may instead be central (Super, 1980).

Super contended that individuals experience job satisfaction in a variety of settings. Although many factors influence the degree of satisfaction, the extent that individuals are able to develop and implement self-concepts is proportionately related to job satisfaction. Super's work suggests that job satisfaction for temporary workers is dependent on the extent to which individuals are able to meet their needs in the workplace.

Schlossberg's Theory of Transitions

Cabral and Salomone (1990) stated that there is a need for a model of adult career development that includes the role that chance and personal characteristics play in decision making. How individuals attempt to understand these influences and cope with chance events needs to be considered. Schlossberg (1984) established a framework for adult career development based on the notion that adults need to be approached as individuals, not in terms of predictable behavior stemming from early childhood experiences nor by age or stage but in terms of transitions. Included in the definition of transition are obvious life changes, such as job entry, and less obvious changes, such as loss of career aspirations. Also to be considered as career transitions are anticipated events that did not come to pass, such as an expected promotion that was never offered. "Thus a transition can be both an event and a nonevent—if it results in change" (Schlossberg, 1984, p. 43). Spierer (1977) claimed that "a transition is any change that has important consequences for human behavior" (p. 6). If an individual does not change previously held assumptions or relationships, then there is no transition. For example, if a worker is not affected by the denial of a promotion and continues to work at the same position, then the worker did not experience a career transition. However, if the worker reacts to the nonevent by deciding to quit the job, then the worker has entered a transition. The goal is for individuals to be able to balance assets and liabilities and, thus, workers should be able to explore goals, narrow choices, and evaluate actions in order to be planful when encountering a career transition (Schlossberg, 1972).

Schlossberg (1984) contended that transitions are "a process of continuing and changing reactions over time—for better or for worse—which are linked to the individual's continuous and changing appraisal of self-in-situation" (p. 56). Each individual's ability to satisfactorily resolve transitions depends on personal traits as well as the nature of the contexts in which the transition takes place. It is possible that individuals are not able to satisfactorily resolve the transition and may face a deterioration of circumstances. If successful, individuals will be able to resolve the transition in a manner that allows the individual to integrate it into the self-concept (Schlossberg, 1984).

Temporary work can be a viable option for individuals experiencing anticipated events such as transitioning from the role of student to the role of worker and transitioning from the role of worker to the role of pensioner. Temporary work can also provide an option for individuals experiencing unanticipated events such as a job layoff or sudden single parenthood (Ryan, 1991). Is it possible to use assessment to estimate if any of these individuals might find job satisfaction with temporary work? To answer this question, it is first necessary to examine the connection, if any, between temporary work and job satisfaction.

Job Satisfaction and Temporary Workers

There are no well-defined theories of job satisfaction regarding temporary workers because few researchers have examined the job satisfaction of temporary workers. In a literature review, Henson (1993) found evidence that the growth of the temporary work industry is driven by employment demands. Henson concluded that workers seek temporary employment for its schedule flexibility and for its varied and satisfying work.

Jackle (1993) studied the factors that influenced the choice to choose temporary work among nurses. She also found that most contingent nurses prefer the work flexibility. Barrett (1993) conducted a study regarding the satisfaction of temporary workers with their brokering agency. A total of 330 employees from two agencies were surveyed. They expressed moderate satisfaction with their agency, and 80% stated they would recommend temporary employment to a friend.

Blai (1991) used Maslow's theory of human motivation as the basis for a study aimed at predicting job satisfaction of 412 temporary government workers. The study explored the hypothesis that self-assessed job satisfaction varies in relationship to the degree that psychological needs are satisfied in the workplace. Results indicated that the strongest psychological needs that influence job satisfaction include interesting duties, job security, and self-actualization.

Lewis (1992) found that variables such as job satisfaction influence temporary workers' organizational commitment. Temporary workers tended to hold more organizational commitment and job satisfaction in regards to flexibility than full-time workers when allowed to work preferred schedules, although most viewed temporary work as a compromise to permanent employment.

Surveys conducted by the BLS regarding the job satisfaction of temporary workers found that the highest level of dissatisfaction occurred when individuals were seeking permanent employment directly prior to entering the contingent workforce. A plausible reason for their dissatisfaction may be that these individuals had hoped for a permanent job. Temporary workers who reported being satisfied with their choice tended to be enrolled in educational programs (Polivka, 1996b).

Preston (1995) surveyed 100 workers in a pool for temporaries at a large rural university and found the temporary workers reported being satisfied with the pay, supervisors, coworkers, and the job in general. The temporaries reported dissatisfaction with promotion possibilities, which suggests that they did not find that temping was leading to permanent positions with the university.

A review of the few job satisfaction studies that have focused on temporary workers suggests that it is possible to identify factors that may indicate satisfaction with temporary work. For example, individuals choosing temporary work for reason such as the flexibility in scheduling and variation of job tasks it affords may find the work more satisfying than those who entered temporary work as a consequence of not finding permanent employment. Knowing these factors, it may be possible to assist individuals contemplating entering temporary work in assessing their potential for job satisfaction.

Counseling Individuals Considering Temporary Work

Individuals experiencing a transition may seek a counselor for assistance in seeking a resolution to their present circumstances. Schlossberg and Robinson (1996) described a strategy for dealing with transitions titled the "Dream Reshaping Process" (p. 52). Individuals must first acknowledge the transition and then ease the distress associated with experiencing a transition. The next step is to refocus by letting go of old expectations and, finally, reshape the future by taking stock and regaining control. An instrument, the McDaniels Career Transitions Consideration Form (McDaniels, Hedricks, & Watts, 1991) may assist with this last task. The self-report form is intended to serve as an impetus for self-discovery of the issues that are most salient for individuals experiencing transitions. Once this process has been completed, it is possible for individuals to explore temporary work as an option that will be consistent with their needs.

The form consists of nine factors that individuals should consider when experiencing a career transition:

- Health (How much is your health a consideration for you?)
- Finances (How much is your financial situation a consideration for you?)
- Family (How much is your family situation a consideration for you?)
- Place of residence (How much is your geographical location a consideration for you?)
- Work options (How much are your work options a consideration for you?)
- Leisure options (How much are your leisure options a consideration for you?)
- Personal issues (How much are your personal issues a consideration for you?)
- Networking issues (How much are networking issues a consideration for you?)
- Other issues (How much are other issues a consideration for you?)

Individuals are first instructed to rate how much they are considering each factor by using a rating scale with setpoints at 0 (*very little*), 25 (*little*), 50 (*somewhat*), 75 (*much*), and 100 (*very much*). Individuals are then requested to rank order the factors in order of importance, ranging from 1 (*most important*) to 9 (*least important*). As a result of this exercise, individuals should be able to identify the factors that are most salient to them. Once the factors have been identified, the likelihood that temporary work will adequately address their career transition considerations can be explored.

Preston (1995) utilized the form in a study of 100 workers employed in a pool of temporary workers at a large rural university. The temporary workers reported that the factors they most considered while in a transition were finances, family, and work options. It was also found that temporary workers who had given more consideration to these factors were more satisfied with temporary work. Thus, the McDaniels Career Transitions Consideration Form (McDaniels et al., 1991) is a nonstandardized assessment tool that may have promise for assisting individuals learn more about their concerns as they attempt to resolve a career transition.

Conclusion

The temporary work industry is a significant force in the labor market, with over 1 million daily participants. The typical temporary worker is between the ages of 18 and 24 years, minority, and female. Temporaries are often attending educational program and are thus more likely to be experiencing a transition such moving from school into the workforce. Another likely characteristic of temporary workers is that they may serve as primary caretakers of their families (DiNatale, 2001). Temporary employment allows these workers the flexibility in scheduling periods of work so as to meet family obligations (Rothausen, 1994). Perhaps for these reasons, the percentage of temporary workers who report that they prefer temping is increasing (DiNatale, 2001).

Another factor contributing to the rise of temporary work to an industry is the restructuring of U.S. corporations. For some companies, temporary work has become a permanent fixture in modern business-staffing schemes (Collins, 1994). The use of contingent workers allows businesses to concentrate their resources on core employees, outsource routine tasks, and utilize specialized temporaries for unique projects (Melchinno, 1999; Steinberg, 1993).

It seems plausible to expect that temporary work will remain a staple of the labor force, and it is also plausible to believe that temping is a viable option for those seeking to resolve a career transition. It may also be possible to use assessment to determine how satisfied individuals may be with their choice to enter temporary work. The assessment should begin with an exploration of transition concerns and then continue with an analysis of the individuals' expectations that temporary work will solve those concerns (Schlossberg & Robinson, 1996). The McDaniels Career Transitions Concerns Form (McDaniels et al., 1991) is a tool that can help individuals with these steps and become more planful during the transition. Most likely, the more planned the transition, the more satisfied the individual will be with temporary work.

The concept of career transitions was first explored by theorists Donald Super (1976, 1980) and Nancy Schlossberg (1972, 1984). From this viewpoint, counselors should use a life-span/life-space developmental approach with clients. Helping professionals should assist individuals in understanding that career decisions are not isolated, singular events but evolve through the progression of life. Counselors should also teach their clients transition adaptation strategies. Building on the knowledge that career development is a lifelong process, individuals can be guided to expect and appreciate changing roles and develop coping skills for managing these changes. Finally, counselors should continue to develop assessment instruments to assist individuals with deciding if temporary work will resolve their career transition needs.

References

Allan, P., & Sienko, S. (1998). Job motivations of professional and technical contingent workers: Are they different from permanent workers? *Journal of Employment Counseling, 35,* 169–179.

Barrance, R. G. (1994). It's not just "temping" anymore. *The Secretary, 54*(8), 16.

Barrett, G. J. (1993). Job satisfaction in the temporary workforce (Doctoral dissertation, George Washington University, 1993). *Dissertation Abstracts International, 54,* 1866.

Belous, R. S. (1989). How human resource systems adjust to the shift towards contingent workers. *Monthly Labor Review, 112*(3), 7–12.

Blai, B. (1991). *Predicting job satisfaction.* Philadelphia: EDRS.

Bridges, W. (1994). *Job shift.* Reading, MA: Addison-Wesley.

Brown, D. R., & Gray, G. R. (1991). Rethinking the contingency workforce: Why not hire the retired? *SAM Advanced Management Journal, 56*(2), 4–9.

Bureau of Labor Statistics. (1992). *News* (USDL No. 92-179). Washington, DC: U.S. Department of Labor.

Bureau of Labor Statistics. (2000). *Occupational outlook handbook*. Indianapolis, IN: JIST.

Burge, P. L. (1987). *Career development of single parents*. Columbus, OH: ERIC.

Cabral, A. C., & Salomone, P. R. (1990). Chance and careers: Normative versus contextual development. *Career Development Quarterly, 39*(1), 15–70.

Clemons, C. R. (1988). The relationship of occupational stress and certain other variables to job satisfaction of licensed professional counselors in Virginia (Doctoral dissertation, Virginia Polytechnic Institute and State University, 1988). *Dissertation Abstracts International, 50,* 360.

Cohany, S. R. (1998). Workers in alternative employment arrangements: A second look. *Monthly Labor Review, 121*(11), 3–22.

Collins, S. (1994, July 4). The new migrant workers. *US News and World Report,* 53–55.

DeCotis, T. A., & Summers, T. P. (1987). A path analysis of a model of the antecedents and consequences of organizational commitment. *Human Relations, 40,* 445–470.

DiNatale, M. (2001). Characteristics of and preference for alternative work arrangements, 1999. *Monthly Labor Review, 124*(3), 28–48.

Feldman, D. C., & Doerpinghaus, H. I. (1992). Missing persons no longer: Managing part-time workers in the '90s. *Organizational Dynamics, 21*(1), 59–72.

Friedman, D. E. (1987). Work vs. family: War of the worlds. *Personnel Administrator, 32*(8), 36–39.

Gardner, J. M. (1994). The 1990–91 recession: How bad was the labor market? *Monthly Labor Review, 117*(6), 3–11.

Greenhaus, J. H. (1988). The interaction of work and family roles: Individual, interpersonal, and organizational issues. *Journal of Social Behavior and Personality, 3*(4), 23–44.

Greenwald, J. (1994, November). The new service class. *Time, 144,* 72–74.

Grossman, M. E., & Magnus, M. (1989). Temporary services: A permanent way of life. *Personnel Journal, 68*(1), 38–40.

Hanisch, K. A., & Hulin, C. L. (1990). Job attitudes and organizational withdrawal: An examination of retirement and other voluntary withdrawal behaviors. *Journal of Vocational Behavior, 37*(1), 60–79.

Hendrix, W. H., Steel, R. P., & Schultz, S. A. (1987). Job stress and life stress: Their causes and consequences. *Journal of Social Behavior and Personality, 2,* 291–302.

Henson, K. D. (1993). Just a temp: The disfranchised worker (Doctoral dissertation, Northwestern University, 1993). *Dissertation Abstracts International, 54,* 1969.

Hipple, S. (1998). Contingent work: Results from the second survey. *Monthly Labor Review, 121*(11), 22–36.

Hipple, S. (2001). Contingent work in the late 1990s. *Monthly Labor Review, 124*(3), 3–27.

Hoppock, R. (1935). *Job satisfaction*. New York: Harper & Row.

Jackle, M. J. (1993). Contingent employment in nursing: Factors affecting career choice (Doctoral dissertation, University of Texas at Austin, 1993). *Dissertation Abstracts International, 54,* 1198.

Judy, R. W., & D'Amico, C. (1997). *Workforce 2020: Work and workers in the 21st century*. Indianapolis, IN: Hudson Institute.

Kesler, K. D. (1990). Burnout: A multimodal approach to assessment and resolution. *Elementary School Guidance and Counseling, 24*, 303–311.

Kornhauser, A. W. (1965). *Mental health of an industrial worker*. New York: Wiley.

Lawlor, J. (1994, May 3). More men lured to temp work. *USA Today*, p. B2.

Lewis, R. R. (1992). Dimensions of commitment: An examination of worker–organization linkages in a large bureaucracy (Doctoral dissertation, Virginia Polytechnic Institute and State University, 1992). *Dissertation Abstracts International, 53*, 3690.

Lewis, R. (1994). Escaping from the jobless maze. *National Retired Teachers Association Bulletin, 35*(9), 2.

Lexington, A. (1990). Office temporaries are trained for the times. *Office, 111*(2), 36–41.

Losey, M. R. (1991). Temps: They're not just for typing anymore. *Modern Office Technology, 36*(8), 58–59.

McDaniels, C. (1989). *The changing workplace*. San Francisco: Jossey-Bass.

McDaniels, C., Hedrick, D., & Watts, G. (1991). *A career success formula*. Garrett Park, MD: Garrett Park Press.

Melchinno, R. (1999). The changing temporary work force: Managerial, professional, and technical workers in the personnel supply services industry. *Occupational Outlook Quarterly, 43*(1), 24–33.

Mendenhall, H. (1993). *Making the most of the temporary employment market*. Chicago: Betterway Books.

Messmer, M. (1993). When hiring temporaries can be a permanent solution. *Corporate Controller, 5*(3), 36–38.

Millner, G. W. (1989). Professional temps in today's workforce. *Personnel, 66*(1), 26–30.

Moore, R. E. (1992). American labor law and workplace control: Addressing the issues of deindustrialization and the increased utilization of temporary labor (Doctoral dissertation, State University of New York at Buffalo, 1992). *Doctoral Dissertation Abstracts, 55*, 677.

Moreau, D. (1994, June). When temping is a permanent job. *Kiplinger's Personal Finance Magazine*, 95–99.

Naisbitt, J. (1984). *Megatrends*. New York: Warner.

Naisbitt, J., & Aburdene, P. (1990). *Megatrends 2000*. New York: William Morrow.

National Association of Temporary Services. (1994, Summer). Profile of the temporary workforce. *Contemporary Times*, 1–4.

National Association of Temporary Services. (2001). *Staffing firms create 100,000 new jobs: Results of fourth quarter national survey*. Retrieved from http://www.natss.org/staffstats/release03-05-01.htm

Olsen Temporaries. (1994). *Skills for success*. New York: Author.

O'Toole, J. (1973). (Ed.). *Work in America: Report on a special task force to the Secretary of Health, Education, and Welfare*. Cambridge, MA: MIT.

Polivka, A. E. (1996a). Contingent and alternate work arrangements, defined. *Monthly Labor Review, 119*(10), 3–9.

Polivka, A. E. (1996b). Into contingent and alternative employment by choice? *Monthly Labor Review, 119*(10), 55–74.

Polivka, A. E. (1996c). A profile of contingent workers. *Monthly Labor Review, 119*(10), 10–21.

Preston, D. S. (1995). Effects of planned career transitions and job satisfaction (Doctoral dissertation, Virginia Polytechnic Institute and State University, 1995). *Dissertation Abstracts International, 56*(04), 1250.

Richman, L. S. (1994, August 22). The new worker elite. *Fortune,* 56–66.

Rosin, H. M. (1990). The effects of dual career participation on men: Some determinants of variation in career and personal satisfaction. *Human Relations, 43,* 169–183.

Rothausen, T. J. (1994). Job satisfaction and the parent worker: The role of flexibility and rewards. *Journal of Vocational Behavior, 44,* 317–336.

Ryan, A. J. (1991). Temporary work can soothe layoff sting. *Computerworld, 25*(3), 67.

Sacco, S. R. (1989). Staffing for profitability in today's new world economy. *Personnel Journal, 68*(1), 9–10.

Sacco, S. R. (1993). All employment relationships are changing. *Managing Office Technology, 38*(5), 47–48.

Schlossberg, N. K. (1972). A framework for counseling women. *Personnel and Guidance, 51,* 137–143.

Schlossberg, N. K. (1984). *Counseling adults in transition.* New York: Macmillan.

Scholssberg, N. K., & Robinson, S. P. (1996). *Going to Plan B: How you can cope, regroup, and start your life on a new path.* New York: Fireside.

Schultz, D. P. (1982). *Psychology and industry today.* New York: Macmillan.

Spierer, H. (1977). *Major transitions in the human life cycle.* New York: Academy for Educational Development.

Stanley, B. N. (1994, December 26). A year of promise? *Richmond Times Dispatch,* pp. 12D, 14D.

Steinberg, B. (1993, Summer). The temporary help industry: An annual update for 1992. *Contemporary Times,* 1–4.

Super, D. E. (1976). *Career education and the meanings of work.* Washington, DC: U.S. Department of Health, Education, and Welfare.

Super, D. E. (1980). A life-span, life-space approach to career development. *Journal of Vocational Behavior, 16,* 282–298.

Thompson, M. (1992, March 8). Uncle Sam wants who? Not "riffed" soldiers. *The Charlotte Observer,* pp. A1, A8.

Zedeck, S., & Moiser, K. L. (1990). Work in the family and employing organization. *American Psychologist, 45,* 240–251.

Special Problems

16

The Impact of Modern Performance Rankings on Career Counseling and Employee Development in Corporate America

Sherry Knight Rossiter

he practice of periodically evaluating employee performance has been an accepted personnel management tool for more than 50 years, but the practice of using formal performance ranking bands has only become a general practice in the last decade. This chapter explores, through the use of case study and commentary, how the contemporary practice of performance ranking is affecting the nature of career counseling and employee development in corporate America. The names of the employees used in the case studies are fictitious, and certain facts have been changed to maintain client confidentiality. However, each of the case studies presented involves a performance ranking issue of some type and, subsequently, a career counseling challenge.

Introduction

Two years ago, employees still came to my counseling office in a major high-tech company to ask fairly traditional questions about strategies for obtaining a promotion or repositioning themselves within the organization. Now, corporate employees most often come to my office for advice on how to maintain their current performance ranking or how to move up in ranking. One employee actually came in and said, "Hello. My name is Bob. I'm a '2.' How can I become a '3'"?

While Bob's introduction initially made me smile, I only had to take one look at his face, particularly his eyes, to recognize the serious nature of his question. A lively discussion ensued about the company's current ranking system, Bob's past performance ranking, and his current skill set. It did not take Bob long to articulate his feelings about the ranking system and about how his individual contributions were viewed by his manager.

Bob is a network administrator for a high-tech company that has become totally focused on customer service, both internal and external. While Bob's network was only "down" for less than an hour in the past 12 months, it was that 1 hour of downtime that Bob's manager remembered and focused on in Bob's latest performance review. Prior to this latest performance evaluation, Bob had been ranked a "3," or an average performer within the company. Now, Bob's desire was to improve his personal visibility not only in the eyes of his manager but also in the eyes of the other managers, who meet once a year to rank employees.

In the meantime, Bob had been devastated and demoralized by his manager's negative tone during the performance evaluation, and Bob was beginning to believe that he no longer "added value" to the company. Instead of praising Bob for his network being operational 99.99% of the time, Bob's manager focused only on the 1 hour that the network was not operational during the past year. When managers or supervisors conduct employee performance reviews in a negative or insensitive manner, the likely outcome is an employee who now feels inherently bad about his or her performance.

This common tendency in corporate America to focus on personal deficits is not only detrimental to employee well-being but also detrimental to society as a whole, and to businesses in particular. It should be self-evident that employees with low self-esteem and a negative self-image are not as productive as employees with high self-esteem and a positive self-image. However, to better understand the negative impact that performance ranking has on most employees, the basic mechanics of performance ranking must be examined.

Basic Mechanics of Performance Ranking

Some companies like Ford Motor Company rank employees with letter grades similar to those used in American classrooms (A, B, C, etc.), whereas other companies use a numerical ranking system in which the highest number equates with the best performance. For example, both Cisco Systems and Hewlett Packard use a 5-band system, where being ranked as a "5" will ensure top pay and open doors to new promotional opportunities.

According to an article in the May 30, 2001, issue of *USA Today*, "Cisco Systems has set a goal of getting rid of one out of every 20 employees each year, even when it was growing so fast that it could not fill new positions" ("More Firms Cut Workers," 2001, pp. B1–B2). The company's hope is that if employees know this is the company's policy, they will work harder and smarter to help Cisco stay ahead of the competition. However, most American workers do not respond well to such fear-based motivational strategies over the long term.

The lowest performance ranking band ("1") generally makes up 5%–10% of a company's workforce. For the bottom 5%–10% to be accurately identified, the employee group must be large enough and random enough for a meaningful bell-curve distribution. For example, if there are only five salesmen in the company who are ranked together as a group (and who generate approximately the same annual sales revenue), it may not make any sense at all to use this type of performance ranking distribution system. However, if there are 500 salesmen in a company who are ranked together as a group (and who generate vastly difference annual sales revenues), then using this type of performance ranking distribution system may be sensible and cost-effective. Even then, the actual distribution may be a skewed performance curve as opposed to a perfect bell curve.

Employees unlucky enough to be ranked at the low end of the performance curve are generally offered "an opportunity" to leave the company with a small severance package or offered a time-dependent performance contract. Unfortunately, the time frame for remediation is short, typically 30–90 days. At the end of that time, if the employee has not showed substantial improvement in specified areas, the employee will again be asked to leave the company—this time without any severance package, as is the policy at Sun Microsystems.

While the opponents of performance ranking believe the system to be highly subjective, often unfair, and generally inhumane, the proponents of performance ranking believe the system to be inherently objective, usually fair, and very humane. Employees with low performance rankings believe that ranking employees is simply a way for companies to morally rationalize terminations, whereas employees with high performance rankings believe the company has a moral obligation to identify and dismiss the low performers.

When queried, employees with high performance rankings believe they will continue to receive high rankings in the future. It is not until an employee's ranking suddenly drops from a "4" to a "2" or "1," sometimes without any warning, that it occurs to the employee that the company's ranking system may not be as inherently fair as they once thought it was.

On the basis of the number of lawsuits already filed, the impact of performance ranking on career counseling strategies and employee development methodologies is only going to increase in the next decade. In the past 15 months, employees have filed class action suits against Ford, Microsoft, and Conoco alleging discrimination in ranking practices. In each of these cases, a different population is involved: older workers at Ford; Blacks and women at Microsoft; U.S. citizens at Conoco ("More Firms Cut Workers," 2001).

But, no matter if you are a proponent or an opponent of the system, performance ranking will continue to affect the nature of career counseling and employee career development well into the future. In the last half of the 20th century, employees were seeking career counseling to devise a strategy for moving up one rung on the proverbial corporate ladder. Now, at the beginning of the 21st century, employees are seeking career counseling to learn how they can improve their performance ranking because they believe that will ensure long-term employment and a pay increase.

Necessity for Comprehensive, Person-Centered Career Counseling Approach

Although it is no longer a well-kept secret that the psychological contract between employee and employer has been altered significantly over the past 10–15 years, most employees are just now beginning to understand how this altered relationship between employer and employee will affect long-range career planning and job security. A.G. Watts from the

National Institute for Career Education and Counseling says, "The model is no longer a long-term relational contract, based on security and reciprocal loyalty. Now, it tends increasingly to be a short-term transactional contract, based on a narrower and more purely economic exchange (Rousseau, 1995). It, therefore, needs to be constantly re-negotiated" (Fuller & Walz, 1997, p. 231). Because management is now using performance ranking as their primary method for retaining "top performers," employees at all organizational levels are being forced to reevaluate and rethink their own career paths at least annually, if not more often. Job security is a myth gone by the wayside. The new overemphasis on performance ranking engenders a "look out for me" attitude that certainly does not foster collaboration in the workplace.

This new emphasis on performance ranking has necessitated a huge paradigm shift for both employees and counselors of employees. Within the new paradigm, conflicts of workplace values have become an everyday occurrence, and competition, rather than collaboration among coworkers, now flourishes like it never has before. Because of this psychological and ethical "disconnect" between "old" and "new" workplace values, career counselors and employee development specialists must engage in a more comprehensive, person-centered approach to counseling employees than they have used in the past.

I believe a comprehensive, person-centered approach to career counseling in the 21st century requires the counseling professional to look at six specific impact areas: emotional, cognitive, physical, social, spiritual, financial. Furthermore, career counselors and career development specialists must have the courage to ask the tough questions. They must also have the courage to give honest answers to the questions posed by employees. This is especially true in the case of low performance ranking or job loss.

Table 16.1 illustrates the types of questions employees are asking career counselors these days.

According to Howard Figler, "The emotional dimensions of career counseling are quite apparent to any practitioner" (Figler & Bolles, 1999, p. 295), but the other dimensions as outlined in Table 16.1 may not be so apparent. Unless a career counselor has worked with victims of traumatic stress, the counselor may not understand that sudden job loss or major workplace change will affect "the whole person" (i.e., body, mind, and spirit) and not just be cognitively and financially unsettling. For this reason, I advocate and practice a more comprehensive, person-centered

Table 16.1   Typical Questions Clients Often Ask Career Counselors

Emotional

- Why do I feel so angry?
- Why do I feel so worthless and ashamed?
- Why do I feel so guilty?

Cognitive

- Why can't I concentrate or seem to make any decisions?
- What will happen to me and my family if I can't find a new job?
- What should I do now?

Physical

- Is it normal to feel "sick to my stomach" under these conditions?
- How come I feel so physically exhausted?
- Am I too old (or fat or unattractive) to find a new job?

Social

- What will my coworkers think when they hear my performance ranking has dropped?
- How do I break this news about the upcoming "downsizing" to my family?
- Is it socially acceptable to tell my neighbors I'm unemployed?

Spiritual

- Why did this happen to me?
- What did I ever do to deserve this?
- Do you think God is punishing me for some reason?

Financial

- How will I pay my rent next month?
- Can I afford to take a pay cut with my next job?
- What are the ramifications of taking money out of my 401(k) plan before age 59½?

approach to career counseling than the approach I was first exposed to in graduate school.

The easiest way to illustrate the need for a more comprehensive, person-centered career counseling approach in the 21st century is to take a look at four cases studies.

Case Study 1: Bob

Case Study 1 involves Bob, the employee introduced previously in this chapter. Bob was clear about what he wanted to accomplish as a result of career counseling: He wanted to increase his performance ranking from a "2" to a "3." Bob was aware that to increase his performance ranking, he would have to find a way to positively increase his visibility within his entire division. However, Bob believed that his manager should be able to see that he was doing a good job, and it went against his personal value system and work style to have to "fabricate reasons" to draw attention to himself to increase his perceived value to the company.

Nonetheless, Bob agreed to brainstorm with me how he might increase his visibility at work. Of the many ideas we generated, three looked most promising:

1. Volunteer for a special project, especially one that his manager really was not looking forward to doing.
2. Write a "white paper" regarding a process improvement or network redesign.
3. Send his manager a list of his accomplishments monthly or quarterly.

Fortunately, Bob possessed strong analytical and organizational skills, which he used daily as a network administrator, so he decided he would attempt to accomplish all three of these suggestions over the next 3–6 months.

Three months later Bob came back to see me. He reported that he was writing a weekly list of his personal, work-related accomplishments and then sending the list to his manager monthly. Just writing the weekly list had made him realize all the different ways he added value to the company, and that alone had increased his self-esteem and self-confidence.

Also, Bob wrote a white paper on a network problem for which the team had never been able to find a long-term solution. Bob first shared the paper with his manager, and then at his manager's request, Bob shared his paper with his teammates. Another team member made a functional improvement to the solution Bob had suggested, and now Bob was again working collaboratively with his team.

Bob said his manager was still looking for a special project to assign to him, but in the meantime, his manager seemed to be treating him with more respect and appreciation. While there was no way to tell for sure, Bob felt confident that he might be given a higher performance ranking the next time around.

From a corporate career counselor's perspective, Bob's case is not particularly unusual. With or without a performance ranking system in place, Bob might have been identified by his manager as someone performing "below average." Clearly, managers have a responsibility to evaluate the performance of their employees. The real issue here, however, is in how the manager chose to talk with Bob about his performance. Focusing only on the negative (i.e., the 1 hour the network was nonoperational all year) was truly damaging to Bob's self-esteem and sense of worth. Fortunately, Bob had the maturity to recognize that he could benefit from visiting with the career counselor about his work-related situation.

It is important for career counselors to remind their clients that the only real control they have at work (and in life) is over their own attitudes and actions. If an employee wants to influence his or her manager's or coworker's behavior, the employee can only do so by changing his or her own attitude and behavior. In other words, by changing the steps of the dance, the dynamics of the current relationship might well be changed too.

Changing attitudes and behaviors requires cognitive reframing, and that requires a willingness to look at a situation from a new perspective. Instead of viewing a situation in the worst possible light, an effective career counselor can help an employee look at a situation from a more positive perspective. In other words, instead of viewing a work situation from a place of discouragement (i.e., "There is nothing I can do that will change my ranking"), the career counselor can help the client view the work situation from a place of encouragement (i.e., "What new opportunities for professional and personal growth can come from this current work situation?"). With ongoing career counseling support, Bob was able to reframe his initial devastation into new determination to be viewed more favorably in the eyes of his manager and teammates, which he hoped would ultimately result in an increase in his performance ranking.

Case Study 2: Carol

Carol is a 40-year-old software engineer with a master's degree in computer science. When she first came to see me for career counseling at the suggestion of her manager, Carol could only tell me repeatedly that her manager did not like her. Carol viewed that as "extremely unfair" because her manager had never taken the time to get to know her. I mostly listened without interruption as Carol told her story, and finally she divulged that her ranking recently had dropped from a "3" to a "2." Carol was terrified that she would soon be ranked a "1" and then be terminated by the company.

As Carol and I talked, I became aware that she was highly intuitive, verbally expressive, and a good creative problem-solver. In addition, she was spiritually attuned and placed a high value on harmonious relationships both in and out of the workplace. I wondered silently if part of the problem between Carol and her manager was simply a "styles difference." From Carol's description, it sounded like her manager was logic-driven and task-oriented, whereas Carol appeared to be values-driven and relationship-oriented. In other words, Carol and her manager probably had totally opposite personal styles, and these differences were magnified within the confines of a small work group.

By the end of our first session, Carol still was convinced that if her manager would just take the time to get to know her, the performance issues would disappear. However, my experience as a career counselor suggested that the solution was not that simple, and Carol and I began meeting monthly.

Carol was very overweight and fond of wearing large print, oversized blouses. In addition, she wore thick-lensed glasses in the most colorful plastic frames imaginable. Just her appearance made it difficult to take her seriously, and I knew that a large portion of the criteria for ranking had to do with a manager's perception. If Carol's manager perceived her as "different," that alone could cause the manager, even subconsciously, to rank her lower than her peers.

Fortunately, Carol and I were able to have an open and honest discussion about her appearance. Carol agreed to begin dressing in less colorful and more tailored clothing and to purchase a very plain pair of eye glasses to wear to work. The next time I met with Carol, she was smiling and upbeat. She reported that her manager and coworkers seemed to be talking with her more, and they were less critical of her performance.

Throughout our monthly sessions, Carol was reminded that she had no control over her manager's thoughts or actions, but she did have control over her own thoughts and actions. We discussed specifically how to change her own internal dialogue into more positive self-talk based on the suggestions of Shad Helmstetter in his book *Choices* (1989). Carol soon learned that positive self-talk made her feel powerful and in control, whereas negative self-talk made her feel like a victim.

Personal empowerment can take many forms, but one quick way to empower clients who feel like victims is to remind them that they do have choices: They can choose what they think, what they believe, how they act. It was in this context that we devised a plan to change Carol's appearance, which you already know resulted in a positive outcome.

However, Carol had come to realize that the computer programming she was doing in her current job was no longer challenging for her, and she was thinking she would like to try her hand at management. She had been the lead engineer on a number of team-based projects, but she had no formal training as a supervisor or manager. While I had some concerns about her ability to succeed in management in this particular corporation, I kept those concerns to myself and helped revise her resume.

We had planned to work on interviewing skills during our next session, but Carol called a few days before our scheduled meeting to tell me she had been selected for a management position within another division of the company. From her description, this new position sounded like "a good job fit" for her. At that time, I was pleased that Carol's case had such a happy ending, but I was truly elated 6 months later when I saw one of Carol's employees for career counseling and she kept referring to Carol as "an awesome manager."

The reality is that what one manager perceives as "a problem employee," who adds little value to the company, another manager may perceive as "a star performer," who adds tremendous value to the company. The last time I saw Carol, she told me she is now ranked a "4" and loves being a manager of people rather than of projects.

Unfortunately, many companies do not allow "low performers" the opportunity to reposition within the company. Ranking information is usually accessible to hiring managers in most companies, and there is no incentive to hire a "1" or a "2" over a more highly ranked employee, even if the lower ranked employee has more experience or a better skill set.

In summary, Carol had recognized for some time that she should be looking for a new job because she no longer felt challenged by her work, but she had been afraid nobody else would hire her. Once she felt empowered to take more control over her thoughts, feelings, and actions, she was able to conduct a job search without assistance, ace a hiring interview, and secure a new job better aligned with her interests and personal style.

But not all employees with low performance rankings are as lucky as Bob and Carol. Let's now look at the case of Ted.

Case Study 3: Ted

Ted is a 53-year-old engineer who is just 18 months away from retirement. He has worked for XYZ Corporation for 27 years and always assumed he would retire from "the company" at age 55. Within the last 6 months, Ted's performance ranking dropped from a "4" to a "1," and a week ago he received written notice that he is on probation. The letter stated specific areas for improvement but contained no measures of evaluation. At the end of the letter, Ted was informed that he had 30 days "to improve" his performance or he would be terminated. After giving Ted the letter, his boss suggested he might want to visit with someone from the human resources (HR) department. The HR employee Ted talked with suggested that he find a professional career counselor or coach familiar with performance ranking issues. Ted later contacted me in my private practice on the recommendation of a friend.

When Ted first appeared in my counseling office, it was clear that his emotions were running the gamut between anger and devastation. He was rapidly blinking his eyes and flexing and unflexing his neck muscles. My first-things-first philosophy mandated that I deal with Ted's emotions immediately.

Initially, Ted resisted my efforts to get him to talk about his feelings, but finally the tears started to flow while his clenched fists gently, but rhythmically, banged on the table where we sat. I sat silently and respectfully with Ted for almost 8 minutes before he was ready to speak. When appropriate, I validated and normalized Ted's feelings about his current work situation. Words Ted used to describe his feelings included *anger, betrayal, disbelief, numbness, confusion,* and *fear*—all words commonly used by victims of trauma produced by rape, assault, or natural disaster.

As Ted's story unfolded, I learned that he had never been ranked lower than a "4" for all the years that the current performance ranking system had been used by his company and that being dropped to a "1" had happened virtually overnight. Ted had been working on an important project for the past 2 years, and that project was now almost completed. He rarely received any feedback from his manager, and when he did, it was positive—that is, until his last performance review a week ago. Ted said he could hardly believe what his manager was telling him about his performance over the last year. Ted noticed that his manager had a hard time making eye contact and kept clearing his throat, all behaviors that Ted translated as nervousness on his manager's part. At the end of the performance review, his manager had told him he was now ranked a "1" and handed him the probation letter. Ted walked out of his manager's office in shock.

Ted said it took a few days for him to really comprehend the significance of his circumstances. When he finally realized he was close to being terminated, he said denial initially took over, but soon he became angry, then depressed, and now just plain scared. Ted said, "It feels like my spirit is dying and I don't know how to stop it."

Ted did not think there was any way he could improve his performance in the short time allotted. Moreover, it was still unclear to him what the performance issues really were. Even after talking a second time with his manager at my suggestion, and again to the HR representative, Ted still did not understand specifically what performance areas needed improvement or what the evaluation criterion would be, and neither did I.

Ted and I discussed his options:

1. He could attempt to improve his performance in all areas over the next 30 days and hope for the best.
2. He could make no changes in his performance for the next 30 days and probably be asked to leave the company without any severance pay
3. He could be preemptive and ask for a severance package right now.
4. He could ask if the company might consider accelerating his retirement considering his age and longevity with the company.
5. He could immediately start looking for another job externally.

Ted was aware that trying to obtain another job within XYZ Corporation while on probation was not even a possibility.

With essentially only 3 weeks left to take action, Ted decided he would first ask the company if they would accelerate his retirement. If they refused to do that, then he would ask for 18 months severance knowing that the company would probably counter that request with an offer of 12 months severance. In the meantime, he would begin revising his résumé on the basis of my specific recommendations and post the résumé on a number of well-known Internet Web sites.

Whereas Bob's and Carol's cases were resolved fairly quickly and in a positive manner, resolution to Ted's case is still pending. XYZ Corporation chose not to give Ted any severance package. Two months ago, Ted decided to file an age discrimination suit against the company knowing that it will be several more months before the case can be heard. Concurrently, Ted moved his family to a smaller house, sold one of his classic cars to generate some cash flow, and started working out of his home as a contract employee for a temporary help agency.

The emotional, cognitive, physical, social, spiritual, and financial issues faced by Ted are manifold. He has maintained contact with me via e-mail and telephone because he knows he needs the emotional support and encouragement that a career counselor can provide. Meanwhile, Ted is continuing to look for another career-oriented job, but he is being very selective about his next employer. Ted still feels betrayed by his former employer of 27 years, and he is leery about working for another large corporation.

Case Study 4: Alice

Alice is a 21-year-old woman who is working in a customer support center. When she first contacted me by e-mail indicating she was interested in returning to college, I asked her what she planned to study in college. Her response was brief: "I don't know. That's why I want an appointment to meet with you." We set an appointment for the next week.

When Alice came to our meeting, she initially appeared self-assured and mature. However, as we talked, it became apparent that she wanted to return to college for all the wrong reasons. She let me know that she was not willing to spend significant time pursuing an education because she "had a life" outside of work that was very important to her. She also said she could not understand why she was not being offered opportunities for advancement even though she had only worked for the company 6 months.

The bottom line was that Alice only wanted to return to college so she could "move up in performance ranking and make a lot of money." She believed that she should be making twice the amount she was making in her entry-level position and that obtaining a college degree would allow her to move more quickly up the corporate ladder. Although Alice did not seem to understand the promotional structure within this particular company, she did realize that pay raises were based on performance ranking. Alice's past work experience included teaching aerobics and working as a waitress. Three years ago, she had dropped out of college after only 1 week because "the classes weren't interesting."

Individuals like Alice, who were born between 1965 and 1975, have been referred to simultaneously by sociologists, journalists, and the media as Baby Busters, Twentysomethings, or Generation X'ers. Because many of these workers do not look at work in the same way that the Baby Boomer generation looks at work, "companies particularly feel a cultural shift as they attempt to hire this generation into entry-level positions" (Fuller & Walz, 1997, p. 285).

Typical complaints from employers about this generation include a lack of maturity, unrealistic salary expectations, a poor work ethic, no loyalty, and a general lack of professionalism. For a generation that grew up with television, computerized games, and microwaves, this generation appears to be short on patience, long on self-interest, and very confused about values and identity. But hidden beneath the surface of most Generation X'ers is a passionate caring for humankind and the environment, a desire to live their lives to the fullest, and a willingness to put health and family ahead of money and work—values that many Baby Boomers have set aside to become upwardly mobile.

In summary, it is the difference in values that creates challenges to employers and career counselors when working with Generation X'ers like Alice. Many Generation X'ers believe they should be promoted and receive pay raises simply because they have showed up at work on time for the past 6 months. Career development for this generation of workers should include a good deal of education about the expectations of the company in terms of performance, an explanation of company policy regarding promotions and ranking, and a healthy dose of economic reality in terms of entry-level salaries.

Conclusion

Jean Houston summarizes it well in *Jump Time* (2000, p. 70) when she wrote, "Take this little story to another plane, and you have the trauma of the twentieth century—our tendency to see people as ciphers and statistics to be manipulated, the feeling tones of their lives unremarked and dis-repected." More and more organizations are now referring to their employees as "headcount" or "expendable resources," meaning that employees are as easily replaceable as office supplies.

The widespread practice of openly referring to performance ranking band 1's and 2's as "low performers" or "slackers" (as one Fortune 50 CEO told the media) not only is degrading and dehumanizing but also is send-ing a distressing message to employees—a message that they are no longer valued by their employer. This is especially true when training, coaching, and mentoring opportunities within a company have been taken away from employees under the guise of cost cutting or "benchmarking."

Modern business strategy can be summed up by "faster, better, cheaper." This management philosophy requires that employees work harder and faster, but with fewer resources. Global companies are extremely concerned about "time to market" and essentially expect their engineers to release products that are not complete. One department head actually told his team that if the product would generate only 5% com-plaints from the consumer, the product was complete enough to be on the market. Needless-to-say, that created a definite values conflict for some of the age 40+ engineers working on that R&D team. When employees voice ethical concerns about their work, they are most likely told that every company is doing it and their company also needs to do it to be competitive or, worse yet, they are told they are negative and not team players. Neither explanation bodes well with quality-driven employees.

At the present time, corporate career counselors, career development specialists, and HR personnel are spending a great deal of time counseling and coaching employees in how to tiptoe around "the elephant in the liv-ing room" rather than how to identify and confront the elephant (as taught in Twelve Step programs). In other words, instead of identifying and confronting behaviors that would be considered dysfunctional in any other setting, career counselors and HR professionals are now expected to teach employees how to function, cope, and optimally produce in work environments that are often hostile, nonencouraging, and highly compet-itive. This expectation creates confusion, stress, and values conflicts not only for the employees but also for career counselors and HR profession-als hired to foster employee career development and enhance human performance in the workplace.

Finally, how can career counselors and employee development special-ists continue to work effectively with employees in the contemporary workplace with the current emphasis on employee performance ranking? While there is no easy or succinct answer to that question, I do believe the answer for both counselor and employee lies in clarifying personal values, in understanding the pervasive and often negative impact that modern performance ranking systems have on employee development and employee morale, and in encouraging employees to find work that supports their chosen lifestyle rather than trying to build a life in the spaces between work and sleep.

The case studies of Bob, Carol, Ted, and Alice all have one thing in common: Each client or employee was dealing with the impact of contemporary performance ranking on his or her career path. Although these employees might have faced the same issues in a corporation without an employee ranking system, I believe the impact of what they were dealing with would have been less intense psychologically speaking if performance ranking numerics had not been involved.

Generally speaking, most well-adjusted employees can receive, process, and act on constructive feedback when they feel they are working in an essentially positive and supportive environment. It has been my experience that the majority of employees do want to contribute to their employer's success in positive ways and that they do their work to the best of their abilities. However, most employees who are truly low performers also know when they are not working up to their employer's expectations. It would seem that a more humane and psychologically sound method of weeding out "the low performers" could save corporations time and money in the long run while salvaging the employees, who are teachable and retrainable.

Performance ranking is not and never will be a neutral process because there are too many variables for managers—who are still fallible human beings with prejudices, biases, and blindspots—to objectively consider and access. But, until the pendulum swings back to a more person-centered performance evaluation system, employees will continue to seek the guidance of career counselors, coaches, and mentors, hoping they will be able to help them "make sense" of what has shaken up, disrupted or derailed their career track under the guise of employee performance ranking.

In a highly competitive corporate-dominated world in which compassion, cooperation, and common sense are rapidly disappearing, it is even more important for career counselors to focus on the whole person, to listen respectfully to their clients' stories, to answer questions honestly and directly, to be practical in their career counseling approach, and to help employees find or recapture the true meaning of work in their lives.

References

Figler, H., & Bolles, R. (1999). *The career counselor's handbook*. Berkeley, CA: Ten Speed Press.

Fuller, R., & Walz, G. (Eds.). (1997). *Career transitions in turbulent times: Exploring work, learning and careers*. Greensboro, NC: ERIC/CASS.

Helmstetter, S. (1989). *Choices*. New York: Pocket Books.

Houston, J. (2000). *Jump time: Shaping your future in a world of radical change*. New York: Penguin Putnam.

More firms cut workers ranked at bottom to make way for talent. (2001, May 30). *USA Today*, B1–B2.

17

Addressing Depression in the Workplace

Steven J. Morris and Patrick H. Hardesty

epression is the "common cold" of psychopathology (Charney & Weissman, 1988). Like the common cold, it is widespread and costly. Across the life span, males have a 3%–12% risk of major (clinical) depression and females a 7%–21% risk (Clark & Beck, 1999; Kessler et al., 1994). Milder subclinical forms of depression are even more common (Clark & Beck, 1999; Wells et al., 1989). Nearly 11 million people in the United States suffered from major depression in 1990 (Greenberg, Stiglin, Finkelstein, & Berndt, 1993a). In that same year, depression cost the workplace $24 billion as a result of excessive absenteeism and diminished productivity (Greenberg, Stiglin, Finkelstein, & Berndt, 1993b). "The cost of depression to employers, particularly the cost in lost work days, is as great or greater than the cost of many other common medical illnesses" (Druss, Rosenheck, & Sledge, 2000, p. 1274). The odds of decreased effectiveness at work may be seven times as high for employees with depressive symptoms (Druss, Schlesinger, & Allen, 2001). Increasingly, employers have come to recognize that it is to their economic benefit to combat depression (as well as other mental health problems) in the workplace.

The purpose of this chapter is to provide insight into depression to help counselors and employers address the problem of depression in the workplace. In the first section, we explore the nature of depression and consider how the symptoms of depression are manifested in the workplace. In the second section, we examine some causes of depression, including the role of work-related stressors. In the third section, we draw on the previous discussion as well as work on the treatment and prevention of depression to consider ways that employers can deal with depression in the workplace.

The Nature of Depression

Depression has three related meanings. It refers to a symptom, to a syndrome, and to a distinct nosological entity (a diagnostic category). As a symptom, depression denotes a mood of profound sadness or dysphoria. Indeed, the predominant feature of clinical depression is a sustained disturbance in mood that involves severe dysphoria and/or loss of interest or pleasure in nearly all activities (Clark & Beck, 1999). In addition to a mood, depression refers to a cluster of correlated symptoms at a syndromal level: "A syndrome is a group or pattern of symptoms, affects, thoughts, and behaviors, that tend to appear together in clinical presentations" (Frances, First, & Pincus, 1995, pp. 16–17). Syndromes provide the basis for defining the mental disorders catalogued in the *Diagnostic and Statistical Manual of Mental Disorders—Text Revision* (4th ed. [*DSM–IV–TR*]; American Psychiatric Association, 2000). Syndromes constitute a necessary but not sufficient basis for defining a diagnostic category because a particular syndrome might be involved in more than one diagnostic category. The syndrome of depression (i.e., a major depressive episode) is a defining feature of three distinct nosological entities: major depressive disorder, bipolar II disorder, and schizoaffective disorder. In this section, we discuss the symptoms that make up the syndrome of depression, the different depressive disorders, and the symptomatic manifestations of depression in the workplace.

Symptoms of Depression

The syndrome of depression consists of four classes of symptoms: affective, cognitive, motivational–behavioral, and somatic or vegetative (see American Psychiatric Association, 2000). The specific symptoms are

1. persistent depressed mood, which the person may describe as sad, hopeless, empty, discouraged, or the like (dysphoria);
2. loss of interest or pleasure in ordinary activities (anhedonia);
3. feelings of guilt, worthlessness, helplessness, or low self-esteem;
4. difficulty thinking, concentrating, remembering, or making decisions;
5. recurrent thoughts of death or suicide or a suicide attempt;
6. decreased energy, fatigue, or tiredness;
7. psychomotor retardation (e.g., slowed speech) or agitation (e.g., the inability to sit still);
8. sleep disturbances (difficulty with falling asleep, staying asleep, or oversleeping);
9. eating disturbances (loss of appetite and weight or weight gain).

Although dysphoria and/or anhedonia are present in every case of depression, each of the other symptoms may or may not be present (Buchwald & Rudick-Davis, 1993). Thus, clinical presentations of the syndrome of depression display considerable diversity, depending on which symptoms are present. In fact, 10% to 15% of patients with severe depression deny feelings of sadness and only meet mood criteria on the basis of anhedonia (Coyne, 1994). Although feelings of worthlessness (or low self-esteem) are very common in depression, many people suffering from a major depressive disorder do not display these feelings (Buchwald & Rudick-Davis, 1993). A number of other features frequently, but not always, accompany the syndrome of depression, including (a) anxiety, (b) irritability, (c) brooding, (d) excessive crying, (e) complaints of aches and pains, and (f) social withdrawal or impairment. Thus, there is considerable variability in the depressive experience.

Depressive Disorders

Depression is not one nosological entity but several different disorders. All depressive disorders have a disturbance of mood as a core feature, and all are defined in terms of the syndrome of depression. These disorders vary in severity, chronicity, and clinical presentation (Clark & Beck, 1999). The *DSM–IV–TR* identifies several types of depression: major depressive disorder, minor depressive disorder, dysthymic disorder, and, although not a mood disorder per se, adjustment disorder with depressed mood. In addition, the syndrome of depression is a facet of the clinical presentation of bipolar II disorder and may be a part of the clinical presentation of bipolar I disorder. In this section, we briefly describe each of these disorders and then consider the hypothesis that depressive states lie on a continuum of severity.

Major depressive disorder is an episodic disorder involving one or more distinct periods characterized by the depressive syndrome. These periods are referred to as major depressive episodes. To qualify as a major depressive episode, five or more symptoms from the syndrome list must be present during a 2-week period or longer and one of the symptoms must be depressed mood or anhedonia. In addition, the symptoms must cause clinically significant distress or impairment in functioning. Clinical presentations of major depressive disorder vary depending on which particular symptoms are present. The duration of major depressive episodes vary but typically last 6 months or longer if left untreated. In some 5% to 10% of the cases, a major depressive episode persists for 2 or more years. In most cases, there is complete remission of symptoms, but in 20% to 30% of the cases some depressive symptoms persist at a subthreshold level for months to years. Major depression takes a recurring course; approximately 50% to 60% of individuals who experience a major depressive episode also experience a second episode.

Although not an official diagnostic category, minor depressive disorder was introduced in the *DSM–IV–TR* (American Psychiatric Association, 2000) as a provisional category deserving further study. It differs from a major depressive disorder in requiring fewer symptoms and less impairment. The essential feature of minor depression is one or more episodes involving either depressed mood or loss of interest or pleasure and a total of at least two symptoms but less than five from the depressive syndrome list. An episode must be at least 2 weeks in duration. Minor depression is an important diagnostic category because of the prevalence of depressive symptoms and their clinical significance (Clark & Beck, 1999).

Dysthymic disorder is a mild, chronic depressive state. The symptoms of dysthymic disorder are very similar to but less severe and more chronic than those of major depressive disorder. The essential feature is chronically depressed mood that lasts for "most of the day more days than not for at least 2 years" (American Psychiatric Association, 2000, p. 376). This diagnosis requires the presence of at least two of the following additional symptoms: poor appetite or overeating, insomnia or hypersomnia, low energy or fatigue, low self-esteem, poor concentration or difficulty making decisions, and feelings of hopelessness. This symptom criteria set shows considerable overlap with the syndrome of depression. Dysthymic disorder is a chronic, subsyndromal state that involves a dispositional tendency toward dysphoria (Clark & Beck, 1999).

Depression is a common response to psychosocial stressors like divorce, loss of a job, and illness. When a depressed mood (e.g., sadness, tearfulness, and feelings of loneliness) develops in response to a stressor so that there is excessive distress or impairment, a diagnosis of adjustment disorder with depressed mood is indicated. This diagnostic category involves a transient state of dysphoria that persists no longer than 6 months beyond the cessation of the stressor.

A major depressive episode can be a facet of disorders other than major depressive disorder, notably the bipolar disorders. Bipolar I disorder is characterized by one or more manic (or mixed manic and depressive) episodes, usually, but not always, accompanied by major depressive episodes. Bipolar II disorder involves one or more major depressive episodes accompanied by at least one hypomanic episode.

The *DSM–IV* treats depressive disorders as distinct categories that are qualitatively different from a depressed mood state. In contrast to this categorical approach, the continuity hypothesis (Flett, Vredenburg, & Krames, 1997) states that the symptoms experienced in the various dysphoric and depressive states differ in severity (quantitatively) but not in kind (qualitatively). Indeed, there is mounting evidence that depression does lie on a continuum of severity ranging from normal depressed mood to minor depressive states to major depressive states (Cox, Enns, Borger, & Parker, 1999; Ruscio & Ruscio, 2000; see reviews by Clark & Beck, 1999; Flett et al., 1997). In addition, the continuity hypothesis implies that the antecedents, concomitants, and consequences of depression (e.g., work and social impairment) are related linearly to the severity of symptoms (Flett et al., 1997). There is compelling evidence that psychosocial impairment is indeed a linear function of symptom severity (Lewinsohn, Solomon, Seeley, & Zeiss, 2000; see reviews by Clark & Beck, 1999; Flett et al., 1997). In particular, research has shown that work impairment increases across the entire range of depressive states from dysphoric mood to major depressive disorder (Clark & Beck, 1999; Endicott & Nee, 1997; Flett et al., 1997). Thus, minor depression and even dysphoria take a toll on work performance.

Manifestations of Depression in the Workplace

Depressive symptoms are manifested in a number of ways in the workplace. Decreased productivity or work impairment is a global manifestation of depression that reflects specific cognitive, affective, and motivational–behavioral symptoms. Cognitive deficits (impaired ability to think, concentrate, remember, or decide) may be expressed in various ways. For example, these deficits may be expressed in an inability to perform demanding but previously manageable tasks (e.g., writing a computer program). Other manifestations of cognitive deficits include forgetting to make a phone call or to respond to a request, having difficulty following instructions or staying on task, or having trouble organizing work or setting priorities. The inability to make decisions or to concentrate may lead to accidents or to mistakes. Anhedonia may be expressed as a loss of interest in work, an attitude of "not caring anymore" about one's job. Without enthusiasm, job performance inevitably suffers. For example, an avid salesman who previously relished soliciting business with clients may find excuses not to contact them. Feelings of worthlessness and helplessness may involve diminished confidence in the ability to perform work-related tasks. With diminished confidence in ability, a worker is less likely to initiate work-related tasks, to expend much effort on them, or to sustain effort in the face of obstacles (Bandura, 1997). For example, a journalist might procrastinate on writing an article, might not work hard on it, or might not persevere if the sources for the article are not cooperative. With fatigue and decreased energy as well as psychomotor retardation, employees with depression may work slowly and ineffectively. As a result of their cognitive and motivational deficits, depressed employees may even fail to complete assigned tasks. Furthermore, their diminished motivation and energy may lead to absenteeism. In an effort to dull their painful feelings of dysphoria, guilt, and worthlessness, depressed employees may begin to abuse alcohol and other drugs.

It is in the sufferer's social life that depression is often most apparent (see Joiner, Coyne, & Blalock, 1999). Symptoms are often expressed in impaired social behavior. For example, anhedonia may be reflected in withdrawal from social activities. In the workplace, employees with depression might isolate themselves from their coworkers or they might not contribute in meetings. To alleviate doubts about their self-worth, depressed individuals may seek excessive reassurance from others (Joiner et al., 1999). Their ability to collaborate and cooperate with others may decline. Furthermore, the depressed individual's social behavior can have a corrosive impact on others and the interpersonal climate. People in close contact with a person with depression may develop depression themselves (contagious depression; Joiner & Katz, 1999). Furthermore, people with depression elicit resentment and rejection from others (Coyne, 1976; Sacco, 1999; Segrin & Abramson, 1994). Thus, the behavior of a depressed employee can affect the work of others and even disrupt the entire workplace. The depressed employee's impaired performance may breed resentment, creating a hostile work environment. Furthermore, the depressed employee's depression can infect others. Morale may plummet.

The Causes (Etiology) of Depression

Depression results from an interaction between a person's biological and psychological vulnerabilities and the occurrence of stressful events or ongoing life difficulties (Akiskal, 1985; Zuckerman, 1999). In this section, we consider the contributions of biology, stress, and personality to the development and maintenance of depression.

Contributions of Biology

Like other medical and psychiatric illnesses, depression runs in families. Studies of twins and families clearly implicate a genetic component in both major depression and bipolar disorders (Zuckerman, 1999). Thus, there is evidence of an inherited vulnerability to developing depression. Many researchers have attempted to identify the specific physiological malfunctions that contribute to depression (see Howland & Thase, 1999). Much of their research centers on disturbances in the way that neurotransmitters (the chemical messengers in the brain) work. Medical conditions (e.g., diabetes) can contribute to depressive symptoms. For this reason, it is important for people with depression to have a thorough physical examination to rule out possible physiological causes of their depression.

Contributions of Stress

The role of stressors in precipitating episodes of depression is well established.

> Research dealing with the onset of particular episodes of adult depression has concluded that the majority are provoked by life events or ongoing difficulties; the role of events has emerged as clearly the more important of the two. . . . Studies have suggested that about 66%–90% of depressed episodes have a severe event occurring within six months of onset. (Brown, 1996, pp. 151–154)

Work is a significant source of depression-inducing stress. Work-related stress often triggers depression (Baba, Galperin, & Lituchy, 1999; Baba, Jamal, & Tourigny, 1998; Lowman, 1993). Thus, not only does depression lead to problems at work, but also problems at work lead to depression (Lowman, 1993). A vicious cycle can ensue in which depression impairs work performance, thereby generating stressful conditions at work that in turn exacerbate the depression.

Stress and Stressors

Stress refers to negative emotional–cognitive–behavioral–physiological response to a noxious or threatening condition in which the demands of the situation tax or exceed one's resources (see Lazarus, 1993, 1999; Pearlin, 1993). Stressors are the events and the demands that provoke stress reactions. A stress-arousing event for one person might not be stressful for another person. Whether a particular event is stressful or not depends on an appraisal of its personal significance ("Am I in danger?") and on an appraisal of the ability to successfully cope with it ("Am I able to do anything about it?"; Lazarus, 1999; Lazarus & Folkman, 1984). When people appraise a situation as a personal threat (rather than a challenge) and doubt their ability to cope with it, stress ensues. One salesman might approach a sales quota with stress, believing that he will be fired if he does not meet the quota and believing that he is not capable of meeting it. A saleswoman might approach the same sales quota with enthusiasm, viewing it as challenge that she can meet.

Burnout and Work-Related Stressors

There is evidence that job burnout mediates the relationship between work-related stress and depression (Baba et al., 1999; see also Glass & McKnight, 1996; Maslach, Schaufeil, & Leiter, 2001). That is, work-related stress may lead to burnout that in turn may lead to depression and a resulting impairment in work performance. "Burnout is a prolonged response to chronic emotional and interpersonal stressors on the job" (Maslach et al., 2001, p. 397). Burnout can spread from the work context to other life domains and give rise to depression.

The empirical literature on burnout provides insight into specific work-related stressors that generate burnout and thus that may contribute to the development of depression. Research has shown that the following work-related stressors precipitate burnout: excessive workload (Arsenault, Dolan, & Van Ameringen, 1991; Baba et al., 1999; Maslach et al., 2001);

underutilization of skills and abilities (Baba et al., 1998; Feltham, 1997); limited participation in decision making (Arsenault et al., 1991; Baba et al., 1998; Feltham, 1997; Maslach et al., 2001); work role ambiguity (lack of clarity about job expectations; Arsenault et al., 1991; Lowman, 1993; Maslach et al., 2001); work role conflict (conflicting job expectations; Arsenault et al., 1991; Baba et al., 1999; Lowman, 1993; Maslach et al., 2001); and a lack of feedback (Maslach et al., 2001). In addition, lack of social support is linked to burnout with the support of supervisors being more critical than that of coworkers (Baba et al., 1999; Lowman, 1993; Maslach et al., 2001).

Contributions of Personality

Most people do not become clinically depressed even when they confront serious stressors (Coyne & Downey, 1991; Monroe & Simons, 1991). Stress alone is not a sufficient condition for the development of depression. Personal and social vulnerabilities also play a role. In particular, various personality characteristics predispose people to depression (Akiskal, Hirschfeld, & Yerevanian, 1983; Clark, Watson, & Mineka, 1994; Gruen, 1993). Typically, these personality characteristics are viewed as diatheses, or predispositions to developing a disorder (in the present case, depression). From the perspective of a diathesis-stress model, these diatheses give rise to a disorder only when triggered by a matching stressor. Neither the diathesis nor the stressor alone is sufficient to cause the disorder. Researchers have proposed a variety of personality characteristics as diatheses for depression, including low self-esteem (Strauman & Segal, 2001), perfectionism (Blatt, 1995), neuroticism (Clark et al., 1994), and a depressogenic attributional style (Abramson, Alloy, & Metalsky, 1995). In this section, we consider three personality characteristics related to depression: coping style, negative thinking patterns, and the personality orientations of sociotropy and autonomy.

Coping Styles

Coping consists of cognitive and behavioral efforts to manage the demands of situations that tax or exceed the person's resources (i.e., stress; Gruen, 1993; Lazarus, 1993). People vary in their coping styles, their characteristic strategies for coping with stress. Coping strategies that involve approach as opposed to avoidance (such as direct problem solving and seeking information from others) can buffer people against the depression-inducing effects of stress (Holahan, Moos, & Bonin, 1999;

Nezu, Nezu, & Perri, 1989). By contrast, avoidant coping strategies (e.g., denial of problems and social withdrawal) is associated with depression (Holahan et al., 1999). Maladaptive coping may perpetuate depression through difficulties in decision making (Coyne, Aldwin, & Lazarus, 1981) and poor social problem-solving skills (Nezu et al., 1989).

Negative Thinking Patterns

People with depression are plagued by disparaging and gloomy thoughts about themselves and their lives. Cognitive therapy proposes that this negatively biased thinking plays a central role in the development and treatment of depression (Clark & Beck, 1999; Young, Weinberger, & Beck, 2001). The biased thinking of people with depression reflects the "negative cognitive triad": a negative view of self, personal world, and future (Clark & Beck, 1999; Young et al., 2001). Thus, people with depression view themselves as worthless, inadequate, and unlovable. They view the world as harsh, overwhelming, and depriving. They view the future as hopeless. These fundamental beliefs or assumptions about themselves, the world, and the future are referred to as schemas. People with depression bias their interpretations of events to be consistent with their schemas, resulting in their distorted thinking (Clark & Beck, 1999; Young et al., 2001). For example, a new teacher who mistakenly believes she is incompetent may misinterpret favorable feedback from her principal to be harsh criticism. This distortion of "reality" may precipitate a bout of depression. Presumably, maladaptive schemas remain latent in the depression-prone individual until activated by a stressor. For example, the teacher's "incompetence" schema may have been latent until activated by a parent who challenged her teaching methods.

Personality Orientations of Sociotropy and Autonomy

Beck (1983; Clark & Beck, 1999) distinguished two schematic personality orientations that determine what kinds of stressors are most likely to activate the latent schemas to produce depression: sociotropy and autonomy. The sociotropic personality strongly values close interpersonal relationships so that self-worth and a sense of well-being are based on being loved, accepted, and intimate with others. The autonomous personality strongly values mastery and independence so that self-worth and a sense of well-being are based on achievement and control. Sociotropy and autonomy are diatheses that interact with matching stressors to precipitate a depressive reaction. Matching stressors for the sociotropic person involve a perceived loss of social acceptance or attachment (e.g., perceived rejection), whereas for the autonomous person matching stressors involve a perceived loss of independence, control, or accomplishment (e.g., perceived failure at work). After experiencing these stressors, the sociotropic person's thinking is characterized by thoughts like "I am unloved" and "Nobody likes me," whereas the autonomous person's thinking is dominated by thoughts like "I am a failure" or "I am helpless." Often these negative patterns in thinking reflect distortions of reality (e.g., misjudging how other people feel about one's self or underestimating one's competence). Nonetheless, these negative thoughts give rise to depression.

Dealing With Depression in the Workplace

The role of supervisors is to promote the productivity of their employees. Toward this end, supervisors identify and correct problems that impair work performance. One such problem is depression. As noted earlier, it is a problem that commonly afflicts employees and that impairs their productivity. Supervisors can contribute to both the treatment and to the prevention of depression in the workplace. They can do this by focusing on the employee or on working conditions, as we show below.

Focusing on Employees

There are three ways that supervisors can deal with depression in the workplace at the level of individual employees. First, they can foster conditions that encourage employees with depression to seek treatment. Second, although they are not therapists, supervisors can interact with depressed employees in ways that are "therapeutic." Third, to prevent depression, they can offer stress management programs that improve the ability of employees to cope with stressors that can precipitate depression.

In dealing with employees with depression, one's primary objective is to get them into treatment. With appropriate treatment, 80% to 90% of people with a major depressive disorder can be successfully treated (Greenberg et al., 1993a). Effective treatments include psychotherapy (notably cognitive therapy, behavioral therapy, and interpersonal therapy) and medication (DeRubeis & Crits-Christoph, 1998; Roth & Fonagy, 1996). Successful treatment leads to improvements in work functioning by providing symptom relief (Mintz, Mintz, Arruda, & Hwang, 1992).

Despite the availability of effective treatments, most people with depression do not get professional help (Frank & Thase, 1999). People do not seek help for a variety of reasons (see Kanfer & Schefft, 1988). First, people may fail to recognize the symptoms of depression in themselves or to realize their serious consequences (Greenberg et al., 1993a; Kanfer & Schefft, 1988). Second, the stigma of depression may inhibit people from seeking treatment (Greenberg et al., 1993a; Young et al., 2001). Third, people with depression may exaggerate the "costs" of treatment and may not be confident that it will help (Kanfer & Schefft, 1988). Finally, people may be unaware of resources for treating depression, or resources may not be readily available to them (Kanfer & Schefft, 1988).

Employers can counter these reasons for not getting help by providing educational programs about depression as well as resources for the treatment of depression. These programs should educate employees and supervisors about the symptoms of depression and their manifestations in the workplace and may include self-assessments of depression. With this information, supervisors and depressed employees themselves are more likely to detect depression. These programs should remove the stigma attached to depression by fostering the view that it is a treatable illness, not a character flaw or a sign of weakness. In addition, these programs should provide realistic information about the costs of treatment and evidence that treatments for depression work. Finally, these programs should provide information about the resources available for treating depression. Ideally, employers would make appropriate treatment available through Employee Assistance Programs (EAPs) and through company-sponsored health benefits. These activities should increase the percentage of employees with depression who are treated.

Although supervisors are not therapists, they can be therapeutic. Supervisors can help employees they suspect are depressed by encouraging them to talk about their feelings—preferably to a trained mental health professional. Not only can talking lead to therapy, but it can be therapeutic in itself. "The instinctive 'cheer up' approach may not work very well, but a willingness to listen, to be available and to offer any necessary practical help can go a long way" (Feltham, 1997, p. 161). Such support can begin to counteract the depressed individual's tendency to suffer in isolation due, in part, to eliciting rejection from others. Further along this line, supervisors can offer kind words and genuine compliments, demonstrating that they respect and value employees. The relationship with the supervisor may be particularly salient for the sociotropic person, whereas the performance feedback that the supervisor provides may be most salient for the autonomous person. (In treatment, the therapist would address the socioptropic individual's excessive dependence on others and the autonomous individual's excessive need for achievement.) Although empathic supervisors can acknowledge their employees' pain, they should refrain from moralizing or offering a diagnosis. Supervisors should be careful about giving personal advice that might be construed as "none of their business." Employees are particularly likely to resent the intrusion of a supervisor when they did not volunteer to discuss their depressed feelings or related work problems. In this delicate situation, the supervisor can make employees aware that problems in their functioning are noticeable, can express concern, and can encourage them to seek help to deal with any personal issues that might be affecting their work. Supervisors should be alert for any signs that an employee is suicidal because depression is associated with an elevated risk of suicide. Supervisors should take even mildly suicidal comments seriously (e.g., "life is not worth living") and should consider contacting an EAP counselor or other mental health professional.

Supervisors can be helpful by pointing out to employees with depression that their thinking is distorted and negative without being critical or disapproving of them but by encouraging them to consider objectively the evidence that contradicts their negative thinking (e.g., an award for sales excellence contradicting a negative self-image that "I am a poor salesman"; see Young et al., 2001). In light of the common problem-solving deficits associated with depression (Nezu et al., 1989), a supervisor can be helpful to employees by guiding them in a systematic problem-solving process (e.g., generating alternatives) to cope with stressful life problems.

As a preventive strategy, supervisors can provide systematic training in coping skills. Stress management programs (e.g., D'Zurilla & Nezu, 1989; Nezu & Nezu, 2001) focus on the development of a repertoire of skills that assist in coping with stressful situations (e.g., relaxation training). There is evidence that stress-management training is an effective intervention for treating and preventing depression, anxiety, and burnout (D'Zurilla, 1990; Jones & Johnston, 2000; Nezu et al., 1989; Rowe, 2000).

Focusing on Working Conditions

"Some employers assume that stressful working conditions are a necessary evil—that companies must turn up the pressure on workers and set aside health concerns to remain productive and profitable in today's economy. But research findings challenge this belief" (Sauter et al., 1999). Stressful working conditions are counterproductive, leading to absenteeism and diminished productivity. Indeed, work-related stress precipitates and exacerbates depression, resulting in impaired work performance.

It makes sense, therefore, to identify stressful aspects of work and to reduce or eliminate them. Some of a supervisor's efforts may be designed to improve the working conditions of a particular depressed employee. Other efforts may be designed to create healthy working conditions that minimize stress for all employees.

In modifying stressful working conditions that contribute to an employee's depression, a supervisor should collaborate with the employee. Together they should identify the source of the stress (e.g., the wrong occupation or position, conflict with a supervisor, and unsupportive coworkers), and together they should engage in problem solving to find a solution. The supervisor may decide to make "reasonable accommodations" (e.g., a flexible schedule) as required by the Americans With Disabilities Act of 1990.

The process of changing an organization to prevent job stress involves three steps: problem identification, intervention, and evaluation (Sauter et al., 1999). Based on evidence of the deleterious effect of some common work-related stressors, Sauter, Murphy, and Hurrell (1990) made a number of recommendations concerning working conditions to prevent job stress:

1. The workload should be compatible with workers' capabilities and resources.
2. "Jobs should be designed to provide meaning, stimulation, and opportunity to use skills" (p. 1149).
3. Workers' roles and responsibilities should be clearly defined.
4. Workers should be given the opportunity to participate in decisions and actions affecting their jobs.
5. Jobs should provide opportunities for social interaction among workers.
6. Employers should make work schedules that are compatible with demands and responsibilities outside the job.

Steps like these can create a healthy work environment that minimizes the corrosive effect of stress.

Conclusion

Depression in the workplace is a major occupational health problem. It is in the enlightened self-interest of employers to address this problem, which afflicts millions of workers and which impairs their productivity. In this chapter, we have presented ideas to help employers understand the nature of depression and to help them develop a strategy for addressing depression in the workplace. We have paid particular attention to how depression is manifested in the workplace, how the workplace contributes to the development of depression, and how employers can manage depression in the workplace.

References

Abramson, L. Y., Alloy, L. B., & Metalsky, G. I. (1995). Hopelessness depression. In G. M. Buchanan & M. E. P. Seligman (Eds.), *Explanatory style* (pp. 113–134). Hillsdale, NJ: Erlbaum.

Akiskal, H. S. (1985). Interaction of biologic and psychologic factors in the origin of depressive disorders. *Acta Psychiatrica Scandinavica, 74*(Suppl. 319), 131–139.

Akiskal, H. S., Hirschfeld, R. M. A., & Yerevanian, B. I. (1983). The relationship of personality to affective disorders. *Archives of General Psychiatry, 40*, 801–810.

American Psychiatric Association. (2000). *Diagnostic and statistical manual of mental disorders—Text Revision* (4th ed.). Washington, DC: Author.

Arsenault, A., Dolan, S. L., & Van Ameringen, M. R. (1991). Stress and mental strain in hospital work: Exploring the relationship beyond personality. *Journal of Organizational Behavior, 12*, 483–493.

Baba, V. V., Galperin, B. L., & Lituchy, T. R. (1999). Occupational mental health: A study of work-related depression among nurses in the Caribbean. *International Journal of Nursing Studies, 36*, 163–169.

Baba, V. V., Jamal, M., & Tourigny, L. (1998). Work and mental health: A decade in Canadian research. *Canadian Psychology, 39*(1–2), 94–107.

Bandura, A. (1997). *Self-efficacy: The exercise of control.* New York: Freeman.

Beck, A. T. (1983). Cognitive therapy of depression: New perspectives. In P. J. Clayton & J. E. Barrett (Eds.), *Treatment of depression: Old controversies and new approaches* (pp. 265–290). New York: Raven Press.

Blatt, S. J. (1995). The destructiveness of perfectionism: Implications for the treatment of depression. *American Psychologist, 50*, 1003–1020.

Brown, G. W. (1996). Onset and course of depressive disorders: Summary of a research programme. In C. Mundt, M. J. Goldstein, K. Hahlweg, & P. Fiedler (Eds.), *Interpersonal factors in the origin and course of affective disorders* (pp. 151–167). London: Gaskell/Royal College of Psychiatrists.

Buchwald, A. M., & Rudick-Davis, D. (1993). The symptoms of major depression. *Journal of Abnormal Psychology, 102*, 197–205.

Charney, E. A., & Weissman, M. M. (1988). Epidemiology of depressive illness. In J. J. Mann (Ed.), *Phenomenology of depressive illness* (pp. 45–74). New York: Human Services Press.

Clark, D. A., & Beck, A. T. (1999). *Scientific foundations of cognitive theory and therapy of depression*. New York: Wiley.

Clark, L. A., Watson, D., & Mineka, S. (1994). Temperament, personality, and the mood and anxiety disorders. *Journal of Abnormal Psychology, 103*, 103–116.

Cox, B. J., Enns, M. W., Borger, S. C., & Parker, J. D. (1999). The nature of depressive experience in analogue and clinically depressed samples. *Behaviour Research and Therapy, 37*, 15–24.

Coyne, J. C. (1976). Toward an interactional description of depression. *Psychiatry, 39*, 28–40.

Coyne, J. C. (1994). Self-reported distress: Analog or ersatz depression. *Psychological Bulletin, 116*, 29–45.

Coyne, J. C., Aldwin, C., & Lazarus, R. S. (1981). Depression and coping in stressful episodes. *Journal of Abnormal Psychology, 90*, 439–447.

Coyne, J. C., & Downey, G. (1991). Social factors in psychopathology. *Annual Review of Psychology, 42*, 401–425.

DeRubeis, R. J., & Crits-Christoph, P. (1998). Empirically supported individual and group psychological treatments for adult mental disorders. *Journal of Consulting and Clinical Psychology, 66*, 37–52.

Druss, B. G., Rosenheck, R. A., & Sledge, W. H. (2000). Health and disability costs of depressive illness in a major U.S. corporation. *American Journal of Psychiatry, 157*, 1274–1278.

Druss, B. G., Schlesinger, M., & Allen, H. A. (2001). Depressive symptoms, satisfaction with health care, and 2-year work outcomes in an employed population. *American Journal of Psychiatry, 158*, 731–734.

D'Zurilla, T. J. (1990). Problem-solving training for effective stress management and prevention. *Journal of Cognitive Psychotherapy: An International Quarterly, 4*, 327–354.

D'Zurilla, T. J., & Nezu, A. M. (1989). Clinical stress management. In A. M. Nezu & C. M. Nezu (Eds.), *Clinical decision making in behavior therapy: A problem-solving perspective* (pp. 371–400). Champaign, IL: Research Press.

Endicott, J., & Nee, J. (1997). Endicott Work Productivity Scale (EWPS): A new measure to assess treatment effects. *Psychopharmacology Bulletin, 33*, 13–16.

Feltham, C. (1997). Common mental health concerns. In C. Feltham (Ed.), *The gains of listening: Perspectives on counselling at work* (pp. 155–179). Bristol, PA: Open University.

Flett, G. L., Vredenburg, K., & Krames, L. (1997). The continuity of depression in clinical and nonclinical samples. *Psychological Bulletin, 121*, 395–416.

Frances, A., First, M. B., & Pincus, H. A. (1995). *DSM–IV guidebook* (4th ed.). Washington, DC: American Psychiatric Association.

Frank, E., & Thase, M. E. (1999). *Natural history and preventative treatment of recurrent mood disorders*. London: Gaskell/Royal College of Psychiatrists.

Glass, D. C., & McKnight, J. D. (1996). Perceived control, depressive sympto-matology, and professional burnout: A review of the evidence. *Psychology and Health, 11,* 23–48.

Gruen, R. J. (1993). Stress and depression: Toward the development of integra-tive models. In L. Goldberger & S. Breznitz (Eds.), *Handbook of stress: Theoret-ical and clinical aspects* (pp. 550–569). New York: Free Press.

Greenberg, P. E., Stiglin, M. A., Finkelstein, S. N., & Berndt, E. R. (1993a). Depression: A neglected major illness. *Journal of Clinical Psychiatry, 54,* 419–424.

Greenberg, P. E., Stiglin, M. A., Finkelstein, S. N., & Berndt, E. R. (1993b). The economic burden of depression in 1990. *Journal of Clinical Psychiatry, 54,* 405–418.

Holahan, C. J., Moos, R. H., & Bonin, L. A. (1999). Social context and depres-sion: An integrative stress and coping framework. In T. Joiner & J. C. Coyne (Eds.), *The interactional nature of depression* (pp. 39–64). Washington, DC: American Psychological Association.

Howland, R. H., & Thase, M. E. (1999). Affective disorders: Biological aspects. In T. Millon & P. H. Blaney (Eds.), *Oxford textbook of psychopathology* (pp. 166–202). New York: Oxford University Press.

Joiner, T., Coyne, J. C., & Blalock, J. (1999). On the interpersonal nature of depression: Overview and synthesis. In T. Joiner & J. C. Coyne (Eds.), *The interactional nature of depression* (pp. 3–19). Washington, DC: American Psy-chological Association.

Joiner, T. E., & Katz, J. (1999). Contagion of depressive symptoms and mood: A meta-analytic review and explanations from cognitive, behavioral, and inter-personal viewpoints. *Clinical Psychology: Science and Practice, 6,* 149–162.

Jones, M. C., & Johnston, D. W. (2000). Evaluating the impact of a worksite stress management programme for distressed student nurses: A randomized controlled trial. *Psychology and Health, 15,* 698–706.

Kanfer, F. H., & Schefft, B. K. (1988). *Guiding the process of therapeutic change.* Champaign, IL: Research Press.

Kessler, R. C., McGonangle, K. A., Zhao, S., Nelson, C. B., Eshleman, S., Wittchen, H., & Kendler, K. S. (1994). Lifetime and 12-month prevalence of *DSM–III–R* psychiatric disorders in the United States: Results of the National Comorbidity Study. *Archives of General Psychiatry, 51,* 8–19.

Lazarus, R. S. (1993). Why we should think of stress as a subset of emotion. In L. Goldberger & S. Breznitz (Eds.), *Handbook of stress: Theoretical and clinical aspects* (pp. 21–39). New York: Free Press.

Lazarus, R. S. (1999). *Stress and emotion: A new synthesis.* New York: Springer.

Lazarus, R. S., & Folkman, S. (1984). *Stress, appraisal, and coping.* New York: Springer.

Lewinsohn, P. M., Solomon, A., Seeley, J. R., & Zeiss, A. (2000). Clinical impli-cations of "subthreshold" depressive symptoms. *Journal of Abnormal Psychology, 109,* 345–351.

Lowman, R. (1993). *Counseling and psychotherapy of work dysfunctions.* Washing-ton, DC: American Psychological Association.

Maslach, C., Schaufeli, W. B., & Leiter, M. P. (2001). Job burnout. *Annual Review of Psychology, 52,* 397–422.

Mintz, J., Mintz, L. I., Arruda, M. J., & Hwang, S. S. (1992). Treatments of depression and the functional capacity to work. *Archive of General Psychiatry, 49,* 761–768.

Monroe, S. M., & Simons, A. D. (1991). Diathesis-stress theories in the context of life stress research: Implications for the depressive disorders. *Psychological Bulletin, 110,* 406–425.

Nezu, A. M., & Nezu, C. M. (2001). Problem solving therapy. *Journal of Psychotherapy Integration, 11,* 187–205.

Nezu, A. M., Nezu, C. M., & Perri, M. G. (1989). *Problem-solving therapy for depression: Theory, research, and clinical guidelines.* New York: Wiley.

Pearlin, L. I. (1993). The social contexts of stress. In L. Goldberger & S. Breznitz (Ed.), *Handbook of stress: Theoretical and clinical aspects* (pp. 303–315). New York: Free Press.

Roth, A., & Fonagy, P. (1996). *What works for whom? A critical review of psychotherapy research.* New York: Guilford Press.

Rowe, M. M. (2000). Skills training in the long-term management of stress and occupational burnout. *Current Psychology: Developmental, Learning, Personality, Social, 19,* 215–228.

Ruscio, J., & Ruscio, A. (2000). Informing the continuity controversy: A taxometric analysis of depression. *Journal of Abnormal Psychology, 109,* 473–487.

Sacco, W. P. (1999). A social–cognitive model of interpersonal processes in depression. In T. Joiner & J. C. Coyne (Eds.), *The interactional nature of depression* (pp. 329–362). Washington, DC: American Psychological Association.

Sauter, S. L., Murphy, L. R., & Hurrell, J. J. (1990). Prevention of work-related psychological disorders: A national strategy proposed by the National Institute for Occupational Safety and Health (NIOSH). *American Psychologist, 45,* 1146–1158.

Sauter, S. L., Murphy, L., Colligan, M., Swanson, N., Hurrell, J., Scharf, F., Sinclair, R., Grubb, P., Goldenhar, L., Alterman, T., Johnston, J., Hamilton, A., & Tisdale, J. (1999). *Stress . . . at work* (DHHS Publication No. 99-101). Cincinnati, OH: National Institute for Occupational Safety and Health.

Segrin, C., & Abramson, L. Y. (1994). Negative reactions to depressive behaviors: A communications theories analysis. *Journal of Abnormal Psychology, 103,* 655–668.

Strauman, T. J., & Segal, Z. V. (2001). The cognitive self in basic science, psychopathology, and psychotherapy. In J. C. Muran (Ed.), *Self-relations in the psychotherapy process* (pp. 241–258). Washington, DC: American Psychological Association.

Wells, K. B., Stewart, A., Hays, R. D., Burnam, A., Rogers, W., Daniels, M., Berry, S., Greenfield, S., & Ware, J. (1989). The functioning and well-being of depressed patients: Results from the Medical Outcomes Study. *Journal of the American Medical Association, 262,* 914–919.

Young, J. E., Weinberger, A. D., & Beck, A. T. (2001). Cognitive therapy for depression. In D. H. Barlow (Ed.), *Clinical handbook of psychological disorders* (pp. 264–308). New York: Guilford Press.

Zuckerman, M. (1999). *Vulnerability to psychopathology: A biosocial model.* Washington, DC: American Psychological Association.

18

Working With the White-Collar Substance Abuser: An Intervention Method for Counseling Practitioners

Octavia Madison-Colmore, James L. Moore III, and Scheryl Price

n recent years, there has been growing concern about the use and abuse of alcohol and other drugs in the workplace. This concern has heightened as a result of the high percentage of substance abusers employed in the United States, an increase in the number of injuries and accidents in the workplace due to alcohol and other drug use, and the financial impact substance users and abusers have on the nation's economy. According to the 1999 National Household Survey on Drug Abuse, 12.3 million adults are illicit drug users; 9.4 million or 77% are employed either full time or part time (U.S. Department of Health and Human Services, 2000). Employees who drink and use drugs not only put themselves but also others in harm's way. Alcohol and other drug use can impair one's judgment, which adversely affects one's motor skills and cognitive abilities. It can also cost employers billions of dollars in work errors, wasted materials and supplies, productivity, health care, disability insurance, workers compensation, and personnel time. There are also human costs associated with substance abuse in the workplace, such as physical disputes, conflicts with supervisors, and low morale for employees (Ames, Grube, & Moore, 1997). The U.S. Department of Labor reports alcohol consumption to be associated with 27% of all murders, nearly 33% of all property offenses, and more than 37% of all robberies (Hanson & Venturelli, 1998, p. 20)

Several factors are believed to be attributed to this growing concern, such as workplace culture, workplace alienation, alcohol availability, level of supervision, and alcohol policies (National Institute on Alcohol Abuse and Alcoholism, 1999). Other factors include job-related stress, overwork, social factors outside of work, personality vulnerabilities brought into the workplace (Richman, Flaherty, & Rospenda, 1996), the degree of powerlessness, alcohol beliefs and expectations, and the type of occupation one has (Delaney & Ames, 1995). In a study conducted by Wiebe, Vinje, and Sawka (1995, p. 180), results indicated that blue-collar workers (e.g., construction and utility employees) reported higher quantity or frequency of alcohol consumption on the job than white-collar workers (e.g., management, professional, and sales employees). Wohlfarth and Van Den Brink (1998) found higher rates of alcohol and drug use disorders among the self-employed (e.g., small business owners) than employed workers (e.g., managers and supervisors). However, Richman et al. (1996) stated that problem drinking occurs in high-status as well as low-status occupations. Despite one's occupational status and the higher rates of substance use, most substance abusers do not seek professional help. Richman et al. believed that individuals employed in high-status occupations are least likely to seek professional help because of their level of denial. Bischof, Rumpf, Hapke, Meyer, and John (2001) stated that very few alcohol-dependent individuals seek professional help, and when they do, they go without formal therapeutic assistance.

To reduce the denial and thus encourage more employees, including white-collar workers, to become more knowledgeable about substance abuse and the process of addiction and seek professional help, employers have developed and implemented programs, such as Employment Assistance Programs and wellness programs. These programs provide an array of services, including literature on substance abuse, seminars, one-on-one counseling, family counseling, and referrals to counseling practitioners. Because of one's level of denial, specific intervention strategies, such as psychodrama, expressive art, music therapy, and peer intervention may be incorporated into the counseling session to increase awareness. Another intervention strategy believed to be helpful not only in increasing awareness but also promoting change is the Denial, Awareness, Surrender, and Help (D.A.S.H.) approach. Similar to the process of addiction, in which one's lifestyle continuously crumbles over time until he or she "hit their bottom," the D.A.S.H. approach, which is also a process, works in the opposite direction by putting the crumbling pieces back together without the use of alcohol and other drugs. The D.A.S.H. approach is a four-step, structural process designed to (a) break through the *denial*, (b) increase *awareness*, (c) *surrender* or let go of the desire to drink and use drugs, and (d) be willing to seek professional *help*. The chapter begins with a brief discussion on the impact of alcohol and other drug use in the workplace followed by a discussion on prevention and intervention strategies. The chapter culminates with a discussion on the D.A.S.H. approach, which will be defined and demonstrated using a case study.

Impact of Alcohol and Other Drugs in the Workplace

The use of alcohol and other drugs in the workplace can have devastating effects on both the employee and the employer. As previously mentioned, alcohol and other drug use can impair one's judgment, resulting in poor decision-making skills. It can also impair motor skills and cause accidents and injuries, which can lead to severe and sometimes permanent damage to one's physical health. Additionally, employees who drink and use drugs in the workplace tend to engage in verbal and physical disputes, have problems with their supervisors, and often require special services from EAPs (Ames et al., 1997). Macdonald (1995) noted that whereas some research studies suggest that alcoholics and problem drinkers are more likely to be involved in work-related injuries than nonproblem drinkers, other studies have failed to find a relationship. Macdonald further stated that many job injuries stem directly from the workplace because of dangerous work conditions, noise and dirt on the job, conflicts at work, and sleeping problems.

Prevention Strategies for Reducing Substance Abuse in the Workplace

Several strategies have been implemented to help prevent work-related problems associated with substance abuse. For instance, as part of the federal government's effort to address the issue of substance abuse in the workplace, the Drug-Free Workplace Act of 1988 was enacted requiring contractors and grantees of federal agencies to agree to provide drug-free workplaces as a precondition of receiving a contract or grant from a federal agency (U.S. Department of Labor, 1989). These subcontractors are strongly encouraged and often required to do preemployment drug screening and drug testing for cause (e.g., after an accident or reports from employees). Alles and Zoran (2000) stated,

> Drug testing is the most direct strategy for substance abuse prevention and early intervention testing . . . drug testing can be conducted as a pre-employment screening device, on a random basis, for cause in response to a behavioral problem or suspicion, an incident, or as part of follow-up monitoring of a person. (p. 5)

As a result of the Drug-Free Workplace Act of 1988, approximately 85% of major firms have developed some form of preemployment, for cause, or random drug testing. Although drug testing has become quite popular and useful in reducing drug use, advocates argue that drug testing decreases employee morale, increases crime in society, and prevents companies from attracting qualified applicants (Macdonald, 1995). Also, it is our opinion that there may be employers who administer drug screening disproportionally among applicants and employees. Low-level positions may be screened more frequently than high-level positions.

Another strategy designed to help reduce the use of alcohol and other drugs in the workplace is EAPs. Although the services offered by EAP vary, most provide short-term therapy (one to three sessions) and psychoeducational seminars for employees as well as their family members. They also provide training for supervisors on how to recognize substance abuse problems and how to refer workers to EAP, sponsor prevention programs, and assist problem drinkers in seeking professional help. Wellness programs have also become quite popular in reducing the spread of alcohol and other drugs in the workplace. These initiatives provide workshops on positive work environments, medical screening, and risk factors associated with substance abuse in the workplace (Goldmeier, 1994). They also provide health fairs, seminars on stress management, and parenting programs.

Intervention Strategies

Intervention strategies vary from person to person and may be either formal or informal. Formal interventions generally involve a meeting with the (a) substance-abusing employee, (b) significant people in the employee's life, such as relatives, employers, and friends, and (c) counseling practitioner. Informal interventions involve providing the substance-abusing employee with educational materials. The purpose of the intervention is to get the substance abuser to look at the defense mechanisms he or she uses to justify the substance use and to get the individual to agree to seek treatment (Stevens & Smith, 2001). Intervention methods commonly used by counseling practitioners to assist substance abusers with defense mechanisms are psychodrama, expressive art, music therapy, and peer intervention.

Psychodrama is a group activity in which an individual acts out or dramatizes life situations using several scenes in an attempt to gain deeper understanding, achieve catharsis, and develop behavioral skills (Corey, 1995). The expressive arts model integrates techniques from psychodrama, music therapy, and art therapy. Through symbolic modes of expression, such as "The Wall" exercise, an individual presents his or her defenses and receives feedback from group members. The following are questions that group members typically ask: What are my defenses doing for me? What are they costing me? How do they help me keep using my drug of choice despite severe negative consequences? (Adelman & Castricone, 1986). Music therapy is another method, in which individuals hear, read, and discuss lyrics using a chart, which illustrates the progression of addiction. The goal of music therapy, as with the previous methods discussed, is to increase personal understanding and, thus, change behavior (Mark, 1986). Another method is peer intervention, in which individuals with similar experiences share their experiences with the substance abuser. Similar to the peer intervention method, the D.A.S.H. approach consists of a dialogue between the substance abuser and the counseling practitioner. The D.A.S.H. approach blends together the formal and informal methods of intervention and may or may not include acting-out scenes, using symbolic imagery, and lyrics from a song.

The D.A.S.H. Approach: An Intervention Method for Practitioners

Depending on the individual, the intervention process can be exhausting and time consuming. Hence, to help alleviate the fatigue and time involved in the process, we developed the D.A.S.H. approach, a four-step, structural intervention method designed especially for the white-collar worker. The first step in the model involves breaking through the *denial.*

Denial, sometimes referred to as "tunnel vision," is a defense mechanism, thought to operate unconsciously, that allows the individual to avoid recognizing the reality of his or her addiction (Doweiko, 1999). One way to break through denial and, thus, increase *awareness*, which is the second step in this approach, is to educate the individual about alcohol and drug addiction. Education manifests in the form of literature, psychoeducation seminars, individual and/or group counseling sessions, and attending Alcoholics Anonymous (AA) meetings. It may also involve a formal meeting of family members or significant others who are aware of the individual's use of alcohol and other drugs. Once the individual becomes aware of his or her addiction and the dangers associated with the process of addiction, he or she is encouraged to make a conscious decision to either accept or reject the notion of being an addict or alcoholic. For those who accept their addiction, they must make a decision to stop drinking and using drugs, or to *surrender*, which is the third step in this approach. For those who reject their addiction, further education to increase awareness is suggested. The fourth and final step is to assist the individual with seeking professional *help*. In the case study that follows, the therapist uses the D.A.S.H. approach in working with Dave, a 20-year veteran of the police department, who is in denial about his use of alcohol and cocaine.

Case Study

Dave is a 45-year-old police officer employed with one of the largest police departments on the East Coast. Dave, who was recently promoted to lieutenant, is a 20-year veteran with the police department. He is married and has three daughters. Dave's wife, Sue, is also a police officer but has not worked since the birth of their second daughter. Dave describes his marriage as "stormy," with arguments brewing almost daily, namely around finances. According to Sue, Dave is irresponsible when it comes to paying the bills.

Twenty-five years ago, Dave began snorting cocaine with some friends in college. During this time, Dave claimed that he consumed less than a gram of cocaine on a monthly basis. However, as time passed, his use of cocaine escalated from 1 gram per month to 1 gram per week. Dave also drinks alcohol, consuming nearly a six-pack of beer per day. On weekends, his use of alcohol included both beer and a pint of liquor. Dave attributes his use of cocaine and alcohol to the constant stressors he experiences at work and home.

Two weeks ago, before going to work, Dave decided to have a few drinks with some colleagues to celebrate his promotion. According to Sue, Dave generally consumes one to two beers prior to leaving for work and maybe a beer or two during his shift, especially if he is working overtime. While celebrating with his colleagues, Dave drank six beers and eight shots of liquor. Although Dave was feeling quite toasted, he was convinced that he could drive and perform his daily duties at work. The celebration ended with Dave getting in his cruiser and heading to work. Unfortunately, Dave's judgment was quite impaired and, as a result, he hit and killed four family members as they crossed a busy intersection. When the paramedics arrived, Dave was found in his cruiser unconscious and smelling of alcohol. Dave was transported to the hospital, where a blood test was taken to determine the amount of alcohol in his system. Dave's blood alcohol content was .16, twice the legal limit of .08. Following his release from the hospital, Dave was arrested and charged with four counts of vehicular manslaughter. The next day, Dave appeared before the judge and was released on his own recognizant. A court date was scheduled 3 months later. Dave's attorney suggested that he seek professional help for his drinking before his scheduled court appearance. However, Dave denies having a drinking problem. Dave states, "I made a foolish mistake and I am sorry, but I don't have a problem with alcohol." A few weeks later, Dave decides to take the advice of his attorney and seek help through the EAP. What follows is his conversation with the EAP counselor.

Therapist:	Hi Dave, my name is Katherine. What brings you in today?
Client:	My attorney thought that it would be a good idea if I came in to see someone.
Therapist:	What concerns does your attorney have?
Client:	Well, I was celebrating a promotion I had received with my job and I probably had a bit too much to drink. While I was driving to work after the celebration, they said I hit and killed four family members. I don't remember doing something so drastic. All I remembered was waking up in the hospital feeling awful. The officers who came with the paramedics to the hospital told me what had happened. I am still having a hard time digesting this because I have never done something so stupid like this in my entire life. Yes, I have gone to work after having a couple of beers, but it has never been a problem.

Therapist:	So other than the alleged accident, have you ever had any problems with alcohol?
Client:	No.
Therapist:	What about at home? Has your wife ever commented on your drinking?
Client:	Yes, my wife complains all the time that I drink too much.
Therapist:	Anyone else?
Client:	Yes. A couple of the guys at work made a remark about my drinking, they said I drink too much.
Therapist:	So your wife and a couple of guys at work report that you drink too much.
Client:	Yes.
Therapist:	What do you think? Do you think you drink too much?
Client:	Heck no! I drink a couple of beers before coming to work, I drink a few beers when I get home from work, I get pretty toasted on the weekends, and when I hang out with the fellows at work, I drink just as much as they do. But I don't have a problem with alcohol. I just made a big mistake and I am truly sorry.
Therapist:	Dave, you said earlier that your wife complains about the amount of alcohol you consume. Does she complain about anything else?
Client:	Yes, she claims that I don't pay enough attention to her and that I am irresponsible when it comes to paying the bills. She claims that my alcohol and drug use is getting in the way of my being a responsible husband and father.
Therapist:	Drug use! Tell me about your drug use.
Client:	Well, I started using cocaine during my college years, snorting about a gram of powdered cocaine a month. As time progressed, I probably snorted about a gram or two, which isn't much by the way, on a weekly basis.
Therapist:	Dave, had you used cocaine on the day of the accident?
Client:	Yes, I snorted a few lines. Nothing much. But, believe me, I don't have a problem with cocaine.
Therapist:	Any other drugs that you used in the past or are currently using?
Client:	No.
Therapist:	Dave, one of the things that we do here to determine if someone has a problem with alcohol and other drugs is to give them an assessment. If you are willing, I would like to have you take the Short Michigan Alcoholism Screening Test (SMAST). It only takes about 5 to 10 minutes to complete.
Client:	Sure, I'll be happy to take the assessment. It is going to tell you that I do not have a problem with alcohol.

[After the test, the counselor informs Dave of the results.]

Therapist: Dave, according to your responses, you scored 6 points, which indicates a strong probability of alcoholism.

Client: So, are you saying that I have a problem with alcohol?

Therapist: The results of the assessment seem to confirm that you do.

Client: But what do you think?

Therapist: Well, my thoughts are not really important right now. What is important is helping you understand your addiction. You see, Dave, sometimes the person who is doing the drinking is unaware of what he or she is doing or how much they are consuming because of their level of *denial*.

Client: Are you saying that I am in denial?

Therapist: That is a possibility. A large percentage of people who are addicts and alcoholics are in denial about their drinking and drug use. Denial is a defense mechanism that people use to avoid dealing with oneself or the truth about their drinking or drug use. One way to help break through the denial is to increase one's *awareness* about substance abuse. I would like to give you some literature on alcohol and cocaine to read and I would also like for you to attend an AA meeting. Next week when you come in, we will discuss the information that you read and your thoughts about the AA meeting.

[The next session:]

Therapist: Dave, what a pleasure to see you again. I was wondering what you thought about the information I gave you and the meeting you attended?

Client: Well, it was an eye-opener. You know when I think about addicts and alcoholics, the first thought that comes to mind is what they call "skid row bums." However, in the meeting I attended, the people seemed normal, just like you and me. In fact, I saw one of my old college buddies there. He told me that he has been alcohol and drug free for 5 years. I never thought that he would graduate from college and become an alcoholic. Even though I know it could happen to anyone, I still worked everyday and cared for my children. I don't think that I fall into the category of those people at the meeting. Heck, I just received a promotion. I don't think an alcoholic or an addict could have accomplished what I have done.

Therapist: Alcohol and drugs may not have an effect on every area of your life, but according to the results of the SMAST, the information you shared about your wife and your friends' reaction to your drinking, alcohol and drugs seem to have an impact on many areas of your life. Remember the accident?

Client: As a policeman, I know that accidents happen. Some can be avoided, others may not. We aren't sure yet as to what happened in my case. Besides, I do not want to talk about the accident or even think about it.

Therapist: You are right. We are not here to discuss the accident, but we are here to discuss your possible abuse of alcohol and drugs. Can we agree that you will attend another AA meeting and spend time talking and listening to other members? Maybe you will find something in common with your college buddy or some other member.

[Next session:]

Therapist: Dave, thanks for coming in. So how was the AA meeting you attended this time?

Client: From what I heard, observed, and read, I can see why my colleagues and my wife saw things that I could not see. Although I am still not comfortable with the term "addict" or "alcoholic," I can say that I am perhaps a problem drinker. As they said in the meeting, "if it causes a problem, then it is a problem!"

Therapist: Now that you have identified yourself as a problem drinker, I am wondering if you are willing to stop drinking and using cocaine.

Client: I know I can give up the cocaine, but I think the alcohol will be a struggle.

Therapist: So, you are ready to *surrender* or give up the cocaine, but you are not sure about the alcohol.

Client: Yes.

Therapist: What would make you sure about the alcohol?

Client: I don't know. I guess I am afraid of letting go.

Therapist: Afraid?

Client: Yes, afraid that people might not like the new me.

Therapist: Do people like the way you are now?

Client: Well, no. I guess I am still searching for excuses.

Therapist: You know, Dave, making the decision not to drink and use drugs is perhaps one of the hardest decisions to make. But if we were to look at the advantages and disadvantages of not using, the advantages will certainly outweigh the disadvantages.

Client: I guess you are right.

Therapist: So, Dave, are you ready to seek professional *help* for your addiction?

Client: I guess I am. My college buddy told me about a 28-day treatment program he attended.

Therapist: Yes, there are 28-day programs and programs that last as long as 6 months. But for now, I would like to enroll you in a 28-day program.

Client: That's fine, but what about my family and my upcoming court date?

Therapist: Your family can come and visit. In fact, they may be involved in your treatment to some extent. As far as court goes, if all goes well, you will be out of the treatment program before your court date.

Client: That sounds good.

Therapist: I'll contact the treatment center and make the arrangements for you to get admitted.

Client: The sooner, the better! If I think about this too much longer, I may lose my nerve.

Conclusion

Drinking and using drugs in the workplace is a serious problem that affects millions of people. Although efforts have been made to reduce substance abuse in the workplace, there are some employees who simply cannot stop drinking or using drugs. The D.A.S.H. approach is one method designed for working with the white-collar addict. Breaking through the *denial*, increasing *awareness*, making the decision not to drink or use drugs, or simply *surrendering*, and assisting the addict with seeking professional *help* is a structural, four-step approach that can be used by novice as well as skilled practitioners. Although the intervention process is not new to most practicing practitioners, we believe that this linear way of thinking may be especially helpful to beginning counselors.

References

Adelman, E., & Castricone, L. (1986). An expressive arts model for substance abuse group training and treatment. *Arts in Psychology, 13*(1), 53–59.

Alles, P. J., & Zoran, B. W. (2000). *Survey results: Substance abuse services for multi employer fund participants.* Brookfield, WI: International Foundation of Employee Benefit Plans.

Ames, G. M., Grube, J. W., & Moore, R. S. (1997). The relationship of drinking and hangovers to workplace problems: An empirical study. *Journal of Studies on Alcohol, 58,* 37–47.

Bischof, G., Rumpf, H. -J., Hapke, U., Meyer, C., & John, U. (2001). Factors influencing remission from alcohol dependence without formal help in a representative population sample. *Addiction, 96,* 1327–1336.

Corey, G. (1995). *Theory and practice of group counseling* (4th ed.). Pacific Grove, CA: Brooks/Cole.

Delaney, W. P., & Ames, G. (1995). Work team attitudes, drinking norms and workplace drinking. *Journal of Drug Issues, 25,* 275–290.

Doweiko, H. E. (1999). *Concepts of chemical dependency* (4th ed.). Pacific Grove, CA: Brooks/Cole.

Goldmeier, J. (1994). Interventions with elderly substance abusers in the workplace. *Journal of Contemporary Human Services, 75,* 624–629.

Hanson, G., & Venturelli, P. (1998). *Drugs and society* (5th ed.). Sudbury, MA: Jones & Bartlett.

Macdonald, S. (1995). The role of drugs in workplace injuries: Is drug testing appropriate? *Journal of Drug Issues, 25,* 703–722.

Mark, A. (1986). Adolescents discuss themselves and drugs through music. *Journal of Substance Abuse Treatment, 3,* 243–249.

National Institute on Alcohol Abuse and Alcoholism. (1999, July). Alcohol and the workplace. *Alcohol Alert, 44,* 1–4.

Richman, J. A., Flaherty, J. A., & Rospenda, K. M. (1996). Perceived workplace harassment experiences and problem drinking among physicians: Broadening the stress/alienation paradigm. *Addiction, 91,* 391–403.

Stevens, P., & Smith, R. L. (2001). *Substance abuse counseling: Theory and practice* (2nd ed.). Columbus, OH: Merrill Prentice Hall.

U.S. Department of Health and Human Services. (2000). *Summary of findings from the 1999 national household survey on drug abuse* (DHHS Publication No. SMA 00-3466). Rockville, MD: Author.

U.S. Department of Labor. (1989). *Drug-Free Workplace Act of 1988.* Retrieved August 10, 2001, from http://www.dol.gov/elaws/drugfree.htm

Wiebe, J., Vinje, G., & Sawka, E. (1995). Alcohol and drug use in the workplace: A survey of Alberta workers. *American Journal of Health Promotion, 9,* 179–181.

Wohlfarth, T., & Van Den Brink, W. (1998). Social class and substance use disorders: The value of social class as distinct from socioeconomic status. *Social Science and Medicine, 47,* 51–58.

Violence in the Workplace: Preventing and Managing the Effects of Critical Incidence Stress in the Workplace

Paige N. Cummins

his chapter focuses on managing the effects of violence on employees before and after a critical incident (i.e., violence in the workplace) has occurred. Because of the prevalence of violence in the workplace, it has become necessary for businesses and agencies to plan for how they will manage their employees prior to and after a critical incident. This chapter examines the history of violence in the workplace, the effects of critical incident stress on employees, and debriefing following a critical incident. In addition, the necessary training and qualifications of Employee Assistance Program (EAP) or mental health personnel to handle such events are discussed.

History of Violence in the Workplace

Workplace violence is becoming an ever-increasing problem for businesses and agencies. Although workplace violence may appear to be a relatively new phenomenon, statistics show that violent acts have occurred at the workplace for several decades now. Workplace violence is defined at "violent acts against a person at work or on duty, including personal assaults, robbery, and homicide" (Bureau of Justice Statistics, 1998, p. 2). A reported 6,956 work-related homicides occurred between 1980 and 1988 (Jenkins, Layne, & Kisner, 1992). More recent figures from the Bureau of Justice Statistics (1998) indicate that 2 million employees were victims of a violent crime while they were working or on duty. Over 1,000 of those employees were victims of homicide. Therefore, homicide was the second leading cause of death in the workplace between 1992 and 1996 (Bureau of Justice Statistics, 1998). Assault or simple assault was the most common act of violence inflicted on employees during 1992 and 1996, with 1.5 million and 396,000 victims, respectively. These statistics suggest violence in the workplace is a growing problem.

More than half of the crimes against employees happen in privately owned companies (Bureau of Justice Statistics, 1998). However, a disproportionate number of workers are employed by federal, state, or county government organizations. Workplace violence occurs at all organizational levels from managerial to frontline staff (Johnson & Indivik, 1994). The majority of these violent acts are perpetrated by strangers (59%), whereas 35% are committed by acquaintances, including disgruntled employees (Bureau of Justice Statistics, 1998).

This violence affects organizations both financially and operationally. The National Safe Workplace Institute estimates an average cost of a single episode of violence to be $250,000 (Anfuso, 1994). Annually, companies lose approximately $5 million a year in lost wages alone (Bachman, 1994). The consequences of this violence for the company can include damaged property, increased insurance costs, legal costs, damaged company image, and low employee morale (Fletcher, Brakel, & Cavanaugh, 2000). More specifically, employees who are directly exposed to the violence cost the company in terms of lost productivity, lost work time, and employee turnover (Fletcher et al., 2000). Because the cost to both the organization and the employee is so high, it is imperative that a plan for managing the effects of a critical incident is in place.

Effects of Critical Incidence Stress

The effect of critical incident stress on employees is well documented in the literature (Carmel & Hunter, 1989; Flannery, Hanson, & Penk, 1994; Nader, Pynoos, Fairbanks, & Frederick, 1990; Pendleton, Stotland, Spiers, & Kirsch, 1989; Terr, 1983). Employees who experience violence at work are affected both personally and professionally. Kinney (1995) asserted that employees who experience violence in the workplace fall into three primary groups: (a) some who appear to recover quickly without mental health intervention but who release those emotions later in a maladaptive manner; (a) some who require modest outpatient counseling to regain a sense of safety and security; and (c) some who develop severe problems requiring long-term therapy. Those employees who experience trauma symptoms past 1 month typically are diagnosed with post-traumatic stress disorder (Flannery, 1995; Miller, 1994, 1998).

The symptoms of these employees can be categorized into several different types. Employees report experiencing physical symptoms such as hypervigilance, exaggerated startle response, difficulty sleeping, impaired concentration, and mood swings (Flannery, 1996; Miller, 1999). Intrusive symptoms are commonly reported, such as recurring or distressing thoughts, flashbacks, and nightmares (Flannery, 1996; Miller, 1999). Employees often experience avoidant symptoms, including withdrawal from daily activities, emotional numbing, and avoidance of reminders of the violent event (Flannery, 1996; Miller, 1999). Symptoms may also be more generalized, such as panic attacks and chronic pain. Some employees may become suicidal (Flannery, 1996). In addition, substance abuse may also increase as a form of self-medication from anxiety (Flannery, 1995). Other research suggests employees who have been the victims of violence may also experience increased worry or fear about being revictimized while on the job; some even consider bringing a weapon to work (Budd, Arvey, & Lawless, 1996). Merely witnessing violence in the workplace can also lead to the aforementioned symptoms (Van der Kolk, 1987). Budd et al. (1996) also reported that employees who are victims of crime in the workplace show a marked increase in job dissatisfaction, which often results in consideration of changing jobs, missed work, and lowered productivity.

Considering the effects of critical incidence stress on employees following violence in the workplace, EAP professionals need to develop a comprehensive plan for addressing the potential for and the aftermath of a violent event.

Managing A Critical Incident

The management of critical incidents in the workplace generally involves a two-pronged approach. The primary approach should be the prevention of violence before it occurs. This is the most cost-effective way to address this problem from a company standpoint. If violence is averted, then companies can avoid the financial and operational costs of "clean-up" following a violent event. A secondary approach involves a comprehensive management plan following the occurrence of an episode to minimize the effects of violence on the employees (Albrecht, 1997; Mantel & Albrecht, 1994).

Violence Prevention Programs

One aspect of a violence prevention program is the development of a *threat assessment team*. This team is interdisciplinary, generally including a human resources manager, an attorney, and a mental health professional or EAP representative (Bush & O'Shea, 1996). The responsibility of the threat assessment team is overall threat management. The team evaluates individual threats to the organization and addresses specific safety needs of the organization. This team is also responsible for training supervisors in the management of potentially violent situations (Overman, 1991, 1993).

Another important responsibility of the team is the development of a crisis management plan. The team drafts policies for the management of a violent episode. Members of a crisis management team could be identified with members of that team coming from the threat management team (Overman, 1993).

Finally, threat management teams can be used to facilitate focus groups to assess employee concerns (Lindsey, 1994). Prevention programs including the one used by the United States Postal Service regularly employ focus groups to discuss present safety concerns of employees and to facilitate employee discussion of violence prevention practices. Hardees Food Systems, Inc. provides employees with informational workshops on personal safety and protection (Nicoletti & Spooner, 1996).

In addition to airing employee concerns about violence, most violence prevention also includes preincident training. Preincident training involves providing employees with the tools to handle all stages of a potentially violent situation (Miller, 1999).

Preincident Training

The focus of preincident training is giving employees (particularly supervisors) skills in crisis intervention training (Bolz, Dudonis, & Schulz, 1996; Caraulia & Steiger, 1997). Employees are taught to use rapport building and active listening skills to defuse a potentially violent situation. Should a situation escalate, employees are taught how to contact authorities in an unobtrusive manner. Prevention training also includes teaching employees how to use communication skills that will ensure that a potentially violent situation will not escalate. Specifically, employees are trained to use empathy and voice tone to reduce the agitation of the potentially violent individual. Control of the scene is also addressed. Control of the scene involves identifying one intervener, not allowing an audience to gather, and the briefing of law enforcement personnel. Preincident training in effect takes the potential intervener (e.g., employee) through the entire process of deescalation of a potentially violent situation. Preincident training is also commonly coupled with other interventions to facilitate a less stressful work environment.

Stress Management

The inclusion of stress management programs in conjunction with preincident training is thought to create an environment where violence is less likely to occur, or if it does occur, it will be handled more effectively (Flannery, 1996). Employees are taught specific stress reduction skills such as adaptive coping skills. Anger management skills are also taught to reduce individuals' level of life stress (Abernathy, 1992). Another benefit of improved anger management skills is that employees will be able to deal with difficult customers or coworkers more effectively, thereby averting workplace violence.

Critical Incident Stress Management

Critical incident stress debriefing (CISD) is the most commonly used intervention following an incident of workplace violence (Bisson, 1999; Flannery, 1996; Hollister, 1996; Miller, 1999). A critical incident is defined as "any situation faced by emergency personnel that causes them to experience unusually strong emotional reactions that have the potential to interfere with their ability to function either at the scene or later" (Mitchell, 1983, p. 36). This definition has now been broadened to include any type of employee who has experienced an event such as workplace violence.

The goals of CISD are both immediate and long term. The most immediate goal of debriefing is to prevent or diminish symptoms of post-traumatic stress disorder (Hollister, 1996; Lane, 1993/1994; Rubin, 1990). Debriefing is also designed to help restore employees' sense of mastery or control over their environment, provide support, and help employees to express feelings of betrayal they may have because the violence happened at their workplace and that they feel they were not protected (Lloyd & D'Antonio, 1992; von Slagmott & Rabobank, 1992). Other goals of debriefing are (a) to help participants to return to a sense of emotional stability, (b) to return participants to an optimal level of functioning, (c) to accelerate recovery, and (d) to ultimately facilitate participants' return to their jobs (Hollister, 1996; Lane, 1993/1994; Rubin, 1990).

Models of CISD

One model of CISD is based on the peer system approach called the Assaulted Staff Action Program, or ASAP. The goal of this model is to restore or instill coping skills in employees who have experienced a critical incident. Debriefing is done both individually and in groups. Families are also debriefed if that is necessary. Referrals are given to participants for further services if they are needed (Flannery, 1995).

Clinicians who use this method need to ensure that they do not stigmatize victims of violence through the use of this intervention. A skilled clinician should be designated as the coordinator of victim assistance. This mental health professional should have no direct involvement with either the event or the supervision of the participants. It is important that the facilitator provide support for the victims. Employees should be given factual information about the incident to dispel rumors that may abound following the violent episode. A group meeting should be used to diffuse any conflict between direct victims and those who may only have been affected by the violence tangentially. Those employees who were not directly affected may avoid direct victims because they feel they are "bad luck" (Brom & Kleber, 1989; Everstine & Everstine, 1993; Flannery, 1995).

Another model of CISD is based on a military model of debriefing, which was developed by General S. L. A. Marshall in Island Victory (Samter et al., 1993). This type of debriefing is done in a group to ensure the accuracy of the information discussed. Participants are asked six or seven open-ended questions regarding the traumatic event. The role each victim played in the event is discussed. Facilitators also encourage participants to discuss the emotions they felt during the traumatic event (Fitzgerald et al., 1993).

The most commonly used model of CISD, however, is based on a model developed by Mitchell and Bray (1990) for CISD with emergency personnel. Since that time, this model has been further developed by Jimmerson (1988) and Spitzer and Burke (1993). This is a comprehensive model for debriefing that is done in a group setting. The entire debriefing process is done during one session. The session is divided into six phases: (a) introductory phase, (b) fact phase, (c) feeling phase, (d) symptom phase, (e) teaching phase, and (f) reentry phase.

The introductory phase consists of setting the ground rules for the debriefing. Participants are informed that what they discuss is confidential and will not be divulged outside of the debriefing session. It is imperative that employees know that no professional grades will be used during the session; all employees are seen as equal. Participants are also instructed that they are not to leave the debriefing so that the facilitator can maintain control of the session. Not allowing premature departures also ensures that no participant leaves in a distressed emotional state without being assessed. Once the ground rules are set for the debriefing, the session then progresses to the fact phase.

The fact phase consists of participants sharing with the group what role each played in the event. With the help of the facilitator, participants are encouraged to reconstruct or reenact the event. The facilitator helps participants to detail where they were during the event. In addition, participants are asked to share what they experienced during the traumatic event. This step is important because telling the details of a trauma helps individuals to heal from the event (Jimmerson, 1988; Mitchell & Bray, 1990).

During the feeling phase, participants are encouraged to retrace their emotional steps during the event. Specifically, the facilitator asks participants to reveal what their feelings were during all phases of the event. Once participants have disclosed how they felt during the event, they are then asked to share how they are dealing with their feelings currently, as victims may experience wild mood swings during the aftermath. It is not uncommon for victims to feel both anger and sadness about what they have experienced. Finally, participants are asked to discuss how these feelings are affecting their job performance and job satisfaction.

The symptom phase is focused on helping participants to explore what problems they are currently experiencing as a result of the trauma. These symptoms are not merely emotional but may also include physical reactions they may be experiencing (e.g., panic attacks, stomach problems, and difficulty sleeping). Symptoms of family and friends who are affected in a tertiary way by the traumatic event are also addressed.

The teaching phase of the debriefing is more didactic in nature. The facilitator teaches participants how to identify the signs and symptoms of stress syndromes. Participants are taught that what they are feeling is normal and to be expected given the event they have just witnessed. Stress reduction techniques are also discussed. Participants are encouraged to use the techniques they have learned after the debriefing.

The reentry phase is designed to help participants to be emotionally able to leave the session. In this final phase, the facilitator brings closure to the session. Participants are given support and are encouraged to support one another. Individual and group goals for dealing with the effects of the traumatic event are identified; for example, participants may decide to call each other to ensure everyone gets the support they need.

The Efficacy of CISD

There is some evidence that CISD is helpful in the recovery from traumatic events. Proper intervention following a violent event results in employees being less likely to develop substance abuse, chronic pain, and somatic disabilities (Miller, 1998; Yandrick, 1996). Appropriate psychological care in the aftermath of a traumatic event results in a reduced number of stress claims (Miller, 1999). Others, such as Dyregrov (1998), have also documented the positive effects of CISD. Western Management Consultants in Canada report positive results of critical incident stress management for nurses. Employee turnover was reduced by 24%. Sick leave use was reduced by 99% (Bisson, 1999).

It should be noted that there is also evidence that CISD has no effect at all on the recovery of employees from a traumatic event. Deahl, Gillham, Thomas, Searle, and Scrinivasan (1994) studied individuals who volunteered for war grave duty during the Gulf War. Part of the sample received debriefing whereas the remainder did not. They found that 50% of the sample reported that the debriefing was helpful; however, psychological measures showed no difference between the group that received a debriefing and the control group at a 9-month follow-up. Kenardy et al. (1996) studied 195 helpers following an earthquake in Australia. Sixty-two of the helpers were debriefed following the earthquake. The remaining 133 were not. Four measures of their rate of recovery over a period of 2 years showed no evidence of an improved rate of recovery.

Similar studies done using individual CISD showed similar results. In a study of road accident victims who received individual debriefing within 24 to 48 hours following the accident, Hobbs, Mayou, Harrison, and Warlock (1996) found that the debriefed group were faring slightly worse overall 4 months later. Bisson, Jenkins, Alexander, and Bannister (1997) studied burn trauma victims admitted to the hospital and found the group that received debriefing were worse at 3 months and 13 months postadmission than those who received no debriefing. An important finding by Dyregrov (1998) is that effectiveness of such programs seems to be related, in part, to the experience of the facilitator.

Members of the CISD Team

Providing facilitation for a CISD team requires extensive training. It is recommended that there be a mental health professional on the debriefing team. (Hollister, 1996; Walker, 1990). This person should have strong crisis intervention skills. Preferably, the mental health professional should be certified in CISD. The mental health professional should have training in group dynamics and leadership as debriefing sessions are often emotionally charged. The facilitator should also be familiar with suicide and homicide assessment as employees may feel like harming themselves or someone else following a violent event. It is important that this person not be affiliated with the organization so those employees will feel free to discuss their feelings and reactions. It is also important that the mental health professional who facilitates the debriefing not have been involved in the direct management of the violent event. The organization may want to contract for services with a mental health professional so that, in the event of a violent event, that person could be contacted immediately to provide debriefing for the employees. If a mental health professional is not contracted for services prior to a violent event, then it should be decided in the critical incident management plan who the individual will be.

If the employees are members of the medical community or emergency services, it is important that a member of the medical community be involved in the debriefing team along with the mental health professional (Clark & Friedman, 1992; Rubin, 1990; Walker, 1990). Having a member of the medical community on the team when working with these employees is important as it is often difficult to develop rapport with individuals in the medical community unless the facilitator has a medical background. Often employees with a medical background feel it is unprofessional to discuss feelings of anger or helplessness they may have felt during the episode of violence. Often this type of disclosure is made easier when there is a person facilitating the debriefing who understands those unwritten rules of the profession.

Long-Term Follow-Up

All of the companies and organizations that employ a critical incident stress management program also provide long-term follow-up services for their employees. These services often include individual counseling services (Flannery, 1995; Miller, 1999). Some organizations provide victim support groups for the employees who were directly affected by the violence. It is important that employee recovery is monitored by trained mental health staff as employees may suffer from symptoms for years after the event has occurred.

Conclusion

If the trend of workplace violence continues, companies will be forced to find ways to protect their employees. It is disturbing to note that, even with the prevalence of workplace violence, companies and organizations are not prepared to deal with violence in the workplace. A survey by Bush and O'Shea (1996) suggests that 78% of insurance and 50% of health care organizations had a clearly defined crisis management plan. None of the pharmaceutical or utility businesses had such a plan in place. In addition, few companies had violence prevention training for supervisors as a part of their preincident training. These skills are critical to the prevention of violence in the workplace. It would seem that companies would want to make use of violence prevention programs versus violence clean-up programs as they are much more cost-effective for the organization. As was mentioned previously, crisis prevention programs mean companies will not lose money on employees who leave or do not function well because of critical incident stress. Counselors and EAP personnel can be instrumental in assisting companies and organization in the development of a crisis management plan. It is also imperative that counselors be an integral part of the crisis management team.

It is clear that preincident training is effective in preventing workplace violence, particularly communication training to defuse potentially violent situations. It also appears that critical incident debriefing following an incident of workplace violence is effective in managing the employees' symptoms of posttraumatic stress. What is less clear is exactly what a violence prevention program should be composed of. In addition, it is not clear which model of critical incident debriefing is preferable. It is not known whether individual debriefing is preferable to group debriefing. Nothing is known as to whether debriefing should be done immediately after the traumatic event or if the debriefing should be done later when employees are not in such a state of shock. There also appears to be some question as to the effectiveness of debriefing over time. Longitudinal studies of employees who have participated in a debriefing program need to be done to determine its long-term effectiveness.

Another area of question remains who specifically should make up the crisis management team and the CISD team. Although it is clear that a mental health professional should be a member of this team, no research has addressed who else might be a part of that team. It is possible that trained peers may be used in conjunction with a mental health professional to lead such debriefing provided that they were not victims of the violence.

In summary, critical incident stress management will become an integral part of corporate and organizational life. Counselors can be an integral part of helping companies to prevent and cope with violence in the workplace.

References

Abernathy, A. D. (1992). *Anger management for law enforcement personnel.* Proceedings of the Second American Psychological Association/National Institute of Occupational Safety Health Conference on Occupational Stress, Washington, DC.

Albrecht, S. (1997). *Fear and violence on the job: Prevention solutions for the dangerous workplace.* Durham, NC: Carolina Academic Press.

Anfuso, D. (1994). Deflecting workplace violence. *Personnel Journal, 73*(10), 66–77.

Bachman, R. (1994). *Violence and theft in the workplace* [Crime Data Brief: National Crime Victimization Survey]. Washington, DC: U.S. Department of Justice, Bureau of Justice Statistics.

Bisson, J. I. (1999). Psychological debriefing: Does it work? In E. J. Hickling & E. B. Blanchard (Eds.), *The international handbook of road traffic accidents and psychological trauma: Current understanding, treatment and law* (pp. 389–396). New York: Elsevier Science.

Bisson, J. I., Jenkins, P., Alexander, J., & Bannister, C. (1997). A randomized study of psychological debriefing for victims of acute burn trauma. *British Journal of Psychiatry, 171,* 78–81.

Bolz, F., Dudonis, K. J., & Schulz, D. P. (1996). *The counterterrorism handbook: Tactics, procedures and techniques.* Boca Raton, FL: CRC Press.

Brom, D., & Kleber, R. J. (1989). Prevention of posttraumatic stress disorders. *Journal of Traumatic Stress, 2,* 335–351.

Budd, J. W., Arvey, R. D., & Lawless, P. (1996). Correlates and consequences of workplace violence. *Journal of Occupational Health Psychology, 1,* 197–210.

Bureau of Justice Statistics. (1998). *Workplace violence, 1992–1996.* Washington, DC: Author.

Bush, D. F., & O' Shea, P. G. (1996). Workplace violence: Comparative use of prevention practices and policies. In G. R. VandenBos & E. Q. Bulatao (Eds.), *Violence on the job* (pp. 283–297). Washington, DC: American Psychological Association.

Caraulia, A. P., & Steiger, L. K. (1997). *Nonviolent crisis intervention: Learning to defuse explosive behavior.* Brookfield, MA: CPI Publishing.

Carmel, H., & Hunter, M. (1989). Staff injuries from inpatient violence. *Hospital and Community Psychiatry, 40,* 41–46.

Clark, M., & Friedman, D. (1992). Pulling together: Building a community debriefing team. *Journal of Psychosocial Nursing, 30*(7), 27–32.

Deahl, M., Gillham, A., Thomas, J., Searle, M., & Scrinivasan, (1994). Sequelae following the Gulf War factors associated with subsequent effectiveness of psychological debriefing. *British Journal of Psychiatry, 165,* 339–344.

Dyregrov, A. (1998). Psychological debriefing—an effective method? *Disaster Management, 2,* 25–30.

Everstine, D. S., & Everstine, L. (1993). *The trauma response: Treatment for emotional injury.* New York: Norton.

Fitzgerald, M., Braudaway, C., Leeks, D., Padgett, M., Swartz, A., Samter, J., Gary-Stephens, M., & Dellinger, N. (1993). Debriefing: A therapeutic intervention. *Military Medicine, 158,* 542–545.

Flannery, R. B. (1995). *Violence in the workplace.* New York: Crossroad.

Flannery, R. B. (1996). Violence in the workplace, 1970–1995: Review of the literature. *Aggression and Violent Behavior, 1,* 57–68.

Flannery, R. B., Hanson, M. A., & Penk, W. E. (1994). Risk factors for inpatient assaults on staff. *Journal of Mental Health Administration, 21,* 24–31.

Fletcher, T. A., Brakel, J. J., & Cavanaugh, J. L. (2000). Violence in the workplace: New perspectives on forensic mental health services in the USA. *British Journal of Psychiatry, 176,* 339–344.

Hobbs, M., Mayou, R., Harrison, B., & Warlock, P. (1996). A randomised study of psychological debriefing for victims of road traffic accidents. *British Measurement, 165,* 1438–1439.

Hollister, R. (1996). Critical incident stress debriefing and the community health nurse. *Journal of Community Health Nursing, 13*, 43–49.

Jenkins, E. L., Layne, L. A., & Kisner, S. M. (1992). Homicide in the workplace: The US experience, 1980–1988. *American Association of Health Nursing Journal, 40*, 215–218.

Jimmerson, C. (1988). Critical incident stress debriefing. *Journal of Emergency Nursing, 14*, 43A–45A.

Johnson, P. R., & Indivik, J. (1994). Workplace violence an issue of the nineties. *Public Personnel Management, 23*, 515–523.

Kenardy, J., Webster, R., Lewin, T., Carr, V., Hazell, P., & Carter, G. (1996). Symptoms and patterns of recovery following a natural disaster. *Journal of Traumatology, 41*, 209–218.

Kinney, J. A. (1995). *Violence at work: How to make your company safer for employees and customers.* Englewood Cliffs, NJ: Prentice Hall.

Lane, P. (1993/1994). Critical incident stress debriefing for health care workers. *Omega, 28*, 301–315.

Lindsey, D. (1994). Of sound mind? Evaluating the workforce. *Security Management, 38*(9), 69–71.

Lloyd, D., & D'Antonio, M. S. (1992). *A petrochemical plan disaster: Initial psychological effects, mental health interventions, and the development of subsequent psychological disorders.* Proceedings of the Second American Psychological Association/National Institute of Occupational Safety and Health Conference on Occupational Safety, Washington, DC.

Mantel, M., & Albrecht, S. (1994). *Ticking time bombs: Diffusing violence in the workplace.* New York: Irwin.

Miller, L. (1994). Civilian posttraumatic stress disorder: Clinical syndromes and psychotherapeutic strategies. *Psychotherapy, 31*, 655–664.

Miller, L. (1998). *Shocks to the system: Psychotherapy of traumatic disability syndromes.* New York: Norton.

Miller, L. (1999). Workplace violence: Prevention, response, and recovery. *Psychotherapy, 36*, 160–169.

Mitchell, J. T. (1983). When disaster strikes: The critical incident stress debriefing process. *Journal of Emergency Medical Services, 8*, 36–40.

Mitchell, J. T., & Bray, G. R. (1990). *Emergency services stress: Guidelines for preserving the health and careers of emergency services personnel.* Englewood Cliffs, NJ: Prentice Hall.

Nader, K., Pynoos, R., Fairbanks, L., & Frederick, C. (1990). Children's PTSD reactions one year after a sniper attack at their school. *American Journal of Psychiatry, 147*, 1526–1530.

Nicoletti, J., & Spooner, K. (1996). Violence in the workplace: Response and intervention strategies. In G. R. VandenBos & E. Q. Bulatao (Eds.), *Violence on the job* (pp. 267–282). Washington, DC: American Psychological Association.

Overman, S. (1991). Crisis management after the smoke clears. *Human Resources Management Magazine, 36*, 43–47.

Overman, S. (1993). Be prepared should be your motto. *Human Resources Magazine, 38*, 210–215.

Pendleton, M., Stotland, E., Spiers, P., & Kirsch, E. (1989). Stress and strain among police, fire fighters and government workers: A comparative analysis. *Criminal Justice and Behavior, 16,* 196–210.

Rubin, J. (1990). Critical incident stress debriefing: Helping the helpers. *Journal of Emergency Nursing, 16,* 255–258.

Samter, J., Fitzgerald, M., Braudawaly, C., Leeks, D., Padgett, M., Swartz, A., Gary-Stephens, M., & Dellinger, N. (1993). Debriefing: From military origin to therapeutic application. *Journal of Psychosocial Nursing, 31*(2), 23–27.

Spitzer, W., & Burke, L. (1993). A critical incident stress debriefing program for hospital-based health care personnel. *Health and Social Work, 18,* 149–156.

Terr, L. C. (1983). Chowchilla revisited: The effects of psychic trauma four years after a school bus kidnapping. *American Journal of Psychiatry, 140,* 1543–1550.

Van der Kolk, B. A. (1987). *Psychological trauma.* Washington, DC: American Psychiatric Press.

von Slagmott, F., & Rabobank, E. (1992). *The Netherlands victim assistance: The Dutch experience.* Proceedings of the Second American Psychological Association/National Institute for Occupational Safety and Health Conference on Occupational Safety, Washington, DC.

Walker, G. (1990). Crisis care in critical incident debriefing. *Death Studies, 14,* 121–133.

Yandrick, R. M. (1996). *Behavioral risk management: How to avoid preventable losses from mental health problems in the workplace.* San Francisco: Jossey-Bass.

Special Programs

....

Reasons, Considerations, and Strategies for Developing and Implementing an Employee Assistance Program in Higher Education

Daya Singh Sandhu and Robert M. Longwell-Grice

uring the mid and late 1900s, Employee Assistance Programs (EAPs) became increasingly common in industry and in higher education as employers sought to improve the job performance of employees who were struggling with a variety of personal issues that may or may not be job related (Carson & Balkin, 1992). EAPs emerged as managers realized that keeping performance high and caring for the social welfare of their employees were not mutually exclusive concerns. EAPs are based on the premise that a company's investment in its employees should be protected and enhanced. By ensuring that employees have access to support systems via EAPs, employers serve both their economic interests and the interests of the society at large. According to Ryan (1997):

> EAPs typically provide counseling, education, and related assistance for a broad range of issues, including job performance problems, alcohol and drug abuse, marital or family problems, stress, emotional or mental health problems, grief and loss, financial troubles, and referrals to community resources. (p. 5)

This chapter describes the historical foundations of EAP programs, especially as they relate to higher education; discusses important issues relating to the potential success of campus EAPs; and outlines some necessary steps that campuses should take when implementing EAPs. The importance of evaluation is also briefly considered.

Historical Foundations of EAP Programs

EAPs began in the 1940s as Occupational Assistance Programs (OAPs; Lew & Ashbaugh, 1992; Masi, 1994). In these programs, assistance was offered to employees with alcohol and drug abuse problems. In the 1970s, OAPs broadened their approach to work with employees who had other problems, and the term Employee Assistance Program came into existence (Masi, 1992; Masi & Goff, 1987).

Several large corporations were among the first to recognize that the negative effect drugs and alcohol had on absenteeism, productivity, morale, and turnover was enough to justify the establishment of workplace EAPs (Pogue, 1994). These early programs focused almost exclusively on alcohol problems and were designed to discover the nature of the problem, its extent, the cost of the problem to the company, and ways to solve the problem. The focus was almost entirely on the decline in work productivity, not the problem itself (Pogue, 1994). Research on these early EAPs over a 20-year period showed that they significantly reduced absenteeism, decreased workplace accidents, increased job performance, and helped problem drinkers overcome their addiction (Asma, Hilker, Shevlin, & Golden, 1980; Hilker, Asma, & Eggert, 1972). These results helped fuel the rapid growth of EAPs beginning in the 1970s that continues today. With the enactment of the Americans With Disabilities Act and the Family and Medical Leave Act, however, not only do employers have a moral obligation to help their employees, but they now have a legal one. With this obligation comes the realization that comprehensive and innovative strategies must be implemented to respond to the needs of individuals in the workplace (Ryan, 1997).

Ryan (1997) stated that well-managed EAPs have at least three significant advantages for organizations that implement them. First, EAPS help to maintain a healthy, motivated, and productive workforce. Losing an employee for 2 hours a week for counseling is far less damaging to overall job performance than allowing a problem to degenerate to the point at which irreparable harm is done—to the organization, to coworkers, or to the individual employee. Second, providing the opportunity for assistance with a range of life and work difficulties clearly shows that an organization makes the effort to provide reasonable accommodations for employees who require it. Third, the availability of comprehensive EAPs and the attitudes that encourage their frequent use may prevent employees from considering legal action for minor, easily resolved disputes.

As effective as EAPs may be, however, higher education appears to have been slower to establish them on their campuses than private industry has (Pogue, 1994). According to Thoreson, Roberts, and Pascoe (1979), one of the first EAPs on a college campus occurred at the University of Missouri–Columbia in 1976 as part of a grant from the National Institute of Alcohol Abuse and Alcoholism (NIAAA). This grant was targeting colleges to implement campus EAPs and was successful in doing so on 5 campuses that year (Masi, 1992). By 1988, 150 colleges had established EAPs (Bureau of National Affairs, 1987; Pogue, 1994; Smewing & Cox, 1998). Currently, there are approximately 250 EAPs on college campuses (primarily at large research universities), representing approximately 5% of all colleges (Stoer-Scaggs, 1999; Wilson, 1997). In contrast, industry EAPS have grown from 300 in 1971 to over 20,000 today, representing approximately 39% of all companies (French, Dunlap, Zarkin, & Karuntzos, 1998; Smewing & Cox, 1998). According to Wilson, EAPS on college campuses have expanded beyond the early days when they simply helped employees with drug or alcohol problems. Campus EAPs now work with individual faculty and staff members on a variety of work-related problems (which may include drug or alcohol problems), and many EAPs also consult with department heads and deans about departmental disputes.

EAPs in Higher Education

Troubled employees in the workforce create a major financial burden on the economy, and institutions of higher education are not immune from inefficiencies and ineffectiveness caused by troubled employees. A faculty and staff survey at the University of Missouri–Columbia indicated that

8% of employees there experienced persistent personal problems, which resulted in poor job performance (Lew & Ashbaugh, 1992). Hampton (as cited in Stoer-Scaggs, 1999) stated that 20% of higher education employees are likely to be affected by personal problems severe enough to affect their job performance. Stress in academia is related to tight financial resources, performance evaluation of faculty and staff by students and supervisors, increased family commitments, the contracting out of services, the "publish or perish" mentality in many academic departments, pressures to adapt to the changing needs of students, a lack of departmental collegiality, professional isolation, and diminishing resources for accomplishing the job, among other issues (dePietro, 1995; Hubbard & Atkins, 1995; Lew & Ashbaugh, 1992; Pogue, 1994; Smewing & Cox, 1998; Stoer-Skaggs, 1999). In addition, many faculty and staff members face the "baby boomer blues" (Johnson & Indvik, 1997) as many boomers feel they are overworked and underpaid, have conflicts with coworkers and supervisors, and are disillusioned with the "glass ceiling" or unfulfilling work. Baby boomers, who make up a large cohort of workers, also have an increasing need for flexible work schedules with time to care for their growing children and their aging parents (dePietro, 1995).

Despite the many stresses faced by college employees, EAPs on college campuses have not evolved to the degree that they have in private industry. There may be several explanations for this. For one, "EAPs in higher education may be viewed as invading the hallowed sanctions of the faculty as well as the directorate of the staff, which may choose to manage their own troubled employees even if that may include enabling problem behavior" (Stoer-Skaggs, 1999, p. 35). Because much of the work performed by campus employees is done independently and out of the sight of the direct supervisor, it could also be that campus supervisors, especially deans and department heads, do not witness behavior that EAPs could help with and are reluctant to confront issues they do not directly observe. In this regard, Besenhofer and Gerstein (1991) found that upper level managers were less likely to refer a hypothetically impaired employee than were lower level managers, with middle managers showing no difference between the upper or lower level managers. Similarly, Shirley (1985) found that upper management tended to cover up for their impaired workers and supervisors, and McClellan (1982) suggested that professionals might prefer to implement peer-helping behaviors instead of using EAP services. Gerstein, Gaber, Dainas, and Duffey (1993), however, found that supervisors were better able to identify impaired workers and suggested more EAP referrals than their employees did. Gerstein et al. also found that middle management staff received services from EAPS more frequently than either upper of lower level personnel. Regardless of the reason colleges have been slow to adapt EAPs—it could also be that colleges have a greater tolerance for varying attitudes and behaviors (Baxter, 1979; Stoer-Skaggs, 1999)—EAPs are increasing in numbers now on college campuses, and there are many issues colleges should consider before establishing one.

Considerations

In establishing an EAP on campus, there are several key ingredients that all EAPs should include if their program is to be successful (Masi, 1992; Smewing & Cox, 1998). These key ingredients include the following:

- Effective training of EAP staff
- Professional staffing of EAP offices
- Ongoing employee education on topical issues
- An advisory service for supervisors
- Training programs for departmental supervisors and managers to help identify and manage troubled employees
- Clear policy statements about the purpose of the EAP and employee eligibility
- Confidentiality in regards to record keeping
- Effective community contacts for referrals
- Adequate funding for staff and programs
- Support from all levels of staff within the college
- Sensitivity to special populations
- Adherence to local, state, and federal laws

Pogue (1994) identified the following as characteristics common to successful EAPs:

- Top management commitment
- Written policies and procedures
- Focus on employee performance
- Professional assistance for departments and individuals
- Involvement of the immediate supervisor
- Confidentiality

Once the decision to have an EAP has been made, the next step is to determine where to house the program. Smewing and Cox (1998) suggested three approaches to draw from in making this decision: (a) run an in-house program that is staffed entirely by employees of the institution, (b) hire the program out to an external agency through a contractual agreement with the university, or (c) adopt a "community network resources" approach that features the best aspects of an in-house program but also uses the wide range of counseling services that generally exist in the college community.

There are pros and cons of having internal and external EAPs. Blum and Roman (1989) reported that when external EAPs are used by an employer, a higher percentage of employees self-refer. Conversely, when internal EAPs are used, there are a greater number of supervisor referrals of employees. Masi (1992), however, feels that in-house services are preferable to external EAPs because off-site locations can be intimidating to clients dealing with sensitive issues that they may not want their employer and supervisor to have knowledge of. Stoer-Scaggs (1999) saw internal EAPs as being beneficial within institutions of higher education because the issues in higher education are different from issues in private industry. According to Stoer-Scaggs, the political climate on campuses can make intervention difficult, and the isolation of faculty and staff can raise unique challenges for supervisors attempting to address problematic behaviors. Moreover, Stoer-Scaggs felt, internal EAPs allow campuses to control the quality of the program, and in-house EAP staff will understand the issues better and will likely be more empathic toward clients because of this mutual understanding of the work situation. Although most colleges appear to run in-house programs, however, the schools that opt for the community network approach do so for three reasons (dePietro, 1995): (a) It is usually less costly, (b) it avoids duplication of services, and (c) it is good public relations to work in a cooperative manner with the local community rather than compete with it.

If the decision is made to have an in-house program, where should it be housed? There does not seem to be any one single place that EAPs are universally housed on college campuses. For example, dePietro (1995) found that the EAPs she researched, especially ones with programs targeted to women and children, were placed in student services, women's studies departments, and even housing offices. She quotes Deborah Kolb, Director of the Simmons Institute on Leadership and Change, who felt that the most effective place for work and family programs is in the president's or provosts' office, with advisory boards to provide guidance, support, and credibility. Smewing and Cox (1998) likewise found no general pattern for where in-house EAPs were housed, finding them within counseling centers, schools of social work, and personnel departments. In addressing this issue, Masi (1992) wrote:

> An EAP should be located with the auspices of the company's human resources or personnel department or occasionally the medical department. It should be situated so that it is accessible to the handicapped and inconspicuous enough to increase confidentiality with well-furnished and maintained surroundings to demonstrate the company's commitment to the EAP. If the EAP is located off-site, there should be an office on the premises where supervisors and clients can meet with the EAP counselors if requested. (p. 9)

We agree with Stoer-Scaggs (1999) that in-house EAPs are more likely to provide better services and a wider range of services to the university community than are external programs or even the resource network programs discussed by Smewing and Cox (1998) and dePietro (1995). We also generally agree with Masi's (1992) opinion that EAPs should be housed within human resource or personal departments because we feel that these departments usually have the experience necessary to deal with the situations that are likely to arise when an EAP's services are used, as well as the paperwork that may be required to deal with leave and medical issues. However, this is not always the case, and it is certainly better to place an in-house EAP program within a department where it is welcomed, sufficiently staffed and fully funded, and supported for its work than to be somewhere that makes sense administratively but where it is ultimately unsupported and ineffective. So, although housing an EAP in another department may not be ideal, it should be placed where it can grow and become a vital part of the campus.

Regardless of where the program is housed, EAPs must be sure that they are targeting their programs accurately to those who need them. Ninety percent of EAP clients are employees who are aware of personal difficulties and self-refer, while only 10% are referred by a supervisor (Cagney, 1999). This points out the need for a strong outreach program that highlights the services provided by the EAP so that employees looking for help can easily find it. The problems faced by employees using EAP services have come from a wide spectrum:

- Alcohol and drug abuse
- Family discord

- Physical illness
- Child-rearing issues
- Career mobility
- Elder care
- Sexual harassment
- Occupational stress
- Financial worries
- Marital problems
- Legal difficulties
- Mental health concerns
- Housing problems (Baxter, 1979; Brunson, 1988; Cagney, 1999; Sullivan & Poverny, 1992)

Because of this wide range of issues EAPs must deal with, it is crucial that they develop a broad-brush approach. Broad-brush programs are generalist in nature, addressing any issues that an employee or employer considers important (Smewing & Cox, 1998). While this broad-brush approach could be criticized as not providing the depth necessary for people with severe problems such as drug addiction, we feel that a broad-brush approach can be more effective because of the range of services they can provide and the ability of the staff to deal with a greater variety of issues simultaneously.

Implementation

Regardless of how these issues are resolved—internal versus external program, within human resources or student life, broad-brush versus focused programs—it is important to keep in mind the goals of the EAP. As Cagney (1999) stated: "Whatever the collateral services offered, and no matter how they are packaged, the core EAP functions must be present" (p. 60). To Cagney (1999), these core functions are the following:

- Consultation with, training of, and assistance to work organization leaders seeking to manage the troubled employee, enhance the work environment, and improve employee job performance; and outreach to and education of employees and their family members about EAP services.
- Confidential and timely problem identification/assessment services for employee clients with personal concerns that may affect job performance.

- Use of constructive confrontation, motivation, and short-term intervention with employee clients to address problems that affect job performance.
- Referral of employee clients for diagnosis, treatment, and assistance, plus case monitoring and follow-up services.
- Consultation with work organizations in establishing and maintaining effective relations with treatment and other service providers and in managing provider contracts.
- Consultations with work organizations to encourage availability of and employee access to health benefits covering medical and behavioral problems, including, but not limited to, alcoholism, drug abuse, and mental and emotional disorders.
- Identification of the effects of EAP services on the work organization and individual job performance. (p. 60)

Masi (1992) felt that it is important not to lose sight of the reasons for establishing an EAP and offered a conceptual framework for an EAP:

- EAPs are based on the premise that work is very important to people (it is ego reinforcing); the work itself is not the cause of the employee's problem. Consequently, the workplace can be a means to get people help.
- The supervisor plays a key role in getting help for the employee. Often, however, the supervisor denies the problem and even enables the troubled employee to continue the problem behavior. The supervisor is critical in the confrontational process with the troubled employee. Therefore, education is necessary to eliminate the supervisor's tendency to enable the employee by denying the problem.
- Information about the employee's job performance is extremely important in diagnosis and treatment. It can be used to measure and track whether treatment is successful.
- Workplace peers and union stewards are very important; however, they too can deny the problem and enable the employee to continue the behavior. Teaching them to confront and consequently break the denial barrier is an important element.
- Job leverage is the key ingredient. The counselor must be able to use this with the supervisor.
- EAPs concentrate on personnel issues and job performance. They are not medical programs.

- Cost-effectiveness is an important consideration and must be addressed with upper management.
- The EAP practitioner's knowledge about addiction is paramount. Every EAP should be staffed by clinically licensed professionals from the mental health field who are familiar with addictions. (p. 5)

Evaluation

For EAPs to be effective, they must conduct thorough ongoing evaluations of their programs. A major weakness of most EAPs is that they rarely conduct the kind of thorough evaluation that allows an EAP to assess how their objectives are being met and what programmatic changes are necessary (Ryan, 1997). Smewing and Cox (1998) recommended evaluating each program within the EAP separately so that "conclusions can be drawn as to which groups of employees benefit most from the programs, which services are the most effective, and what interactions exist between the different parts of the system" (p. 280). Regardless of the type of evaluation used, it is important for EAPs to consider program and staff evaluation as an integral component.

Conclusion

Masi (1992) argued that "by developing and maintaining a strong EAP, an organization significantly reduces the many costs, financial and otherwise, that it would have incurred because of employees' personal problems" (p. 4) and that there is no way to measure the savings in relief for employees from anxieties, fears, and distress. Programs designed to enhance the professional and personal development of college faculty and staff must remember that the faculty and staff are first of all human beings (Hubbard & Atkins, 1995). As universities attempt to meet the changing needs of their employees, it is likely that balanced programs addressing professional, social, personal, familial, health, and prevention issues will have the greatest long-term benefits. Simply exhorting employees to "work smarter, not harder" will not result in the goals many colleges have of high employee performance and healthy employees. Colleges that are increasingly coming to terms with this understanding are beginning to accept and embrace EAPs as an integral part of the campus environment.

References

Asma, F. E., Hilker, R. R. J., Shevlin, J. J., & Golden, R. G. (1980). Twenty-five years of rehabilitation of employees with drinking problems. *Journal of Occupational Medicine, 22,* 241–244.

Baxter, A. K. (1979). University employees as people: A counseling service for faculty and staff. *CUPA Journal, 30,* 44–49.

Besenhofer, D., & Gerstein, L. (1991). Referrals to Employee Assistance Programs (EAPs): Characteristics of hypothetical supervisors. *Employee Assistance Quarterly, 72*(2), 41–62.

Blum, T. T., & Roman, P. M. (1989). Employee Assistance Programs and human resources management. In K. Rowland & G. Ferris (Eds.), *Research in personnel and human resources management* (Vol. 7, pp. 259–312). Greenwich, CT: JAI Press.

Brunson, K. (1988). A cost benefit analysis of the medical center: The University of Michigan. *The Almacan, 18,* 23–30.

Bureau of National Affairs. (1987). *Employee Assistance Programs: Benefits, problems, and prospects.* Washington, DC: Author.

Cagney, T. (1999). Models of service delivery. In J. H. Oher (Ed.), *The employee assistance handbook* (pp. 59–69). New York: Wiley.

Carson, K. D., & Balkin, D. B. (1992). An employee assistance model of health care management for employees with alcohol-related problems. *Journal of Employee Counseling, 29,* 146–156.

dePietro, L. (1995). Campus work and family programs: Passing trend or wave of the future? *CUPA Journal, 46,* 29–33.

French, M. T., Dunlap, L. J., Zarkin, G. A., & Karuntzos, G. T. (1998). The costs of an enhanced Employee Assistance Program (EAP) intervention. *Evaluation and Program Planning, 21,* 227–236.

Gerstein, L., Gaber, T., Dainas, C., & Duffey, K. (1993). Organizational hierarchy, employee status, and use of Employee Assistance Programs. *Journal of Employment Counseling, 30,* 74–78.

Hilker, R. R. J., Asma, F. E., & Eggert, R. L. (1972). A company-sponsored alcoholic rehabilitation program: Ten year review. *Journal of Occupational Medicine, 14,* 769–772.

Hubbard, G. T., & Atkins, S. S. (1995). The professor as a person: The role of faculty well-being in faculty development. *Innovative Higher Education, 20,* 117–128.

Johnson, P. R., & Indvik, J. (1997). The boomer blues: Depression in the workplace. *Public Personnel Management, 26,* 359–365.

Lew, A. T., & Ashbaugh, D. L. (1992). Employee Assistance Programs in higher education. *CUPA Journal, 44,* 33–37.

Masi, D. (1992). Employee Assistance Programs. In D. Masi (Ed.), *The AMA handbook for developing employee assistance and counseling programs* (pp. 1–19). New York: AMACOM.

Masi, D. (1994). *Evaluating your employee assistance and managed care programs.* Troy, MI: Performance Resource Press.

Masi, D. M., & Goff, M. E. (1987). The evaluation of employee behavioral programs. *Public Personnel Management, 16,* 323–327.

McClellan, K. (1982). An overview of occupational alcoholism issues for the 80s. *Journal of Drug Education, 12,* 1–26.

Pogue, G. (1994). The effective use of EAPs. *NACUBO Business Officer, 28*(1), 20–23.

Ryan, K. C. (1997). Evaluate your EAP: Can it help support employee rights legislation? *CUPA Journal, 48,* 5–8.

Shirley, C. (1985). TOPEX study: "Hitting bottom in high places." In S. Klarreich, J. Francek, & C. Moore (Eds.), *The human resources management handbook: Principles and practices of employee assistance programs* (pp. 360–369). New York: Praeger Special Studies–Praeger Scientific.

Smewing, C., & Cox, T. (1998). Employee Assistance Programmes and their place within universities. *British Journal of Guidance and Counseling, 26,* 273–285.

Stoer-Scaggs, L. (1999). Employee Assistance Programs in higher education. In J. H. Oher (Ed.), *The employee assistance handbook* (pp. 35–58). New York: Wiley.

Sullivan, R., & Poverny, L. (1992). Differential patterns of EAP service utilization among university faculty and staff. *Employee Assistance Quarterly, 7*(4), 1–11.

Thoreson, R. W., Roberts, K. S., & Pascoe, E. A. (1979). University of Missouri–Columbia Employee Assistance Program: A case study of implementation and change. In R. W. Thoreson & E. P. Hosokawa (Eds.), *Employee Assistance Programs in higher education* (pp. 179–194). Springfield, IL: Charles C Thomas.

Wilson, R. (1997). Universities turn to psychologists to help dysfunctional departments. *Chronicle of Higher Education, 43*(47), A10–A11.

21

Evaluating
Employee Assistance Programs

Robert M. Longwell-Grice and Daya Singh Sandhu

ll Employee Assistance Programs (EAPs) should be evaluated to justify their existence and to demonstrate their effectiveness" (Masi, 1992, p. 12). A thorough evaluation process enables companies and universities to assess the extent to which an EAP's objectives are being reached and to find ways to improve the effectiveness of an EAP. A thorough evaluation can also ensure that an EAP is legally protected (Masi, 1992). According to Smewing and Cox (1998), evaluation is a necessary component of any EAP, and when properly conducted, "conclusions can be drawn as to which groups of employees benefit most from the programs, which services are the most effective, and what interactions exist between the different parts of the system" (p. 280). Smewing and Cox also contended that EAP evaluations provide useful information as to the needs of different groups of staff and the most appropriate method for delivery of services. This chapter discusses the assessment process, reviews some ways an EAP can be evaluated, and offers some evaluation materials.

Assessment Process

Myers (1984) found no published empirical EAP evaluation studies using social service research methodology, and Lew and Ashbaugh (1992) maintained that EAPs are difficult to evaluate. Likewise, Ryan (1997) argued that a major weakness of most organizations is that they rarely conduct a thorough evaluation of ongoing EAPs, even though evaluation "is the only way in which organizations can assess the extent to which their objectives are being met and identify what improvements are necessary" (p. 7). Upcraft and Schuh (1996) argued that, too often, evaluation occurs as a reaction to a crisis. This crisis can involve threats to funding or by committees questioning the effectiveness of a program. In reacting to the crisis, program administrators often want "quick and dirty" surveys to "prove" that the program in question is indeed worth funding. Unfortunately, Upcraft and Schuh (1996) contended, "Responding to a crisis with a survey is not assessment: it is crisis management" (p. 4). Assessment, Upcraft and Schuh maintained, is a complex process, and mindless surveying in a crisis situation will probably do more harm than good. Crisis assessment can destroy the credibility of assessment as an important tool for gathering information and can destroy the assessment's potential for determining the worth of the programs being assessed. It is unfortunate, Upcraft and Schuh (1996) wrote, that assessment is misunderstood and too often misused (if it is used at all, given the low priority it is usually assigned).

The process of assessment does not begin with simply selecting an assessment instrument and mailing it out. Upcraft and Schuh (1996) formulated six basic questions that help define the assessment process, which they argued need to be asked before the assessment process begins. Although Upcraft and Schuh (1996) wrote these questions for evaluation in student affairs, they are entirely relevant for evaluating EAP programs:

1. Why are we doing this assessment? What is its basic purpose? Why do we need information in the first place? Are we looking to improve a service? Are we trying to justify the existence of a program? Answering questions such as these determines in large part the answers to the subsequent questions.
2. What will we assess? This question helps clarify what information is to be gathered. Do we need information on who uses the

programs, or what they think of the programs, or what type of programs are viewed as most effective?

3. How will we assess? What methodologies will be used to gather the information needed? Will we use qualitative or quantitative methods? Where will we collect the information?

4. Who will do the assessment? Upcraft and Schuh (1996) wrote that there is always controversy over this issue. While some would maintain that assessment should be handled in an objective manner by someone with no connection to the program being evaluated, others argue that assessment should be conducted by those closest to the program who can best interpret the meaning of the results. Regardless, those who conduct the evaluation need to be competent to do so.

5. How will the results be analyzed? Information in and of itself says little—it is the interpretation of the data that is helpful.

6. How will the results be communicated and to whom? Upcraft and Schuh (1996) recommended reporting the results of the evaluation by using multiple formats designed to reach both internal and external audiences. A typical report, they wrote, should include an executive summary, the purpose, design, results of the study, and any recommendations the investigators have to offer. (p. 26)

Upcraft and Schuh (1996) emphasized that it is also very important to consider the timing of communicating the report.

Ryan (1997) described the components of an EAP she maintained should be evaluated:

1. The number and type of cases referred or self-referred each month: Are services accessible to all employees? Are some segments of the workforce over- or underrepresented?

2. How members of the organization perceive the EAP: Do the clients have a high degree of trust in the program? Are the services offered too narrow or too broad in scope?

3. Training provided to supervisors and other organizational members who may make referrals: Is use of the EAP part of an overall management strategy? Are they fully informed about the services the EAP offers?

4. Outcomes of program services: Do treatment and services result in improved work performance, satisfaction, and commitment? Are the goals of the programs being met?
5. Correspondence of EAP services offered to employee rights legislation: Are EAP personnel knowledgeable about laws such as the Americans With Disabilities Act and the Family Medical Leave Act? Does the program offer support for workers with disabilities and for people working with disabled individuals? (p. 8)

Evaluation Methods

Although a variety of evaluation methods can be used to evaluate EAP programs, a truly comprehensive EAP should include the following two components (Masi, 1992): (a) the monitoring of the implementation of the program (a *process* evaluation) and (b) a study of the effectiveness of the program (an *outcome* evaluation). A process evaluation encompasses the review and analysis of monthly EAP statistics, including the number of cases, categories of diagnosis, and supervisory referrals. The purpose of this evaluation component is to ensure (a) that the EAP reaches the appropriate number of employees, including those with alcohol and drug problems; (b) that the client population reflects the workforce composition in regards to age, sex, race, job level, and so forth; and (c) that there is baseline data in job performance for comparing performance after going to the EAP.

An outcome evaluation includes both quantitative and qualitative analysis. Among other things, the quantitative evaluation can determine whether the EAP is cost-effective. In making a cost-effectiveness determination, evaluators measure and compare information on costs incurred before the company EAP was in place, in relation to issues such as absenteeism, leave without pay, sick leave, accidents, and so on (Masi, 1992). Smewing and Cox (1998) contended that cost–benefit analysis is more often applied to industry EAPs, whereas cost-effectiveness is more appropriate within a university setting. In cost–benefit analysis, all of the direct costs and benefits of the EAP are calculated and compared, whereas in cost-effectiveness, costs of the EAP are weighed against the achievement of the EAP stated goals (French, Dunlap, Zarkin, & Karuntzos, 1998; Smewing & Cox, 1998).

In conducting qualitative assessment, Masi (1992) suggested using external experts in the field of psychiatry, psychology, or social work who can provide "professional, comprehensive, and constructive reviews of individual case records" (p. 13). According to Masi, these evaluators should review a number of randomly selected EAP records and provide a written and an oral report to management. Another method of qualitative assessment is the use of individual and group interviews with former EAP clients, a method that is discussed further in the next section. Examples of forms that can be used to conduct qualitative assessment can be found in the Appendix section at the end of this chapter.

How to Evaluate

This section briefly outlines a few methods that are commonly used in conducting evaluation of programs. Some sample forms for possible use in evaluation are provided in the Appendixes.

1. Mailed Questionnaires: One way to evaluate EAP services is to mail out a questionnaire to everyone who has used the EAP services. While this can be one way to gather data from a wide range of people, and potentially a large group of people, traditionally the response rate to these types of questionnaires is fairly low. To truly evaluate an EAP using this methodology, a "good" return rate of 50% would be needed, but a return rate of 25% or 30% is more reasonable to expect (Upcraft & Schuh, 1996). In addition, a cross-section of people using different services would be needed to achieve some level of validity. A sample questionnaire is provided in Appendix A. Appendixes D and E also provide examples of mailed questionnaires. Appendix E is designed to fit onto a postcard for ease of return mailing by the client.

2. Client Satisfaction Surveys: This type of evaluation attempts to obtain client feedback immediately. Clients who use EAP services are asked to complete a brief survey prior to leaving the office or are asked to mail it back. If a survey is not received within 7–10 days, another survey can be mailed to the client with a request that he or she complete it and return it. Although this may improve the return rate because it is more immediate, there may be a tendency to receive these types of forms back only from dissatisfied clients. Again, care must be taken to solicit feedback from different client groups to gain an accurate picture

of how the EAP is perceived and if its programs are effective. A sample satisfaction client survey is provided in Appendix B.

3. Telephone Interviews: Telephone interviews can be used to increase the response rate of mailed questionnaires. The interviews can be done as a separate evaluation, as a follow-up to people who have not responded to the initial questionnaire or satisfaction survey, or as a way to get more information from people who indicate that they wish to talk to someone personally. As Masi (1992) and Upcraft and Schuh (1996) suggested, it is probably best to have the services of trained staff members when conducting a telephone interview, as the interviewers need to be extremely "customer friendly." A suggested "script" for use in conducting telephone interviews is found in Appendix C.

4. Individual Interviews: Individual interviews are more appropriate when discussing sensitive issues that clients may not wish to share with others. They also allow the interview to use scripted questions, to more carefully control the interview, and to develop a close rapport with the interviewee (Upcraft & Schuh, 1996). However, it is more time consuming than focus groups. Ideally, if this method is used, a combination of individual and focus group interviews should be utilized.

5. Focus Groups: Focus groups are small groups (fewer than 10 people) and can be brought together to discuss one specific program that an EAP offers or the EAP as a whole. They can be heterogeneous or homogeneous in nature, depending on the type of data that is sought. Attention must be paid to the dynamics of the group so that an individual does not end up monopolizing the group or attempting to force the group to agree with his or her way of thinking. In addition, the interviewer must be more flexible in how questions may be asked because the group dynamics may shape the interview in an unintended manner.

Conclusion

This chapter discussed the assessment process, reviewed ways that EAPs can be evaluated to improve their effectiveness, and offered some evaluation materials. All EAPs should be evaluated in a thorough manner, on a regular basis. A thorough evaluation process will determine how cost-effective and cost-beneficial an EAP actually is and will provide the EAP with information that will help improve its effectiveness tremendously. Evaluation that is systematic and ongoing, rather than crisis-oriented, is recommended. For that reason, it should be given a higher priority than it normally is.

References

French, M. T., Dunlap, L. J., Zarkin, G. A., & Karuntzos, G. T. (1998). The costs of an enhanced Employee Assistance Program (EAP) intervention. *Evaluation and Program Planning, 21*, 227–236.

Lew, A. T., & Ashbaugh, D. L. (1992). Employee Assistance Programs in higher education. *CUPA Journal, 44*, 33–37.

Masi, D. (1992). Employee Assistance Programs. In D. Masi (Ed.), *The AMA handbook for developing employee assistance and counseling programs* (pp. 1–19). New York: AMACOM.

Myers, D. W. (1984). Measuring cost effectiveness of EAPs. *Risk Management, 31*(11), 56–61.

Ryan, K. C. (1997). Evaluate your EAP: Can it help support employee rights legislation? *CUPA Journal, 48*, 5–8.

Smewing, C., & Cox, T. (1998). Employee Assistance Programmes and their place within universities. *British Journal of Guidance and Counseling, 26*, 273–285.

Upcraft, M. L., & Schuh, J. H. (1996). *Assessment in student affairs: A guide for practitioners.* San Francisco: Jossey-Bass.

Appendix A

Sample EAP Evaluation Form

How did you learn about the EAP?

How did you contact the EAP?

Did you receive timely assistance? _____ yes _____ no

Were you given an appointment that
was convenient for you? _____ yes _____ no

Were you treated professionally and courteously? _____ yes _____ no

Was the EAP setting easy to find? _____ yes _____ no

Was the counselor's office comfortable for you? _____ yes _____ no

Did you feel you received help for your problem? _____ yes _____ no

Was your situation kept confidential? _____ yes _____ no

Was your problem resolved successfully? _____ yes _____ no

Were you referred to another agency? _____ yes _____ no

Overall, how satisfied are you with the service you received through the EAP?
_____ Very satisfied
_____ Satisfied
_____ Unsure
_____ Dissatisfied
_____ Very dissatisfied

I am (circle one):   faculty   staff   hourly employee

My EAP counselor's name was: _____

Please provide any further comments that you wish to share with us about the EAP in the space provided below:

_____

_____

_____

If you wish to have someone contact you about the EAP and the services you received, please leave your name and phone number in the space provided below:

_____

_____

_____

Thank you for your time in completing this form.

Appendix B

Sample Client Satisfaction Survey

How were you made aware of the EAP?

Friend _____   Coworker _____   Supervisor _____
Poster/Brochure _____   Other _____

Did you find the EAP office easy to contact?   Yes _____   No _____
If no, what was the problem you experienced? _____

_____

Was your initial contact satisfactory?   Yes _____   No _____
If no, what was the problem you experienced? _____

_____

Was your counselor helpful?   Yes _____   No _____
If no, what was the problem you experienced? _____

_____

Overall, were you satisfied with the service you received?
Yes _____   No _____
If no, what was the problem you experienced? _____

_____

Would you recommend our services to someone else?
Yes _____   No _____   why/why not? _____

_____

Please use this space to write any comments that you have about the EAP
services: _____

_____

_____

_____

If you would like to speak to someone personally, please write your name,
address and phone number on the spaces provided below and someone
will contact you.

_____

_____

_____

Thank you for your time in completing this form.

Appendix C

Sample Telephone Script

(You might consider sending out a letter or a postcard to the client prior to the phone call, alerting them to the fact that you are going to call. That way, they can be expecting it.)

Hello, my name is _____ and I am conducting a telephone poll on behalf of (name of EAP). I would like to ask you a few questions regarding the EAP services that you recently used. This poll is brief and should only take a few minutes of your time. The information collected will be used to help improve the services that the EAP provides. All information collected from you will be held in the strictest of confidence. Your name and your responses will not be revealed to anyone. May I begin with the poll? (If not, schedule a time that is more convenient or ask if you can mail them a questionnaire.)

(You will want to collect demographic data [name, age, gender, department, job, etc.], what programs they used, as well as the responses to the questions.)

Appendix D

Service Feedback Survey
Employee Assistance Program

Please rate your level of satisfaction (if applicable) and level of importance for the following service areas by circling the appropriate response. The response choices are listed below the survey. Thank you.

Employee Assistance Staff Members*	Satisfaction	Importance
1. *understand university rules and policies	A/D/NB	I/U/NB
2. *are able to answer my questions	A/D/NB	I/U/NB
3. *are flexible in arranging meeting times	A/D/NB	I/U/NB
4. *are readily accessible to assist me	A/D/NB	I/U/NB
5. *treat me with respect	A/D/NB	I/U/NB
6. *maintain confidentiality	A/D/NB	I/U/NB
7. *listen well	A/D/NB	I/U/NB
8. *are friendly	A/D/NB	I/U/NB
9. *are approachable	A/D/NB	I/U/NB
10. *show genuine concern for me	A/D/NB	I/U/NB
11. *return my phone calls promptly	A/D/NB	I/U/NB
12. *provide information in a timely manner	A/D/NB	I/U/NB
13. *provide accurate information	A/D/NB	I/U/NB

Response choices:
Satisfaction:

A = Agree,   D = Disagree,   NB = No Basis on which to judge

Importance:

I = Important,   U = Unimportant,   NB = No Basis on which to judge

(continued)

Appendix D *(continued)*

What do you like most/least about working with the staff at the Employee Assistance Program?

_____

_____

_____

_____

_____

I have participated in a program sponsored by the Employee Assistance Program*

    0   1–2   3–4   5+   *times this year.

I have talked with a staff member in the Employee Assistance Program*

    0   1–2   3–4   5+   *times this year.

Deposit this survey in the nearest on-campus mailbox.
Thank you for your help in improving our program!

Appendix E

Report Card on EAP Services

Please Grade Our Services in Order to Help Us Improve Them
(Please Circle Your Response and Tell Us Why You Circled It)

Knowledge of the EAP staff on relevant policies	A B C D F
Courteousness of EAP staff	A B C D F
Friendliness of the EAP staff	A B C D F
Availability of the EAP staff	A B C D F
Usefulness of the EAP programs	A B C D F

Please list any suggestions that you have to improve our services: _____

_____

_____

_____

Deposit this survey in the nearest on-campus mailbox.

Thank you for your help in improving our program!

(This "report card" could also be reduced to fit on a post card with some modifications)

Index